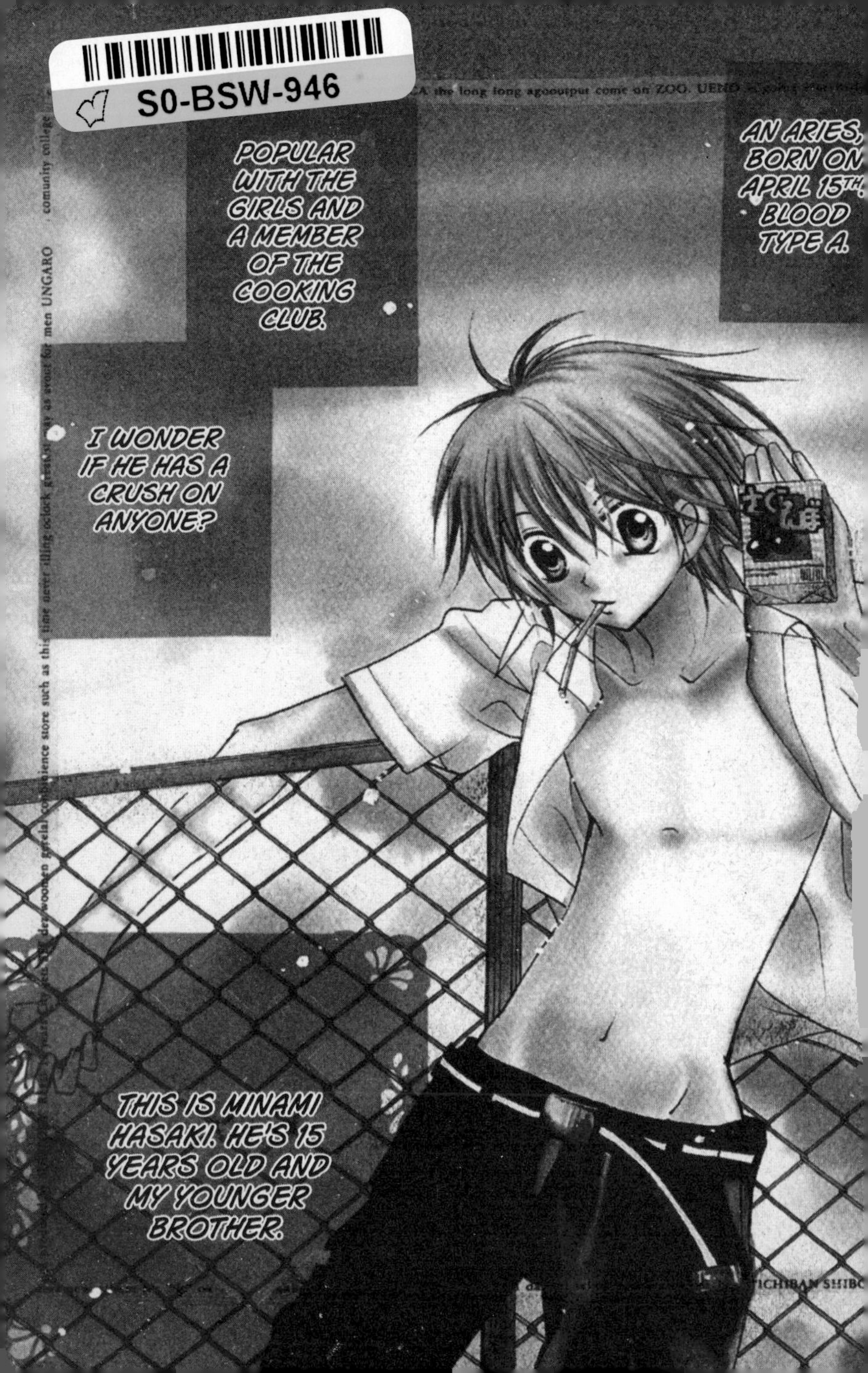
AN ARIES, BORN ON APRIL 15TH, BLOOD TYPE A.
POPULAR WITH THE GIRLS AND A MEMBER OF THE COOKING CLUB.
I WONDER IF HE HAS A CRUSH ON ANYONE?
THIS IS MINAMI HASAKI. HE'S 15 YEARS OLD AND MY YOUNGER BROTHER.

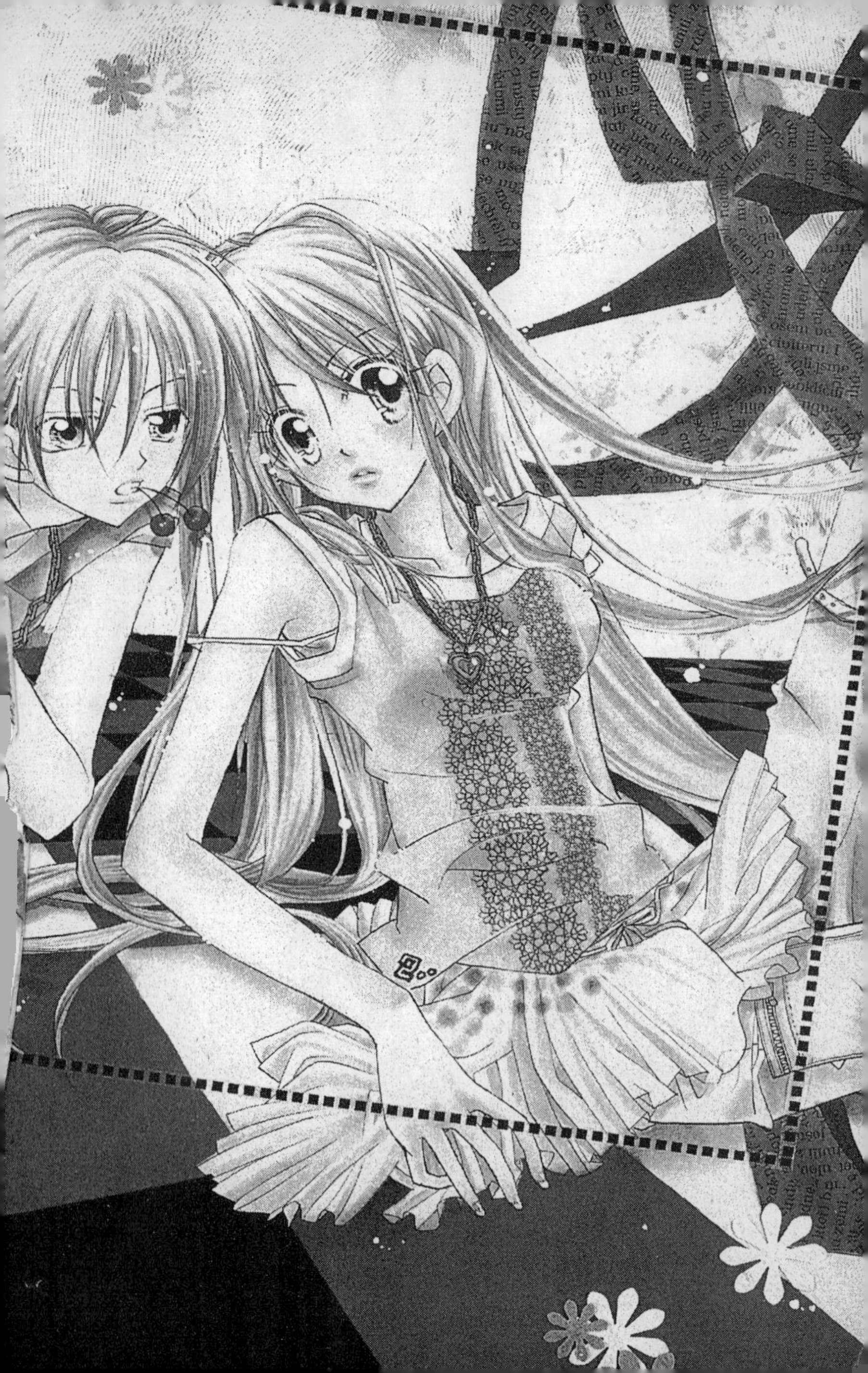

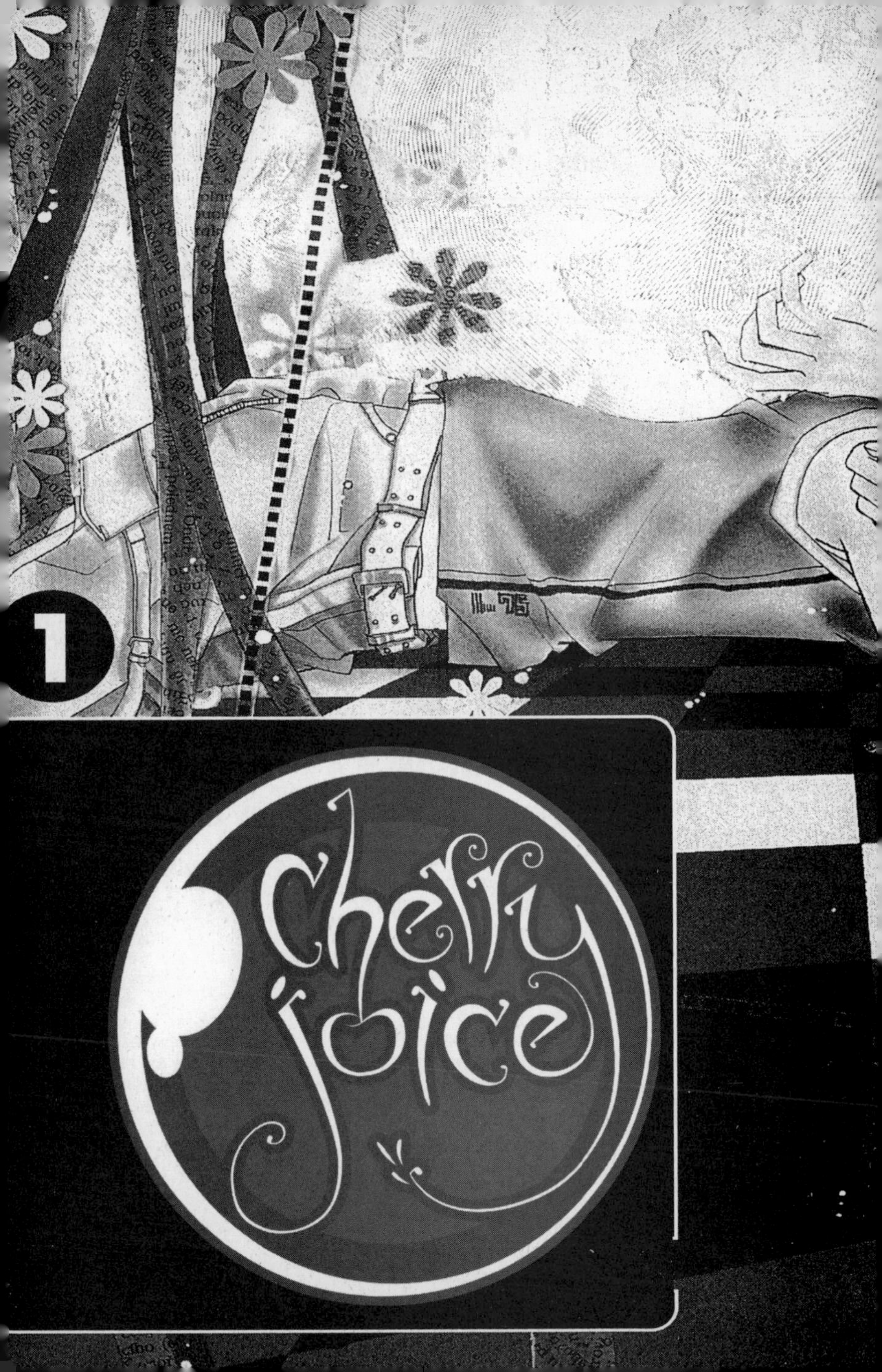
1

cherry juice

Cherry Juice Volume 1
Created by Haruka Fukushima

Translation - Kristy Harmon
English Adaptation - Meadow Jones
Copy Editor - Stephanie Duchin
Retouch and Lettering - Star Print Brokers
Production Artist - Vicente Rivera, Jr.
Graphic Designer - Tomas Montalvo-Lagos

Editor - Lillian Diaz-Przybyl
Digital Imaging Manager - Chris Buford
Pre-Production Supervisor - Erika Terriquez
Art Director - Anne Marie Horne
Production Manager - Elisabeth Brizzi
Managing Editor - Vy Nguyen
VP of Production - Ron Klamert
Editor-in-Chief - Rob Tokar
Publisher - Mike Kiley
President and C.O.O. - John Parker
C.E.O. and Chief Creative Officer - Stuart Levy

A  Manga

TOKYOPOP and ⚙ are trademarks or registered trademarks of TOKYOPOP Inc.

TOKYOPOP Inc.
5900 Wilshire Blvd. Suite 2000
Los Angeles, CA 90036

E-mail: info@TOKYOPOP.com
Come visit us online at www.TOKYOPOP.com

ISBN: 978-1-4278-0286-6

First TOKYOPOP printing: September 2007
10 9 8 7 6 5 4 3
Printed in the USA

BY HARUKA FUKUSHIMA
VOL. 1

HAMBURG // LONDON // LOS ANGELES // TOKYO

For starters!

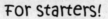

Hello!
Haruka Fukushima here.
Cherry Juice vol. 1 is
my 9th book. It was born
from my earthly desire
of wanting to draw a
story about a boy and
girl living together and
my fantasies about how
nice it would be to have
a hot younger brother.
So, if the hearts of all
you readers out there
will pound along with
mine, I'll be glad. Now,
without further ado...

ENJOY!

04.10.28

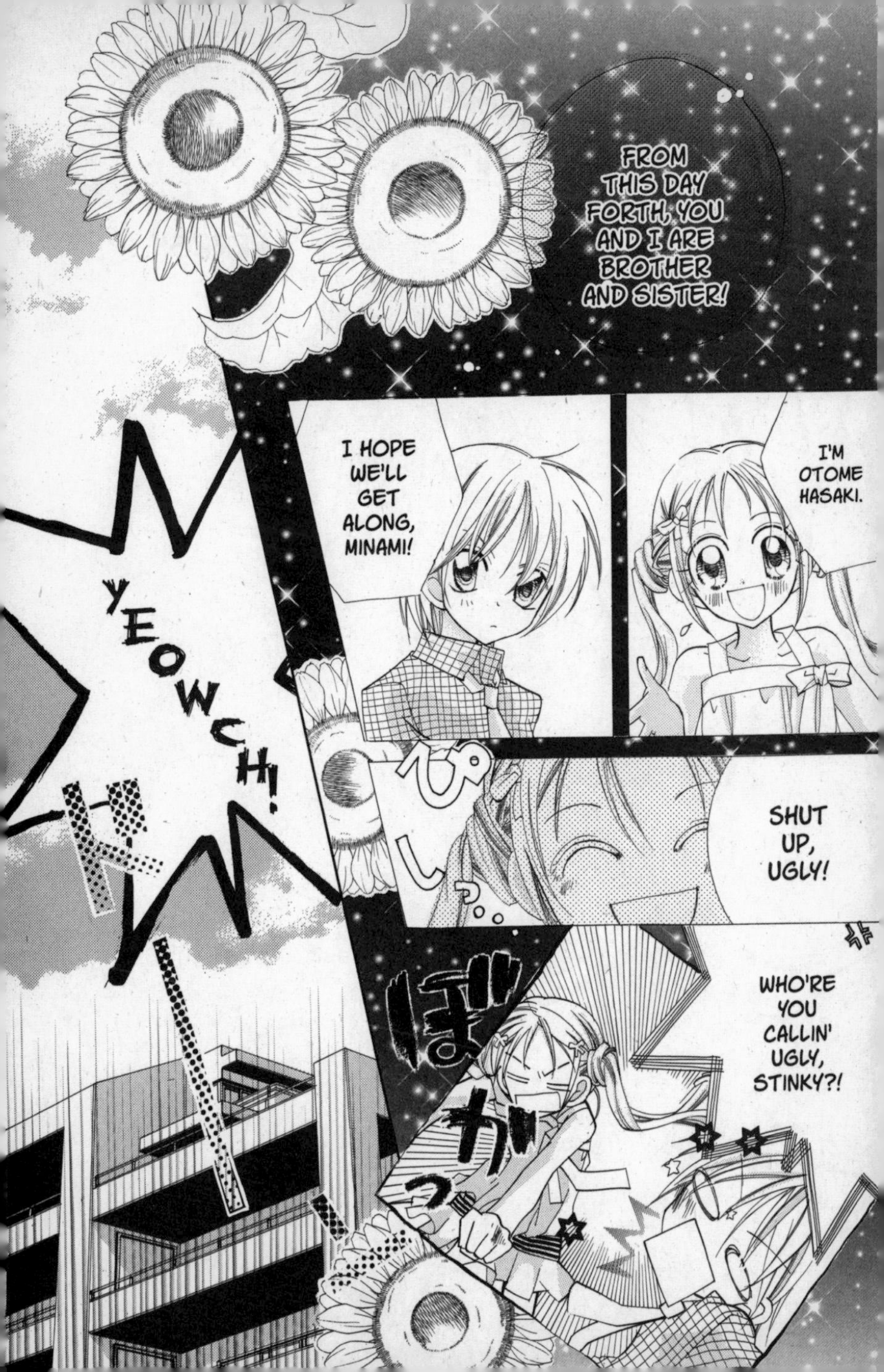
FROM THIS DAY FORTH, YOU AND I ARE BROTHER AND SISTER!
I'M OTOME HASAKI.
I HOPE WE'LL GET ALONG, MINAMI!
ぴしっ
SHUT UP, UGLY!
WHO'RE YOU CALLIN' UGLY, STINKY?!
YEOWCH!

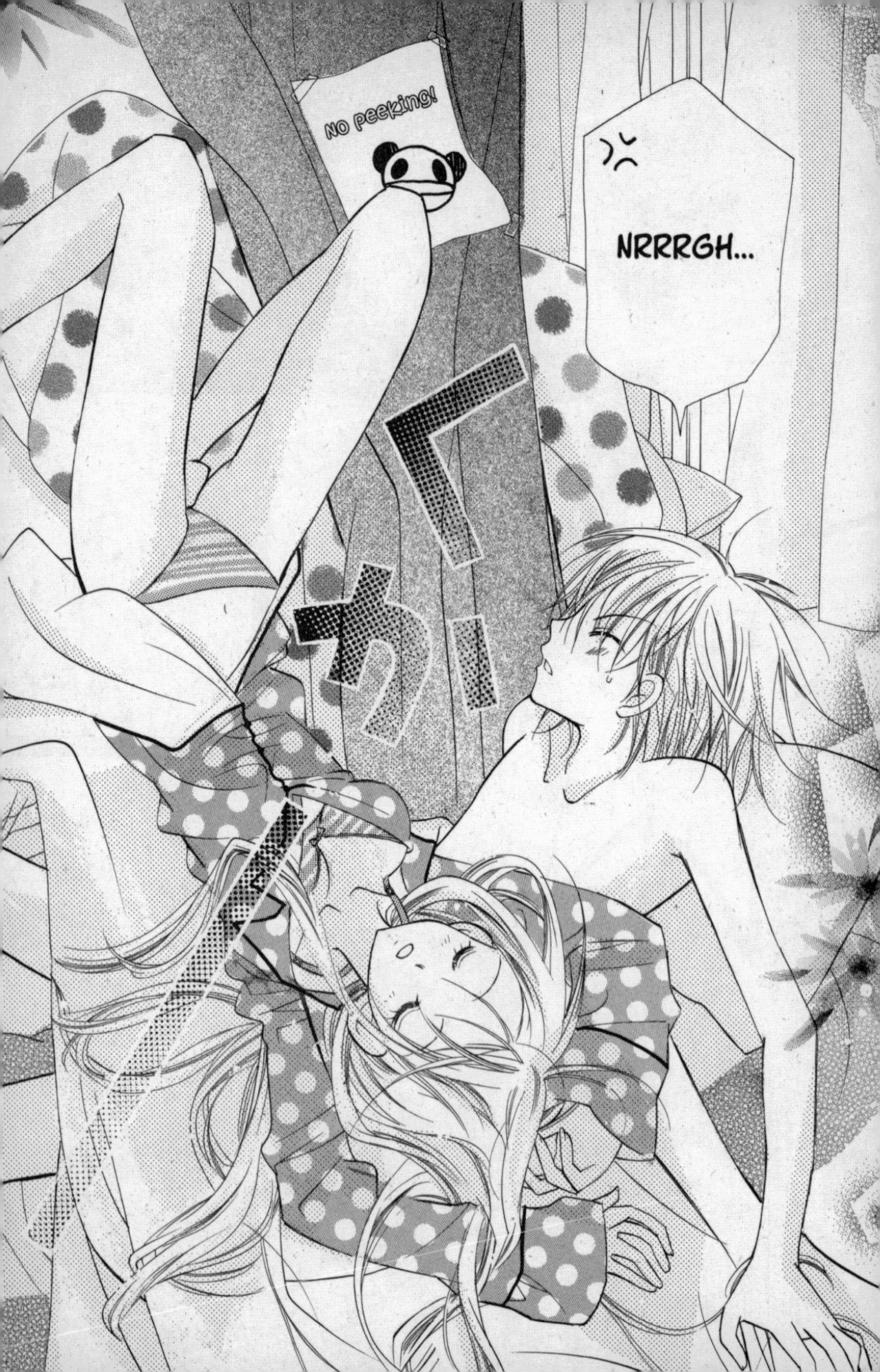
NRRRGH...
No peeking!

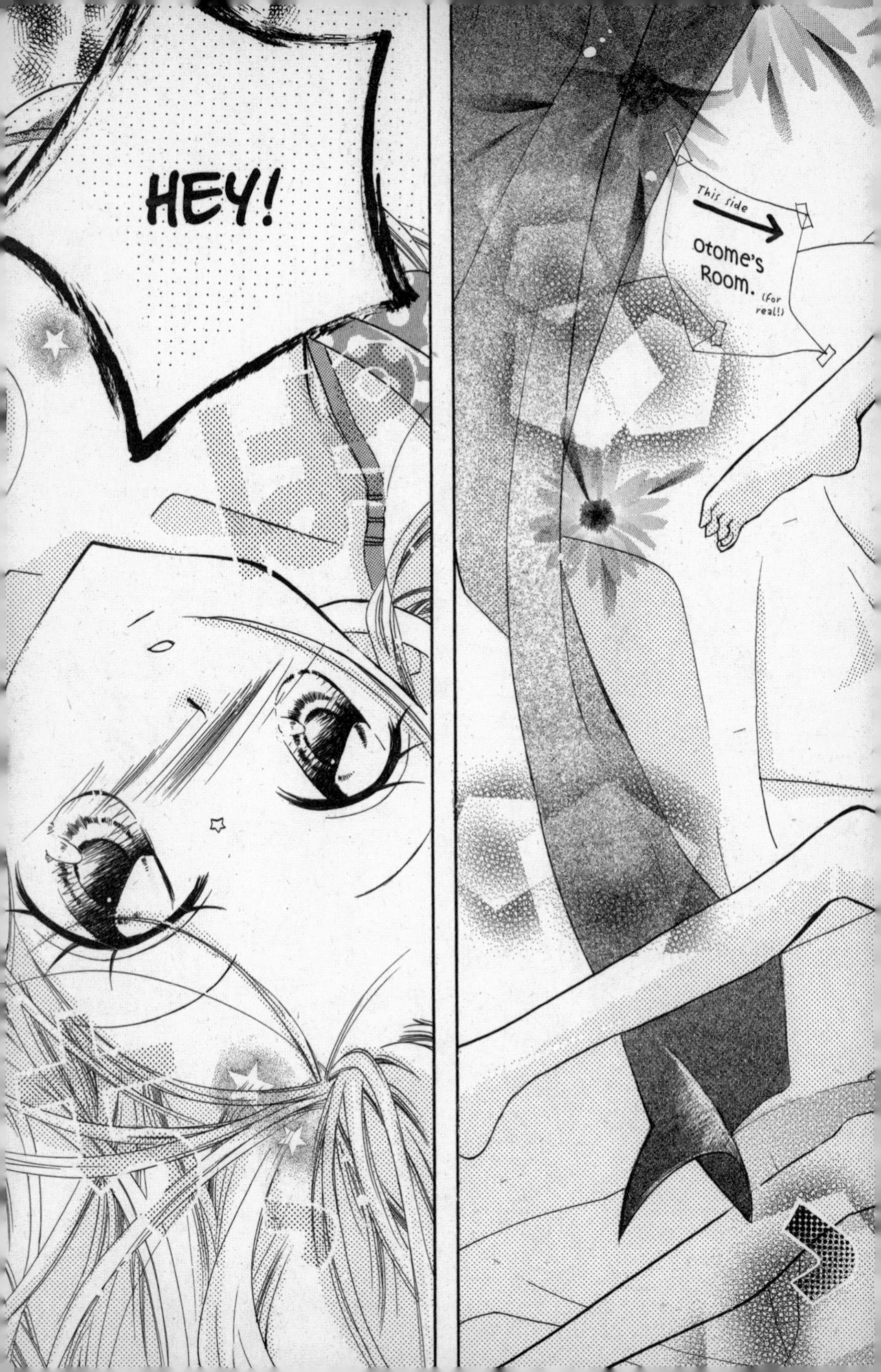
This side
Otome's Room. (for real!)
HEY!

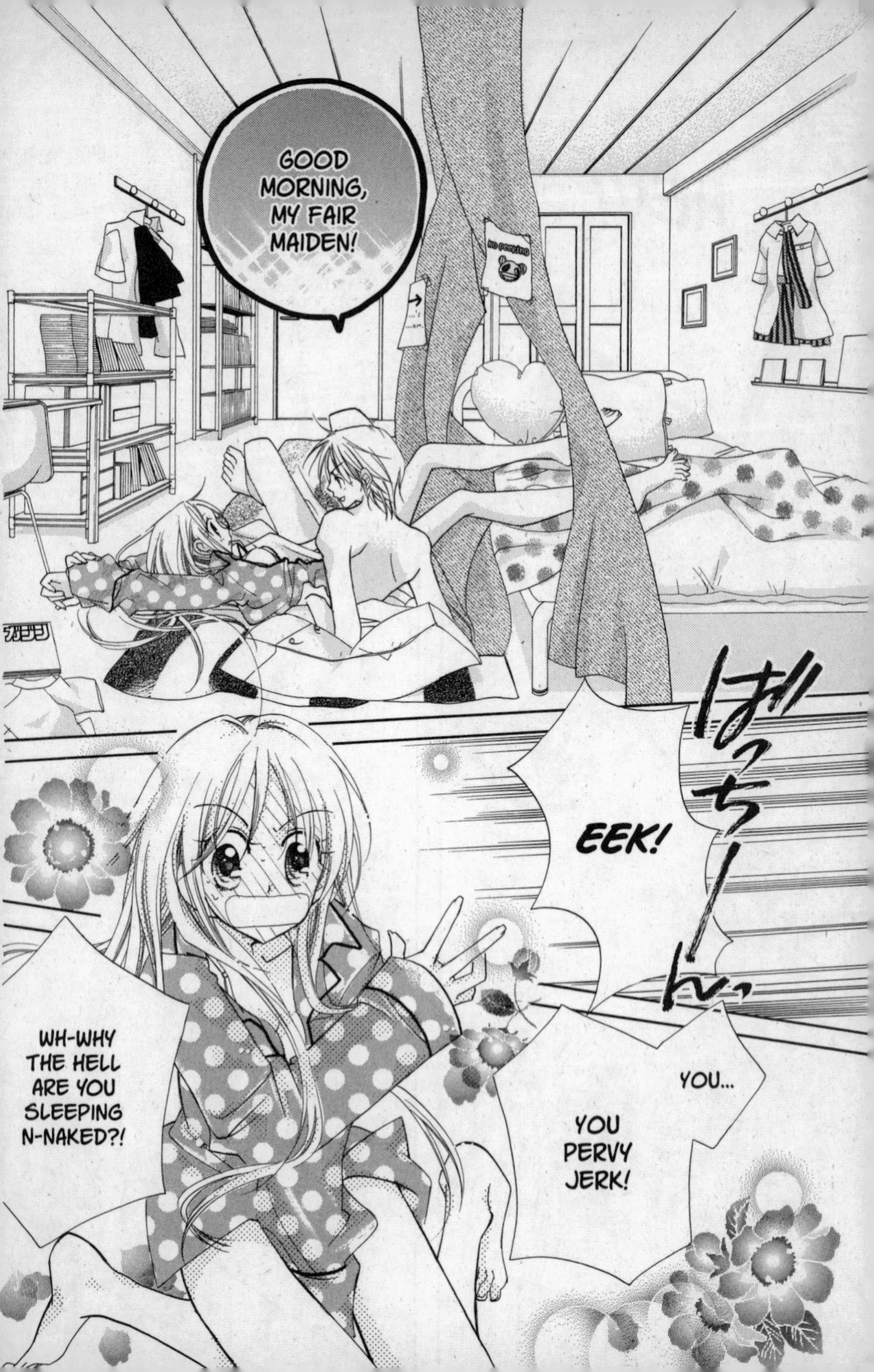
GOOD MORNING, MY FAIR MAIDEN!
ぱっちーん
EEK!
YOU...
YOU PERVY JERK!
WH-WHY THE HELL ARE YOU SLEEPING N-NAKED?!

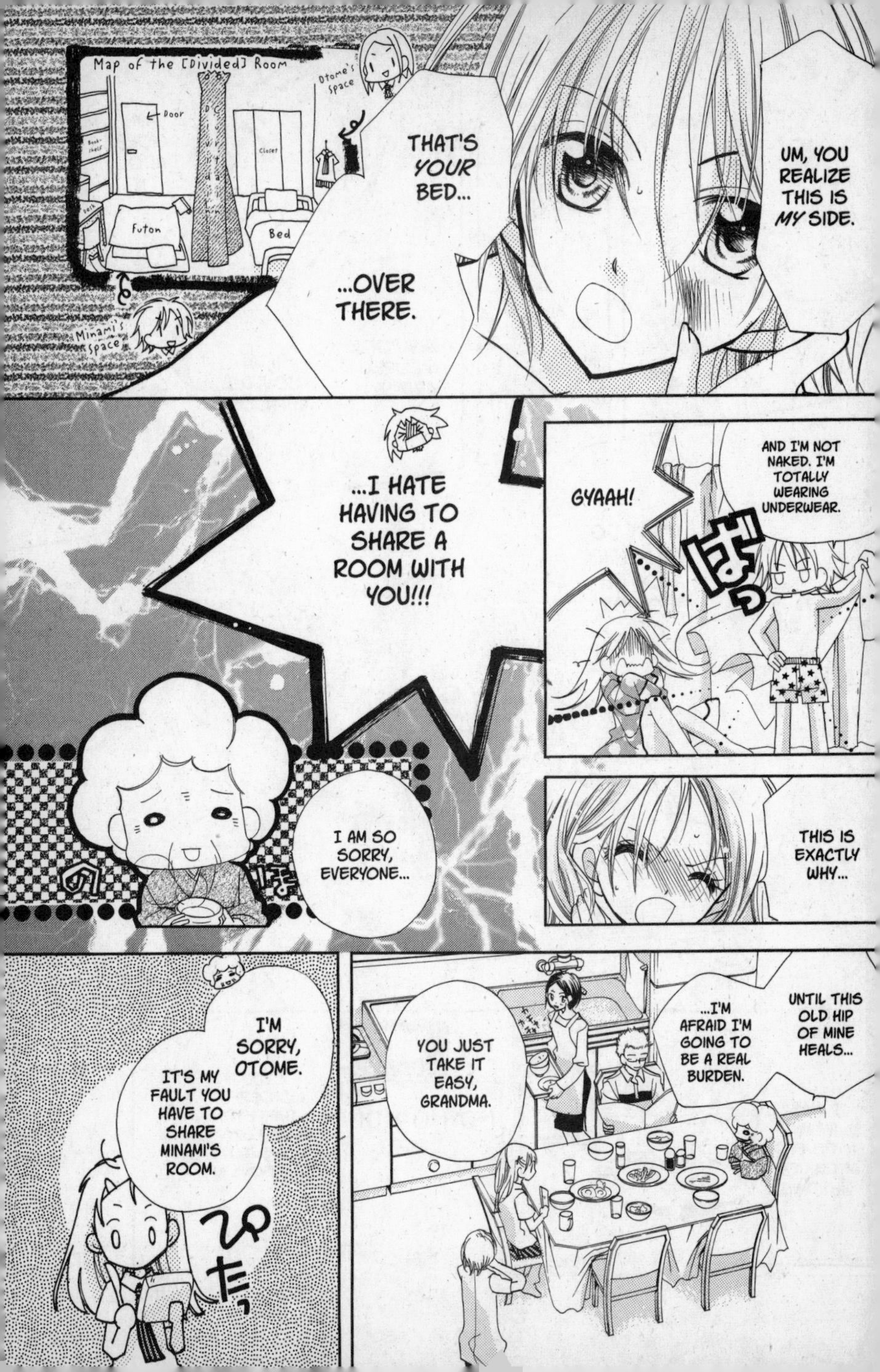
UM, YOU REALIZE THIS IS MY SIDE.
THAT'S YOUR BED...
...OVER THERE.
Map of the [Divided] Room
Otome's Space
Door
Closet
Futon
Bed
Minami's Space
AND I'M NOT NAKED. I'M TOTALLY WEARING UNDERWEAR.
GYAAH!
ばっ
THIS IS EXACTLY WHY...
...I HATE HAVING TO SHARE A ROOM WITH YOU!!!
I AM SO SORRY, EVERYONE...
UNTIL THIS OLD HIP OF MINE HEALS...
...I'M AFRAID I'M GOING TO BE A REAL BURDEN.
YOU JUST TAKE IT EASY, GRANDMA.
I'M SORRY, OTOME.
IT'S MY FAULT YOU HAVE TO SHARE MINAMI'S ROOM.
ぴた

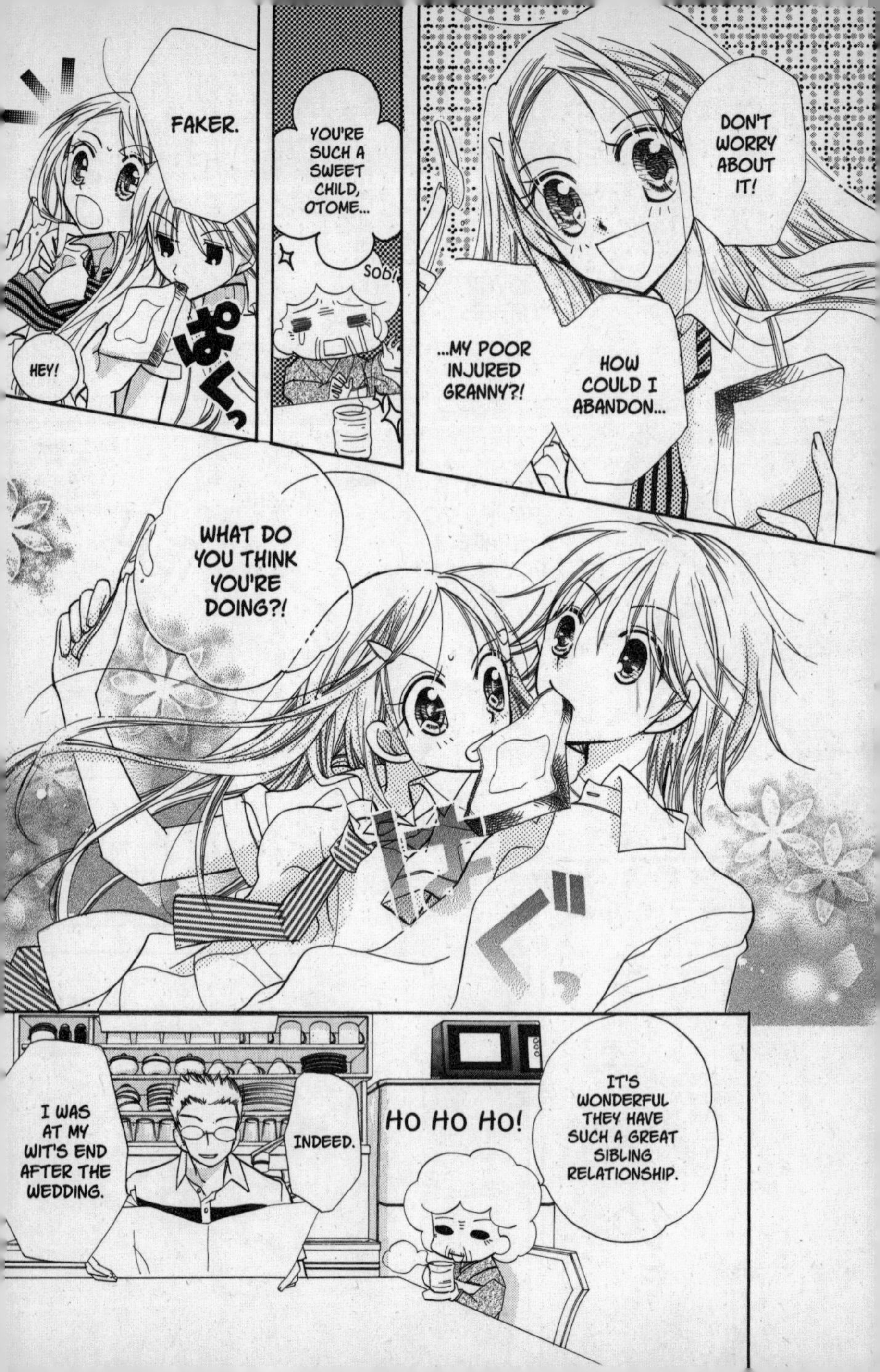
DON'T WORRY ABOUT IT!
HOW COULD I ABANDON...
...MY POOR INJURED GRANNY?!
YOU'RE SUCH A SWEET CHILD, OTOME...
SOB!
FAKER.
HEY!
WHAT DO YOU THINK YOU'RE DOING?!
IT'S WONDERFUL THEY HAVE SUCH A GREAT SIBLING RELATIONSHIP.
HO HO HO!
INDEED.
I WAS AT MY WIT'S END AFTER THE WEDDING.

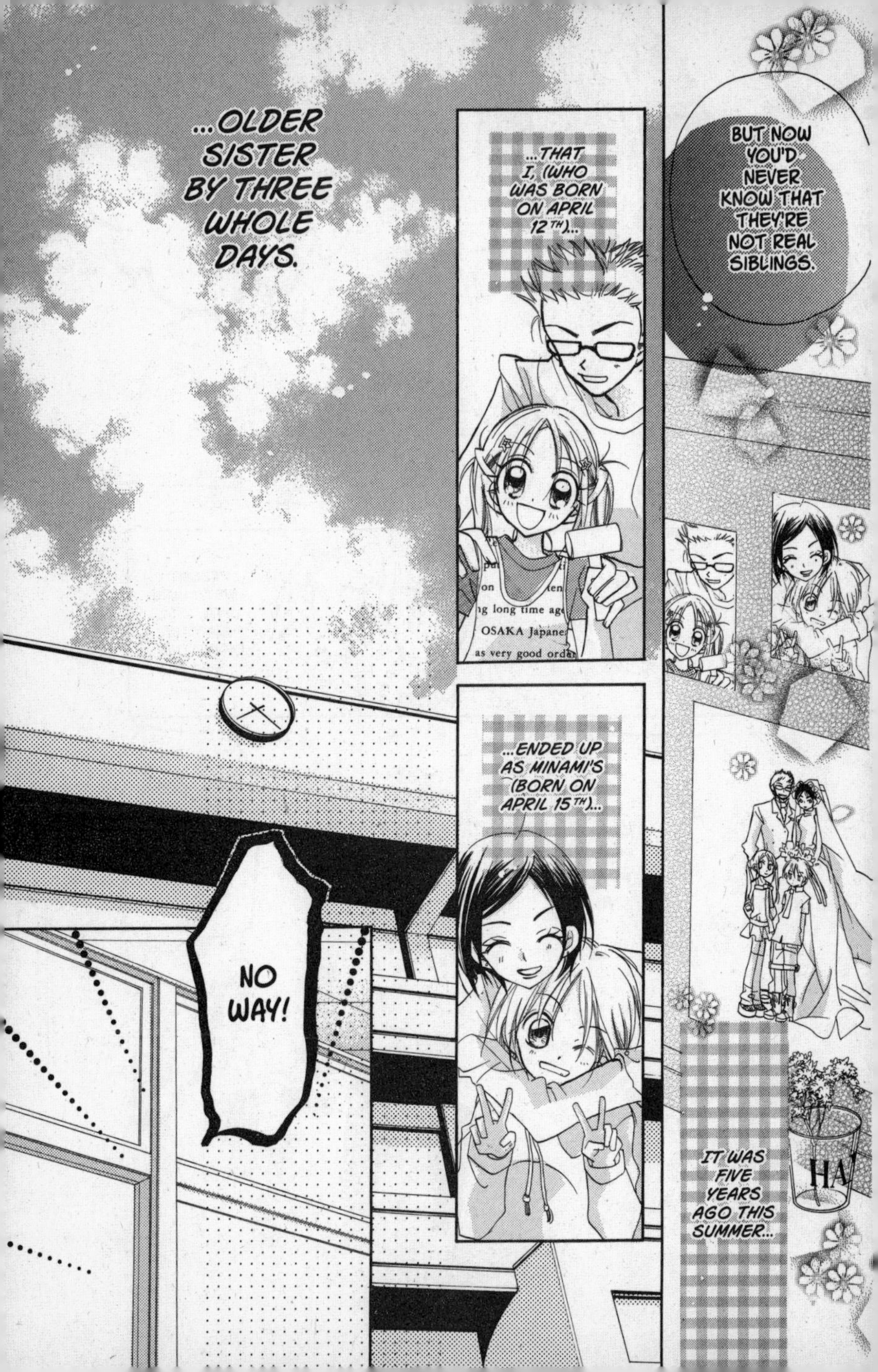
BUT NOW YOU'D NEVER KNOW THAT THEY'RE NOT REAL SIBLINGS.
IT WAS FIVE YEARS AGO THIS SUMMER...
HA
...THAT I, (WHO WAS BORN ON APRIL 12TH)...
...ENDED UP AS MINAMI'S (BORN ON APRIL 15TH)...
...OLDER SISTER BY THREE WHOLE DAYS.
NO WAY!

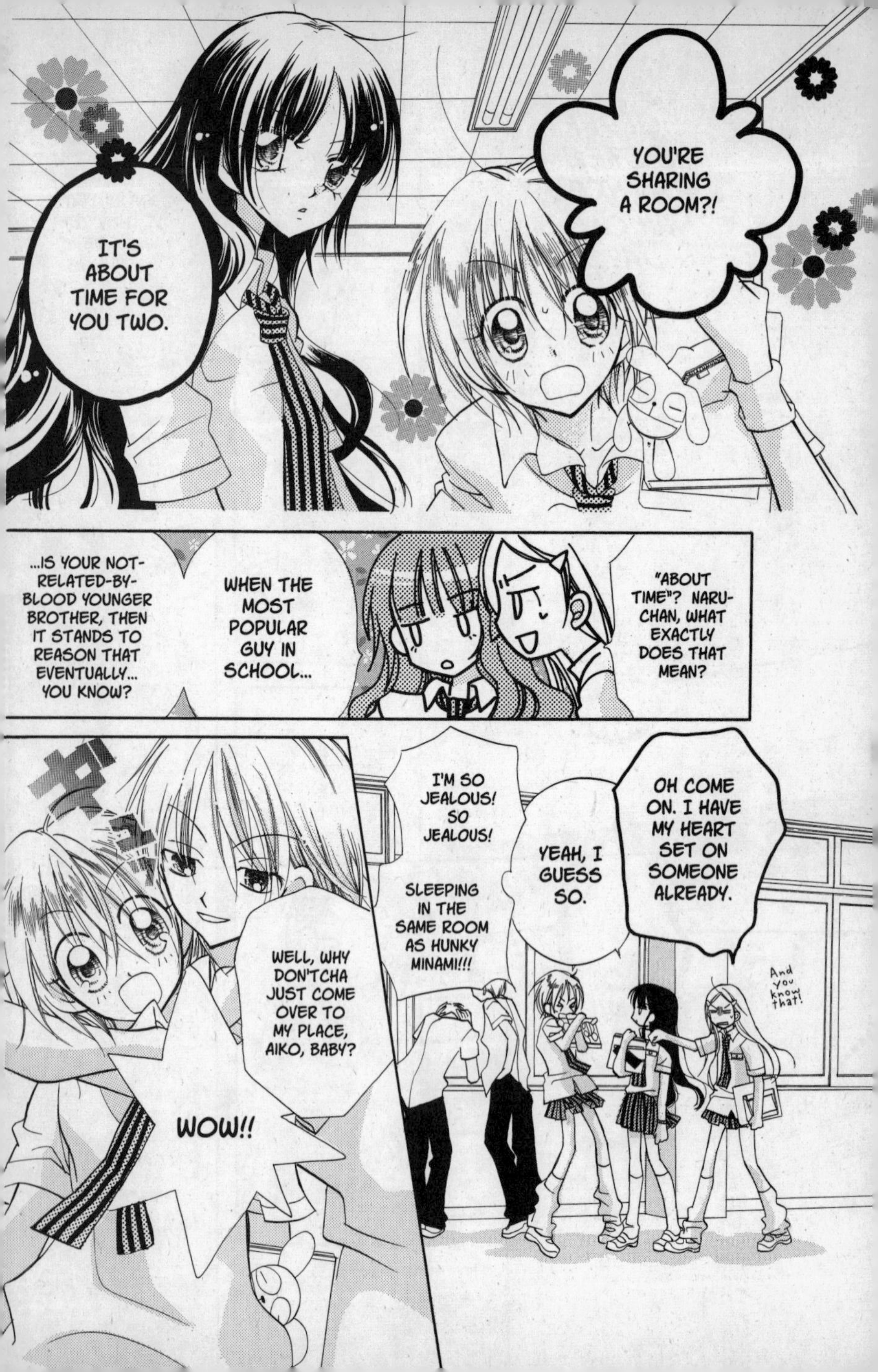
YOU'RE SHARING A ROOM?!
IT'S ABOUT TIME FOR YOU TWO.
"ABOUT TIME"? NARU-CHAN, WHAT EXACTLY DOES THAT MEAN?
WHEN THE MOST POPULAR GUY IN SCHOOL...
...IS YOUR NOT-RELATED-BY-BLOOD YOUNGER BROTHER, THEN IT STANDS TO REASON THAT EVENTUALLY... YOU KNOW?
OH COME ON. I HAVE MY HEART SET ON SOMEONE ALREADY.
And you know that!
YEAH, I GUESS SO.
I'M SO JEALOUS! SO JEALOUS!
SLEEPING IN THE SAME ROOM AS HUNKY MINAMI!!!
WELL, WHY DON'TCHA JUST COME OVER TO MY PLACE, AIKO, BABY?
WOW!!

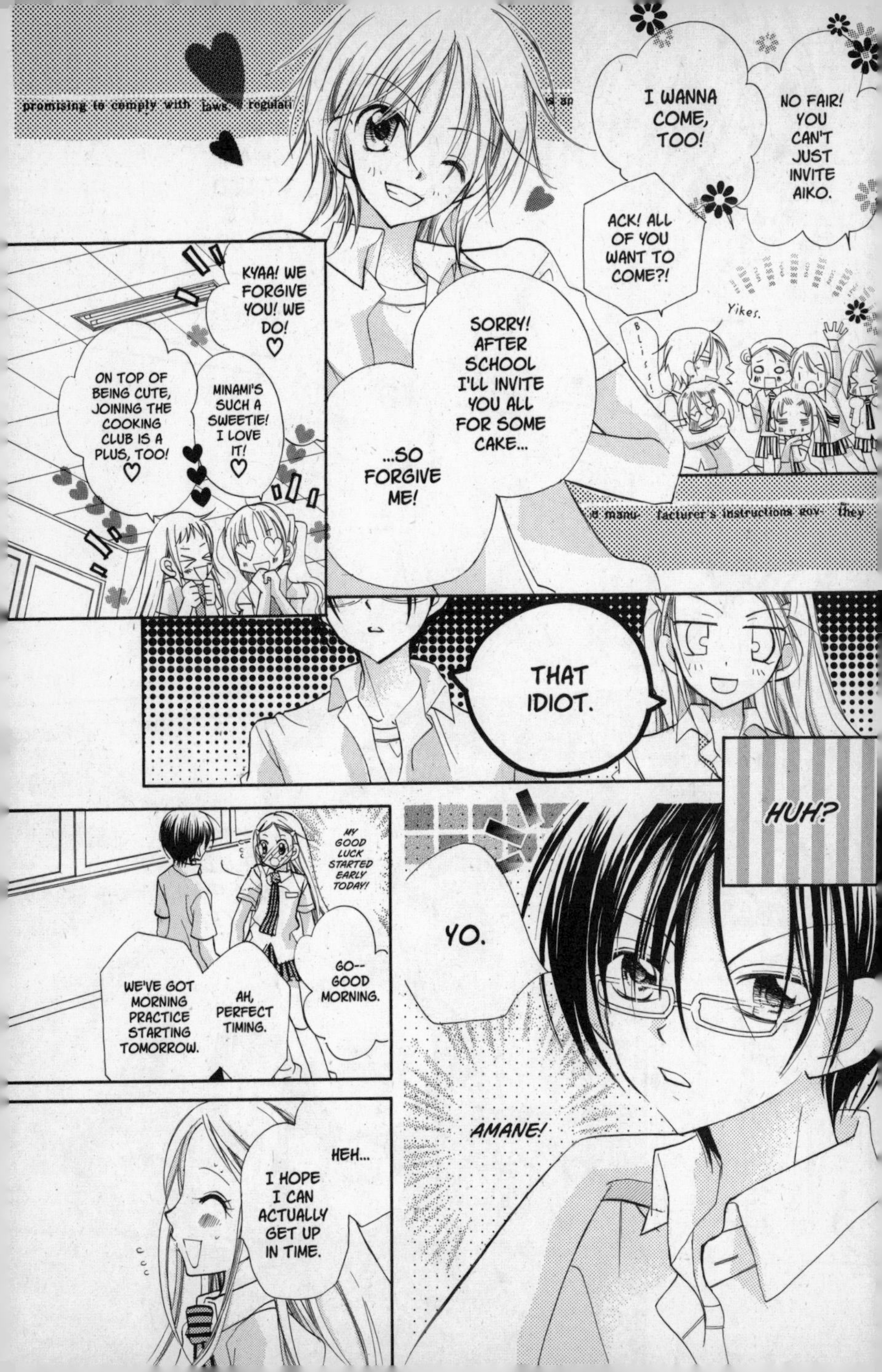
NO FAIR! YOU CAN'T JUST INVITE AIKO.
I WANNA COME, TOO!
ACK! ALL OF YOU WANT TO COME?!
Yikes.
SORRY! AFTER SCHOOL I'LL INVITE YOU ALL FOR SOME CAKE...
...SO FORGIVE ME!
KYAA! WE FORGIVE YOU! WE DO! ♡
MINAMI'S SUCH A SWEETIE! I LOVE IT! ♡
ON TOP OF BEING CUTE, JOINING THE COOKING CLUB IS A PLUS, TOO! ♡
THAT IDIOT.
HUH?
YO.
AMANE!
MY GOOD LUCK STARTED EARLY TODAY!
GO-- GOOD MORNING.
AH, PERFECT TIMING.
WE'VE GOT MORNING PRACTICE STARTING TOMORROW.
HEH...
I HOPE I CAN ACTUALLY GET UP IN TIME.

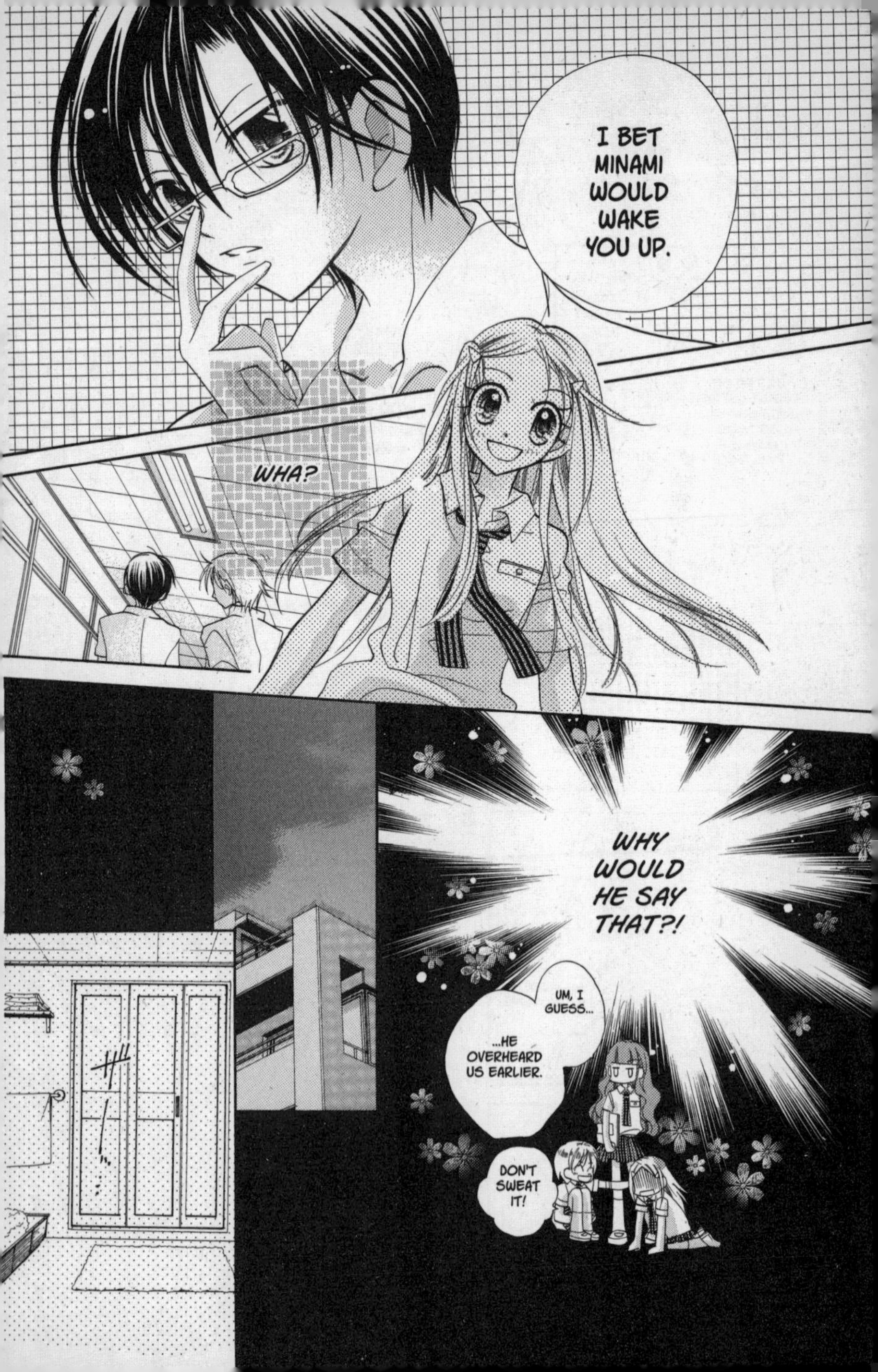
I BET MINAMI WOULD WAKE YOU UP.
WHA?
WHY WOULD HE SAY THAT?!
UM, I GUESS...
...HE OVERHEARD US EARLIER.
DON'T SWEAT IT!

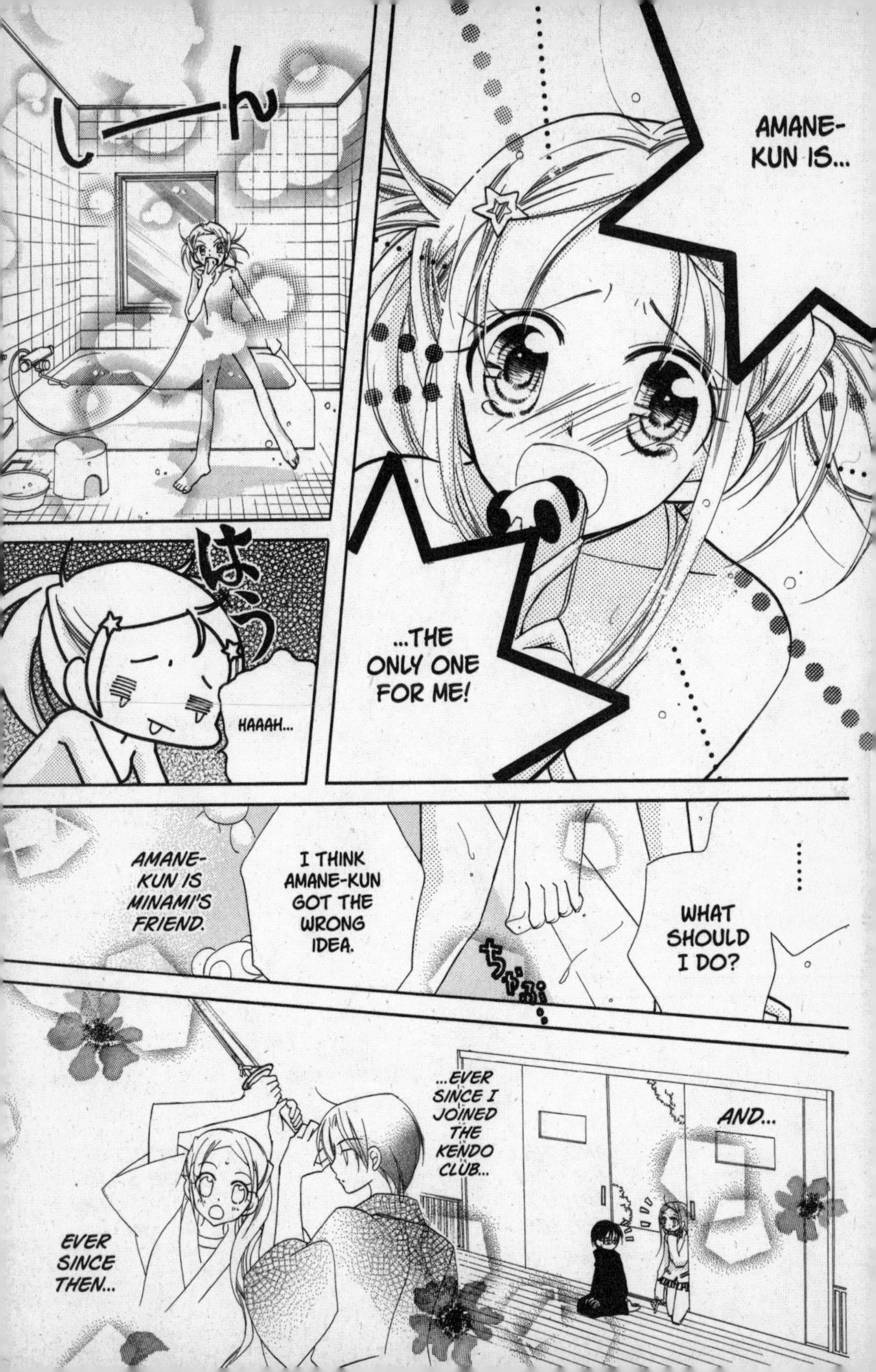
AMANE-KUN IS...
...THE ONLY ONE FOR ME!
しーん
はっ
HAAAH...
......
WHAT SHOULD I DO?
ちゃぷ
I THINK AMANE-KUN GOT THE WRONG IDEA.
AMANE-KUN IS MINAMI'S FRIEND.
AND...
...EVER SINCE I JOINED THE KENDO CLUB...
EVER SINCE THEN...

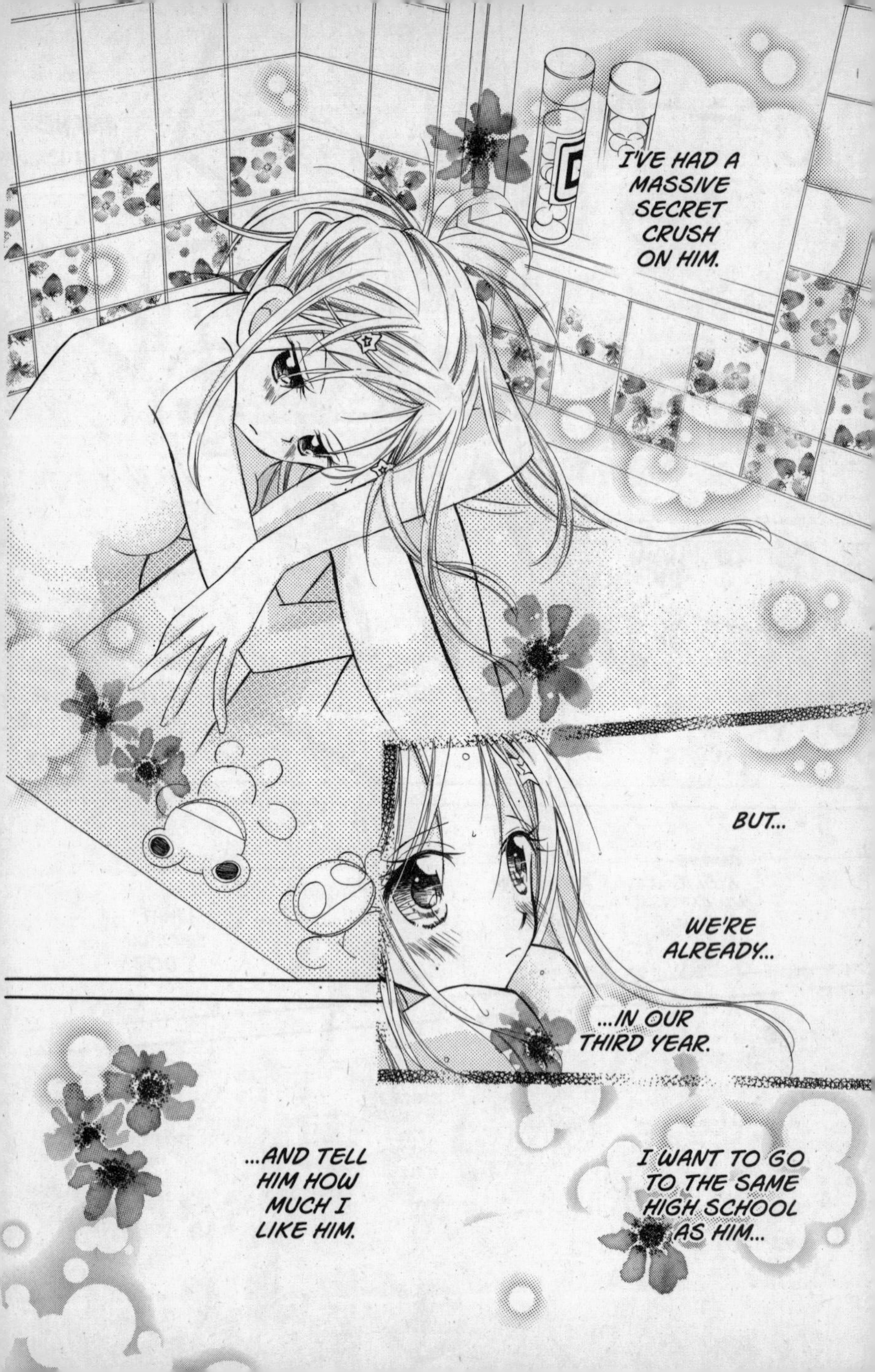
I'VE HAD A MASSIVE SECRET CRUSH ON HIM.
BUT...
WE'RE ALREADY...
...IN OUR THIRD YEAR.
I WANT TO GO TO THE SAME HIGH SCHOOL AS HIM...
...AND TELL HIM HOW MUCH I LIKE HIM.

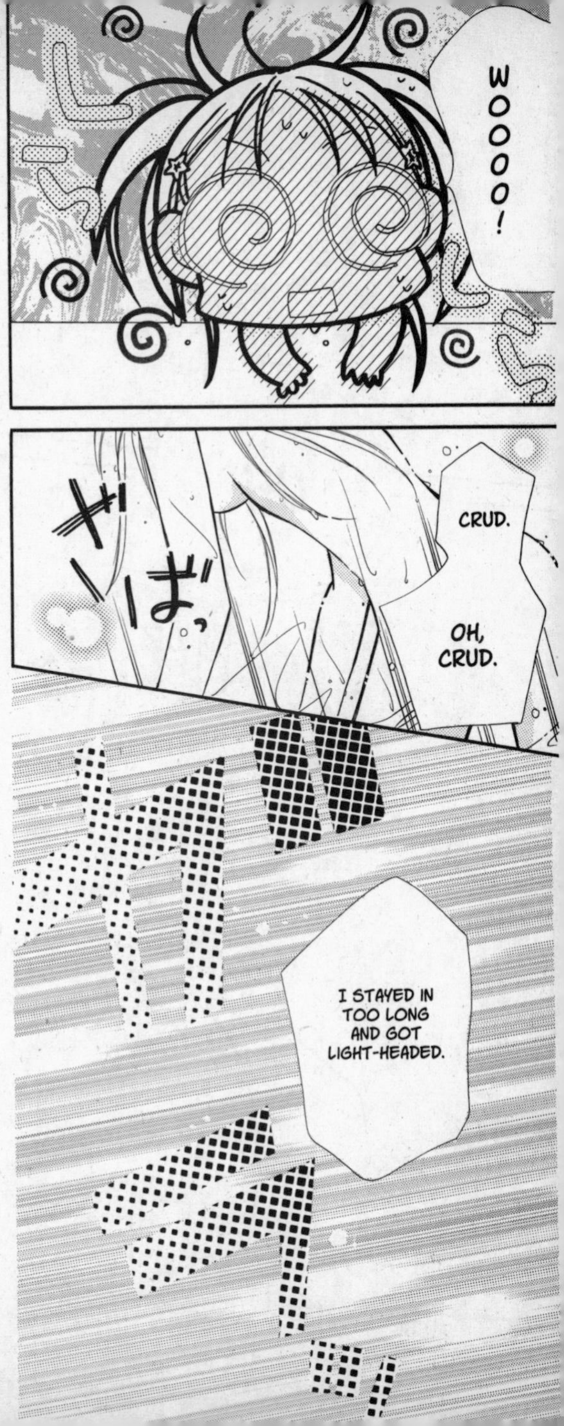
WOOOOO!
CRUD.
OH, CRUD.
ヤばっ
I STAYED IN TOO LONG AND GOT LIGHT-HEADED.

ONE!

WAZZUP?!

Haruka Fukushima here! Nice to meet you! And a

Special Thanks!

to those of you who always read my works! I hope you're doing well. As for me, I just...

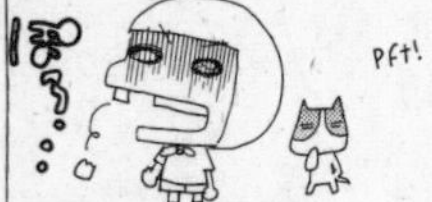
Pft!

...Lost a tooth.

It's this little bugger's fault.

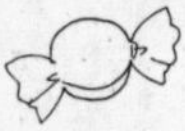

I was eating a certain milk candy as I was drawing just now. It stuck surprisingly hard to my teeth and then one of them fell out.

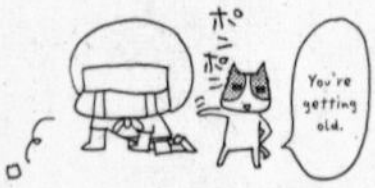
You're getting old.

As soon as I get this manuscript finished, I am going to head over to our swell family dentist to get patched up.

To Two →

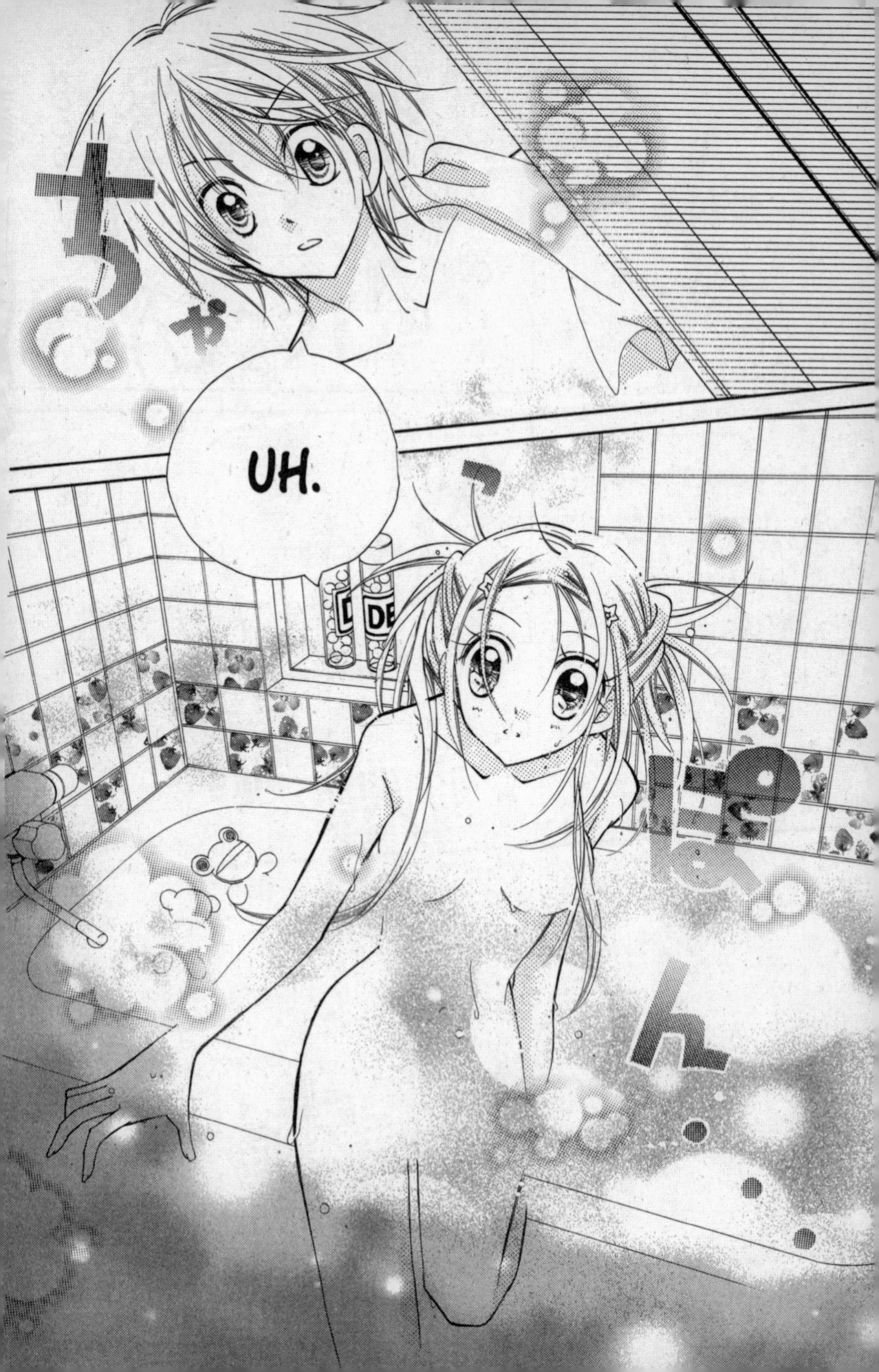
UH.

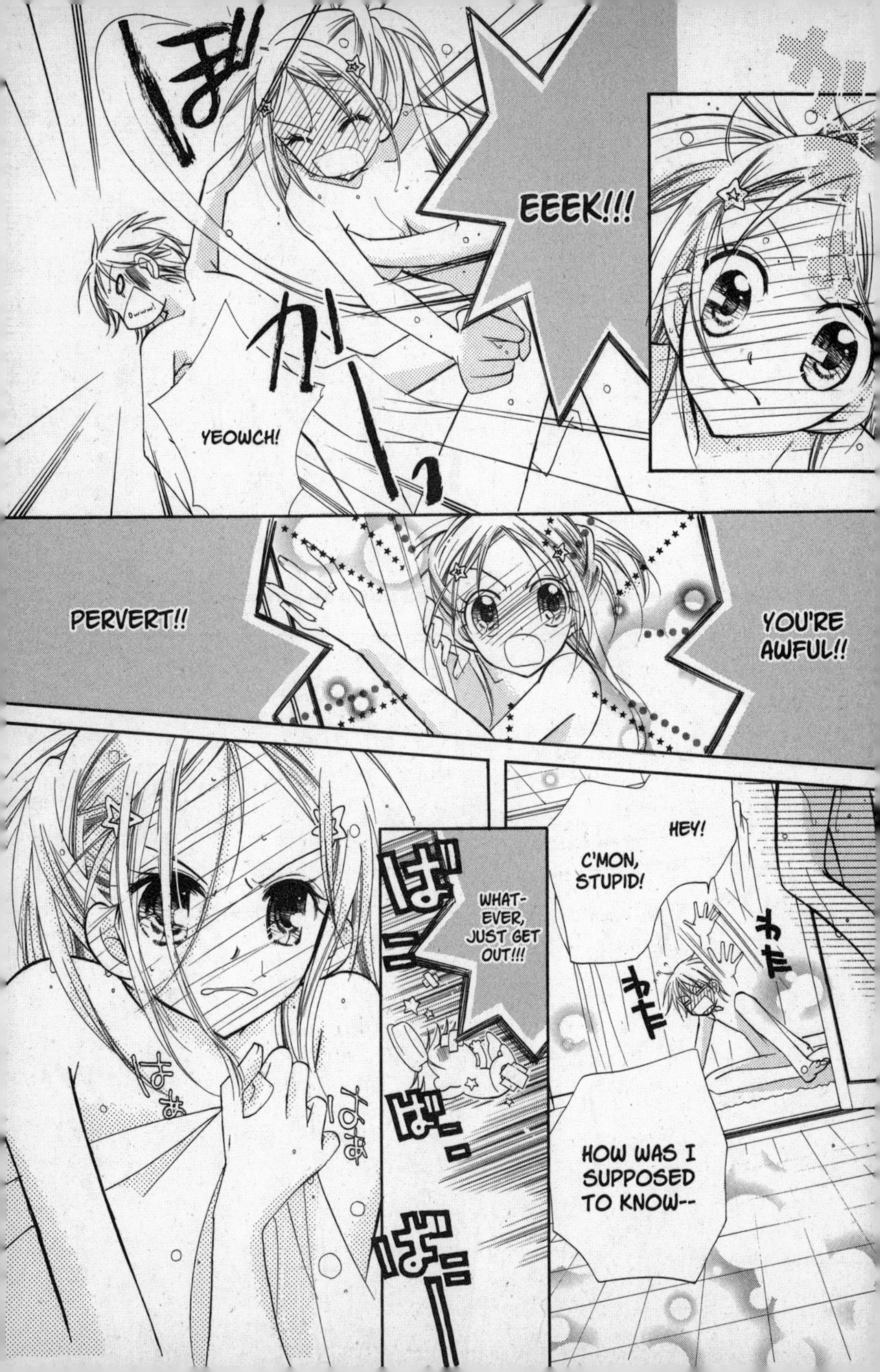
EEEK!!!
Owww!
YEOWCH!
YOU'RE AWFUL!!
PERVERT!!
HEY!
C'MON, STUPID!
HOW WAS I SUPPOSED TO KNOW--
WHAT-EVER, JUST GET OUT!!!

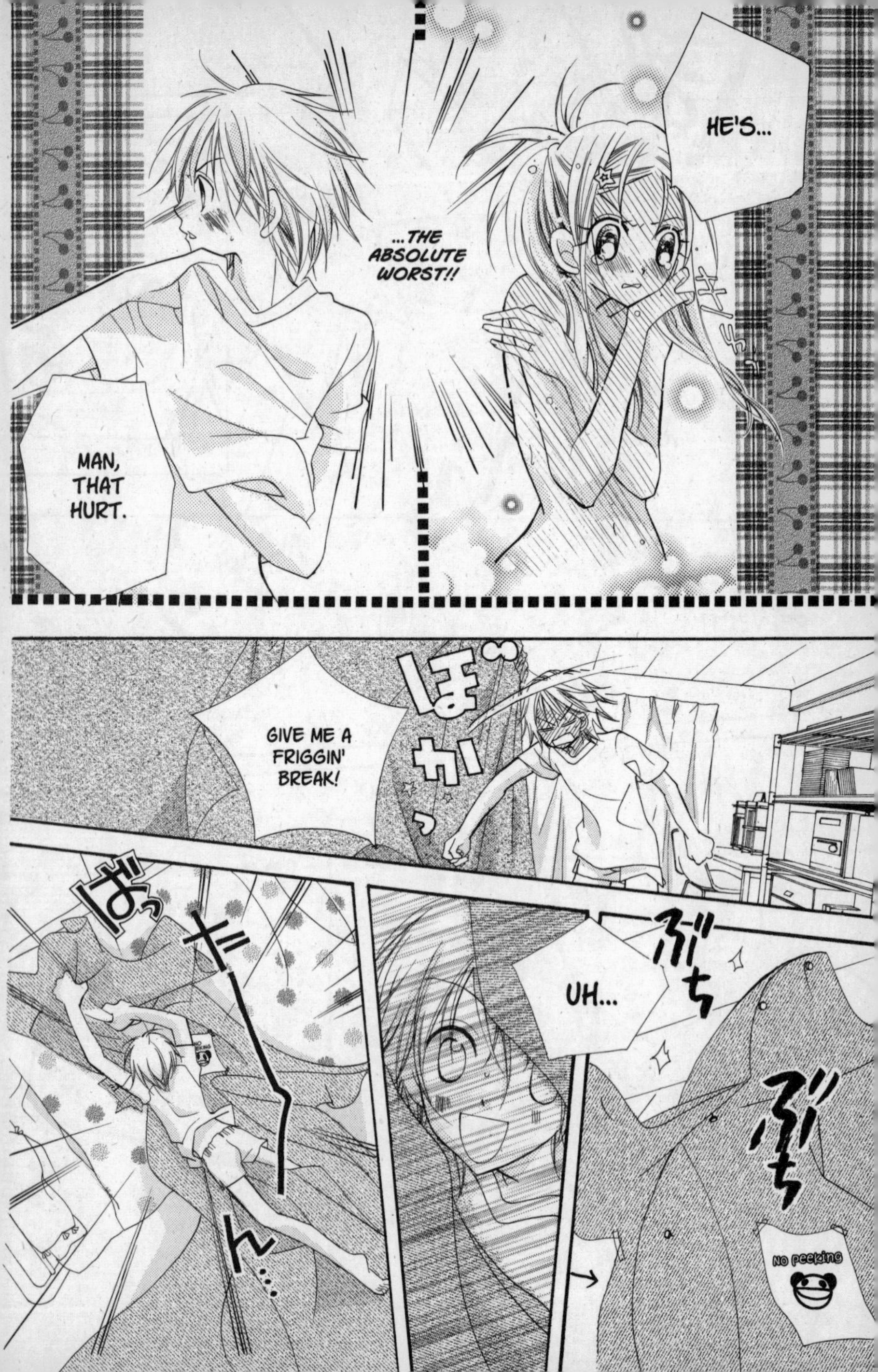
HE'S...
...THE ABSOLUTE WORST!!
MAN, THAT HURT.
GIVE ME A FRIGGIN' BREAK!
UH...
No peeking

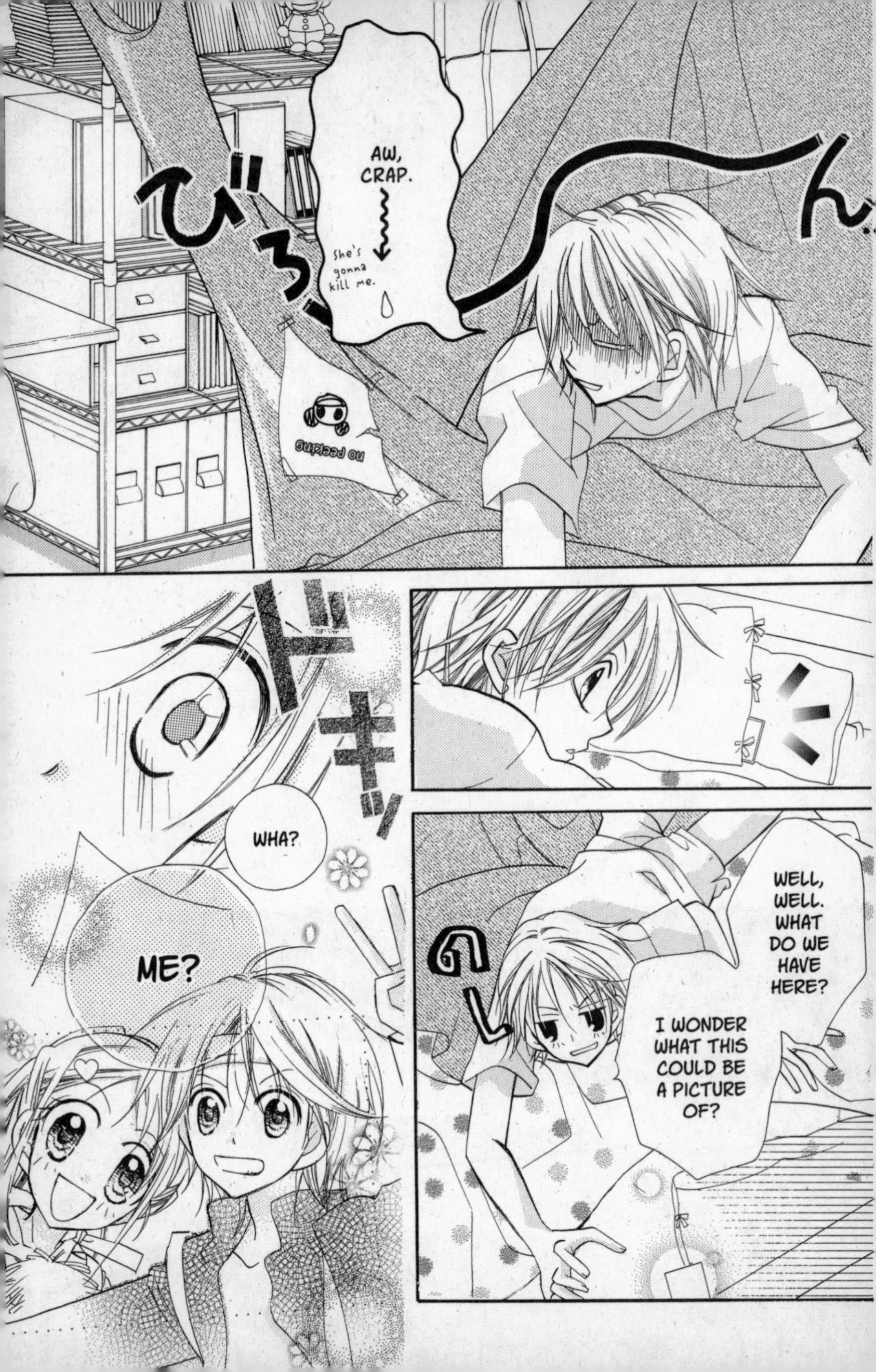
びろ〜〜ん
AW, CRAP.
She's gonna kill me.
no peeking
WELL, WELL. WHAT DO WE HAVE HERE?
I WONDER WHAT THIS COULD BE A PICTURE OF?
ドキッ
WHA?
ME?

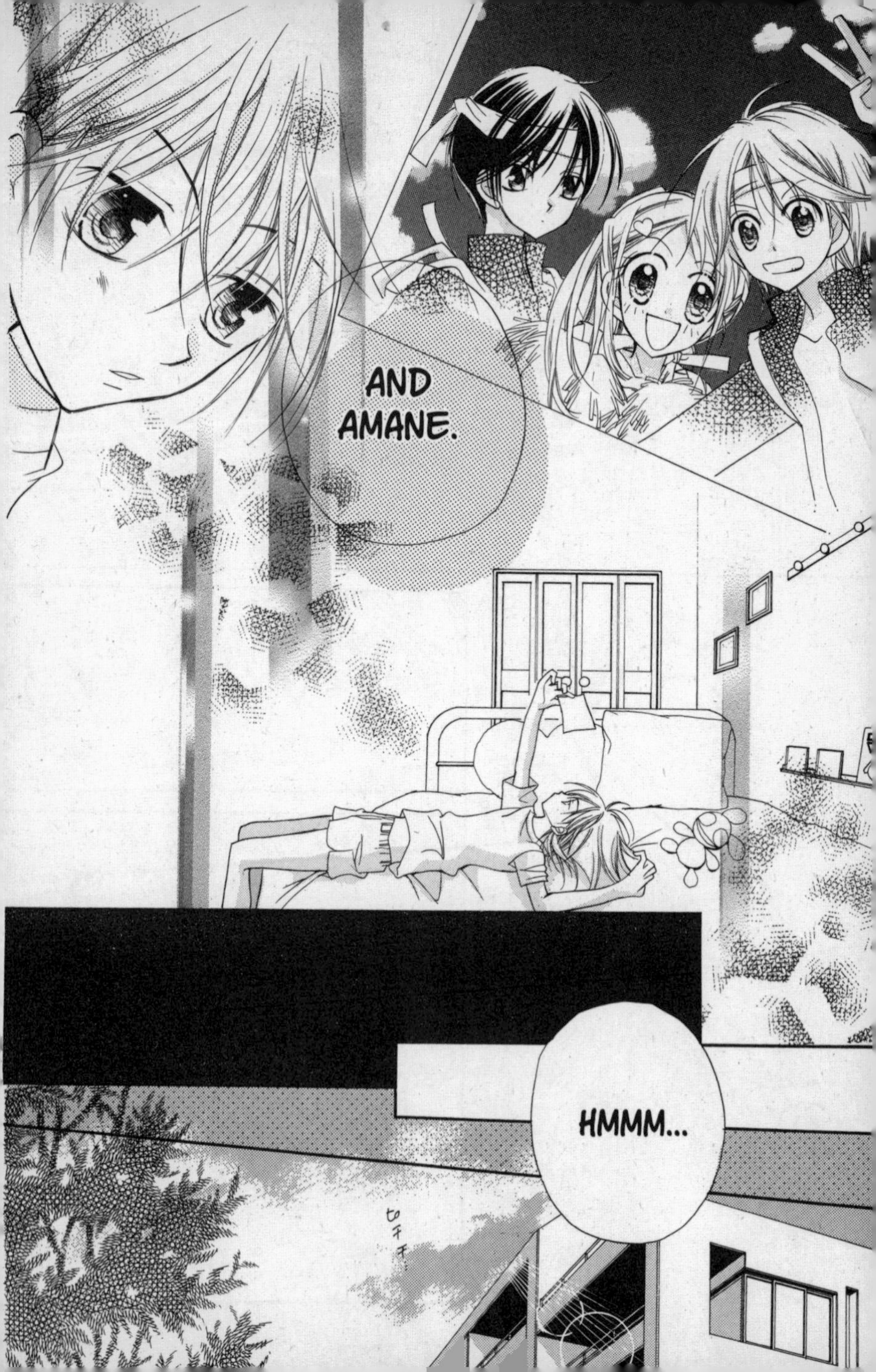
AND AMANE.
HMMM...
ピチチ

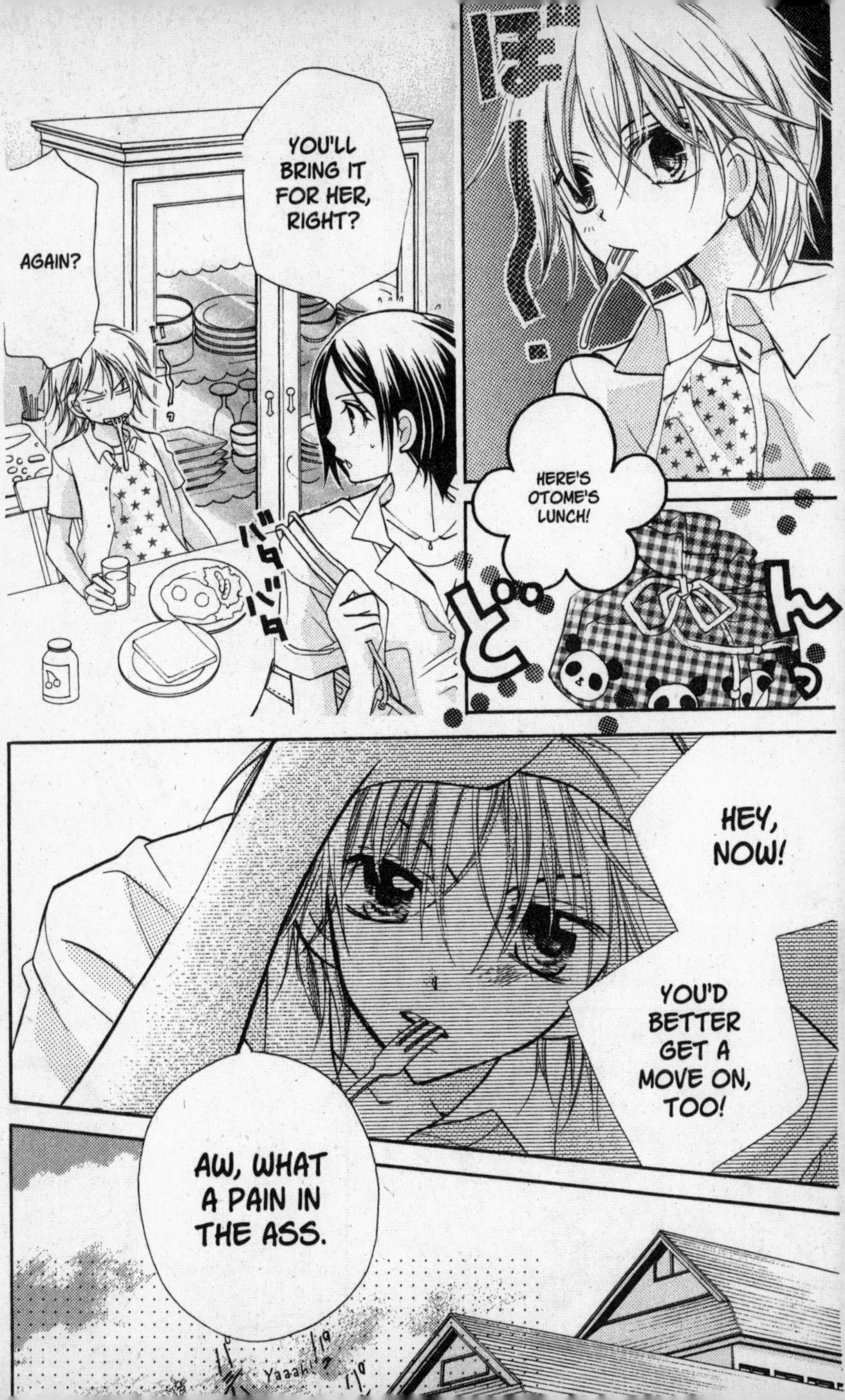
HERE'S OTOME'S LUNCH!
YOU'LL BRING IT FOR HER, RIGHT?
AGAIN?
バタバタ
HEY, NOW!
YOU'D BETTER GET A MOVE ON, TOO!
AW, WHAT A PAIN IN THE ASS.
Yaaah!

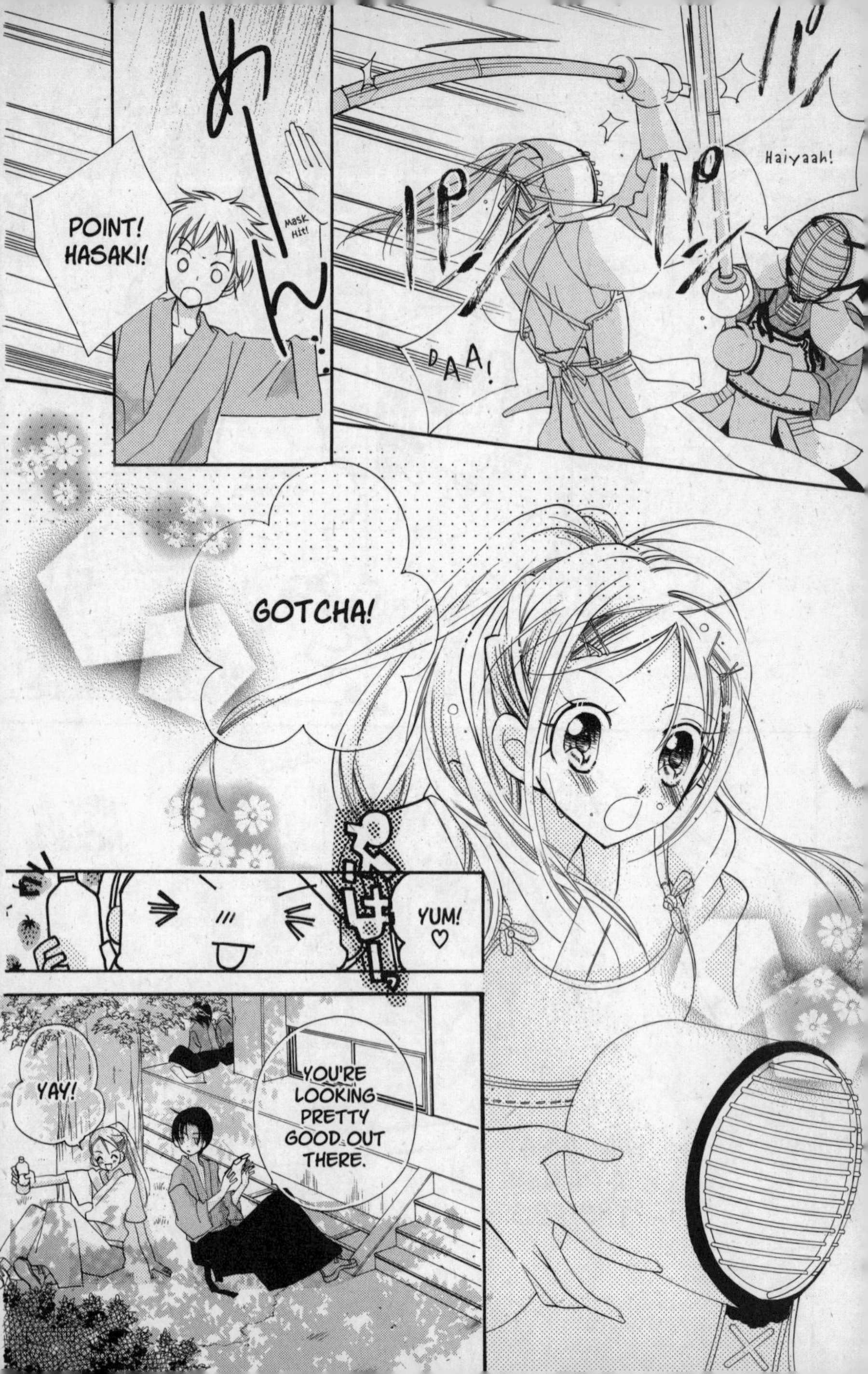
Haiyaah!
DAA!
POINT! HASAKI!
Mask Hit!
GOTCHA!
YUM! ♡
YOU'RE LOOKING PRETTY GOOD OUT THERE.
YAY!

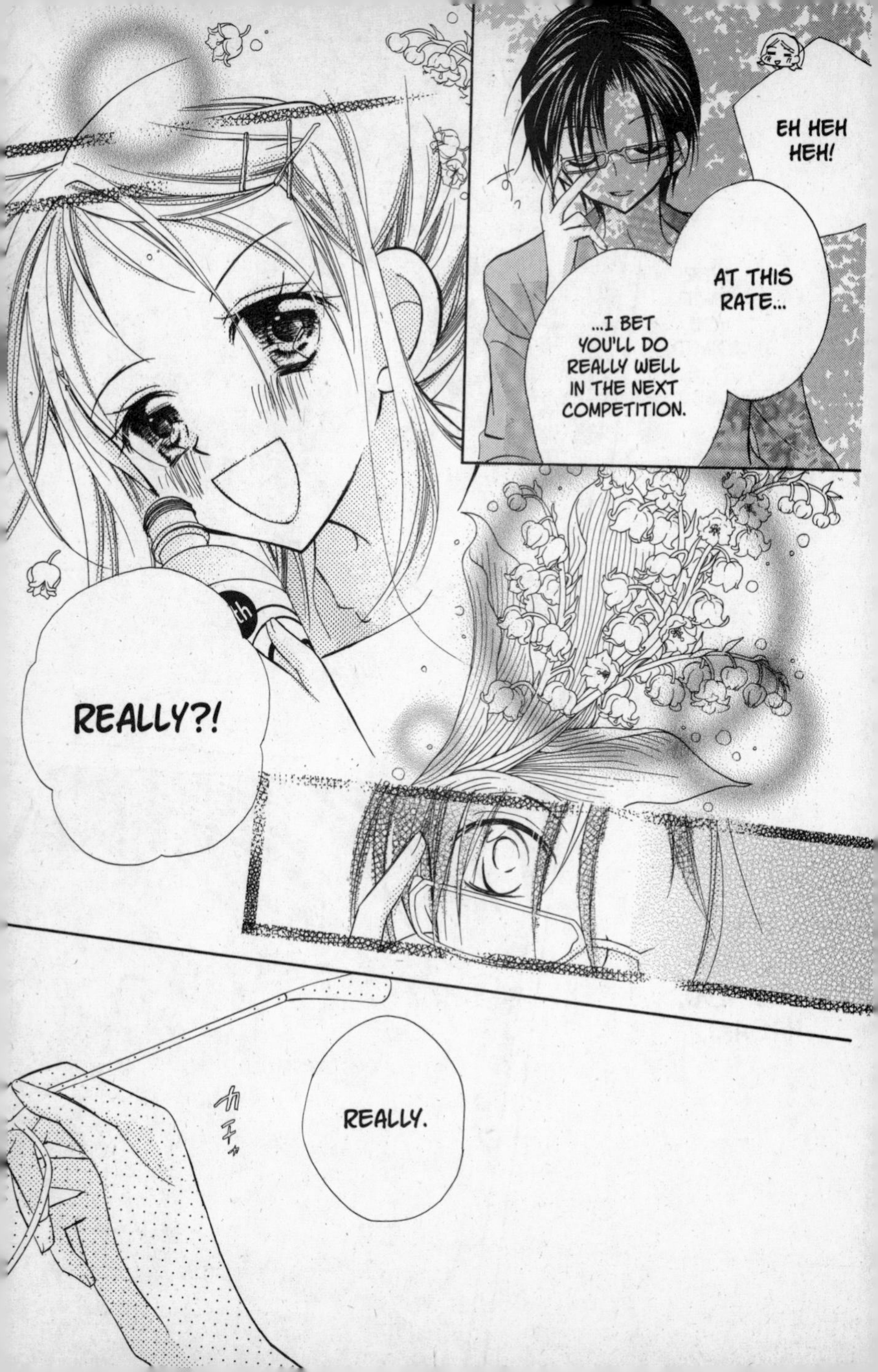
EH HEH HEH!
AT THIS RATE...
...I BET YOU'LL DO REALLY WELL IN THE NEXT COMPETITION.
REALLY?!
REALLY.
カチャ

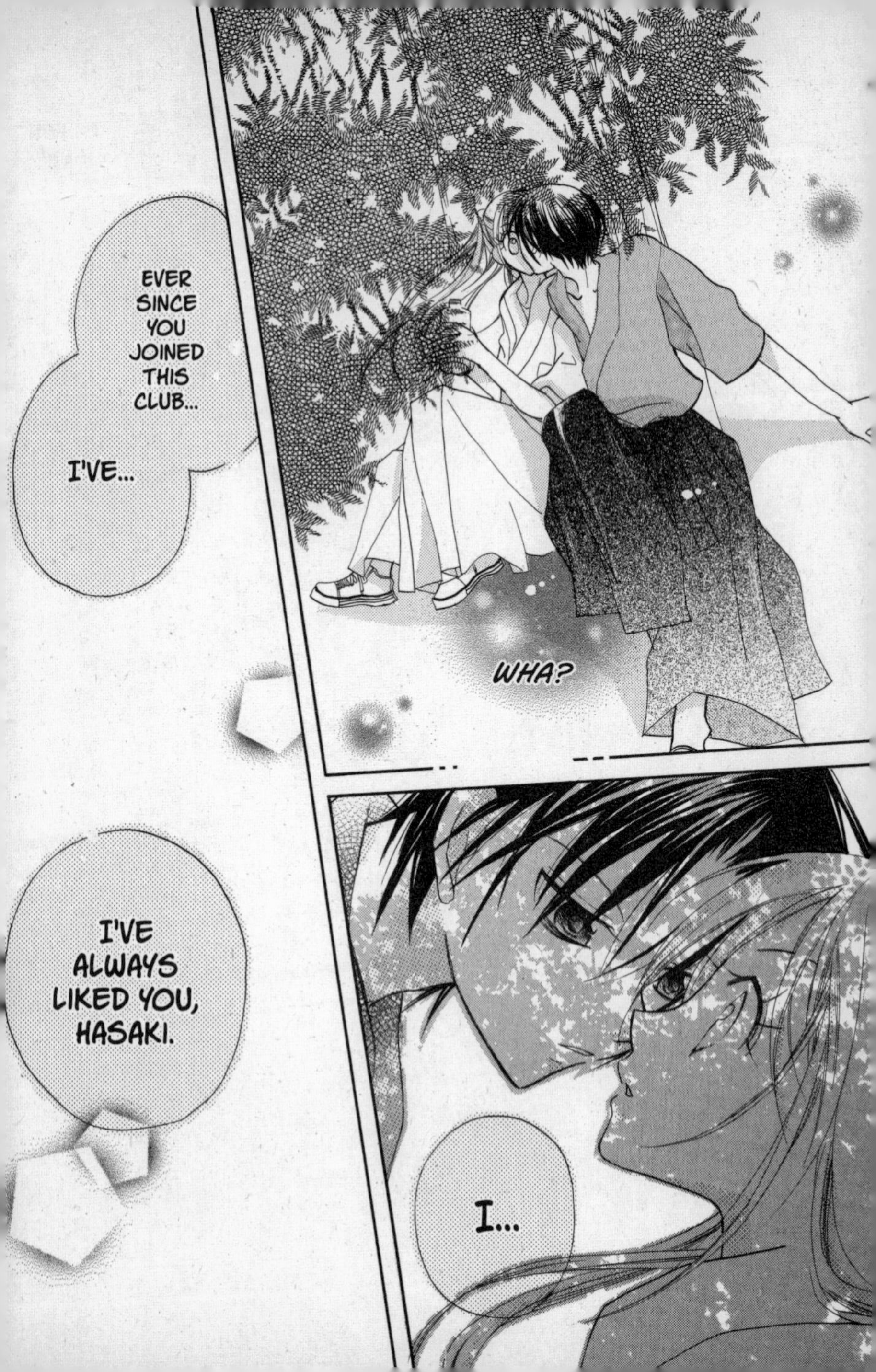
WHA?
EVER SINCE YOU JOINED THIS CLUB...
I'VE...
I...
I'VE ALWAYS LIKED YOU, HASAKI.

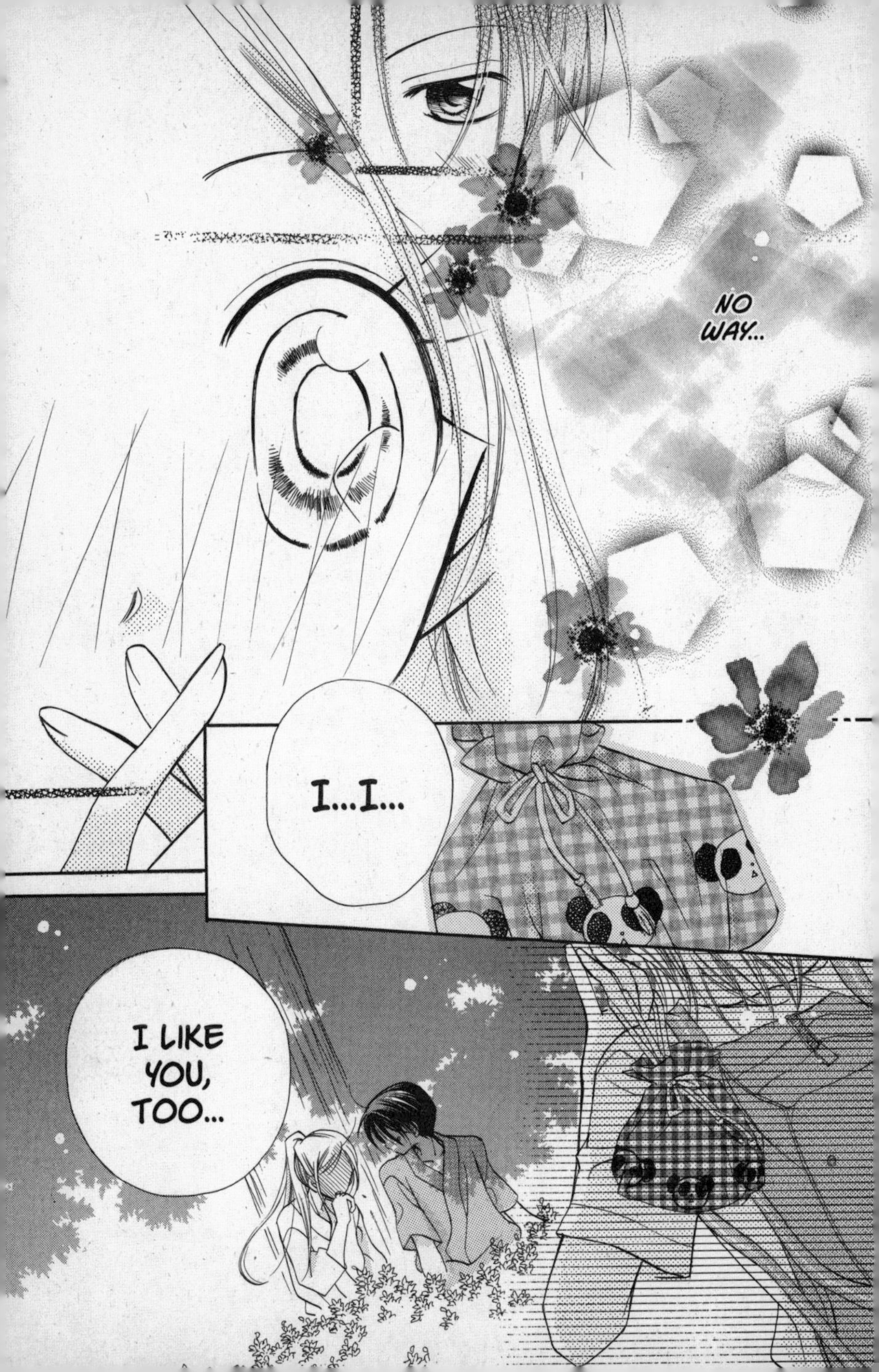
NO WAY...
I...I...
I LIKE YOU, TOO...

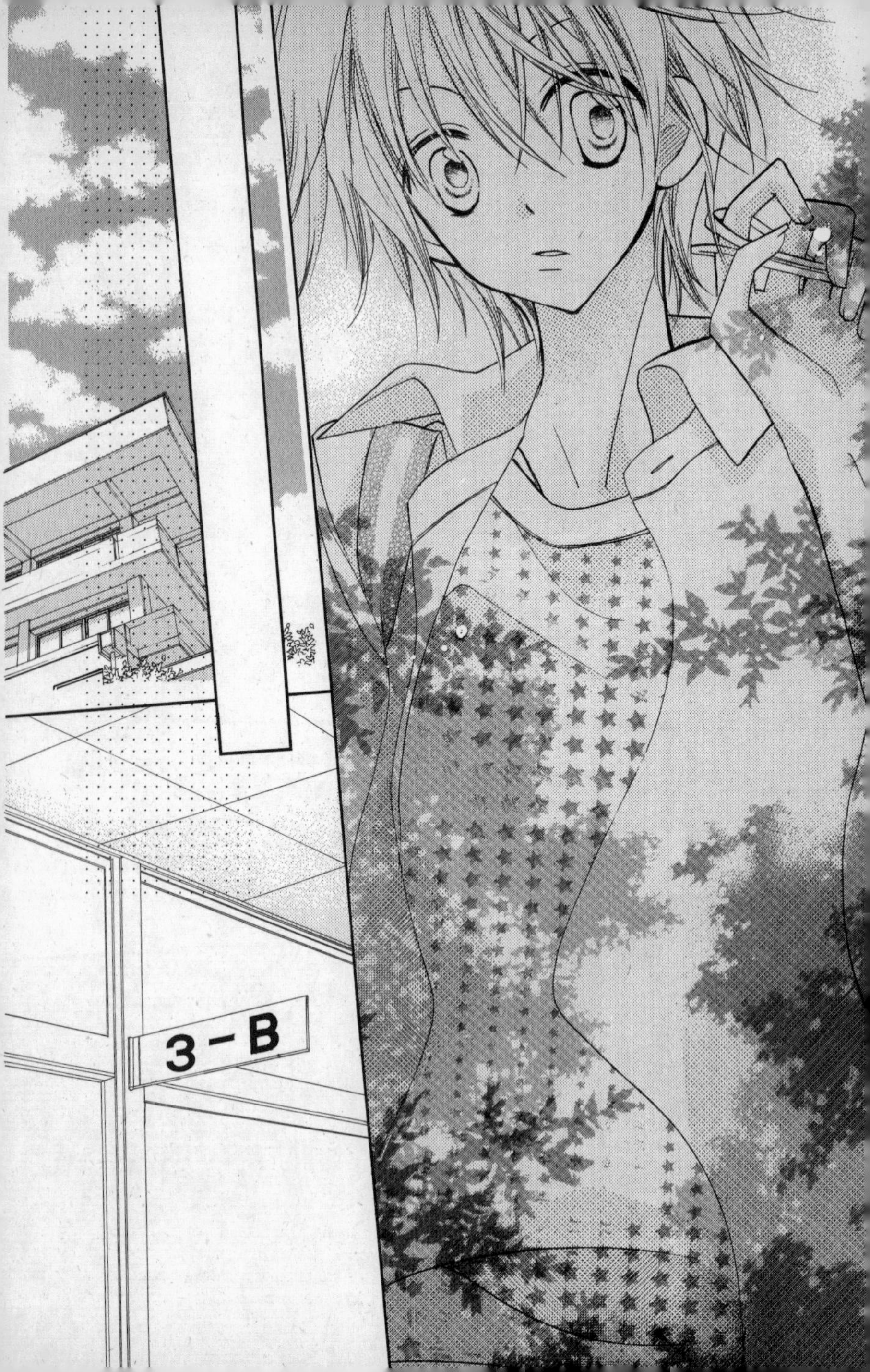
3-B

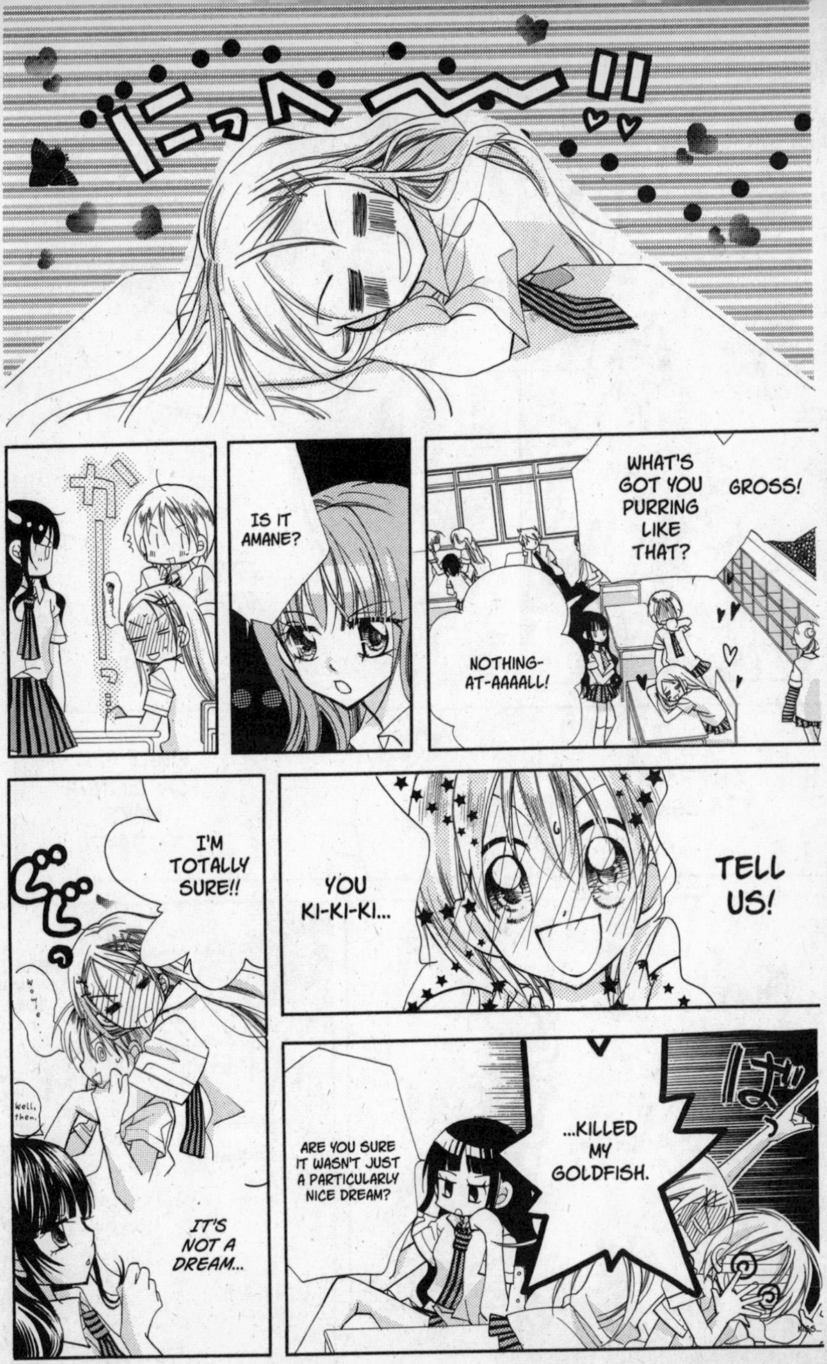
にっへへ〜!!
GROSS!
WHAT'S GOT YOU PURRING LIKE THAT?
NOTHING-AT-AAAALL!
IS IT AMANE?
かー
TELL US!
YOU KI-KI-KI...
ばっ
...KILLED MY GOLDFISH.
ARE YOU SURE IT WASN'T JUST A PARTICULARLY NICE DREAM?
I'M TOTALLY SURE!!
ぐぐっ
Well, then.
IT'S NOT A DREAM...

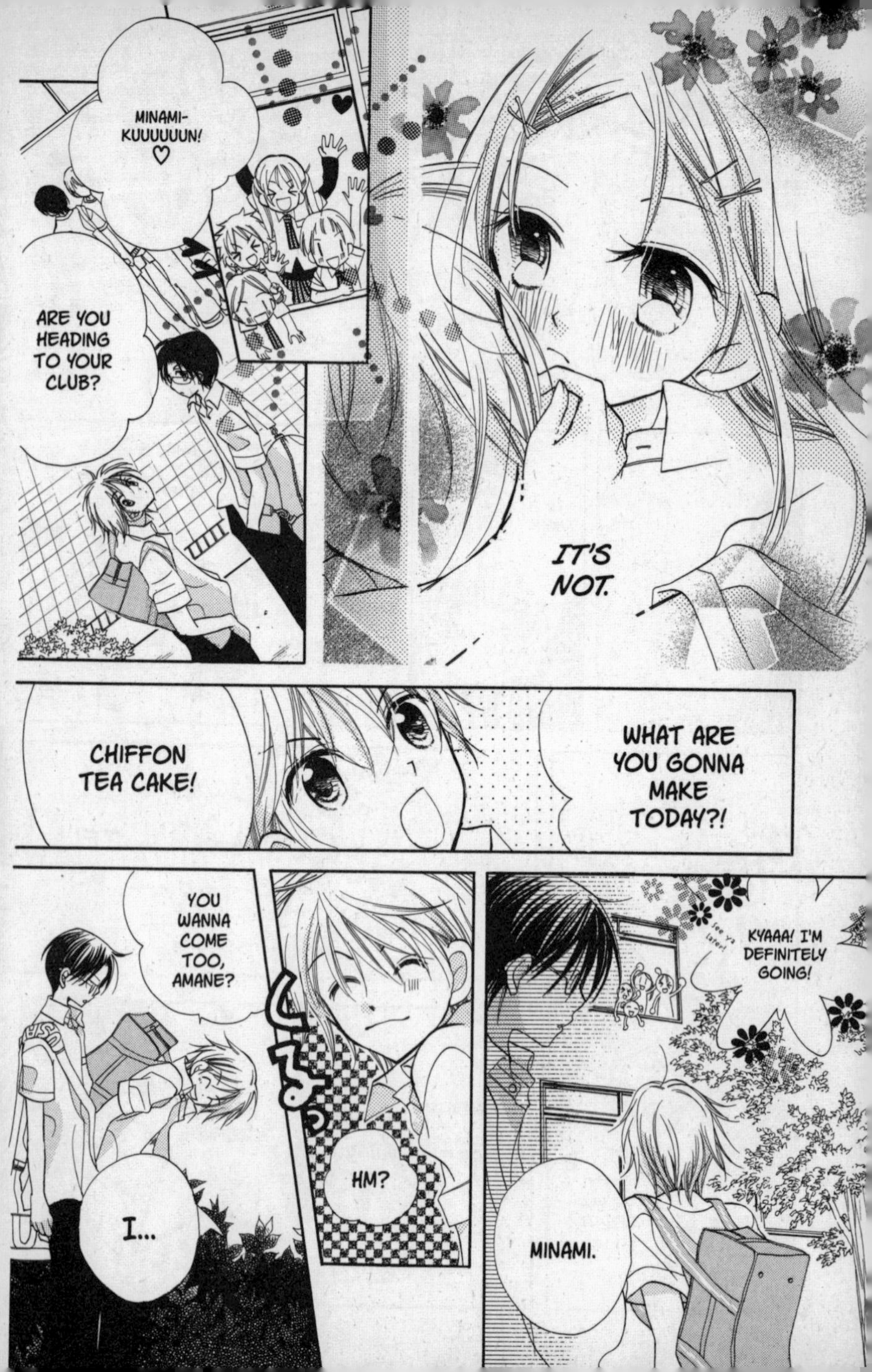
IT'S NOT.
MINAMI-KUUUUUUN! ♡
ARE YOU HEADING TO YOUR CLUB?
WHAT ARE YOU GONNA MAKE TODAY?!
CHIFFON TEA CAKE!
KYAAA! I'M DEFINITELY GOING!
See ya later!
MINAMI.
HM?
YOU WANNA COME TOO, AMANE?
I...

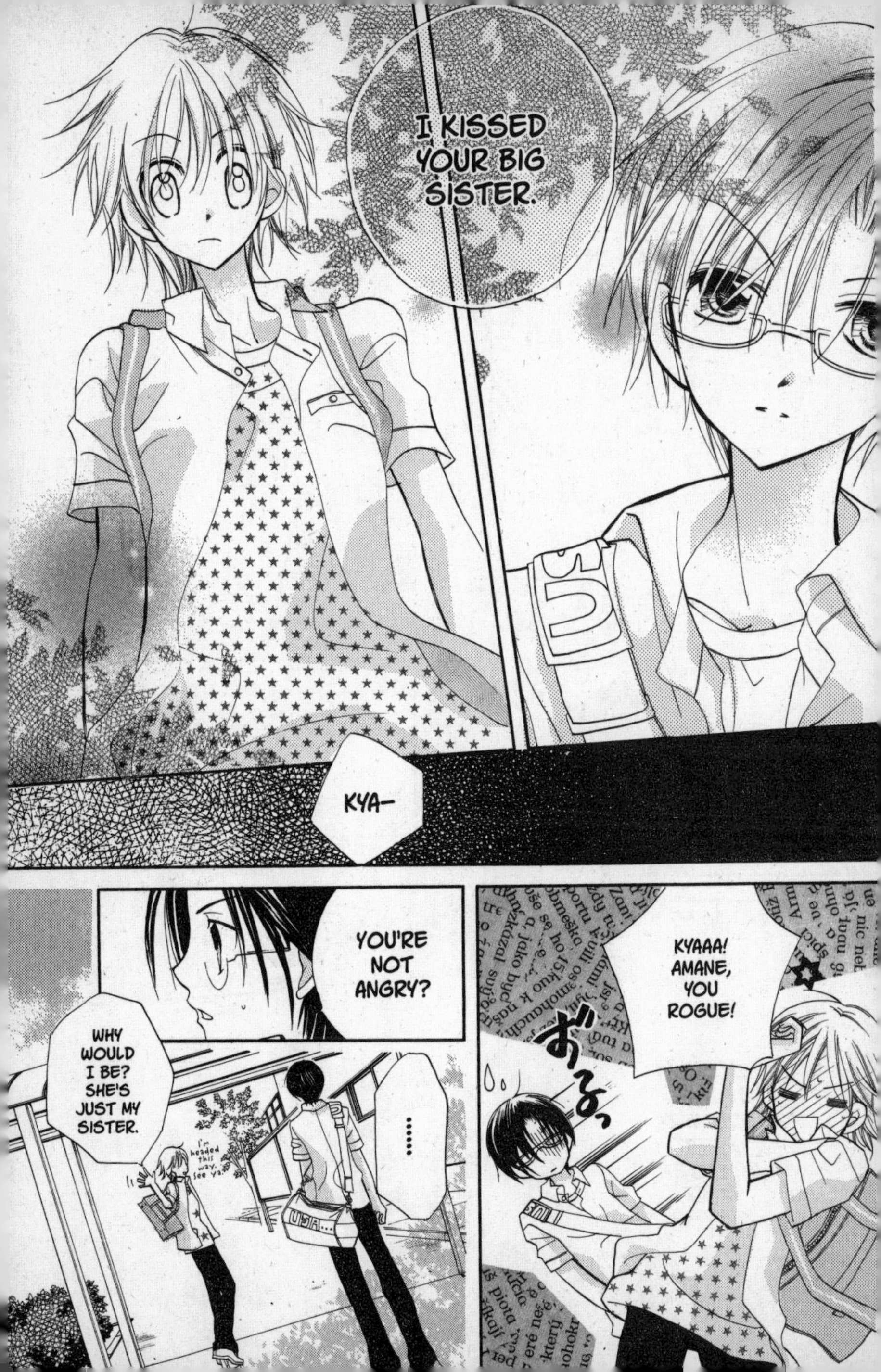
I KISSED YOUR BIG SISTER.
KYA-
KYAAA! AMANE, YOU ROGUE!
YOU'RE NOT ANGRY?
WHY WOULD I BE? SHE'S JUST MY SISTER.
I'm headed this way. See ya.
......

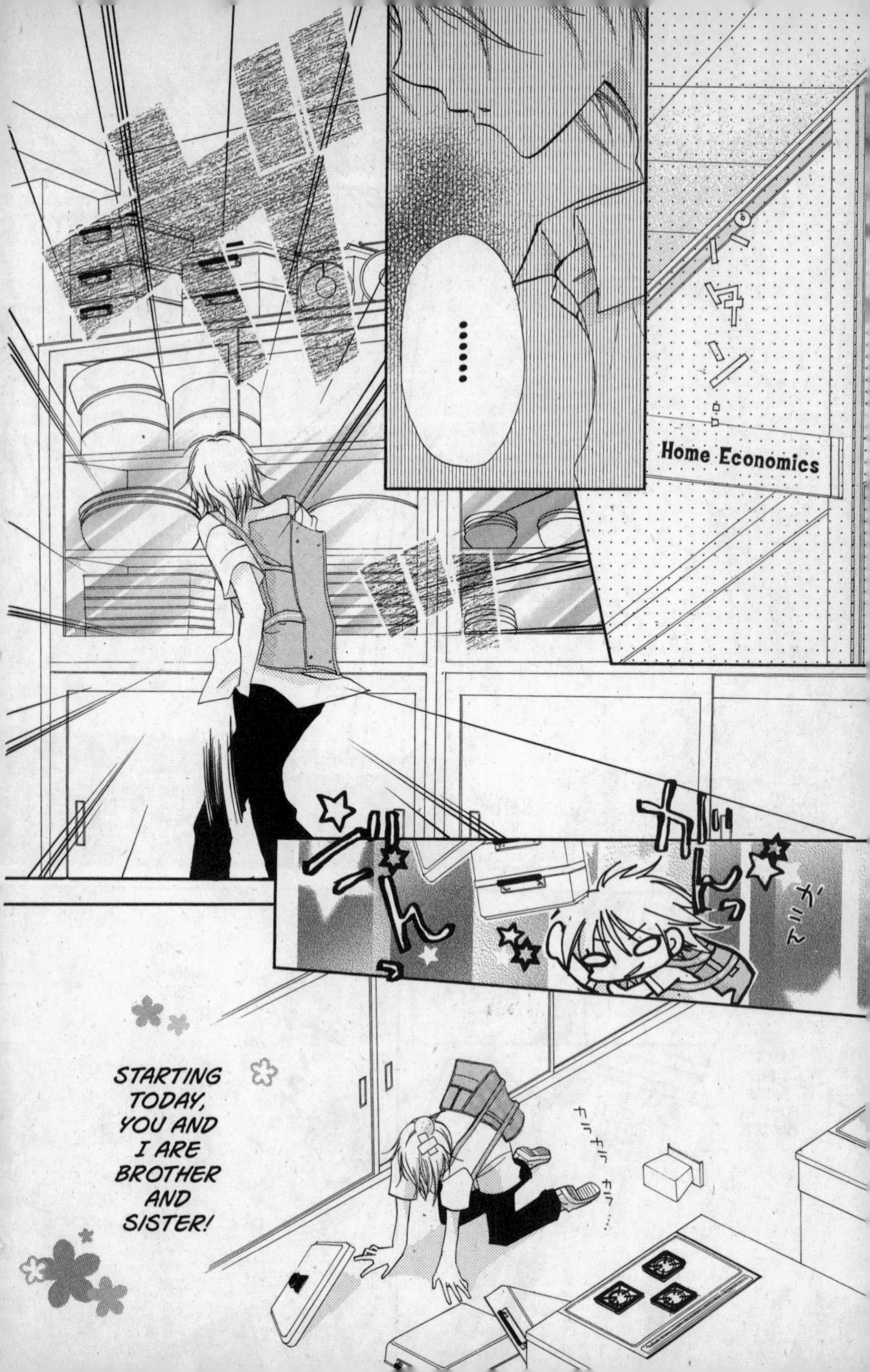
Home Economics
......
STARTING TODAY, YOU AND I ARE BROTHER AND SISTER!
カラ カラ カラ…

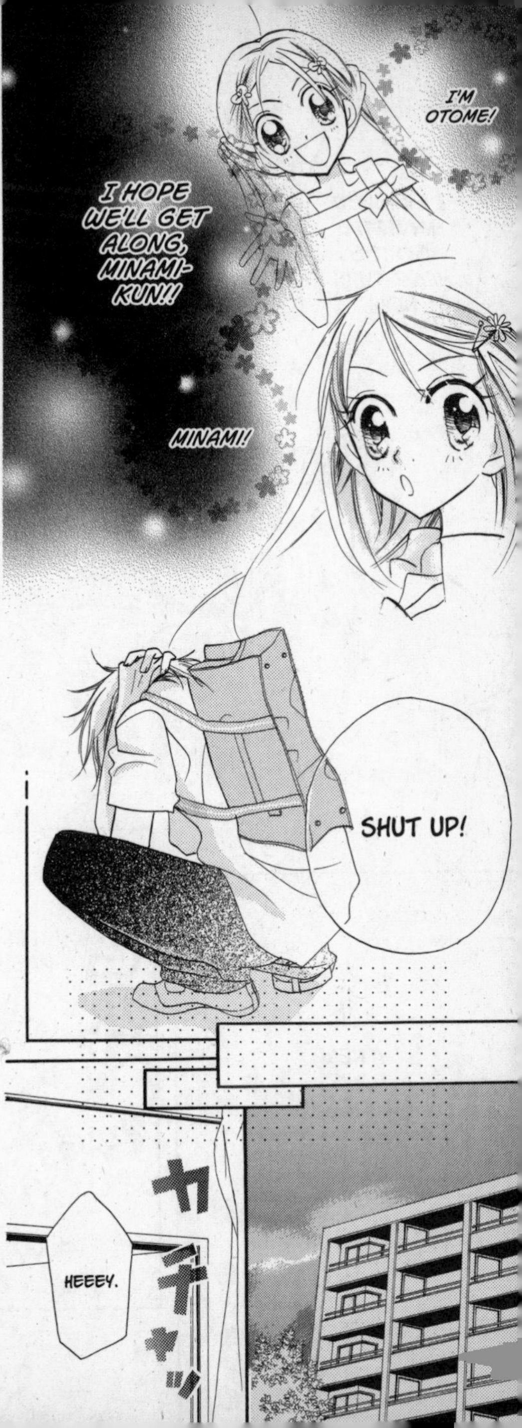
I'M OTOME!
I HOPE WE'LL GET ALONG, MINAMI-KUN!!
MINAMI!
SHUT UP!
HEEEY.

TWO!

- And so it's hello once again! Somehow, I've managed to deliver *Cherry Juice* volume 1 to you all.

- It's been such a long time since I've had a story serialized in the main *Nakayoshi* magazine that...

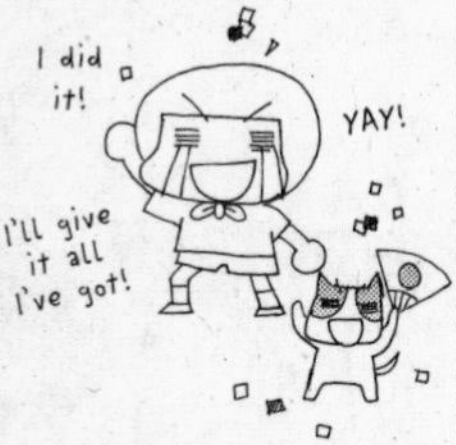
I did it!
YAY!
I'll give it all I've got!

...feelings like this, and...

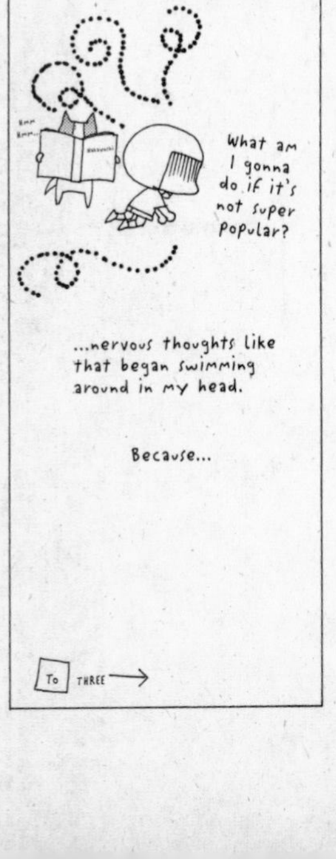
What am I gonna do if it's not super popular?

...nervous thoughts like that began swimming around in my head.

Because...

To THREE →

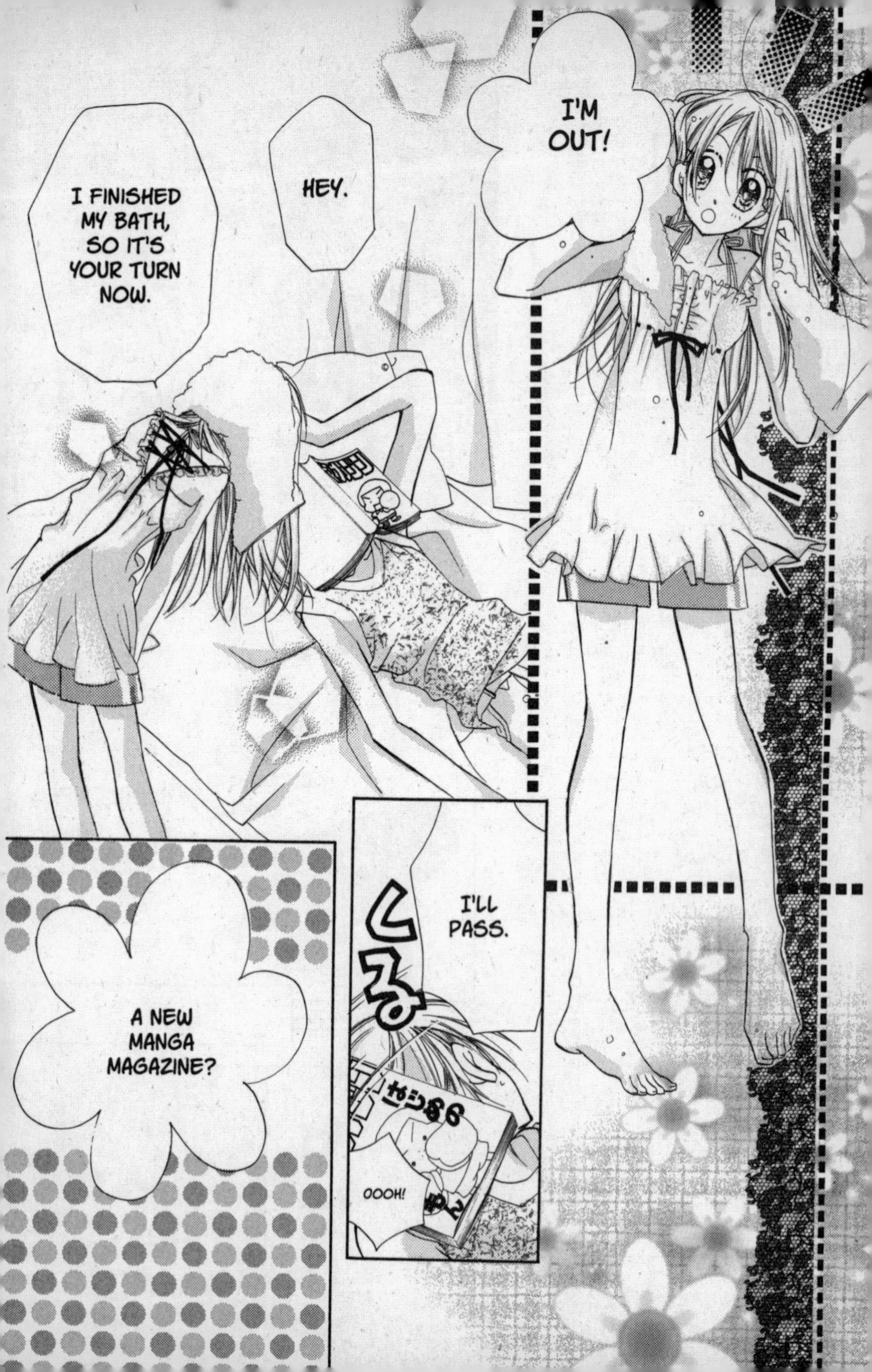
I'M OUT!
HEY.
I FINISHED MY BATH, SO IT'S YOUR TURN NOW.
I'LL PASS.
OOOH!
A NEW MANGA MAGAZINE?

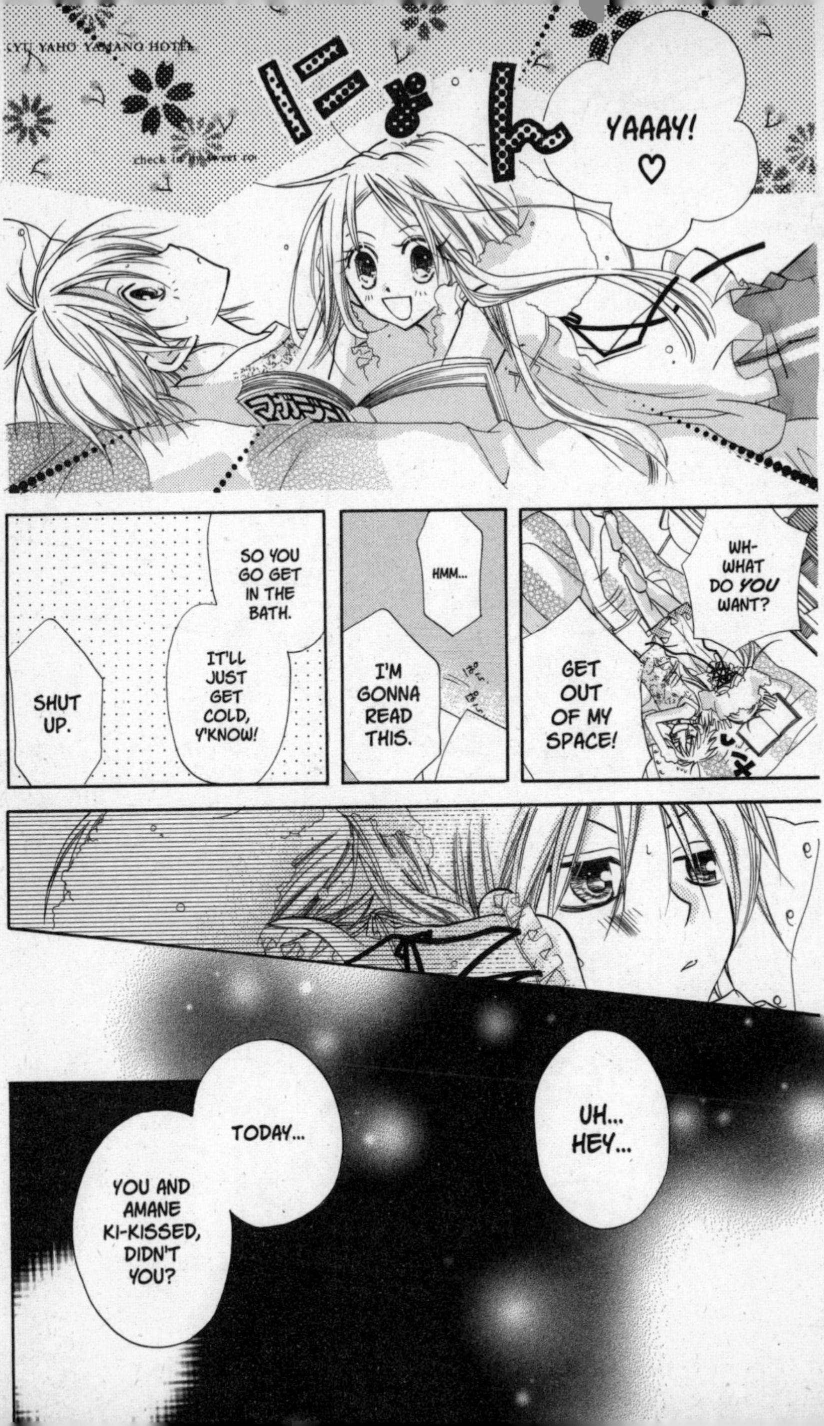
にゃん
YAAAY! ♡
WH-WHAT DO YOU WANT?
GET OUT OF MY SPACE!
HMM...
I'M GONNA READ THIS.
SO YOU GO GET IN THE BATH.
IT'LL JUST GET COLD, Y'KNOW!
SHUT UP.
UH... HEY...
TODAY...
YOU AND AMANE KI-KISSED, DIDN'T YOU?

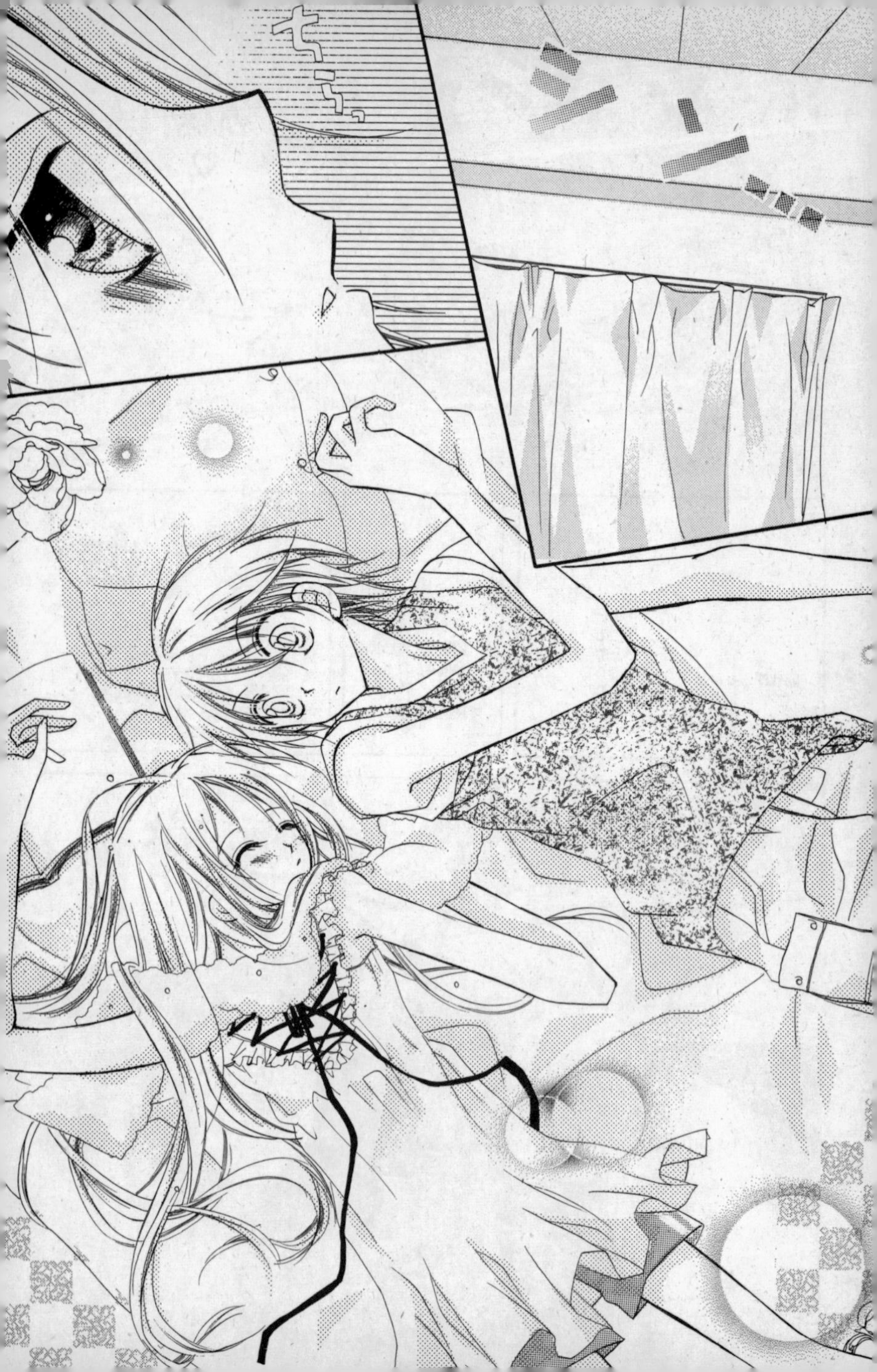
ちーらっ

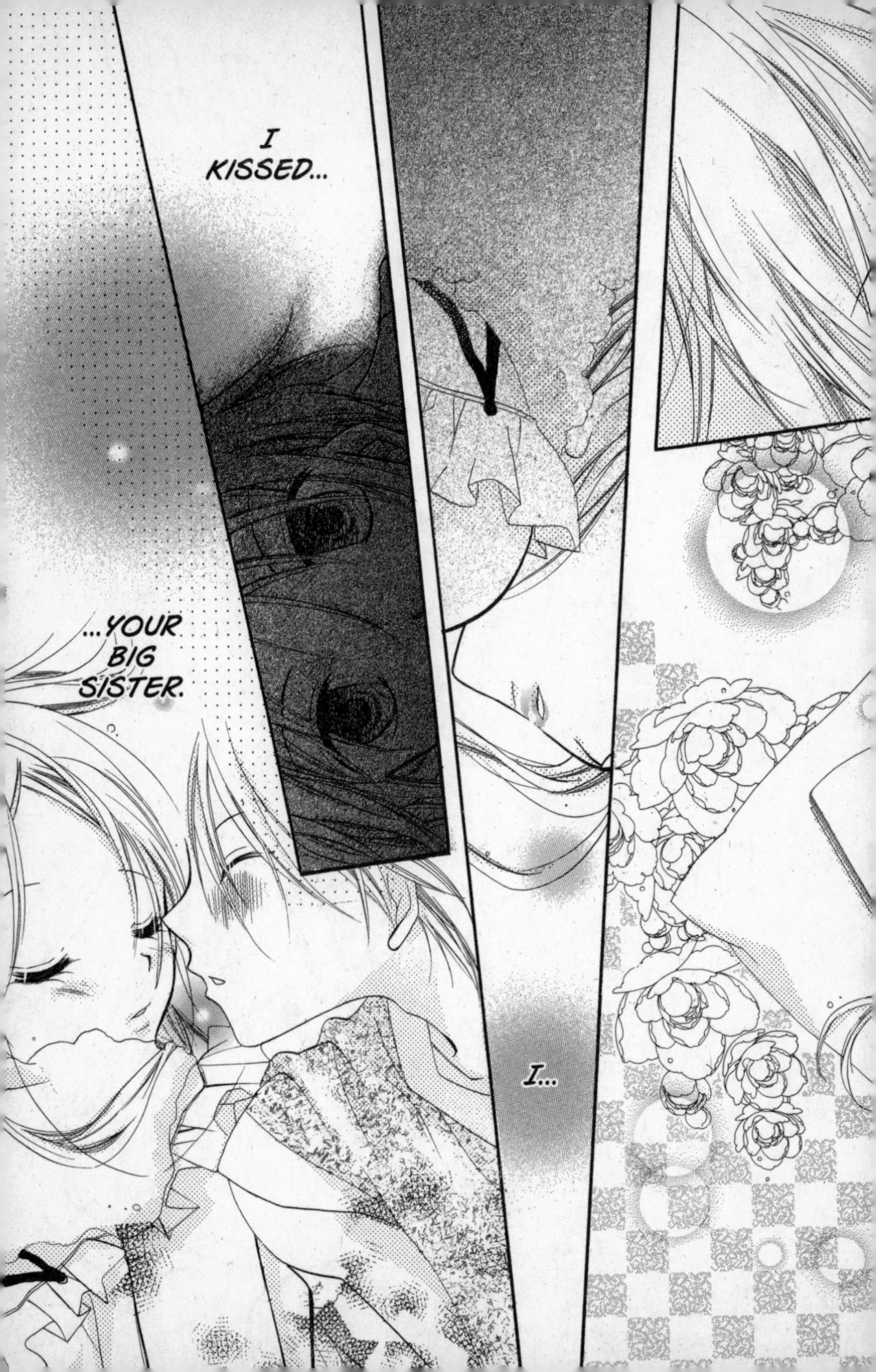
I...
I KISSED...
...YOUR BIG SISTER.

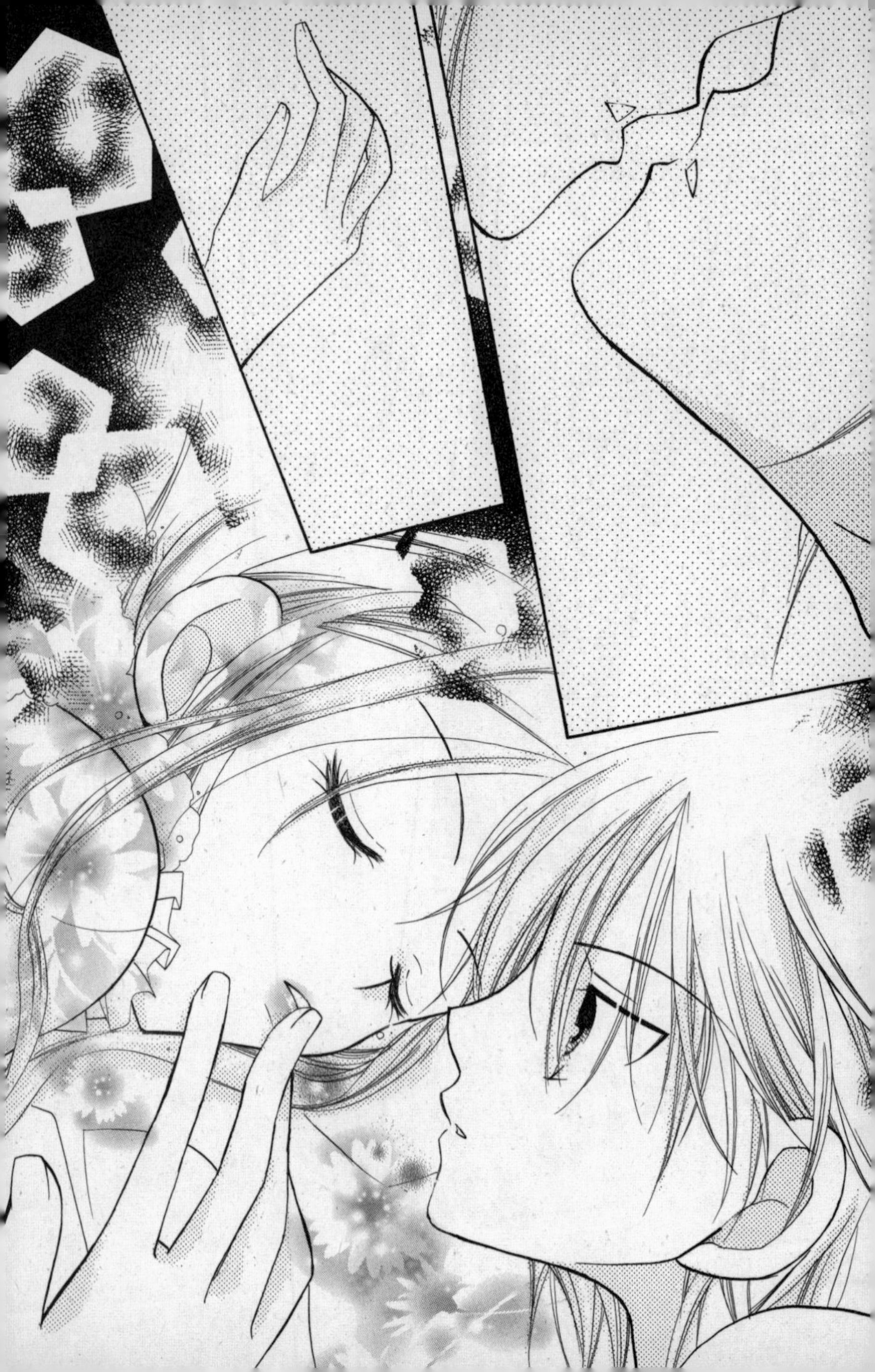

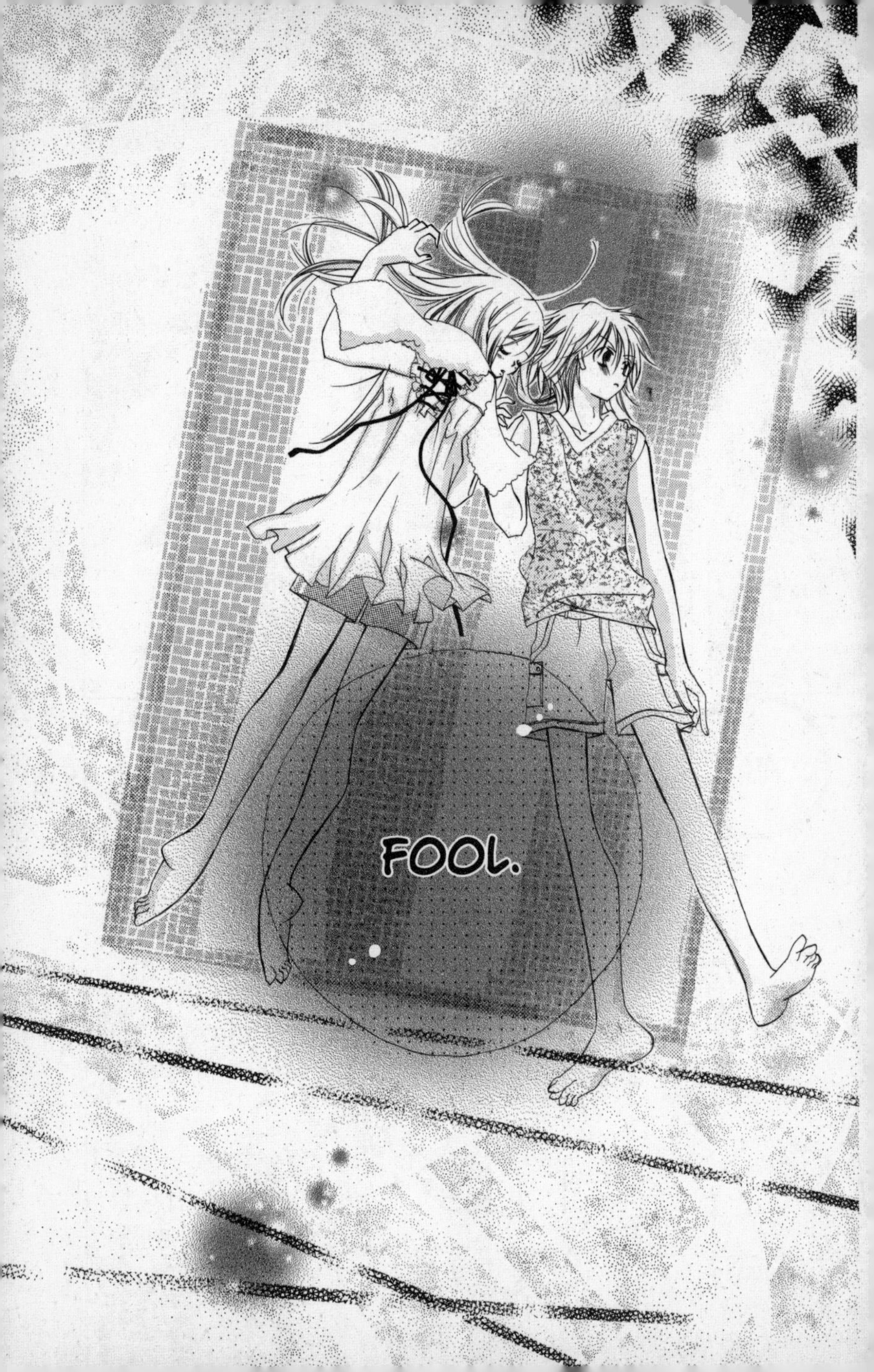
FOOL.

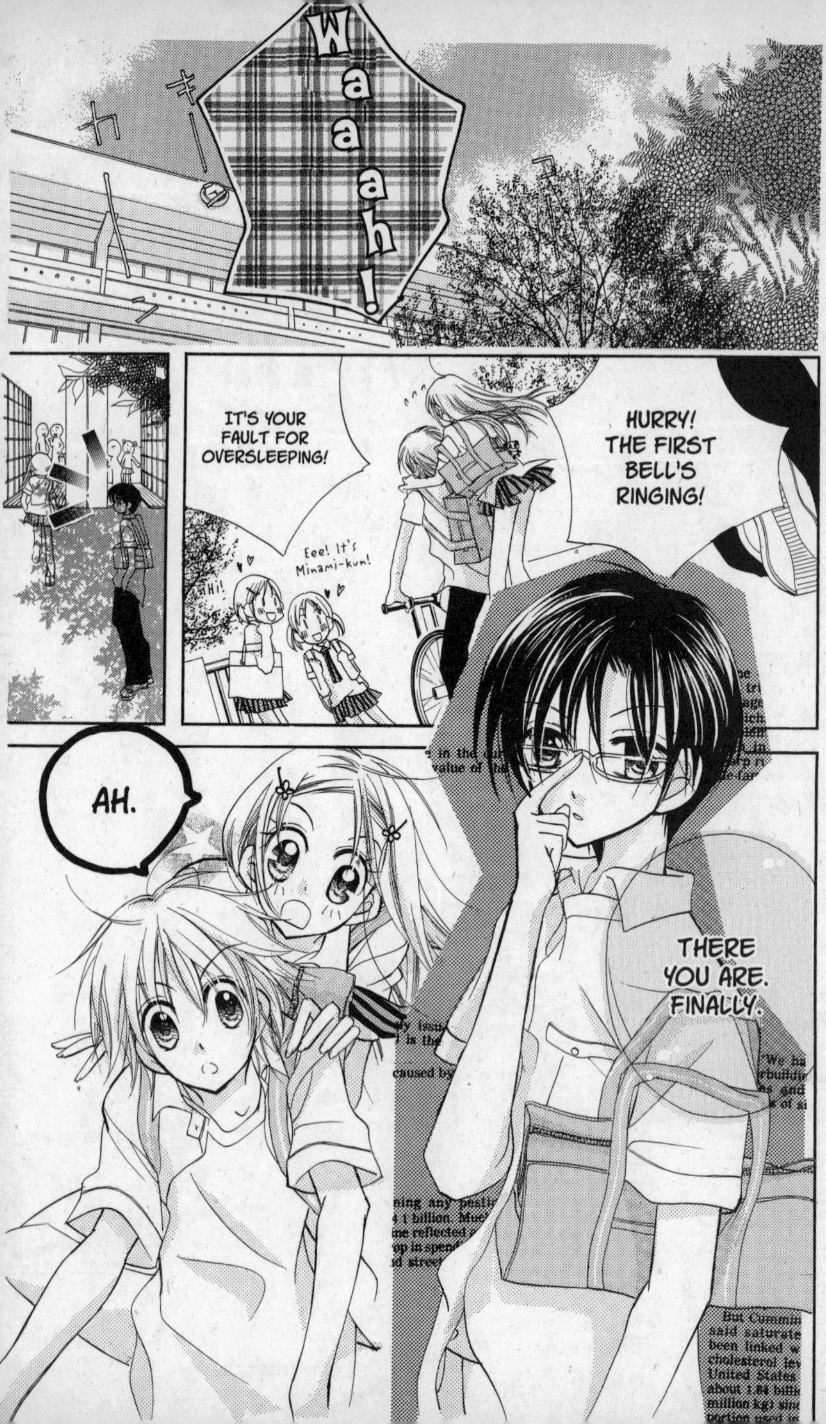
Waaah!
HURRY! THE FIRST BELL'S RINGING!
IT'S YOUR FAULT FOR OVERSLEEPING!
Eee! It's Minami-kun!
Hi!
THERE YOU ARE. FINALLY.
AH.

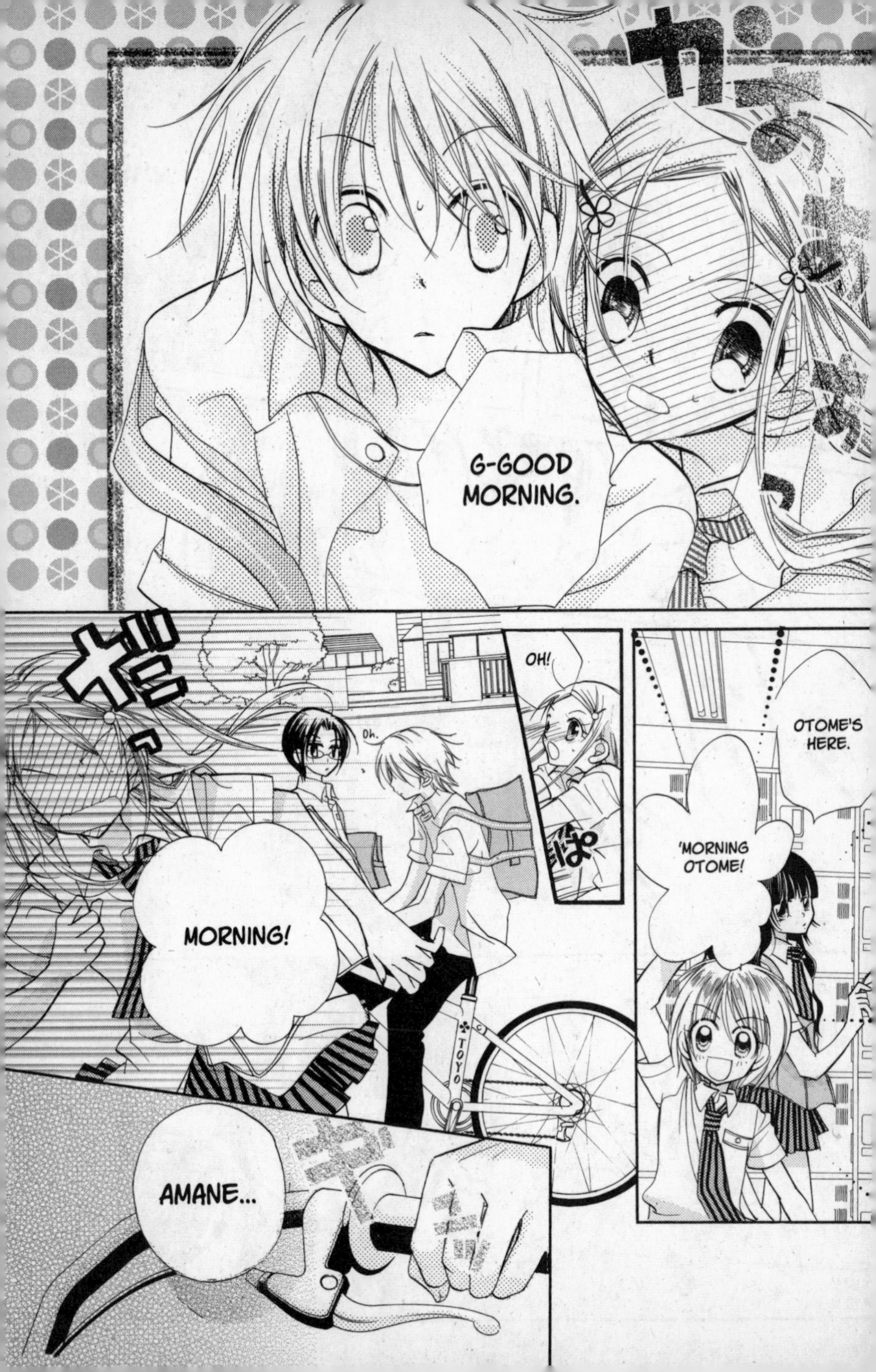
G-GOOD MORNING.
OTOME'S HERE.
'MORNING OTOME!
OH!
Oh.
MORNING!
AMANE...

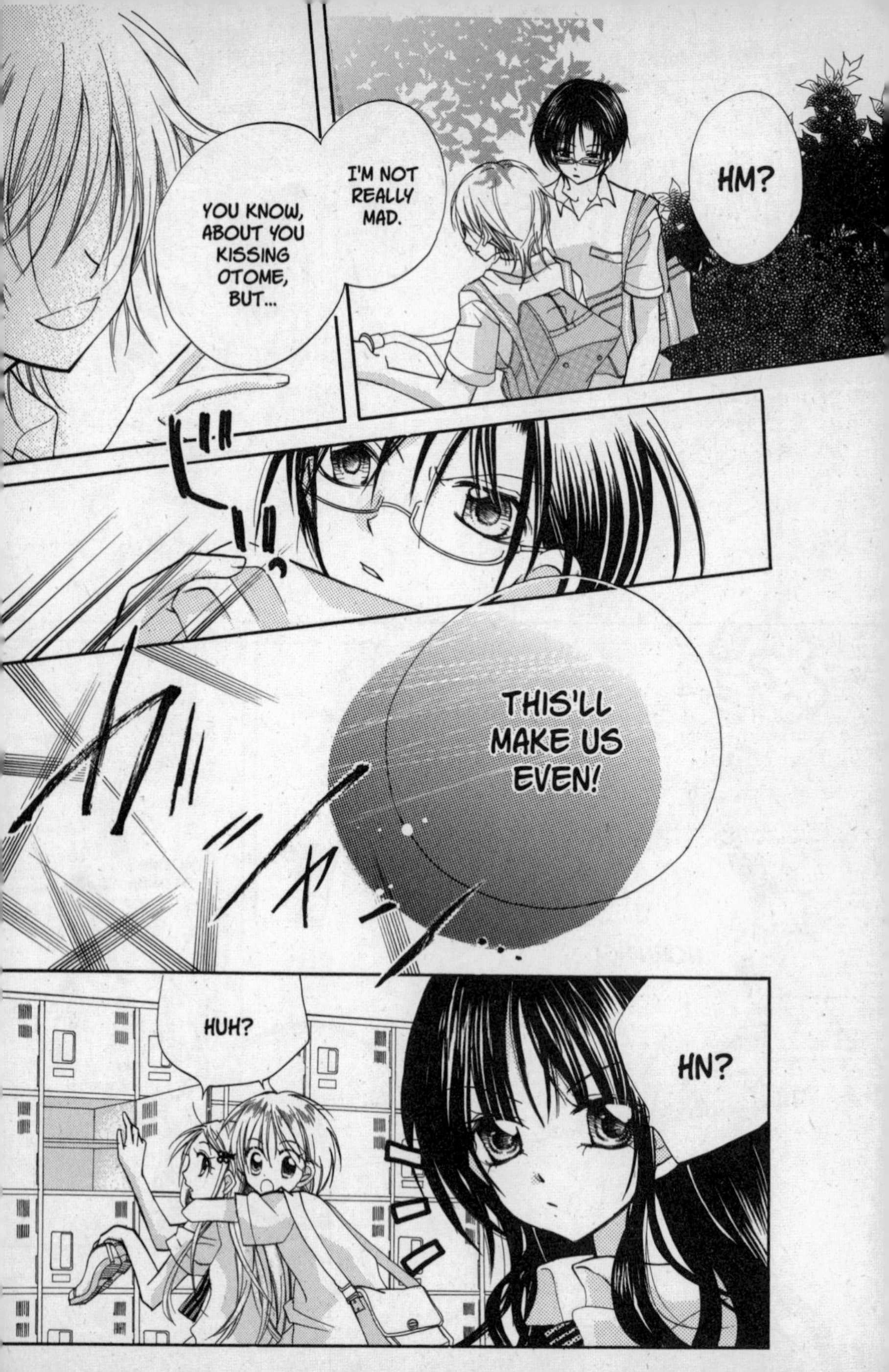
HM?
I'M NOT REALLY MAD.
YOU KNOW, ABOUT YOU KISSING OTOME, BUT...
THIS'LL MAKE US EVEN!
HN?
HUH?

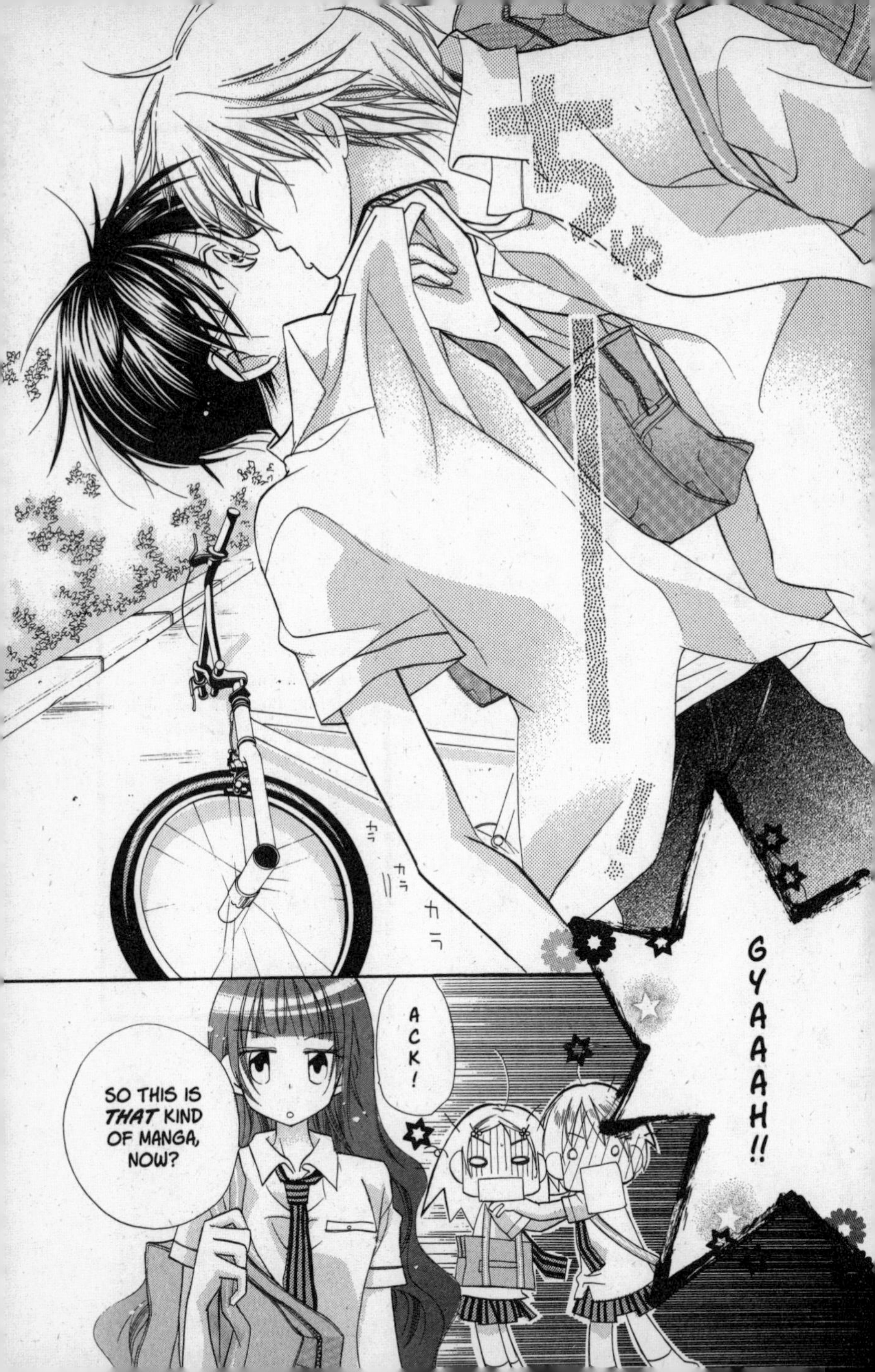
ちゅ!!
カラ
カラ
カラ
GYAAAAH!!
ACK!
SO THIS IS *THAT* KIND OF MANGA, NOW?

By The Way...
My supervisor for
this project, Zusshi, is
putting a special effort
into this. (Heh.)
The "leads," these bits of
writing at the beginning
of each chapter...

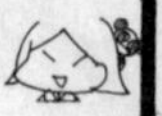

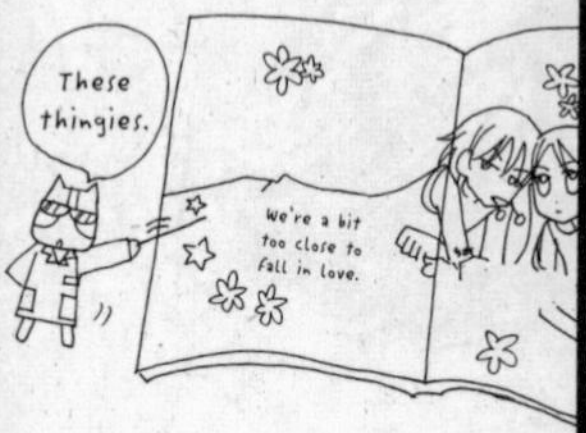
These thingies.
We're a bit too close to fall in love.

...get thought up by her.
She has blessed my work
with these fragments
of Otome's heart.

Normally they'd have been
omitted when the individual
chapters were compiled into
this volume, but because
they were so wonderful, I'll
try putting them here.

Please keep an eye
out for them.

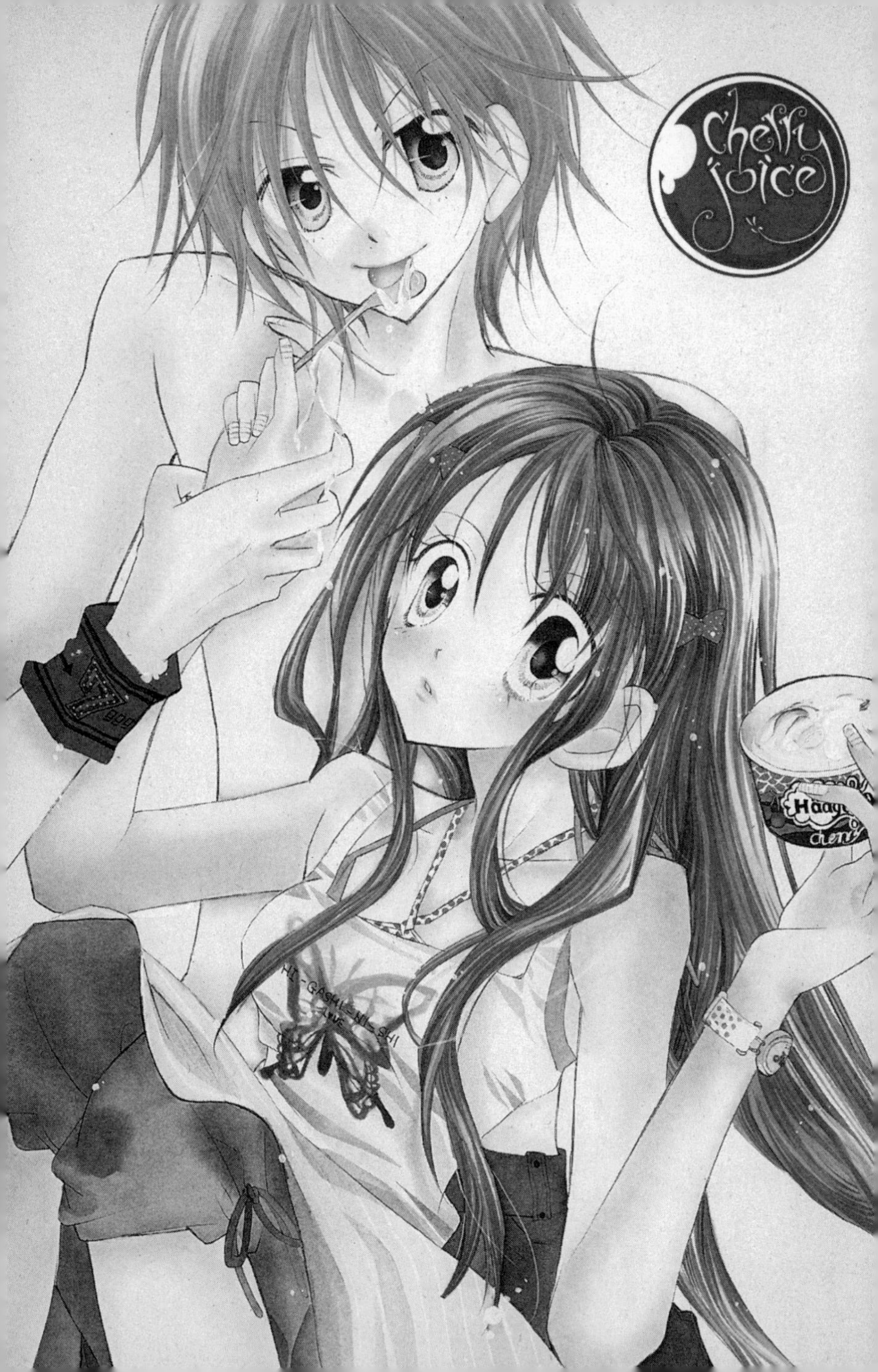
Cherry Juice
HI-GASHI-NI-SHI

We're...

...a bit too close...

...to fall in love.

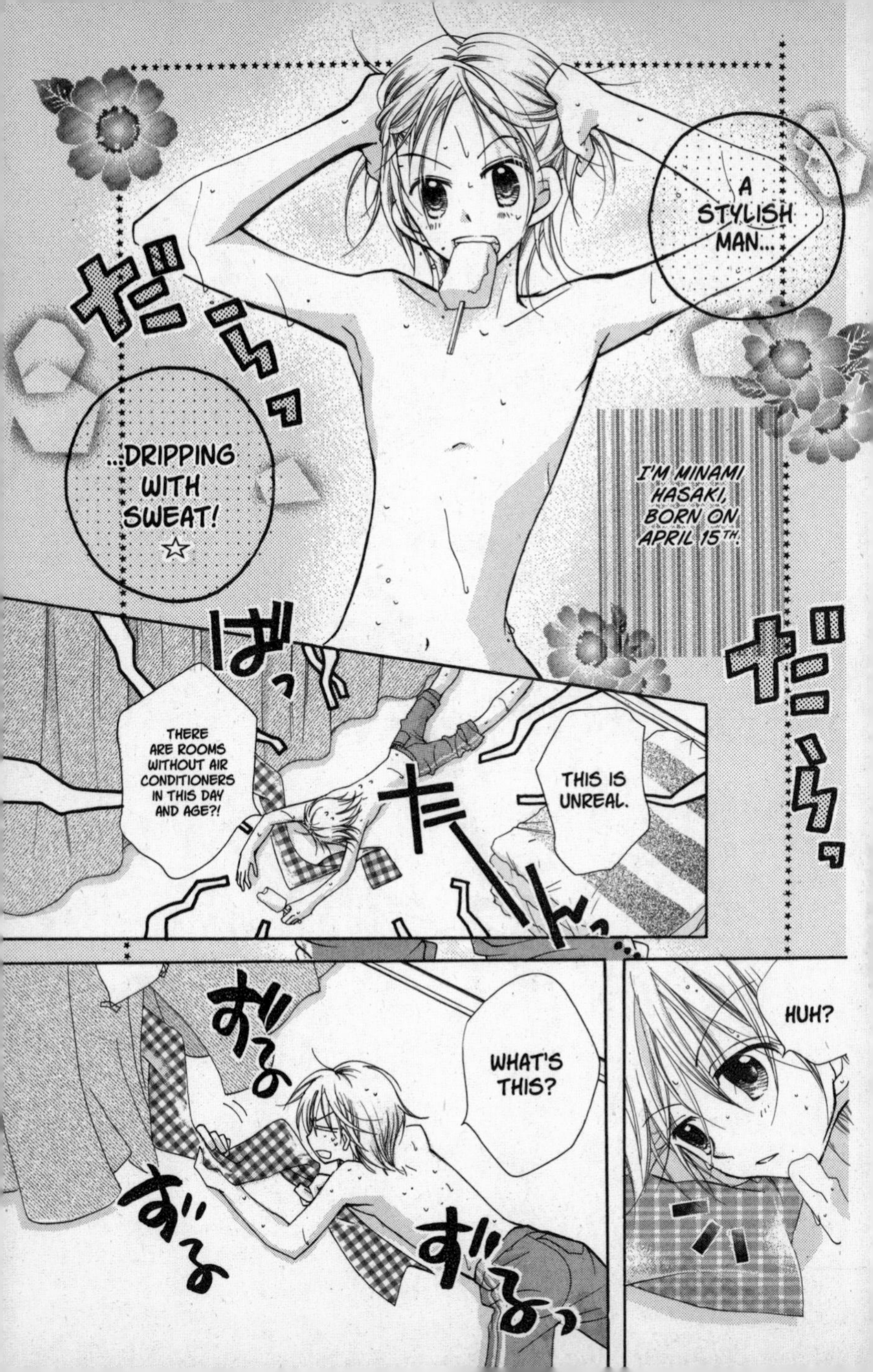
I'M MINAMI HASAKI, BORN ON APRIL 15TH.
A STYLISH MAN...
...DRIPPING WITH SWEAT! ☆
THIS IS UNREAL.
THERE ARE ROOMS WITHOUT AIR CONDITIONERS IN THIS DAY AND AGE?!
HUH?
WHAT'S THIS?

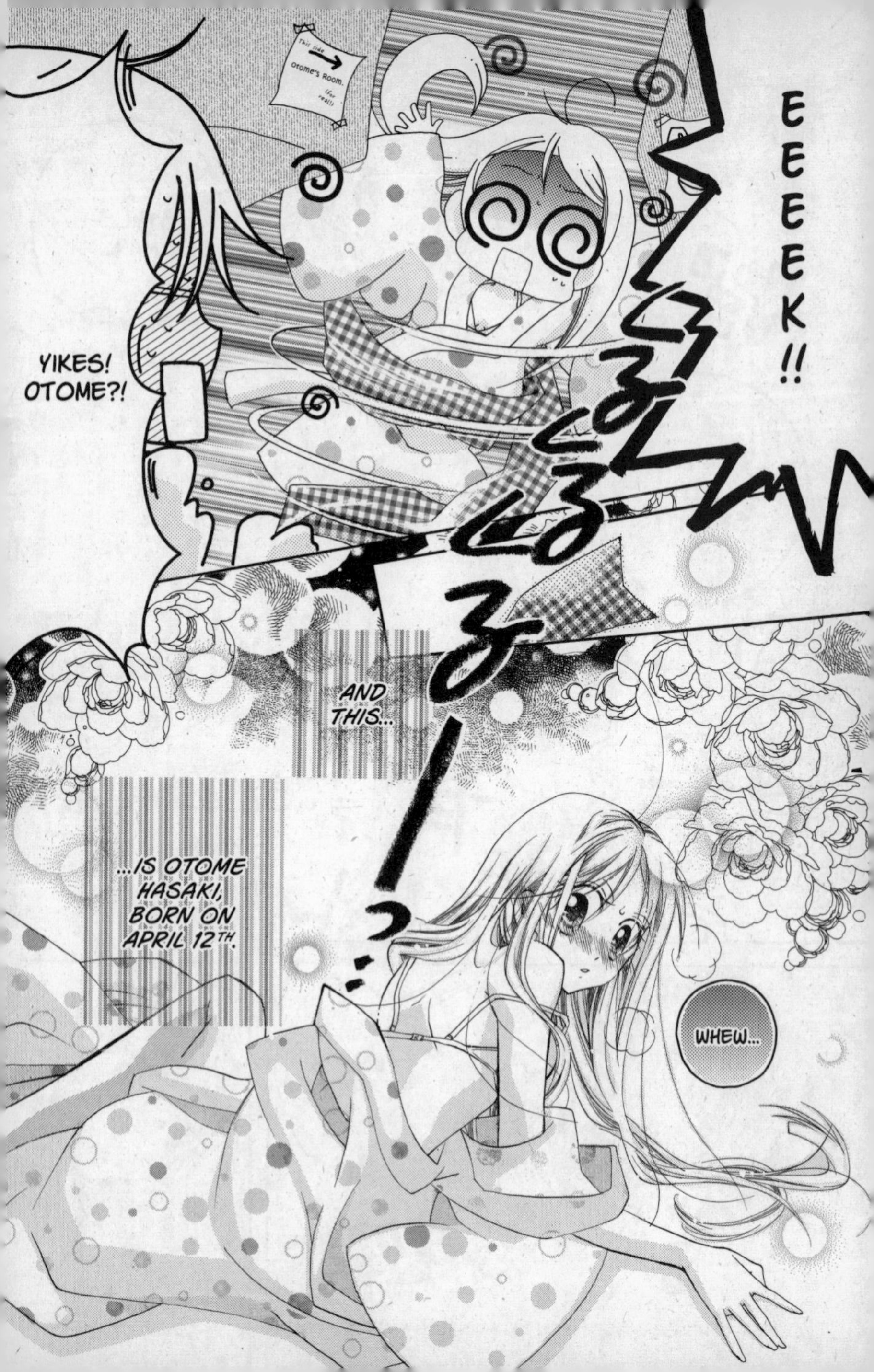
EEEEK!!
This side → Otome's Room. (for real!)
YIKES! OTOME?!
ころころころ
AND THIS...
...IS OTOME HASAKI, BORN ON APRIL 12TH.
WHEW...

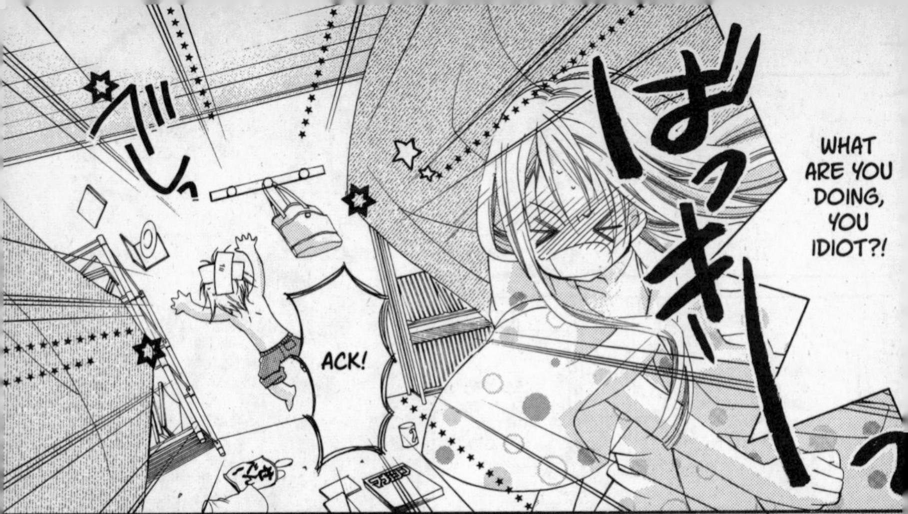
WHAT ARE YOU DOING, YOU IDIOT?!
ACK!

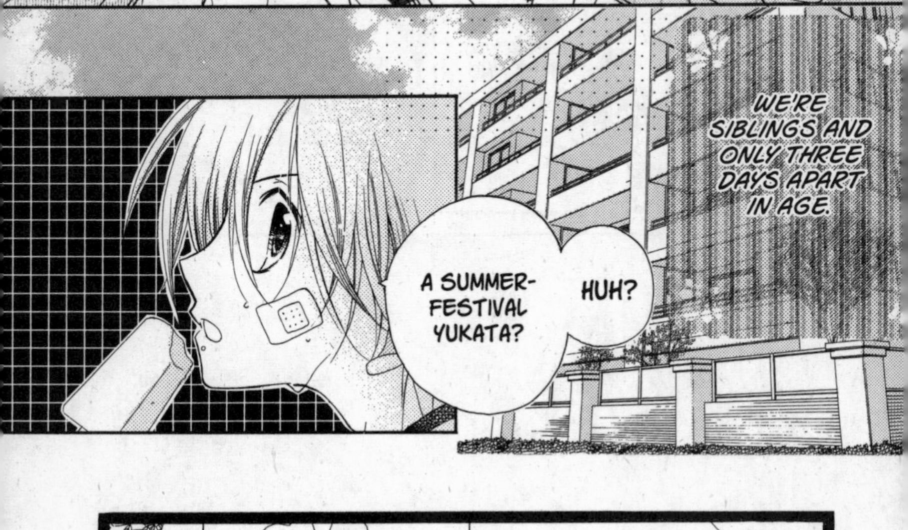
WE'RE SIBLINGS AND ONLY THREE DAYS APART IN AGE.
HUH?
A SUMMER-FESTIVAL YUKATA?

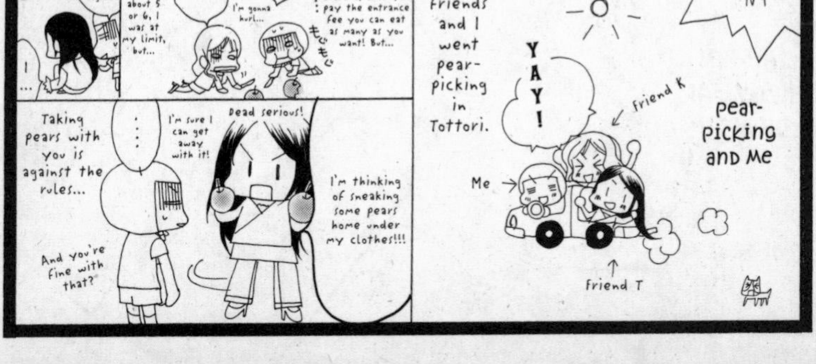
Sunny Country Newsletter IV 1
pear-picking and Me
My friends and I went pear-picking in Tottori.
YAY!
Friend K
Me
Friend T
At the pear orchard, once you pay the entrance fee you can eat as many as you want! But...
Ugh.
I'm gonna hurl...
Not... ...another bite.
After about 5 or 6, I was at my limit, but...
T, are you all right?
I...
I'm thinking of sneaking some pears home under my clothes!!!
Dead serious!
I'm sure I can get away with it!
....
Taking pears with you is against the rules...
And you're fine with that?

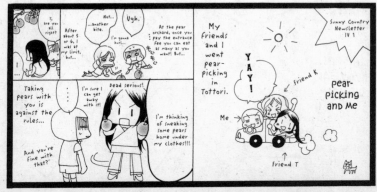

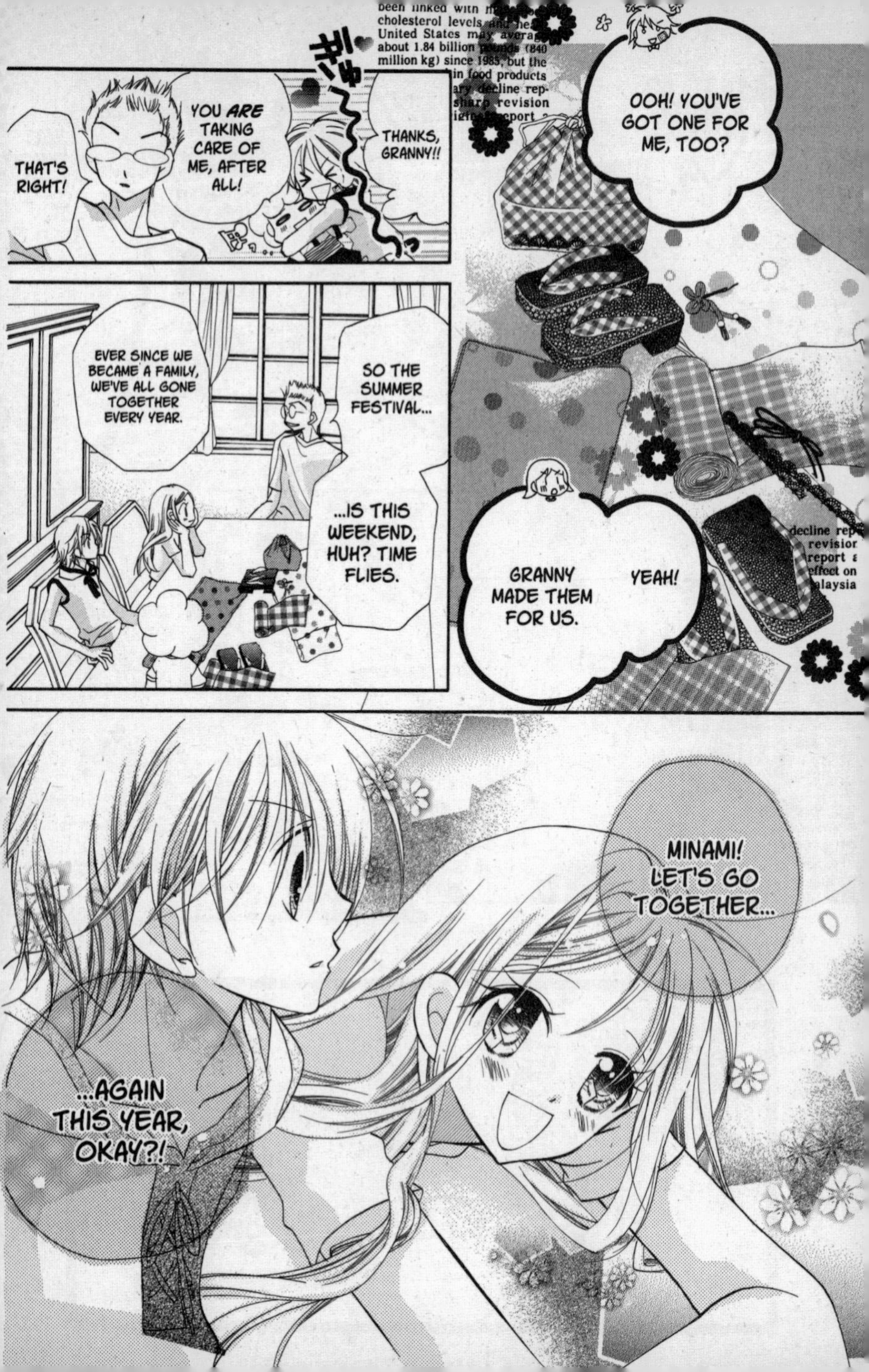
OOH! YOU'VE GOT ONE FOR ME, TOO?
YEAH!
GRANNY MADE THEM FOR US.
THANKS, GRANNY!!
YOU *ARE* TAKING CARE OF ME, AFTER ALL!
THAT'S RIGHT!
SO THE SUMMER FESTIVAL...
...IS THIS WEEKEND, HUH? TIME FLIES.
EVER SINCE WE BECAME A FAMILY, WE'VE ALL GONE TOGETHER EVERY YEAR.
MINAMI! LET'S GO TOGETHER...
...AGAIN THIS YEAR, OKAY?!

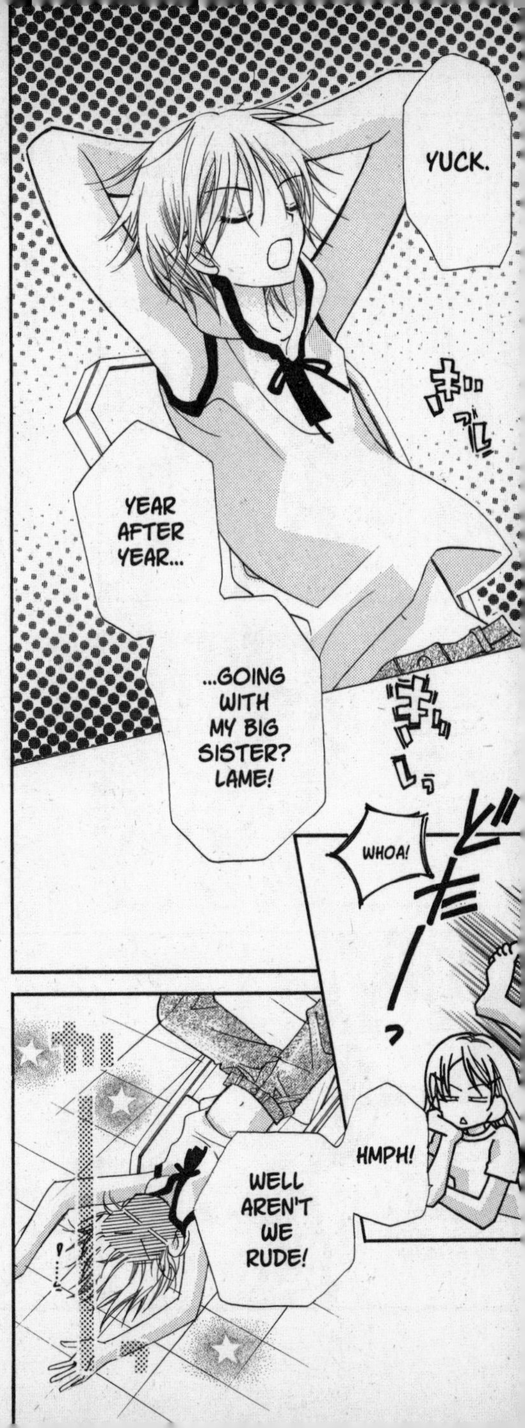
YUCK.
YEAR AFTER YEAR...
...GOING WITH MY BIG SISTER? LAME!
WHOA!
HMPH!
WELL AREN'T WE RUDE!

THREE!

☑ The characters from my series up to now...

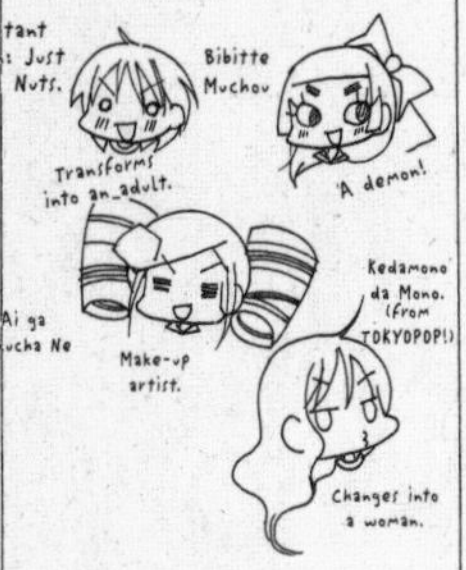
Instant Teen: Just Add Nuts.
Transforms into an adult.
Bibitte Muchou
A demon!
Ai ga Nakucha Ne
Make-up artist.
Kedamono da Mono. (From TOKYOPOP!)
Changes into a woman.

...are different from those in this one. And as this story is predominately a school romance, I worried a lot about the reaction from Nakayoshi's readers. I personally love things like this, so I am quite enjoying it (aside from all the worrying I'm doing about it not being well received)...

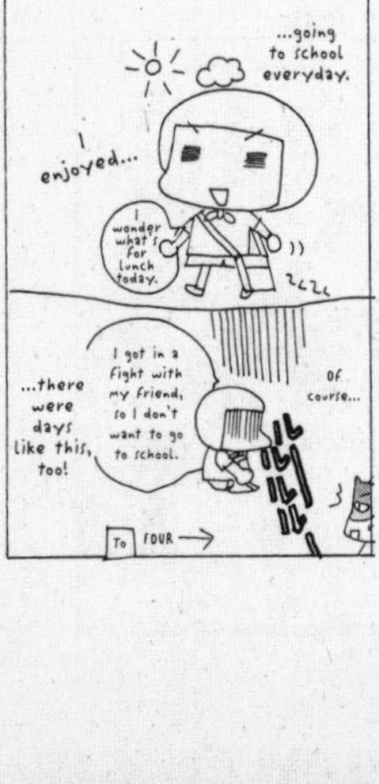
I enjoyed...
...going to school everyday.
I wonder what's for lunch today.
...there were days like this, too!
Of course...
I got in a fight with my friend, so I don't want to go to school.

To FOUR →

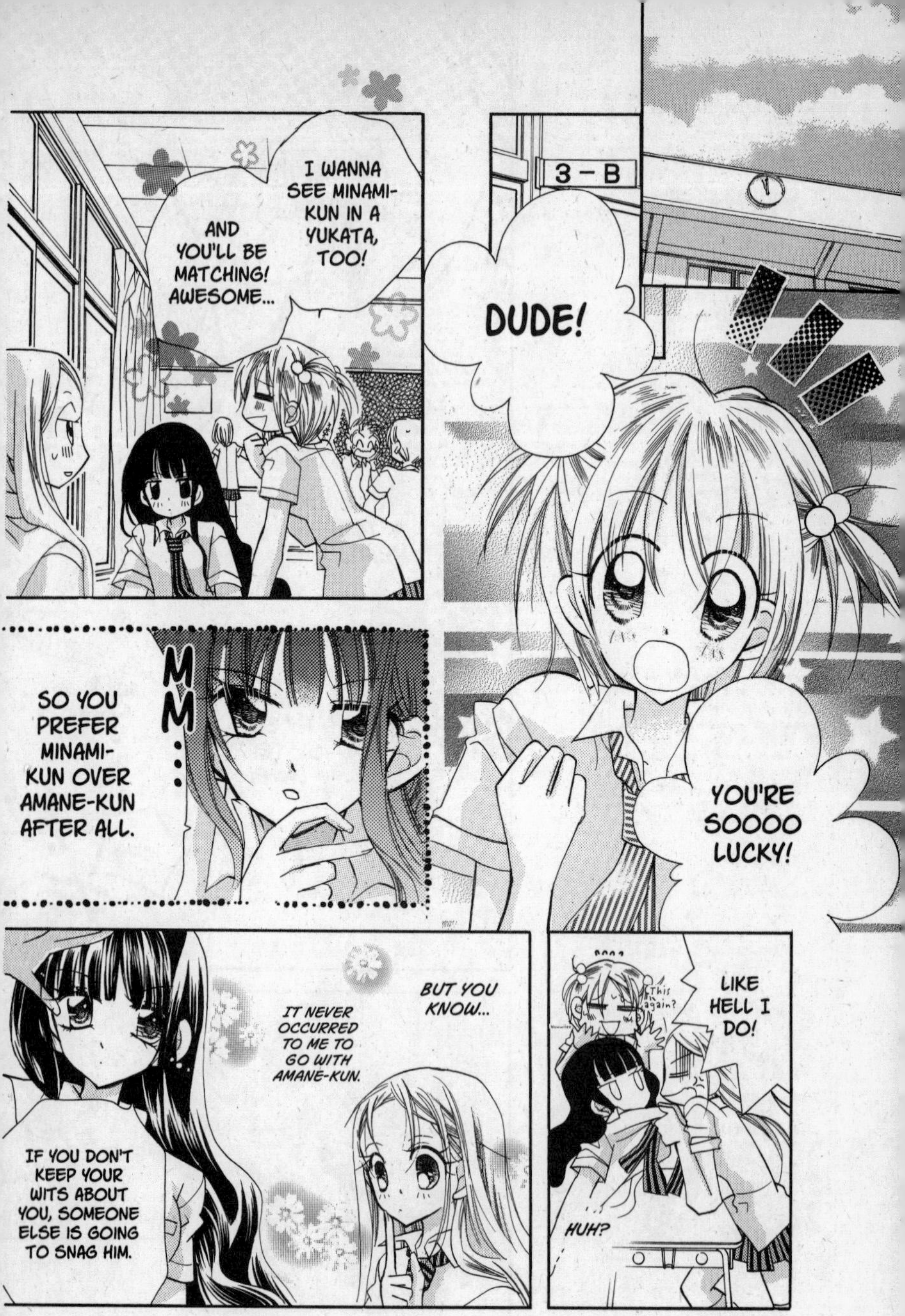
3-B
DUDE!
YOU'RE SOOOO LUCKY!
I WANNA SEE MINAMI-KUN IN A YUKATA, TOO!
AND YOU'LL BE MATCHING! AWESOME...
MM...
SO YOU PREFER MINAMI-KUN OVER AMANE-KUN AFTER ALL.
LIKE HELL I DO!
This again?
HUH?
BUT YOU KNOW...
IT NEVER OCCURRED TO ME TO GO WITH AMANE-KUN.
IF YOU DON'T KEEP YOUR WITS ABOUT YOU, SOMEONE ELSE IS GOING TO SNAG HIM.

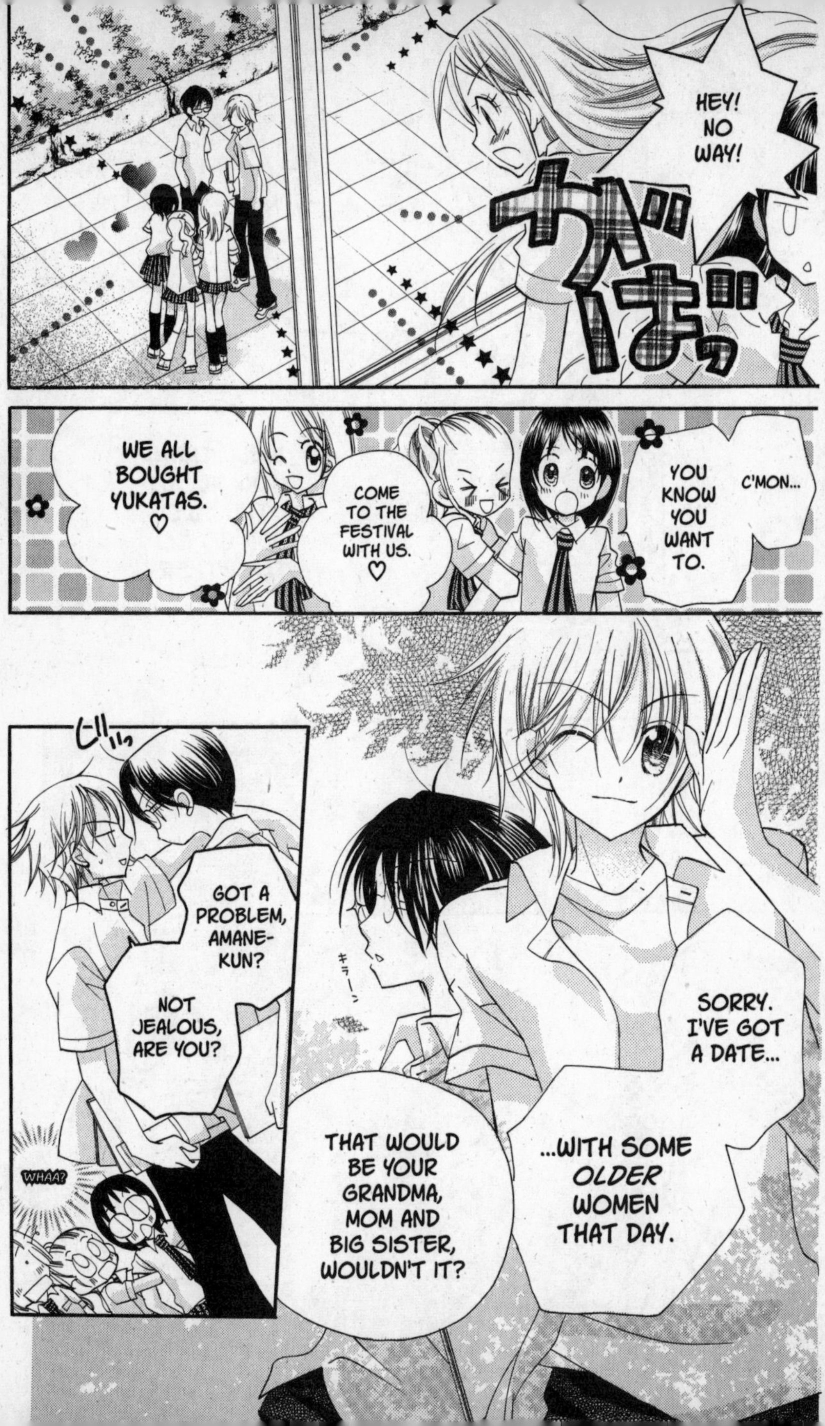
HEY! NO WAY!
C'MON...
YOU KNOW YOU WANT TO.
COME TO THE FESTIVAL WITH US. ♡
WE ALL BOUGHT YUKATAS. ♡
SORRY. I'VE GOT A DATE...
...WITH SOME *OLDER* WOMEN THAT DAY.
THAT WOULD BE YOUR GRANDMA, MOM AND BIG SISTER, WOULDN'T IT?
GOT A PROBLEM, AMANE-KUN?
NOT JEALOUS, ARE YOU?
WHAA?

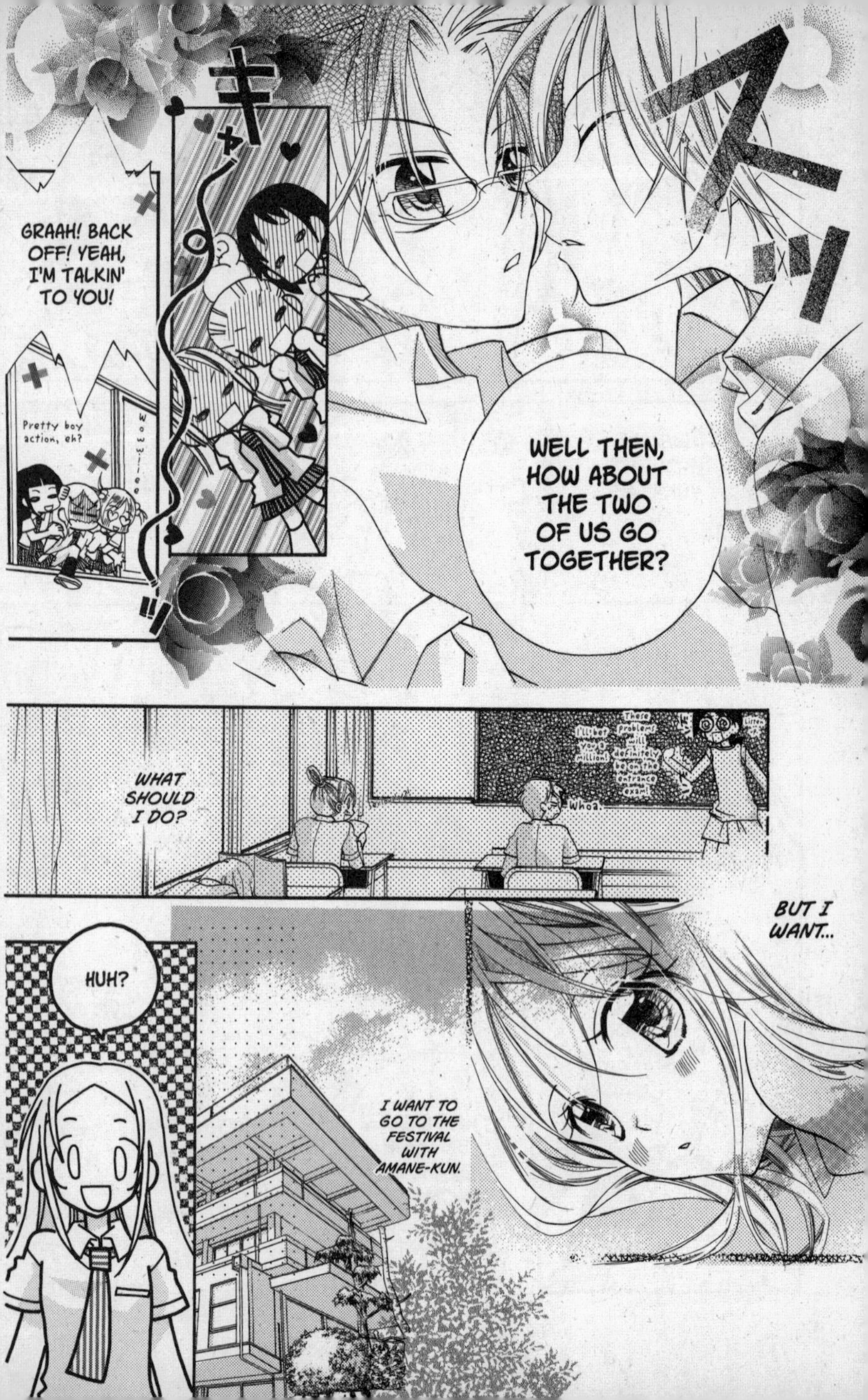
WELL THEN, HOW ABOUT THE TWO OF US GO TOGETHER?
GRAAH! BACK OFF! YEAH, I'M TALKIN' TO YOU!
Wowwiiee
Pretty boy action, eh?
Listen up.
These problems will definitely be on the entrance exam!
I'll bet you a million!
Whoa.
WHAT SHOULD I DO?
BUT I WANT...
I WANT TO GO TO THE FESTIVAL WITH AMANE-KUN.
HUH?

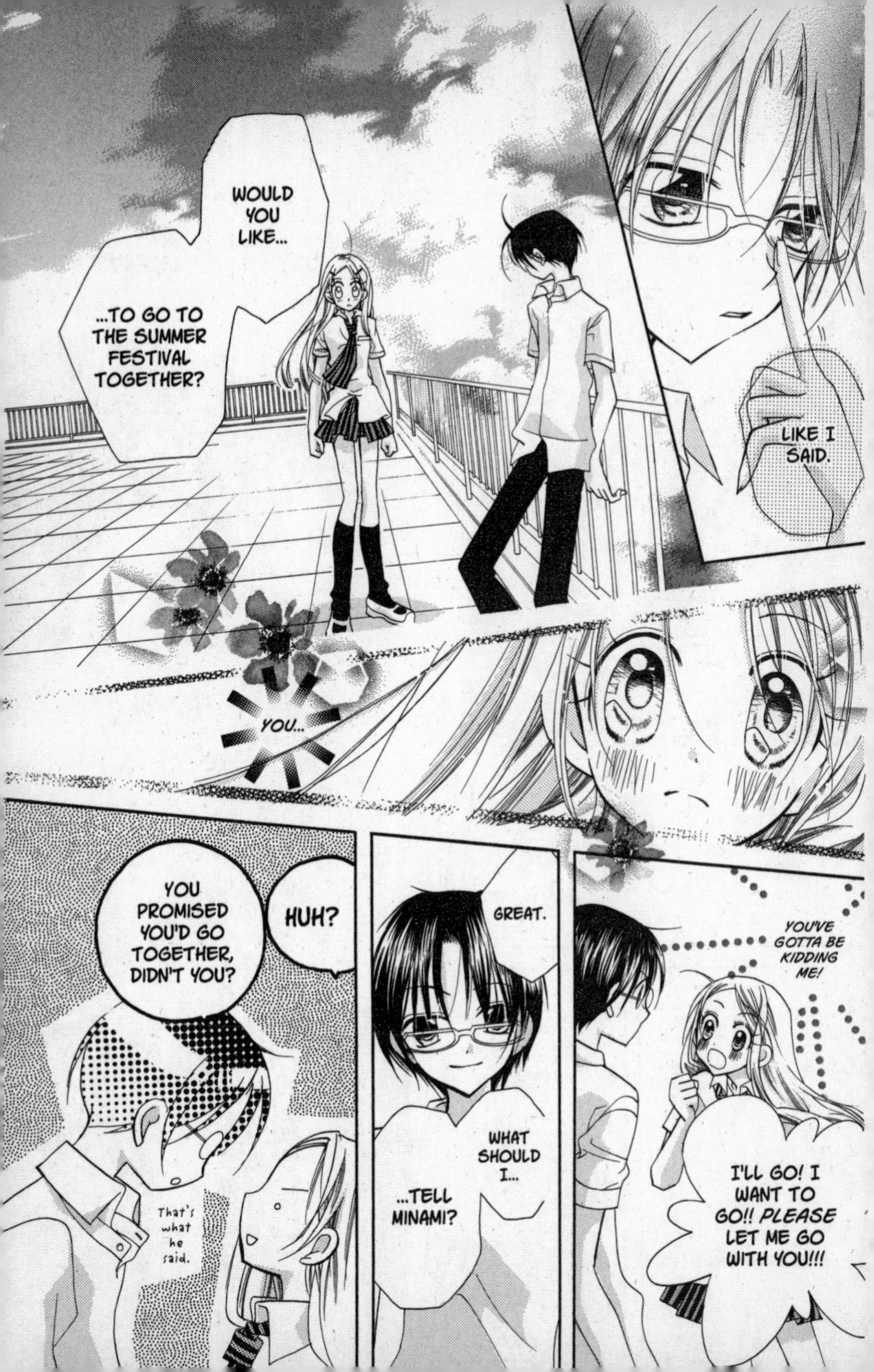
LIKE I SAID.
WOULD YOU LIKE...
...TO GO TO THE SUMMER FESTIVAL TOGETHER?
YOU...
YOU'VE GOTTA BE KIDDING ME!
I'LL GO! I WANT TO GO!! *PLEASE* LET ME GO WITH YOU!!!
GREAT.
WHAT SHOULD I...
...TELL MINAMI?
HUH?
YOU PROMISED YOU'D GO TOGETHER, DIDN'T YOU?
That's what he said.

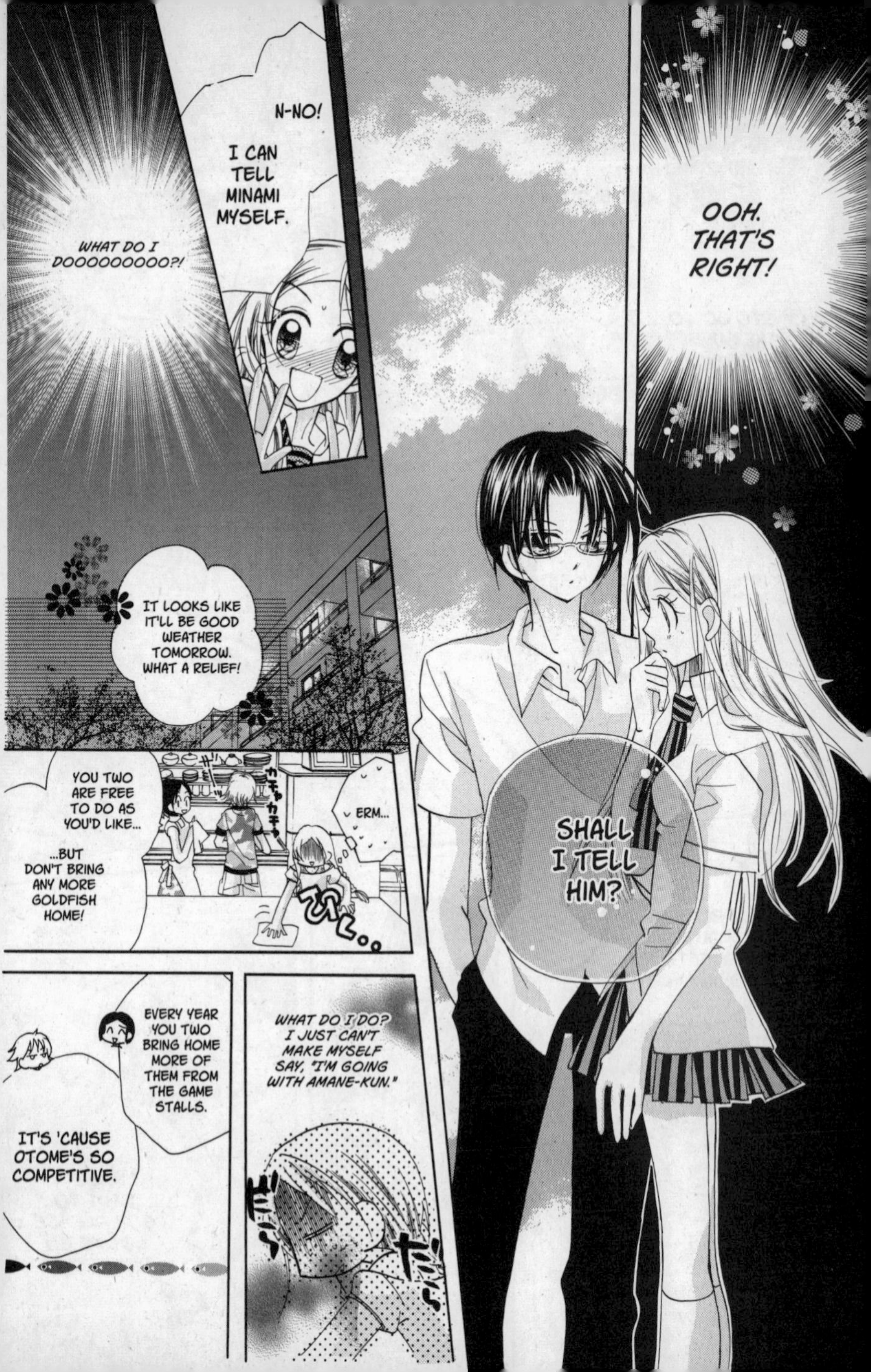
OOH. THAT'S RIGHT!
SHALL I TELL HIM?
N-NO!
I CAN TELL MINAMI MYSELF.
WHAT DO I DOOOOOOOOO?!
IT LOOKS LIKE IT'LL BE GOOD WEATHER TOMORROW. WHAT A RELIEF!
YOU TWO ARE FREE TO DO AS YOU'D LIKE...
...BUT DON'T BRING ANY MORE GOLDFISH HOME!
ERM...
WHAT DO I DO? I JUST CAN'T MAKE MYSELF SAY, "I'M GOING WITH AMANE-KUN."
EVERY YEAR YOU TWO BRING HOME MORE OF THEM FROM THE GAME STALLS.
IT'S 'CAUSE OTOME'S SO COMPETITIVE.

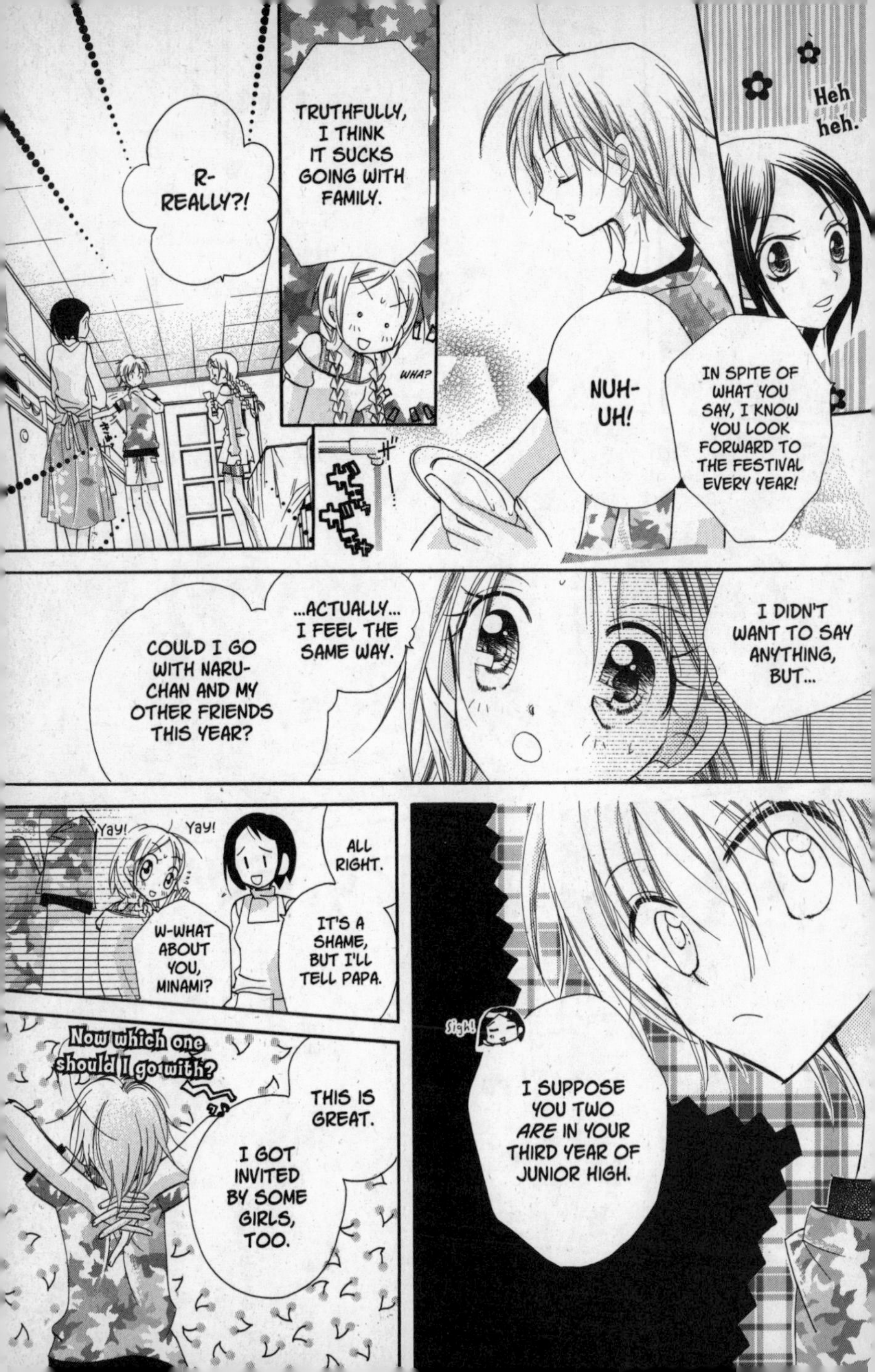
Heh heh.
IN SPITE OF WHAT YOU SAY, I KNOW YOU LOOK FORWARD TO THE FESTIVAL EVERY YEAR!
NUH-UH!
TRUTHFULLY, I THINK IT SUCKS GOING WITH FAMILY.
WHA?
R-REALLY?!
I DIDN'T WANT TO SAY ANYTHING, BUT...
...ACTUALLY... I FEEL THE SAME WAY.
COULD I GO WITH NARU-CHAN AND MY OTHER FRIENDS THIS YEAR?
Sigh!
I SUPPOSE YOU TWO *ARE* IN YOUR THIRD YEAR OF JUNIOR HIGH.
ALL RIGHT.
IT'S A SHAME, BUT I'LL TELL PAPA.
Yay!
Yay!
W-WHAT ABOUT YOU, MINAMI?
THIS IS GREAT.
I GOT INVITED BY SOME GIRLS, TOO.
Now which one should I go with?

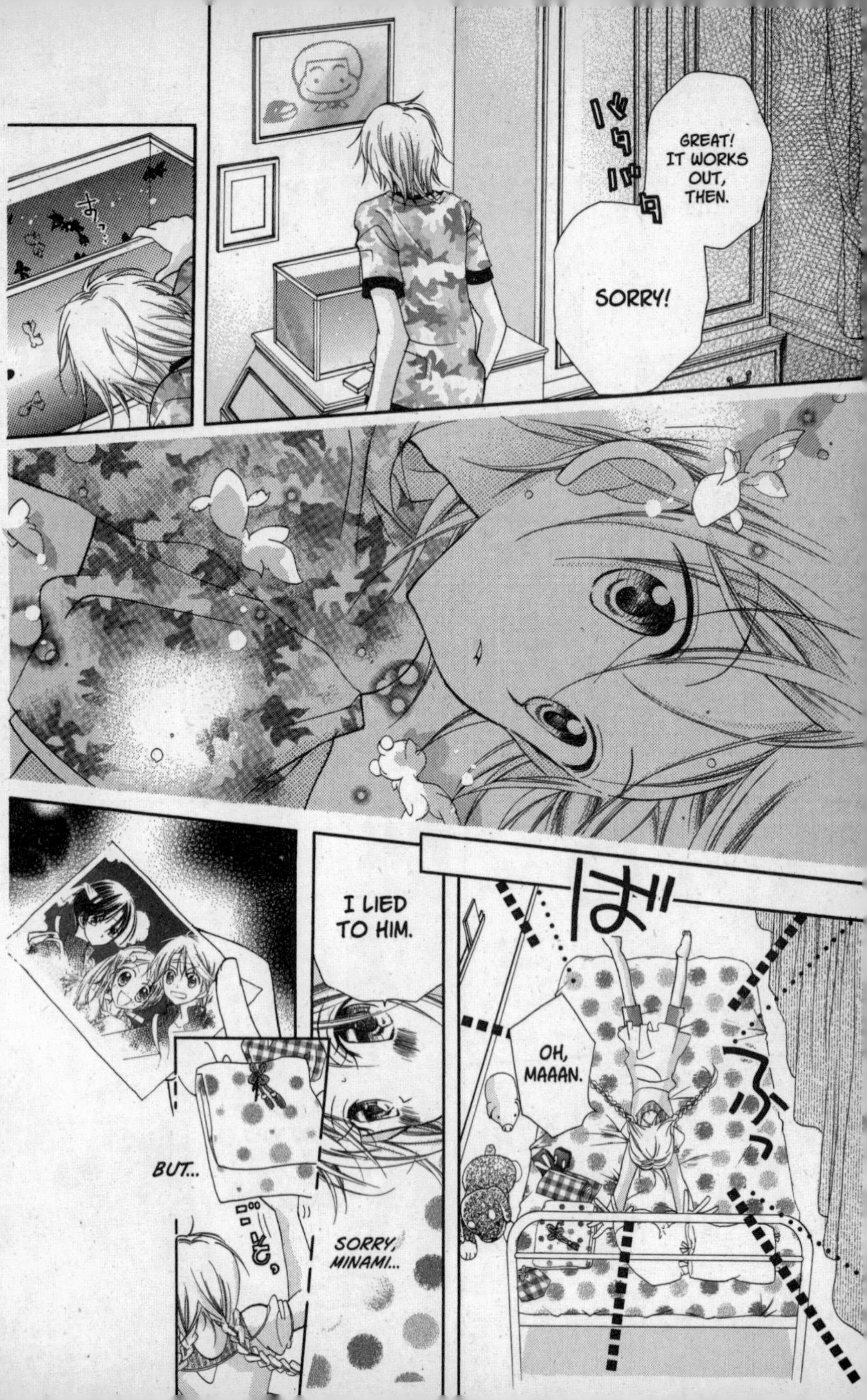
GREAT! IT WORKS OUT, THEN.
SORRY!
OH, MAAAN.
I LIED TO HIM.
BUT...
SORRY, MINAMI...

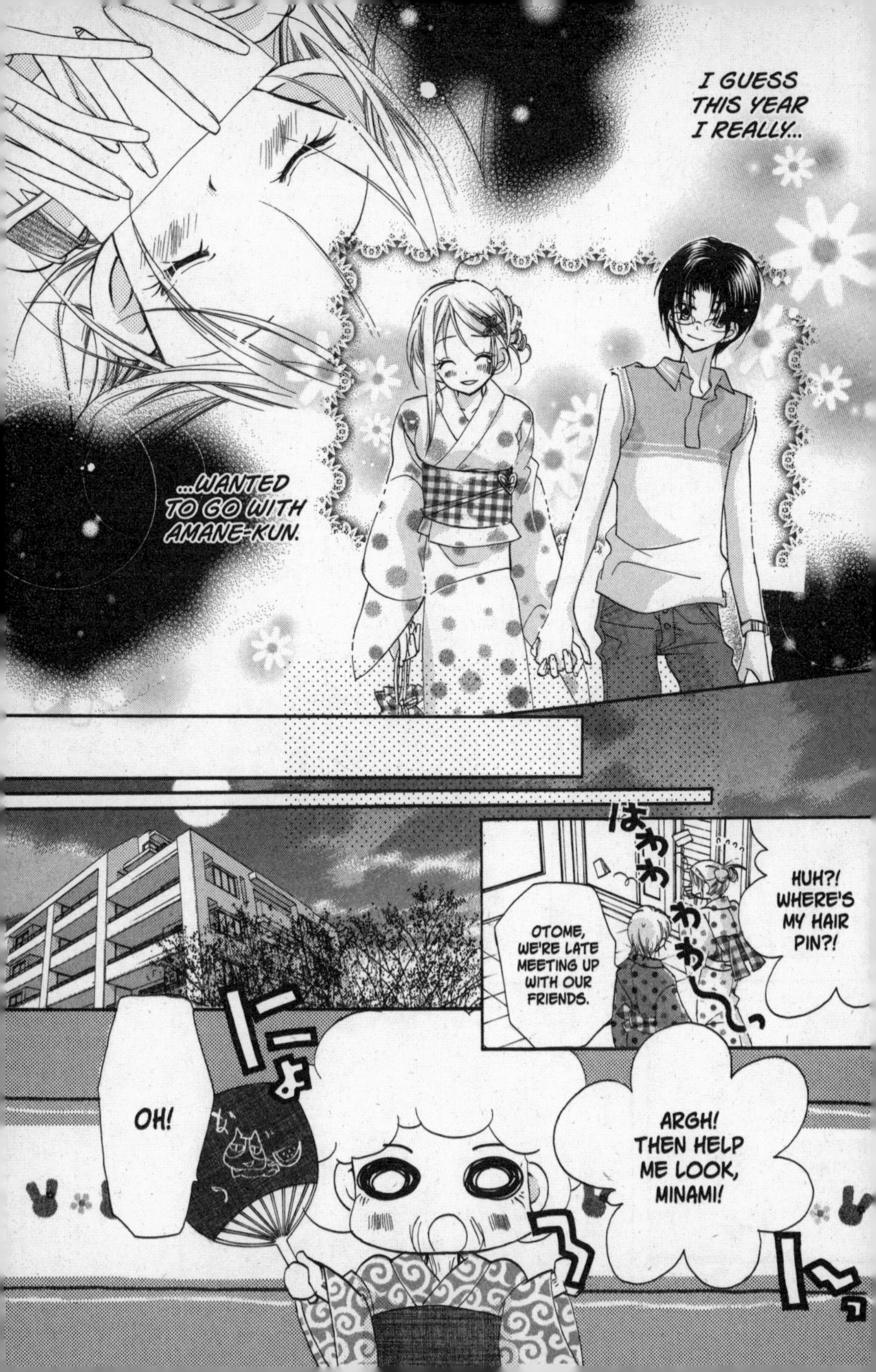
I GUESS THIS YEAR I REALLY...
...WANTED TO GO WITH AMANE-KUN.
HUH?! WHERE'S MY HAIR PIN?!
OTOME, WE'RE LATE MEETING UP WITH OUR FRIENDS.
ARGH! THEN HELP ME LOOK, MINAMI!
OH!

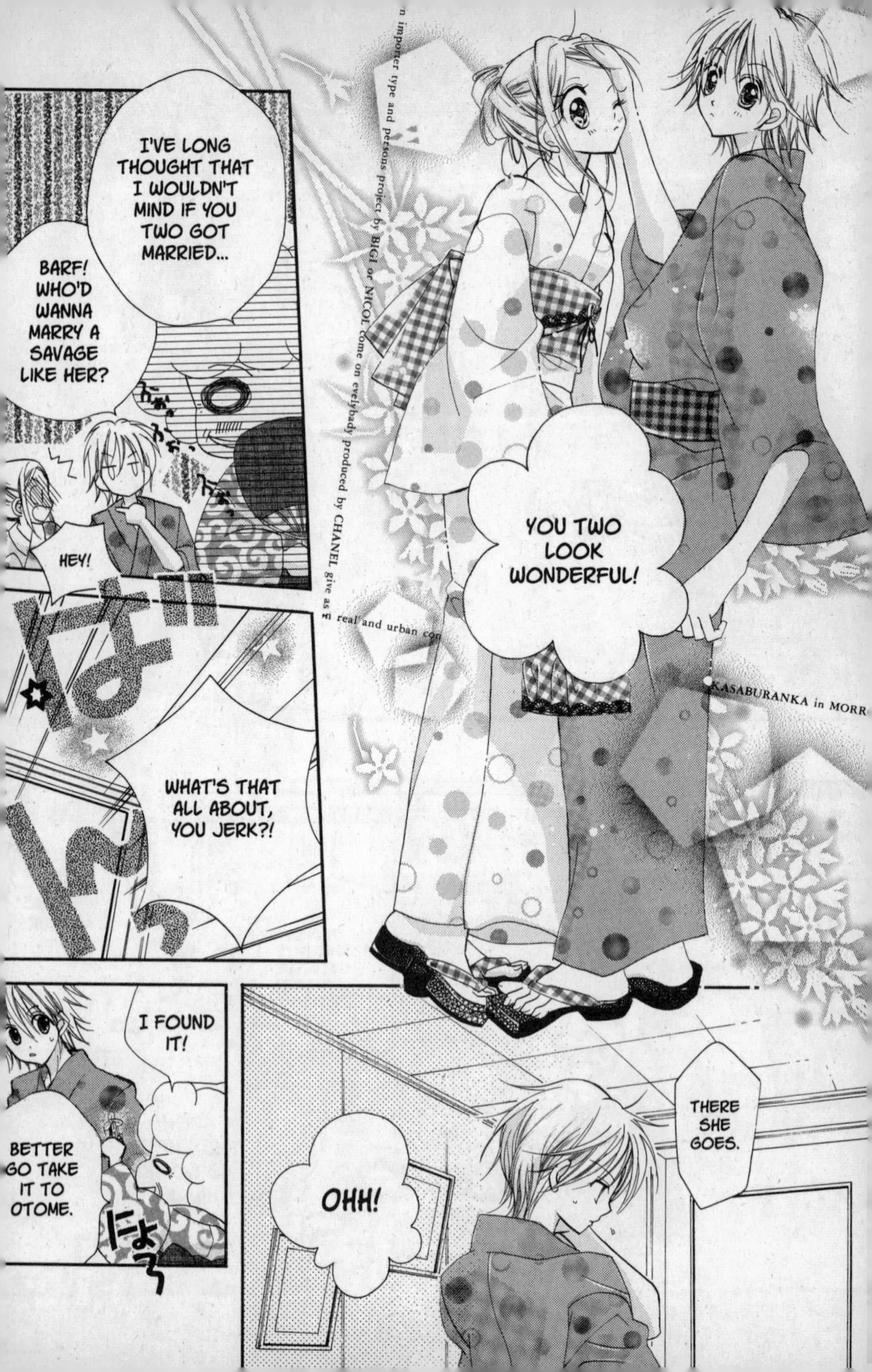
n importer type and persons project by BIGI or NICOL come on evelybady produced by CHANEL give as a real and urban con
KASABURANKA in MORR
YOU TWO LOOK WONDERFUL!
I'VE LONG THOUGHT THAT I WOULDN'T MIND IF YOU TWO GOT MARRIED...
BARF! WHO'D WANNA MARRY A SAVAGE LIKE HER?
HEY!
ば!!ん
WHAT'S THAT ALL ABOUT, YOU JERK?!
THERE SHE GOES.
OHH!
I FOUND IT!
BETTER GO TAKE IT TO OTOME.
にょっ

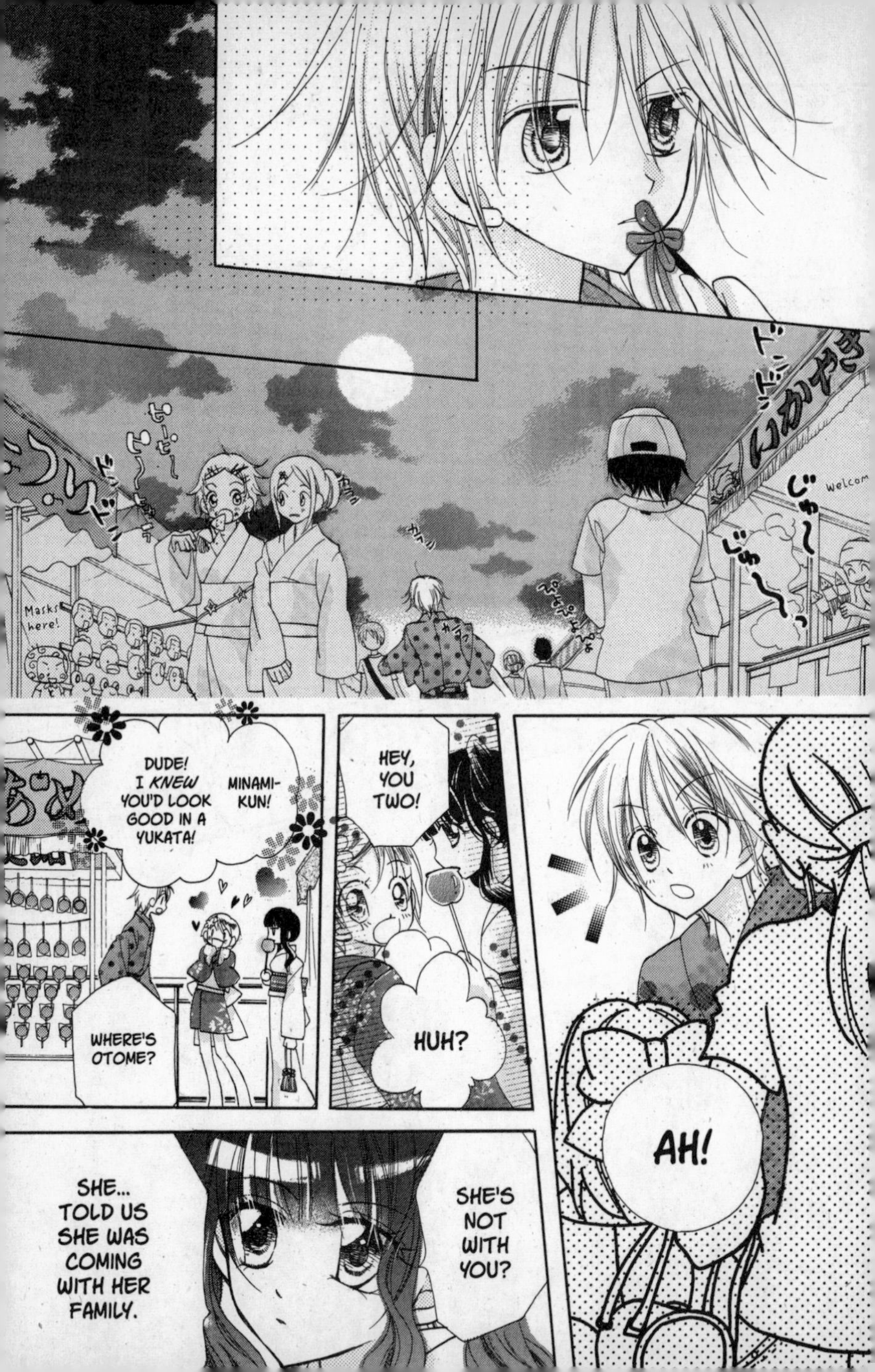
Welcom
Masks here!
AH!
HEY, YOU TWO!
HUH?
MINAMI-KUN!
DUDE! I KNEW YOU'D LOOK GOOD IN A YUKATA!
WHERE'S OTOME?
SHE'S NOT WITH YOU?
SHE... TOLD US SHE WAS COMING WITH HER FAMILY.

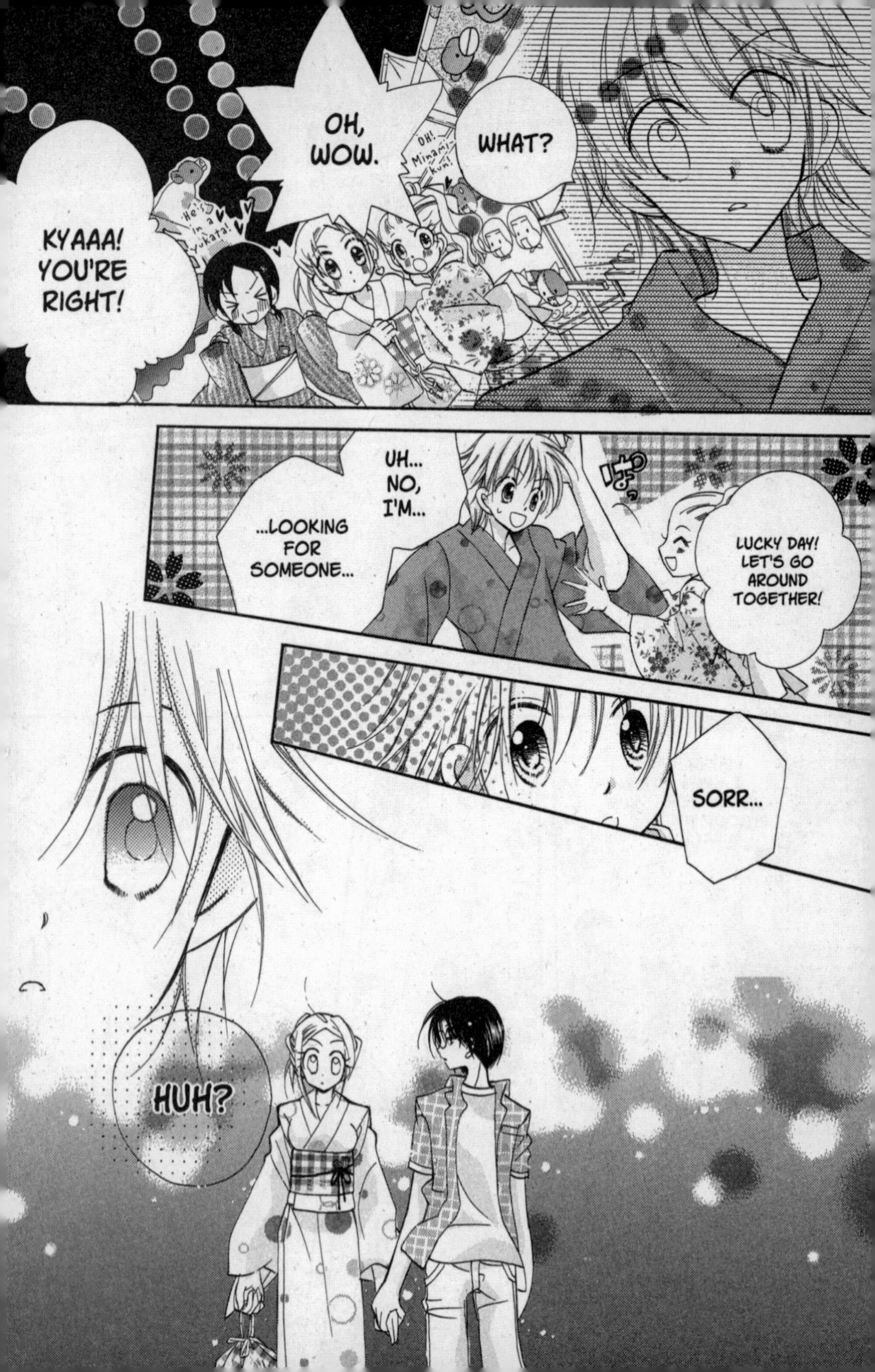
WHAT?
OH! Minami-kun!
OH, WOW.
He's in a Yukata!
KYAAA! YOU'RE RIGHT!
LUCKY DAY! LET'S GO AROUND TOGETHER!
UH... NO, I'M...
...LOOKING FOR SOMEONE...
SORR...
HUH?

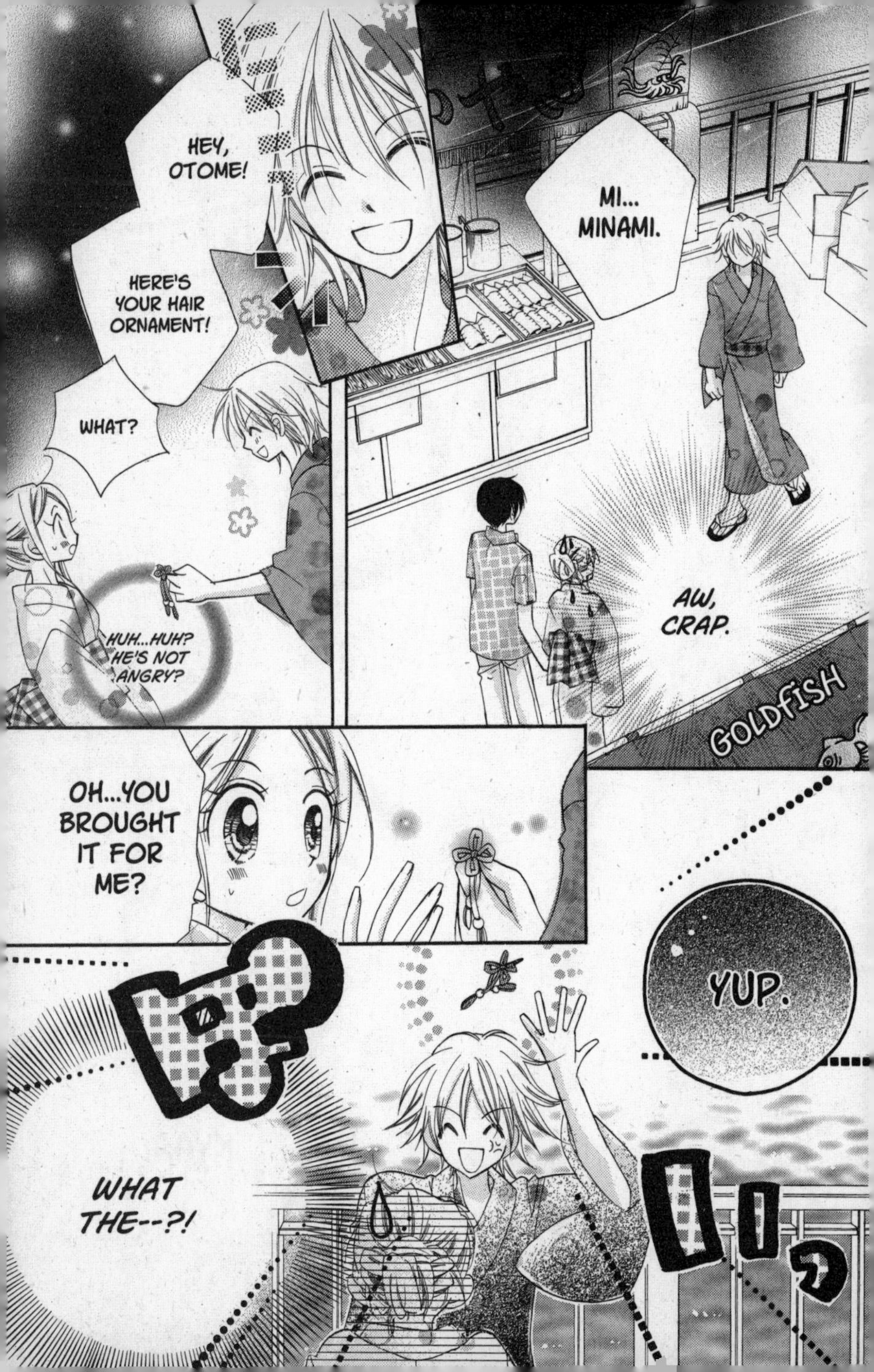
MI... MINAMI.
AW, CRAP.
GOLDFISH
HEY, OTOME!
HERE'S YOUR HAIR ORNAMENT!
WHAT?
HUH...HUH? HE'S NOT ANGRY?
OH...YOU BROUGHT IT FOR ME?
YUP.
WHAT THE--?!

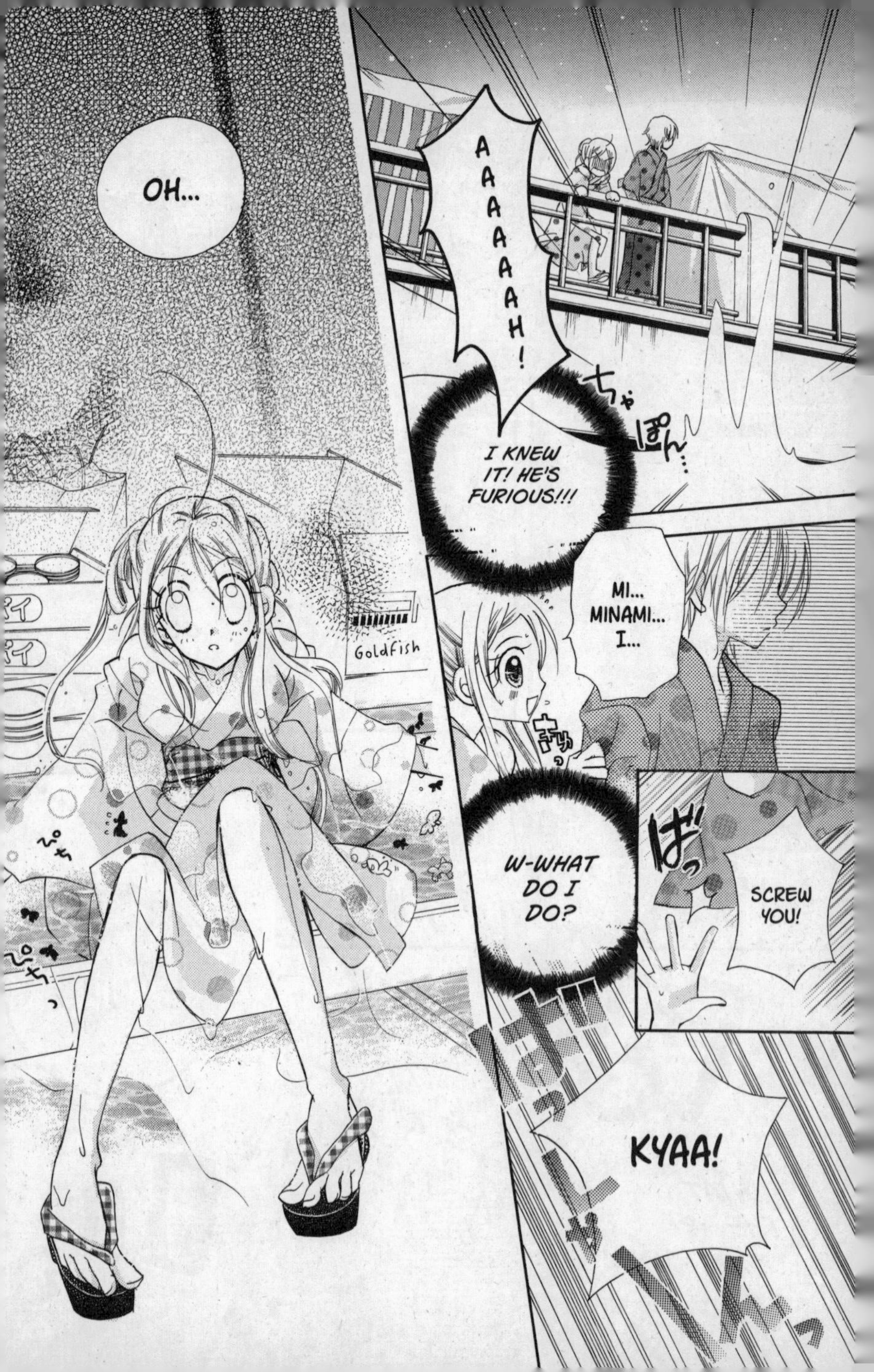
AAAAAAH!
I KNEW IT! HE'S FURIOUS!!!
ちゃぽん…
MI... MINAMI... I...
W-WHAT DO I DO?
SCREW YOU!
KYAA!
OH...
Goldfish

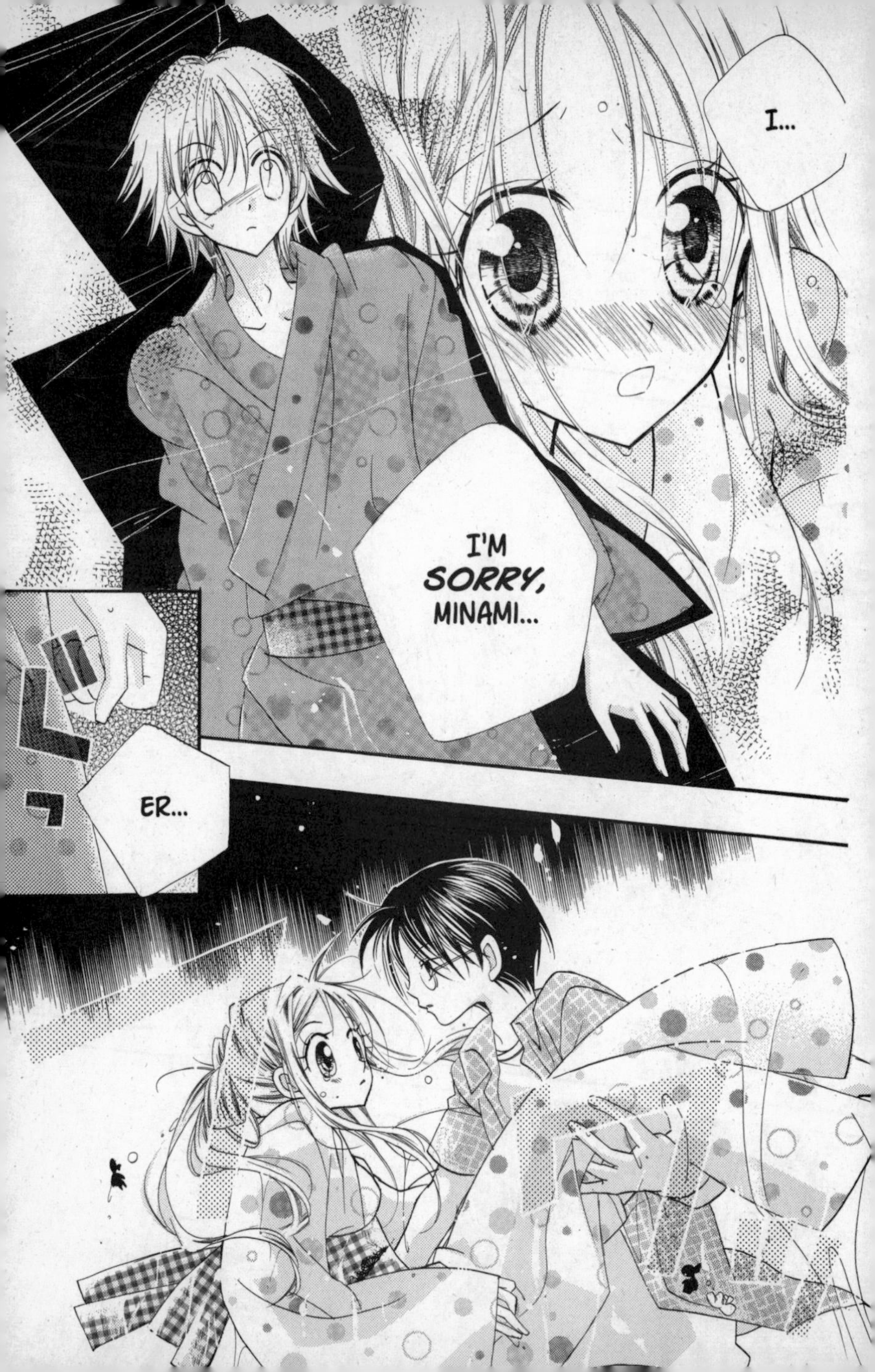
I...
I'M SORRY, MINAMI...
ER...

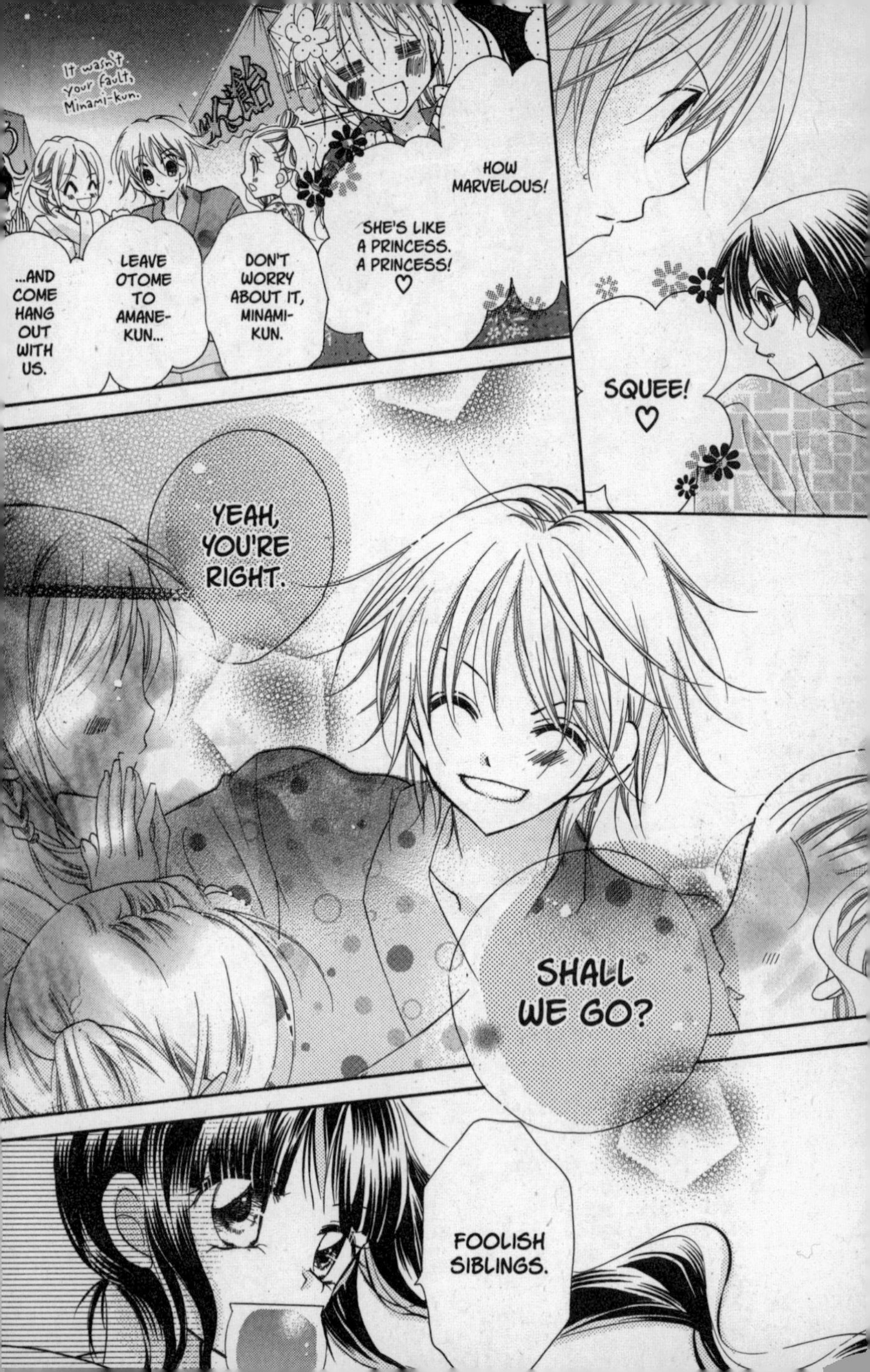
SQUEE! ♡
HOW MARVELOUS!
SHE'S LIKE A PRINCESS. A PRINCESS! ♡
It wasn't your fault, Minami-kun.
DON'T WORRY ABOUT IT, MINAMI-KUN.
LEAVE OTOME TO AMANE-KUN...
...AND COME HANG OUT WITH US.
YEAH, YOU'RE RIGHT.
SHALL WE GO?
FOOLISH SIBLINGS.

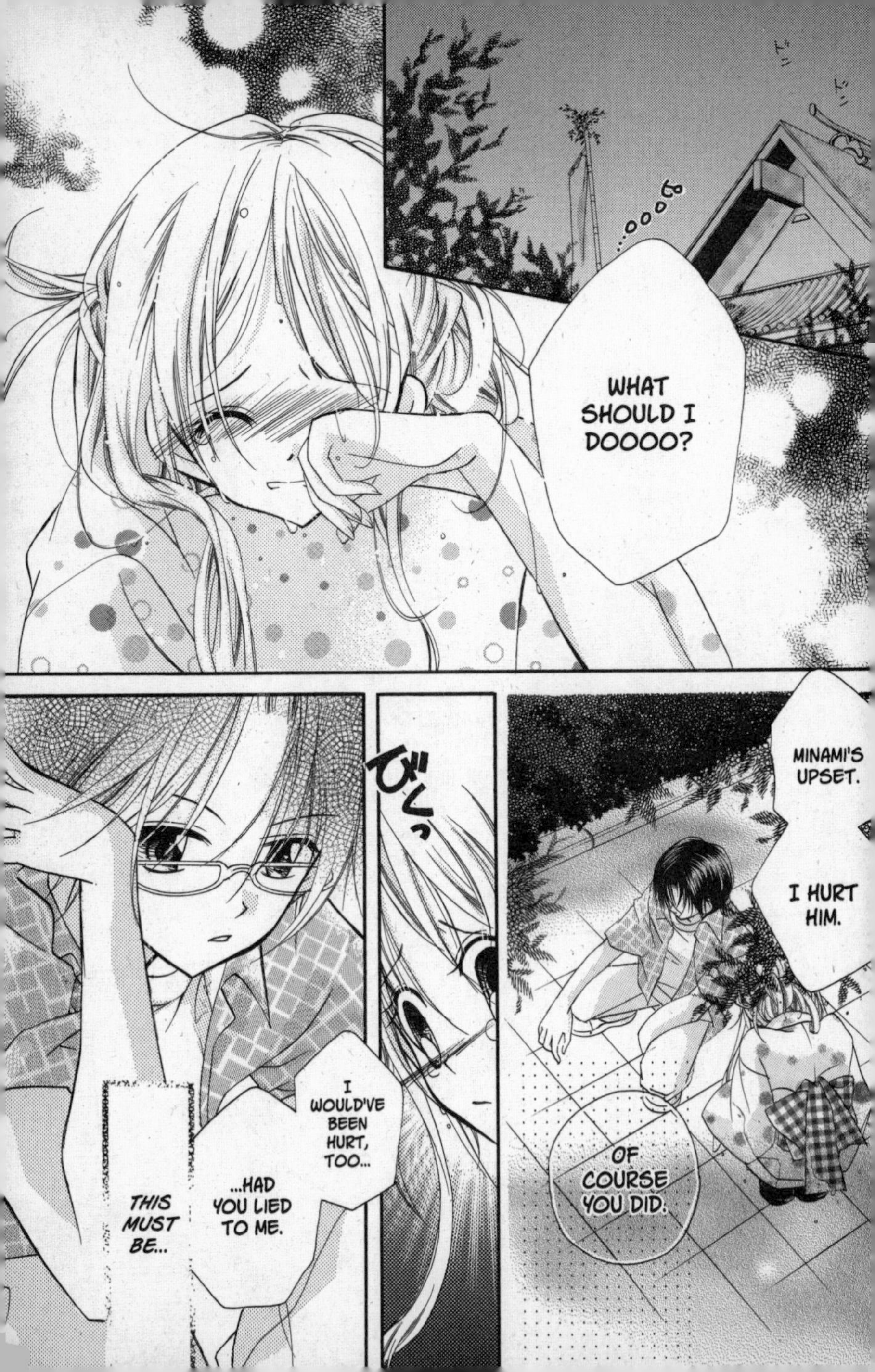

...oooo
WHAT SHOULD I DOOOO?
MINAMI'S UPSET.
I HURT HIM.
OF COURSE YOU DID.
びくっ
I WOULD'VE BEEN HURT, TOO...
...HAD YOU LIED TO ME.
THIS MUST BE...

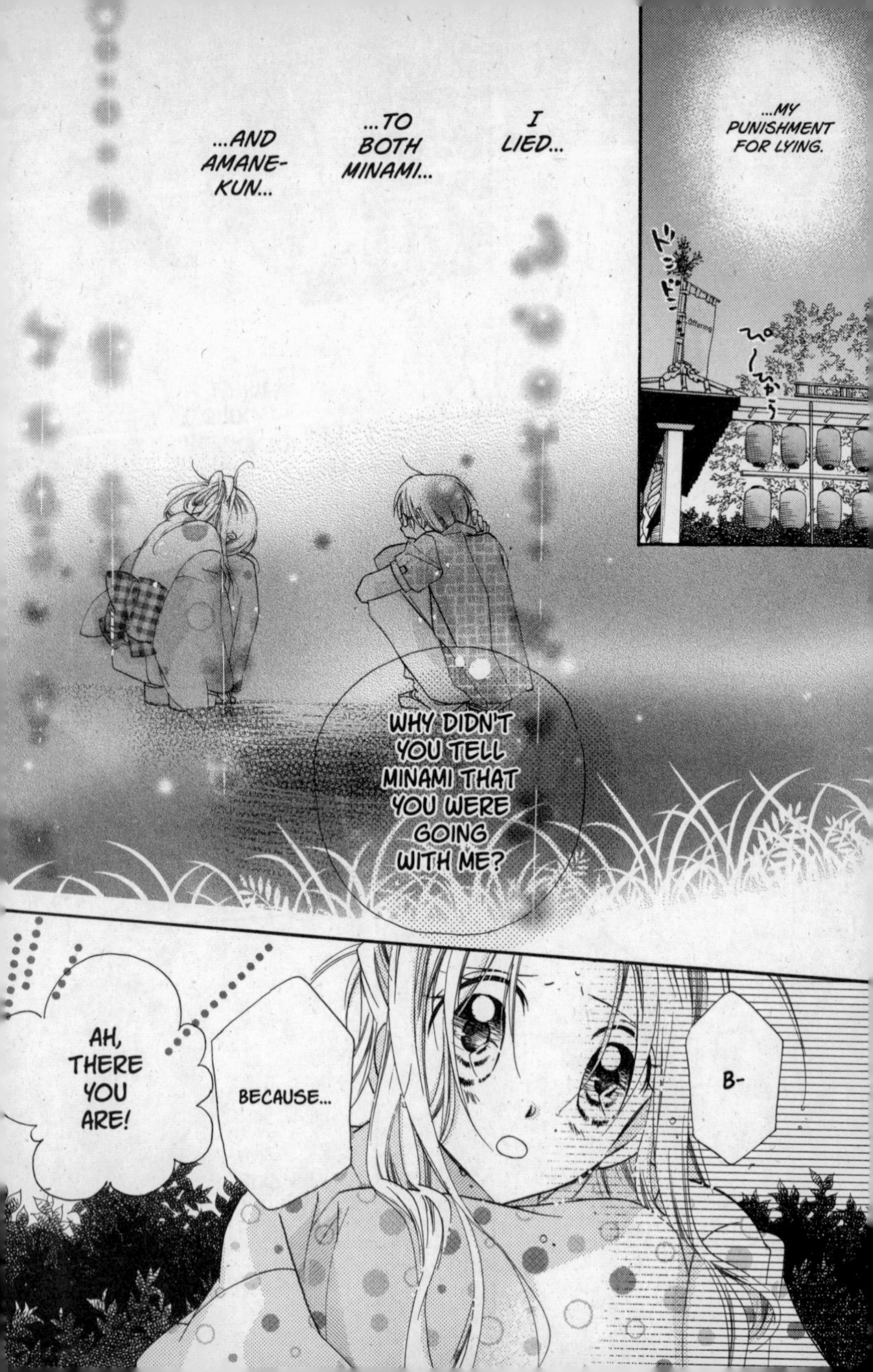
...MY PUNISHMENT FOR LYING.
I LIED...
...TO BOTH MINAMI...
...AND AMANE-KUN...
WHY DIDN'T YOU TELL MINAMI THAT YOU WERE GOING WITH ME?
B-
BECAUSE...
AH, THERE YOU ARE!

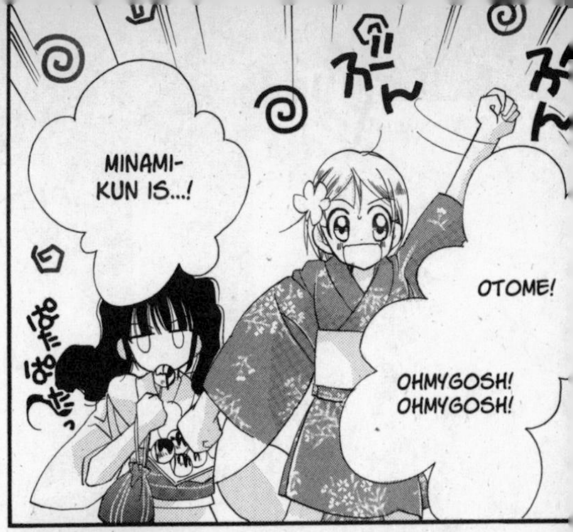
ぶん ぶん
OTOME!
OHMYGOSH!
OHMYGOSH!
MINAMI-
KUN IS...!
ぱたぱたっ

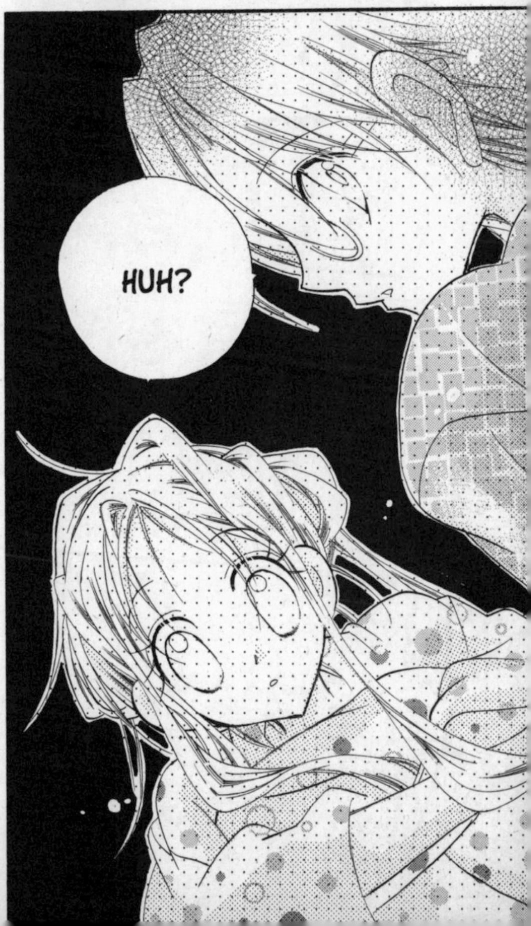
HUH?

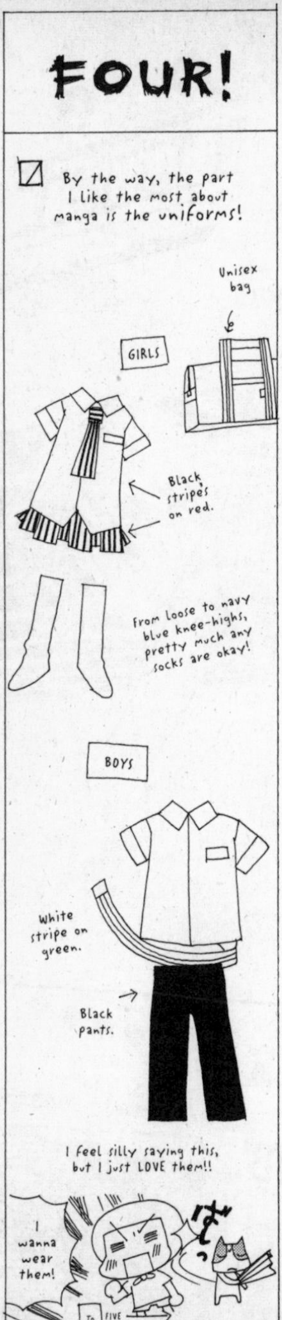
FOUR!
By the way, the part I like the most about manga is the uniforms!
GIRLS
Unisex bag
Black stripes on red.
From loose to navy blue knee-highs, pretty much any socks are okay!
BOYS
White stripe on green.
Black pants.
I feel silly saying this, but I just LOVE them!!
I wanna wear them!
ぱっ
To FIVE

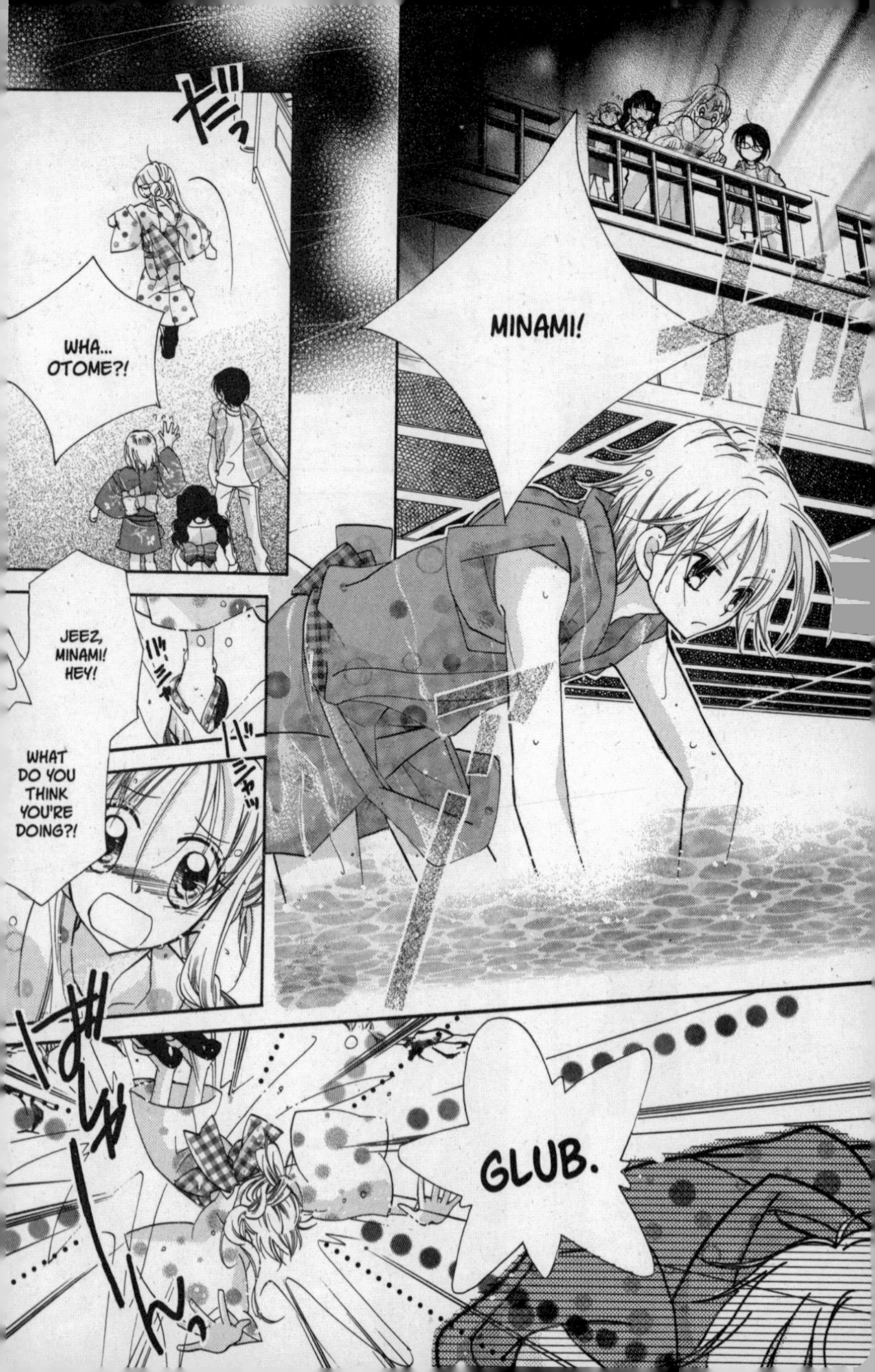
MINAMI!
WHA... OTOME?!
JEEZ, MINAMI! HEY!
WHAT DO YOU THINK YOU'RE DOING?!
GLUB.

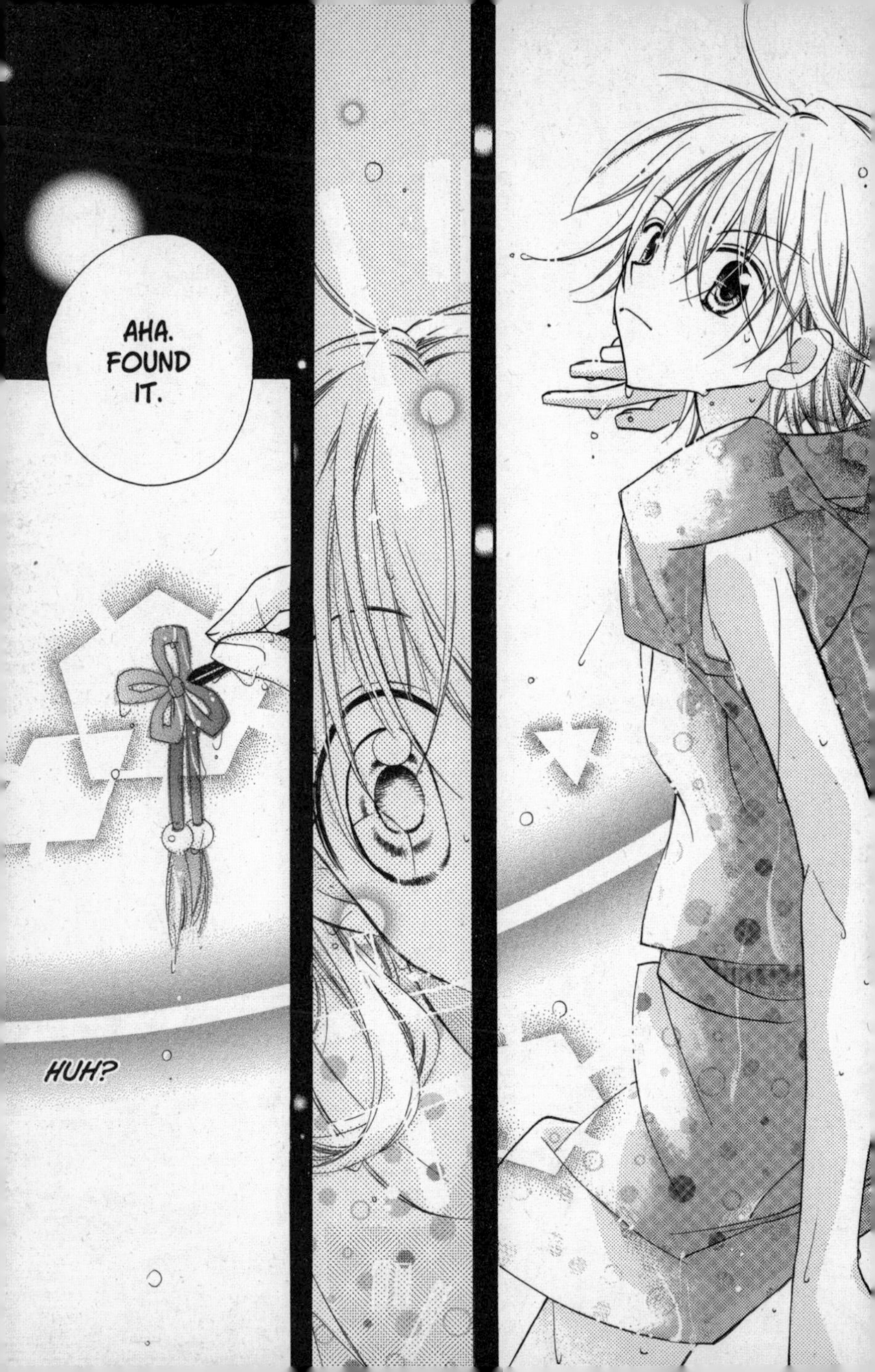
AHA. FOUND IT.
HUH?

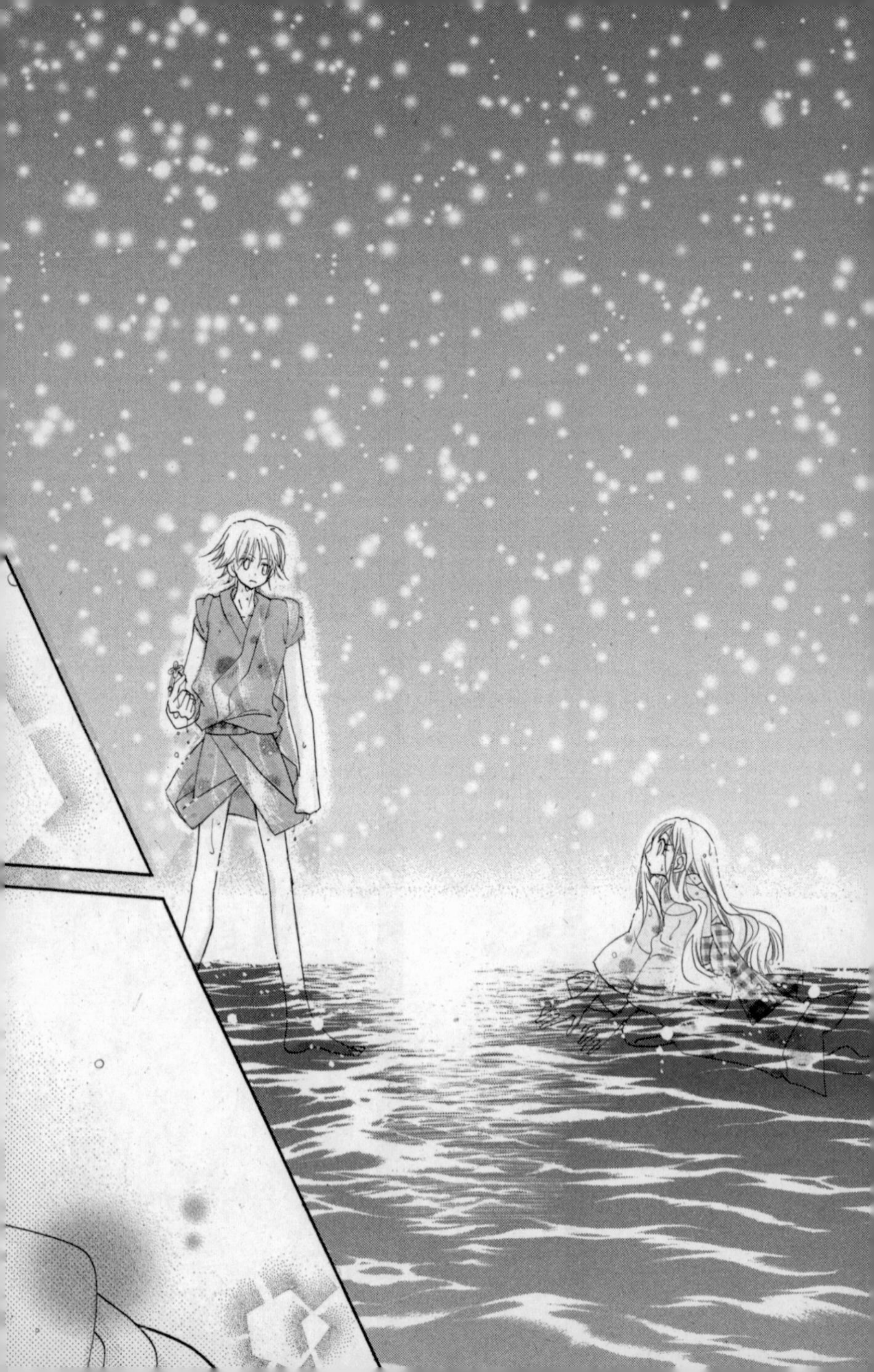

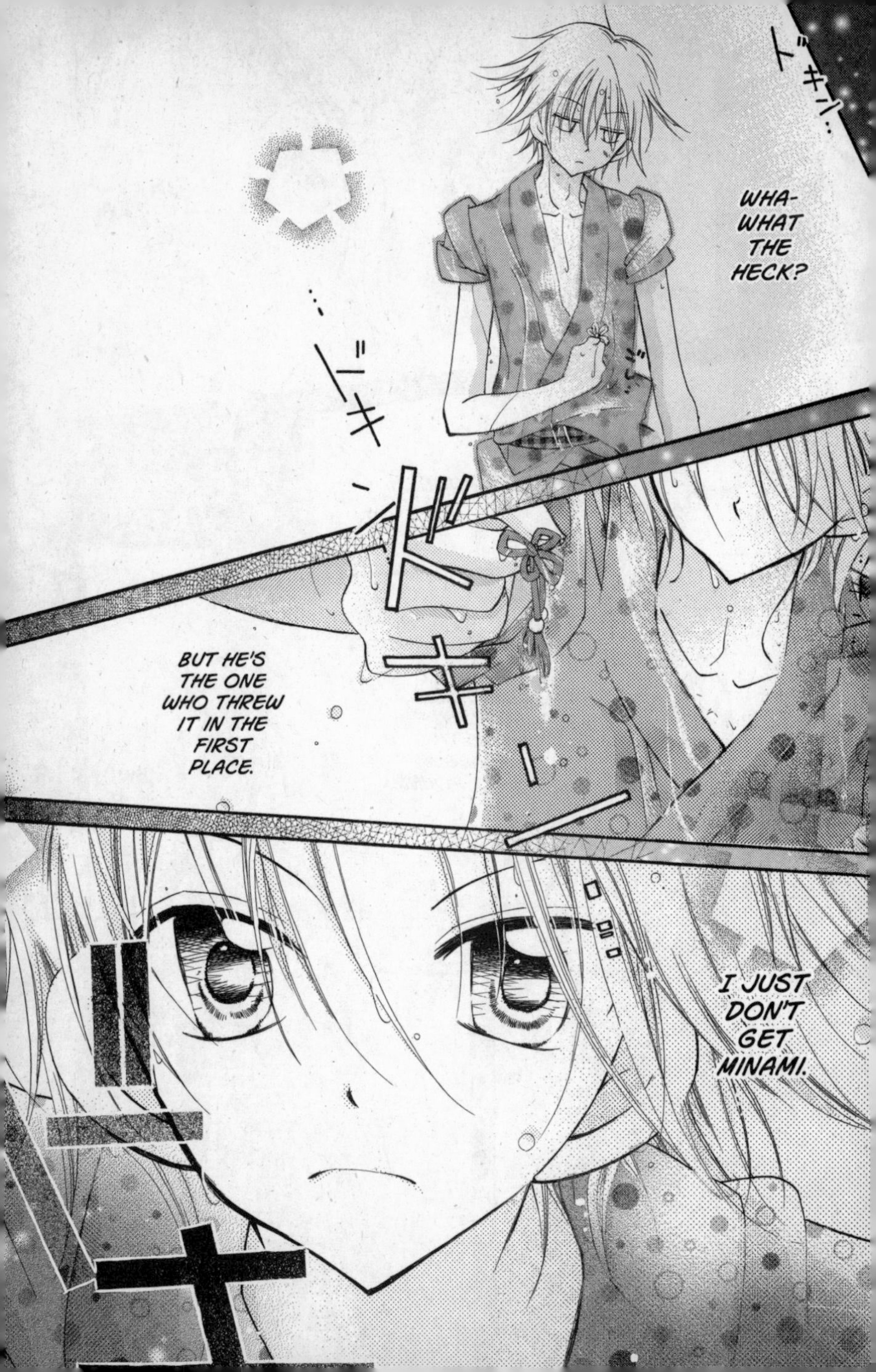
ドキン…
WHA-WHAT THE HECK?
BUT HE'S THE ONE WHO THREW IT IN THE FIRST PLACE.
I JUST DON'T GET MINAMI.

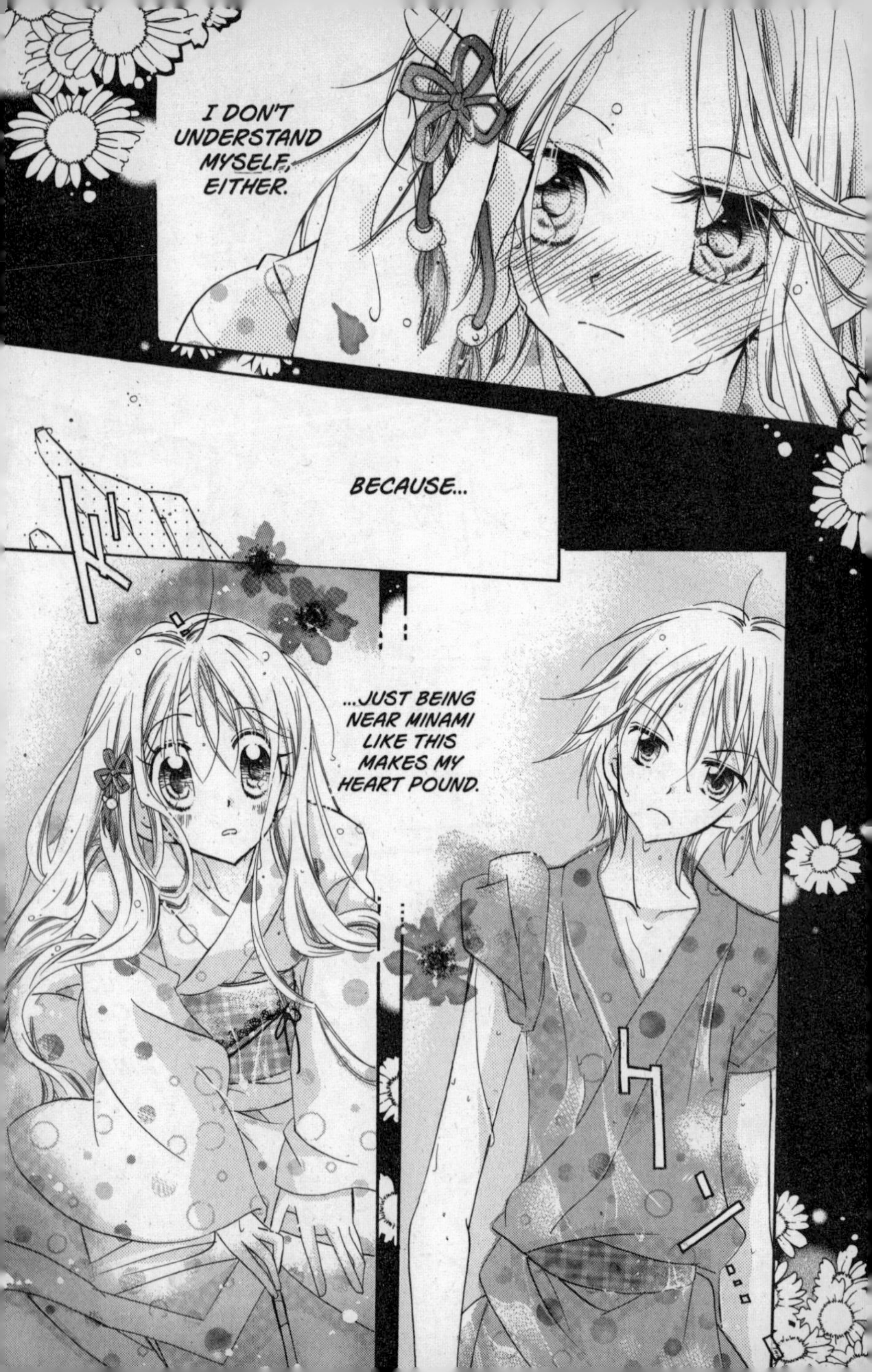
I DON'T UNDERSTAND MYSELF, EITHER.
BECAUSE...
...JUST BEING NEAR MINAMI LIKE THIS MAKES MY HEART POUND.

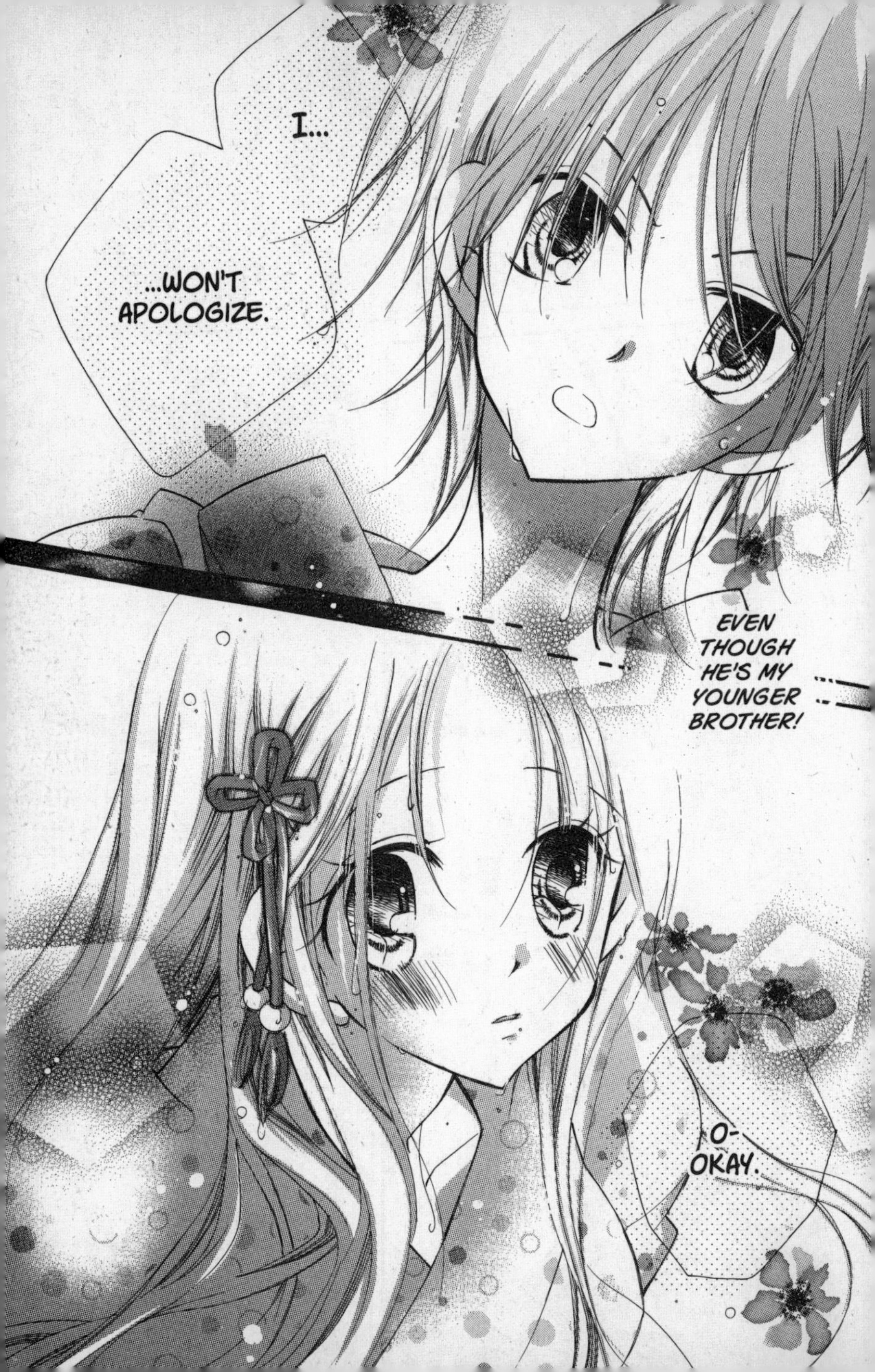
I...
...WON'T APOLOGIZE.
EVEN THOUGH HE'S MY YOUNGER BROTHER!
O- OKAY.

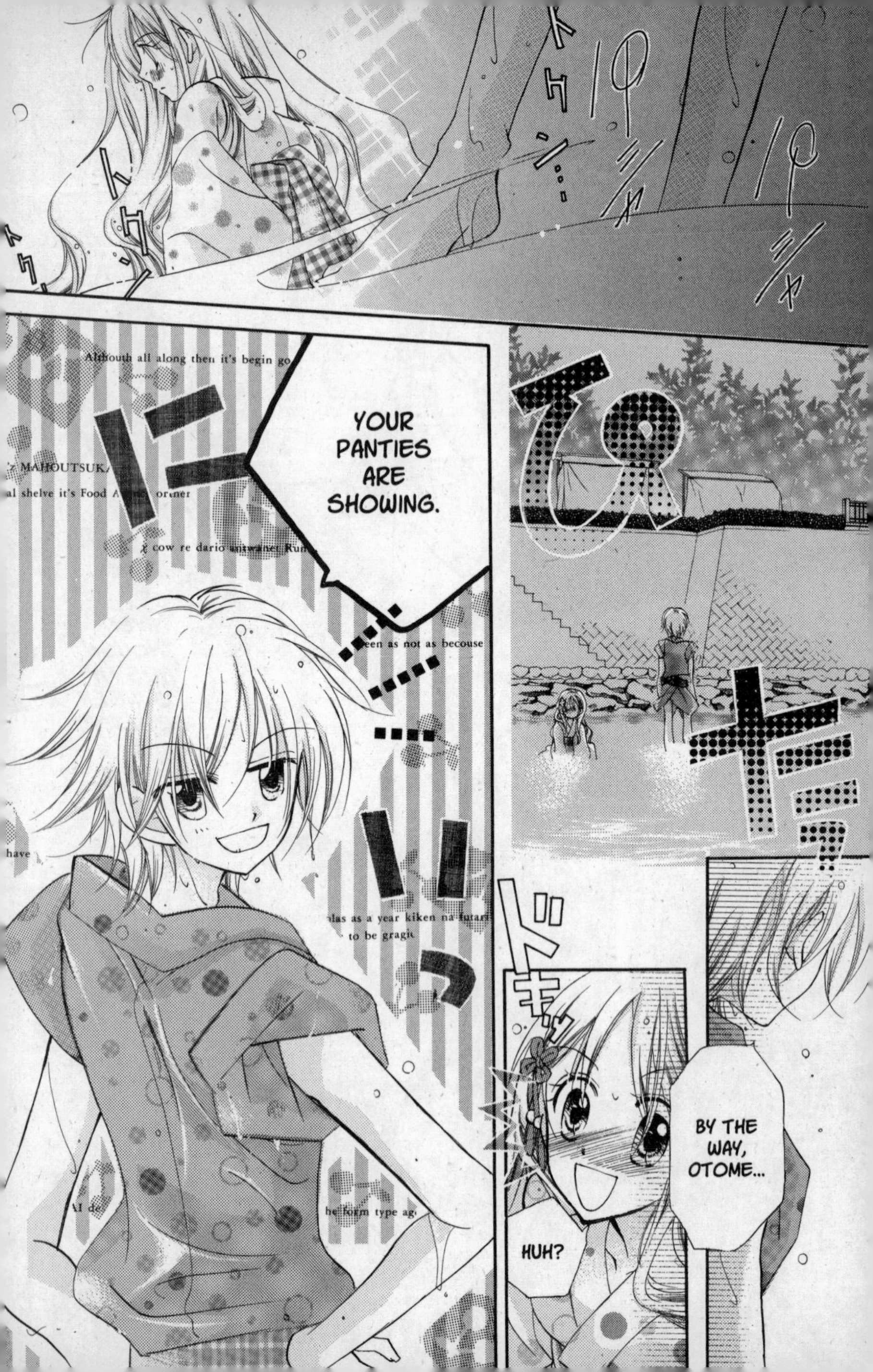
BY THE WAY, OTOME...
HUH?
YOUR PANTIES ARE SHOWING.

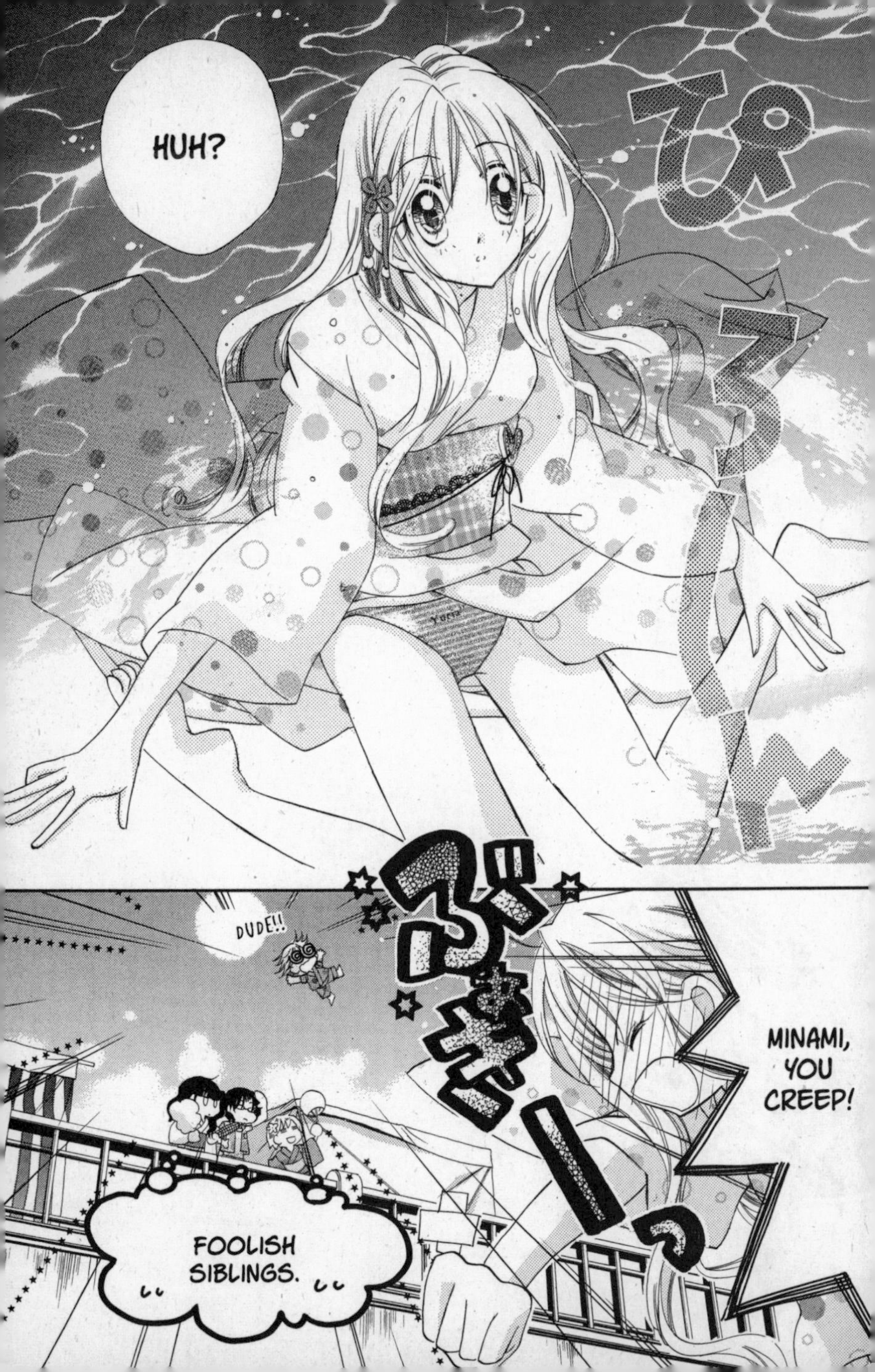
HUH?
MINAMI, YOU CREEP!
DUDE!!
FOOLISH SIBLINGS.

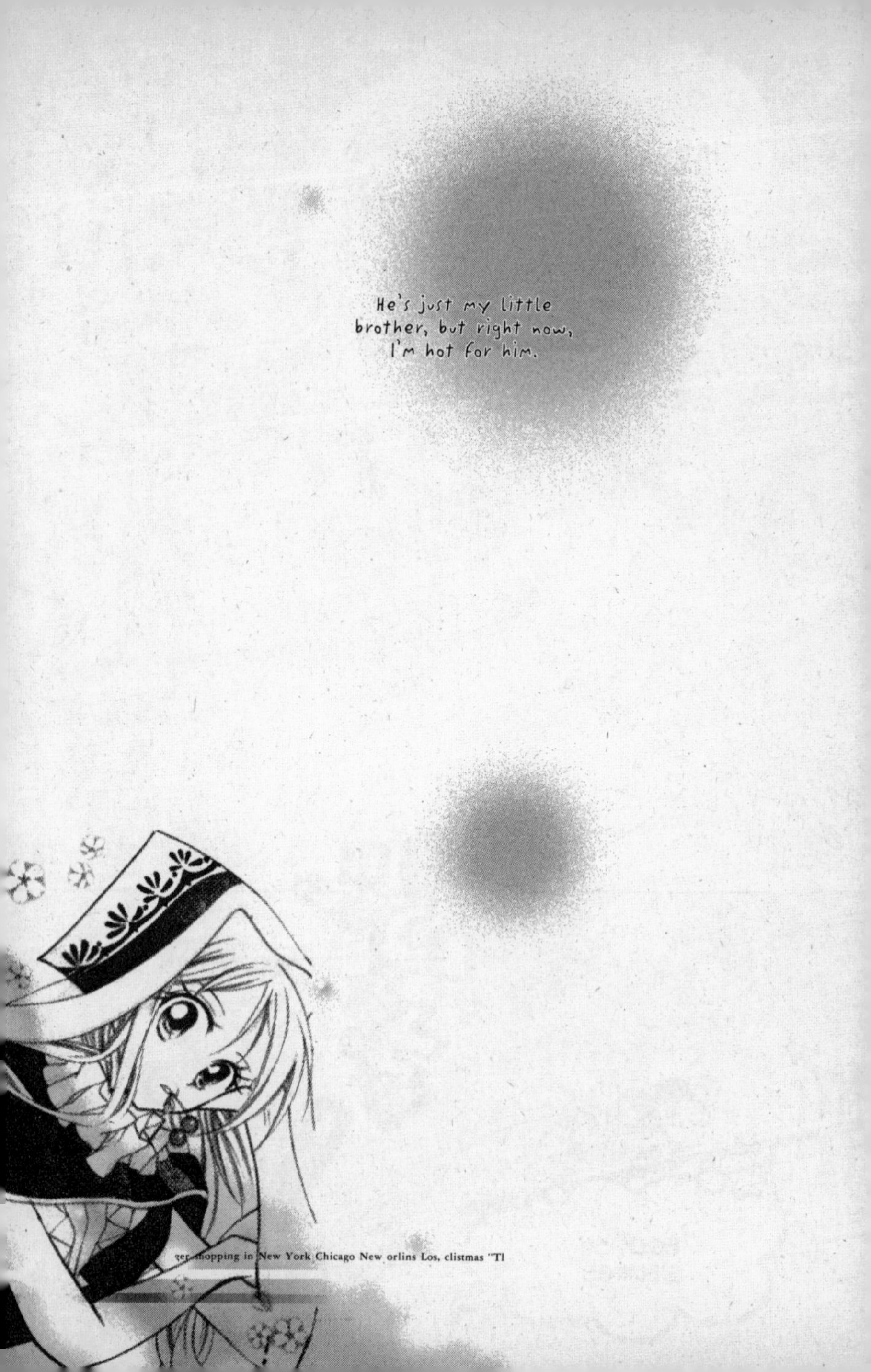
He's just my little brother, but right now, I'm hot for him.
qer shopping in New York Chicago New orlins Los, clistmas "Tl

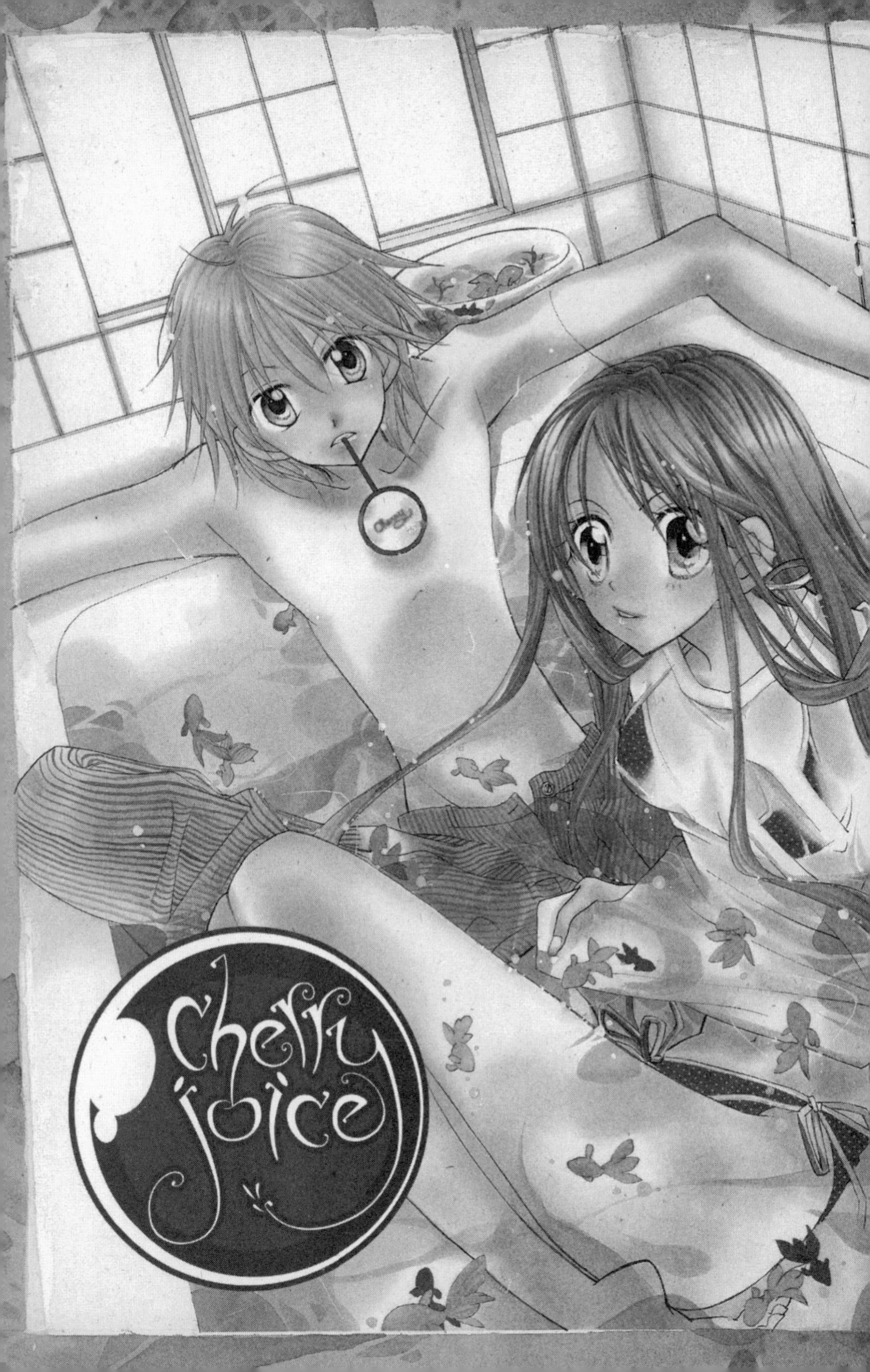
Cherry Juice

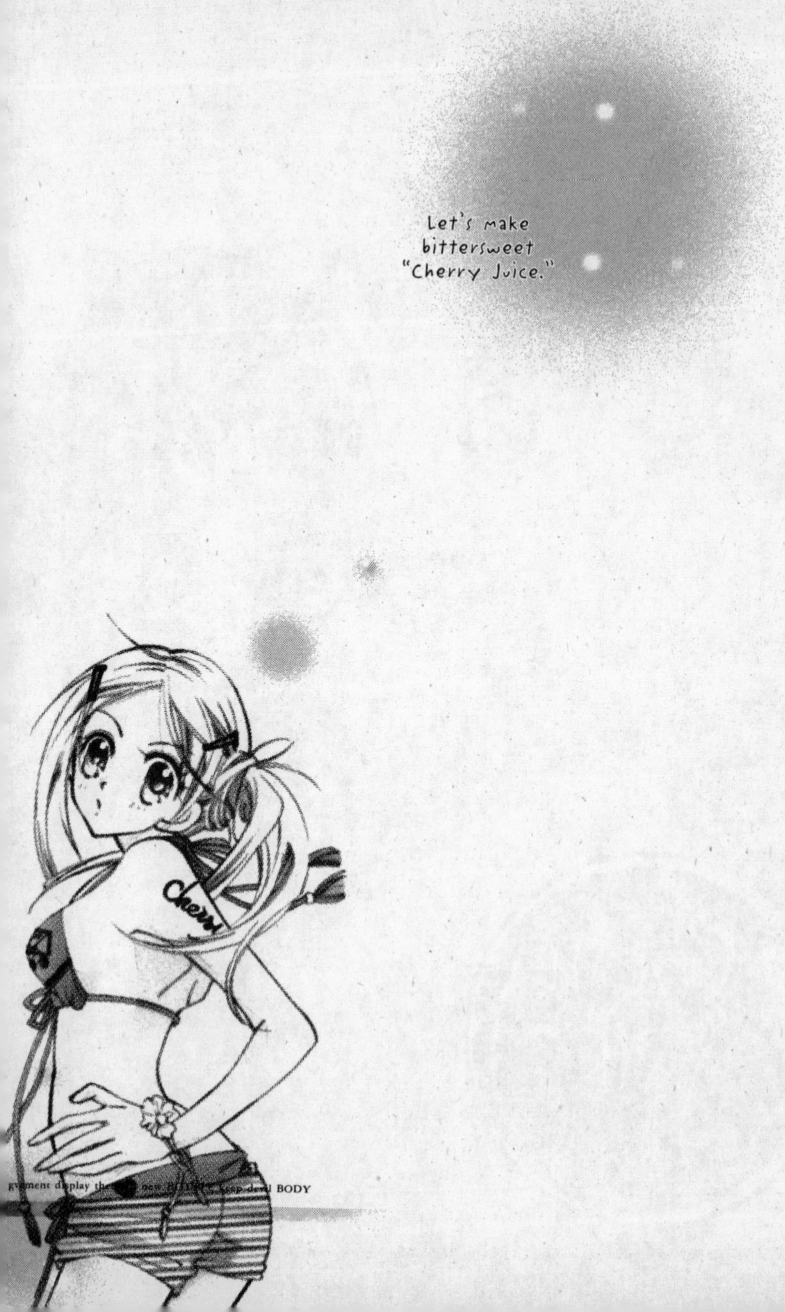
Let's make
bittersweet
"Cherry Juice."
Cherry

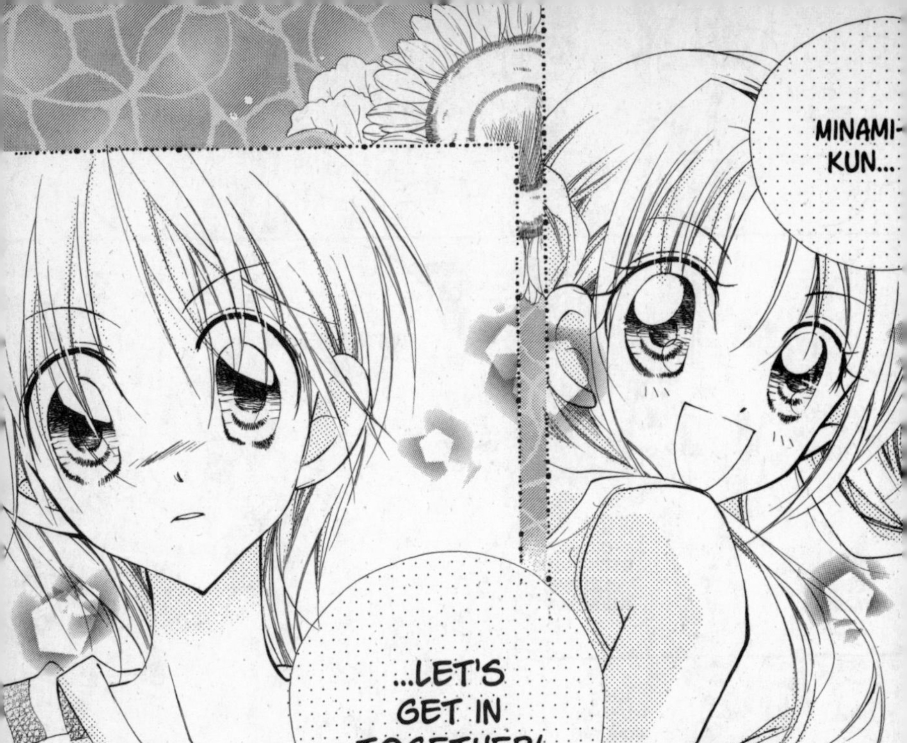
MINAMI-KUN...
...LET'S GET IN TOGETHER!
N.P.

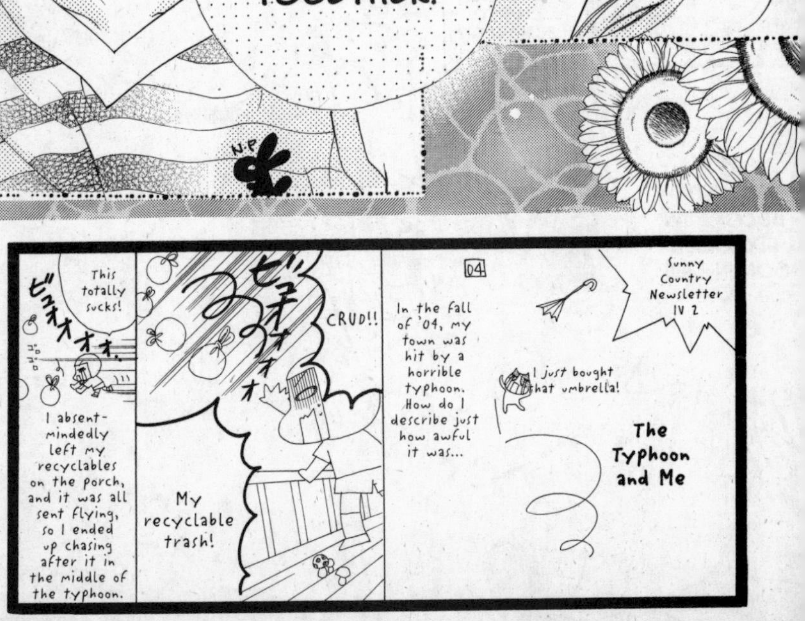
Sunny Country Newsletter IV 2
The Typhoon and Me
I just bought that umbrella!
04
In the fall of '04, my town was hit by a horrible typhoon. How do I describe just how awful it was...
CRUD!!
My recyclable trash!
This totally sucks!
I absent-mindedly left my recyclables on the porch, and it was all sent flying, so I ended up chasing after it in the middle of the typhoon.

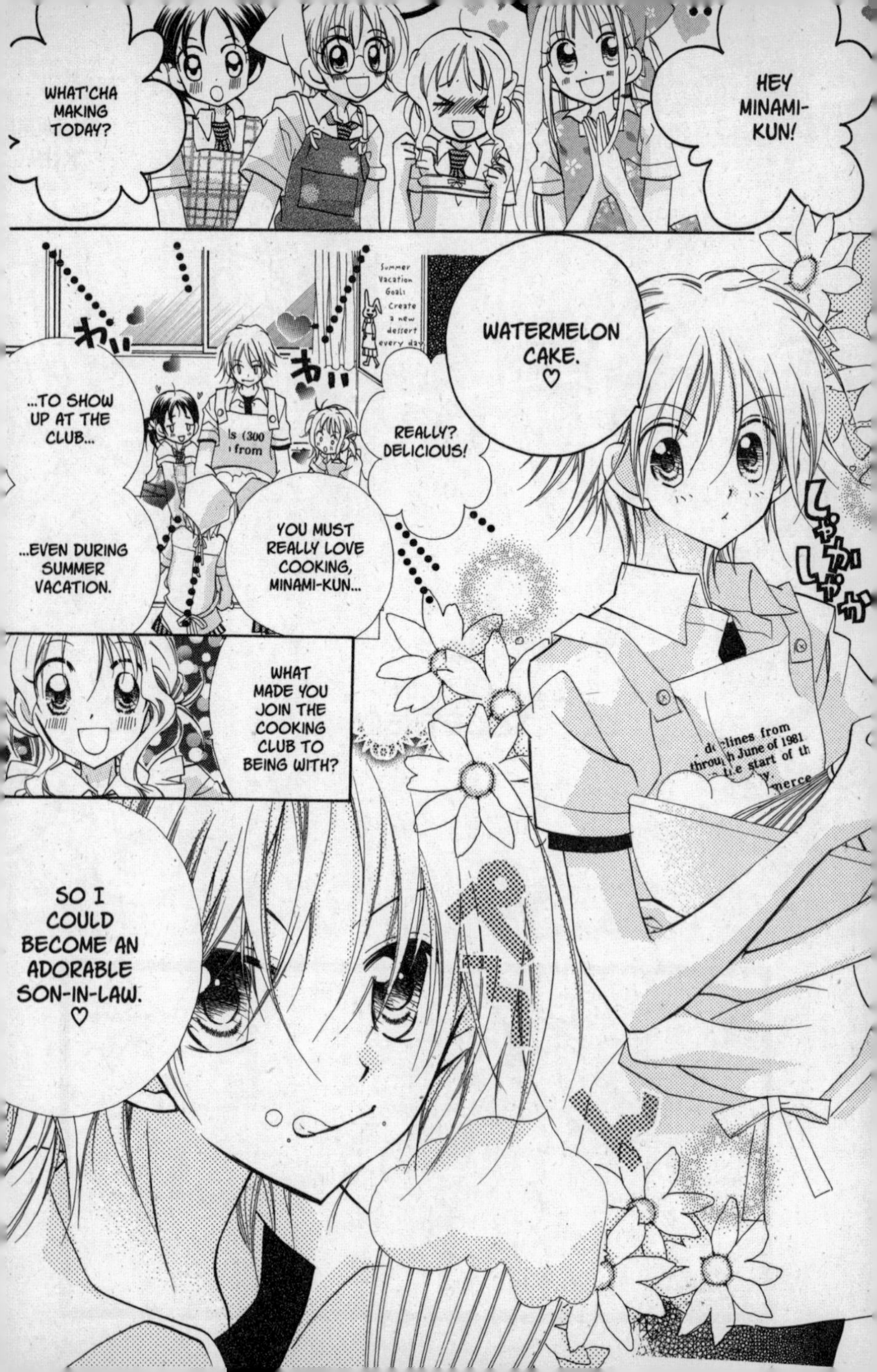
HEY MINAMI-KUN!
WHAT'CHA MAKING TODAY?
WATERMELON CAKE. ♡
しゃかしゃか
REALLY? DELICIOUS!
Summer Vacation Goal: Create a new dessert every day
わい
わい
YOU MUST REALLY LOVE COOKING, MINAMI-KUN...
...TO SHOW UP AT THE CLUB...
...EVEN DURING SUMMER VACATION.
WHAT MADE YOU JOIN THE COOKING CLUB TO BEING WITH?
SO I COULD BECOME AN ADORABLE SON-IN-LAW. ♡

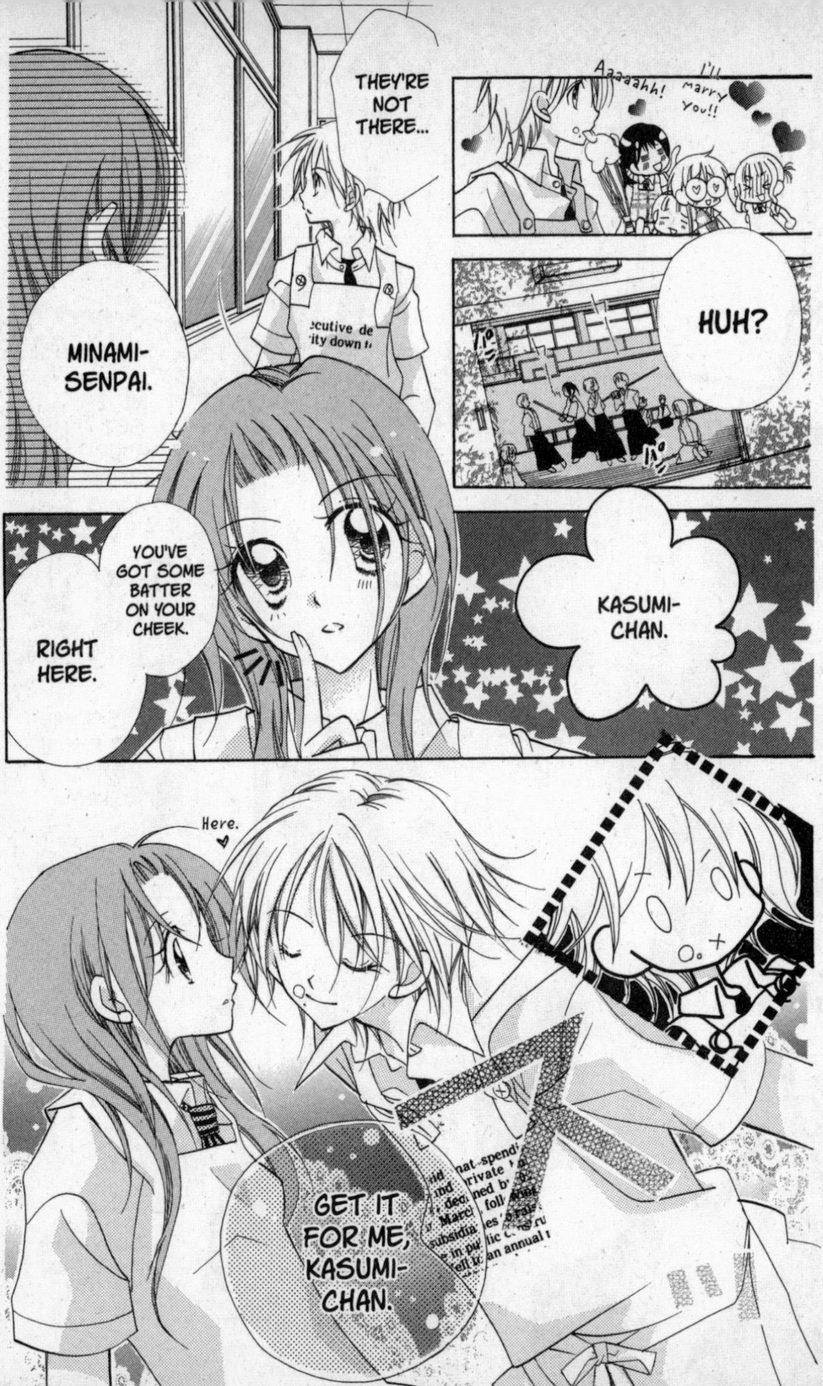
Aaaaaahh!
I'll marry you!!
HUH?
THEY'RE NOT THERE...
MINAMI-SENPAI.
KASUMI-CHAN.
YOU'VE GOT SOME BATTER ON YOUR CHEEK.
RIGHT HERE.
Here.
GET IT FOR ME, KASUMI-CHAN.

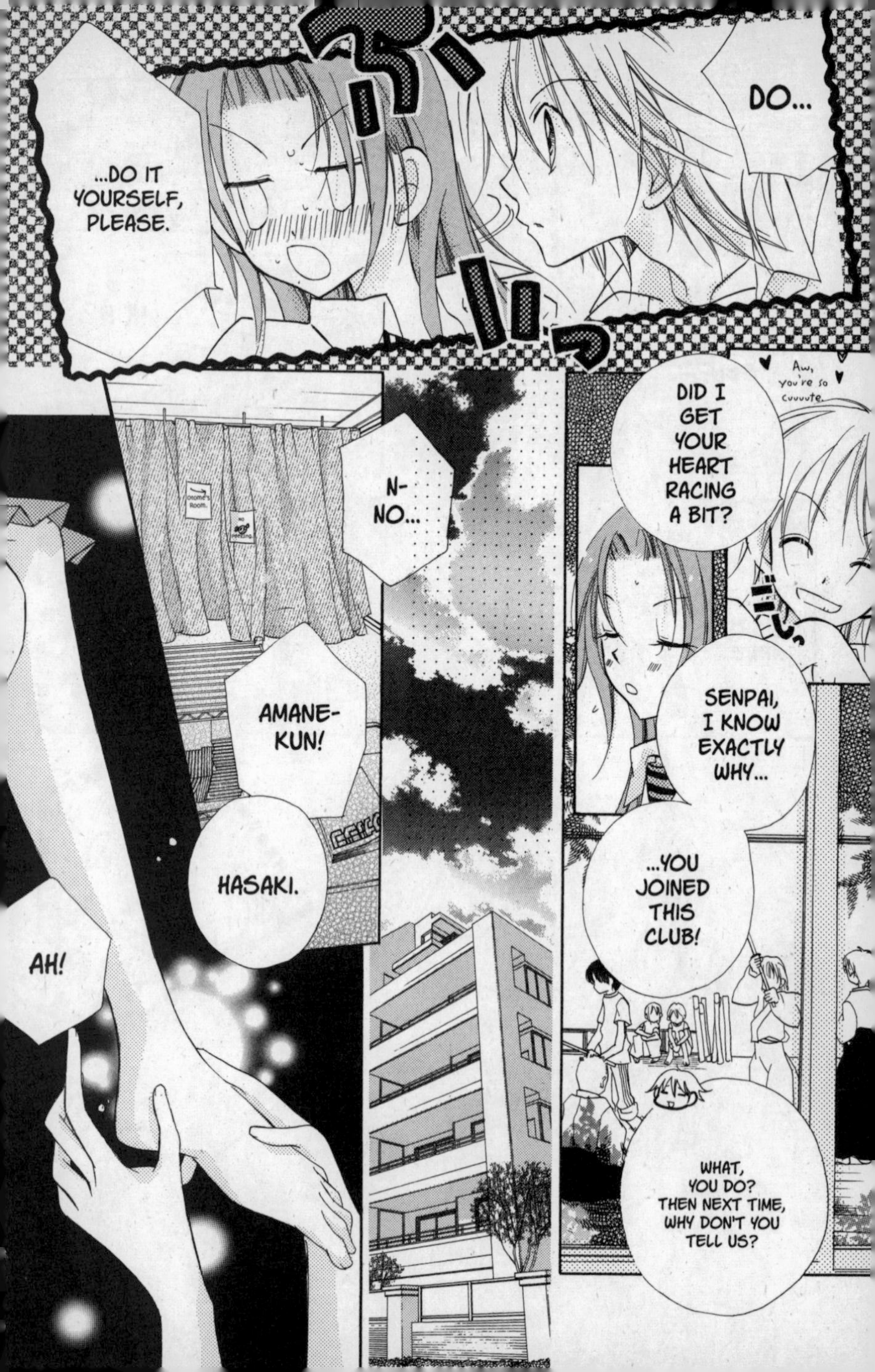
DO...
...DO IT YOURSELF, PLEASE.
Aw, you're so cuuuute.
DID I GET YOUR HEART RACING A BIT?
SENPAI, I KNOW EXACTLY WHY...
...YOU JOINED THIS CLUB!
WHAT, YOU DO? THEN NEXT TIME, WHY DON'T YOU TELL US?
N-NO...
Otome's Room.
AMANE-KUN!
HASAKI.
AH!

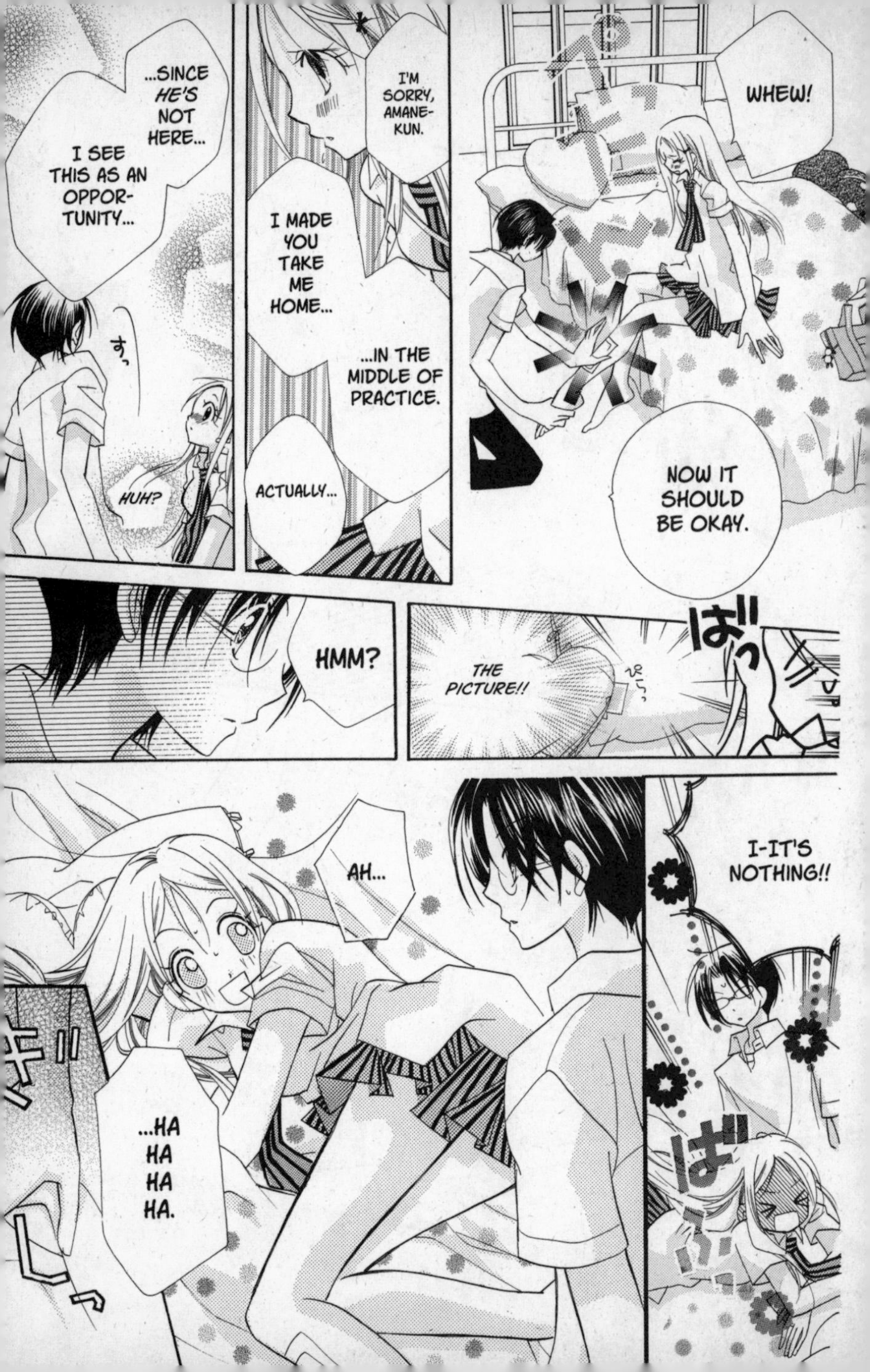
WHEW!
NOW IT SHOULD BE OKAY.
I'M SORRY, AMANE-KUN.
I MADE YOU TAKE ME HOME...
...IN THE MIDDLE OF PRACTICE.
ACTUALLY...
...SINCE HE'S NOT HERE...
I SEE THIS AS AN OPPORTUNITY...
HUH?
ばっ
THE PICTURE!!
HMM?
I-IT'S NOTHING!!
AH...
...HA HA HA HA.

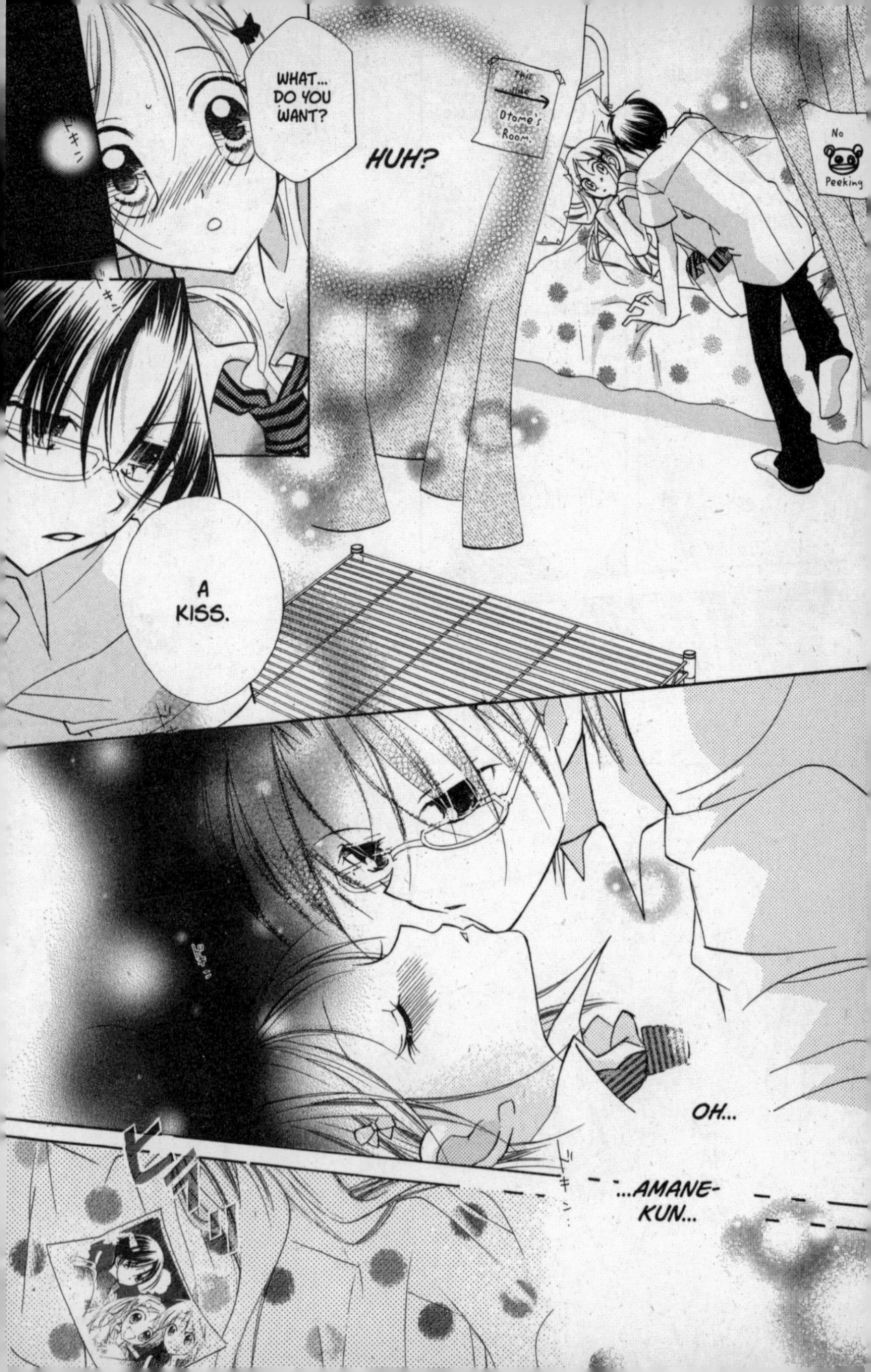
This side
Otome's Room.
No
Peeking
HUH?
WHAT... DO YOU WANT?
A KISS.
OH...
...AMANE-KUN...

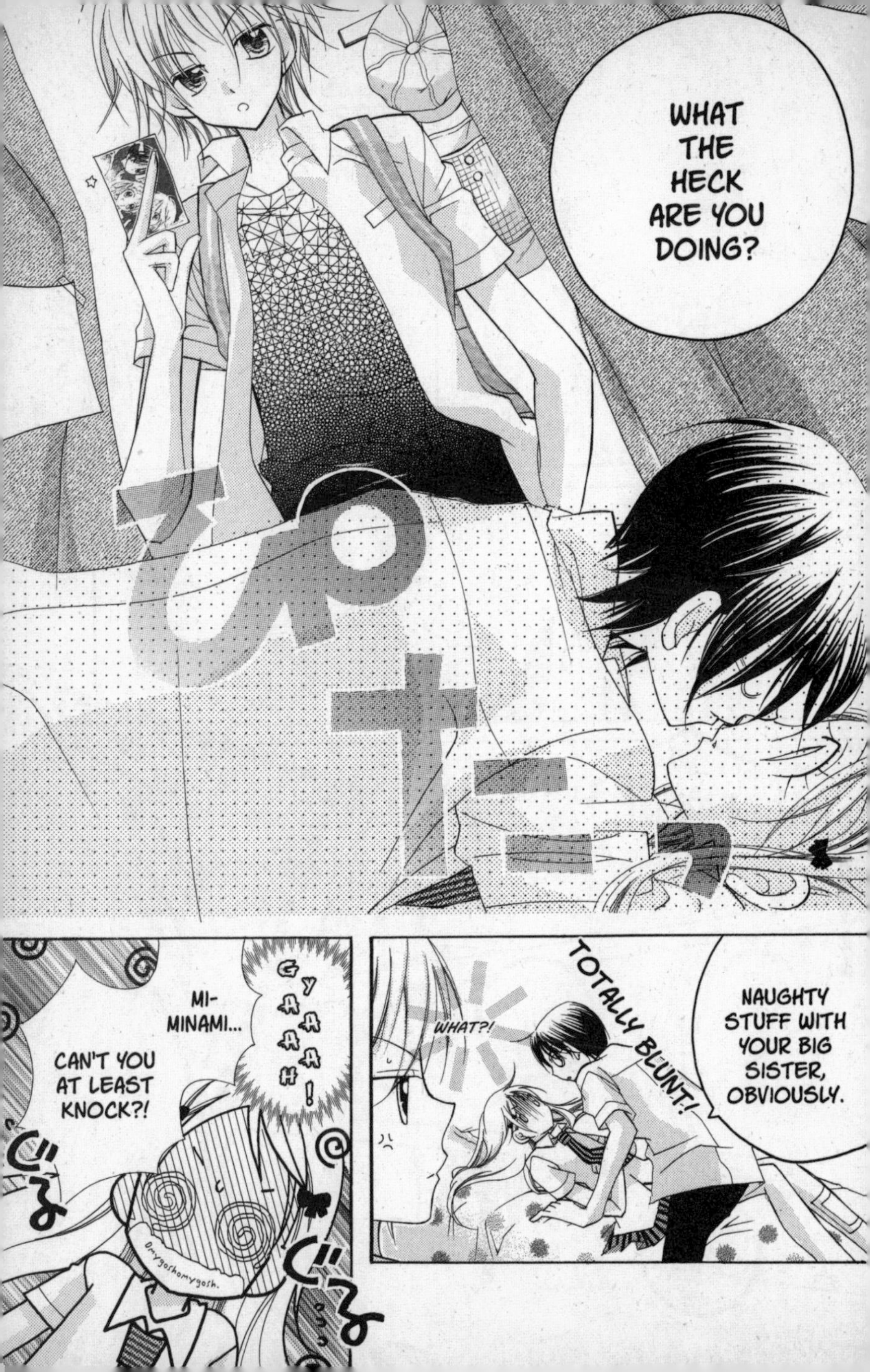
WHAT THE HECK ARE YOU DOING?
NAUGHTY STUFF WITH YOUR BIG SISTER, OBVIOUSLY.
TOTALLY BLUNT.!
WHAT?!
GYAAAAH!
MI-MINAMI...
CAN'T YOU AT LEAST KNOCK?!
Omygoshomygosh.

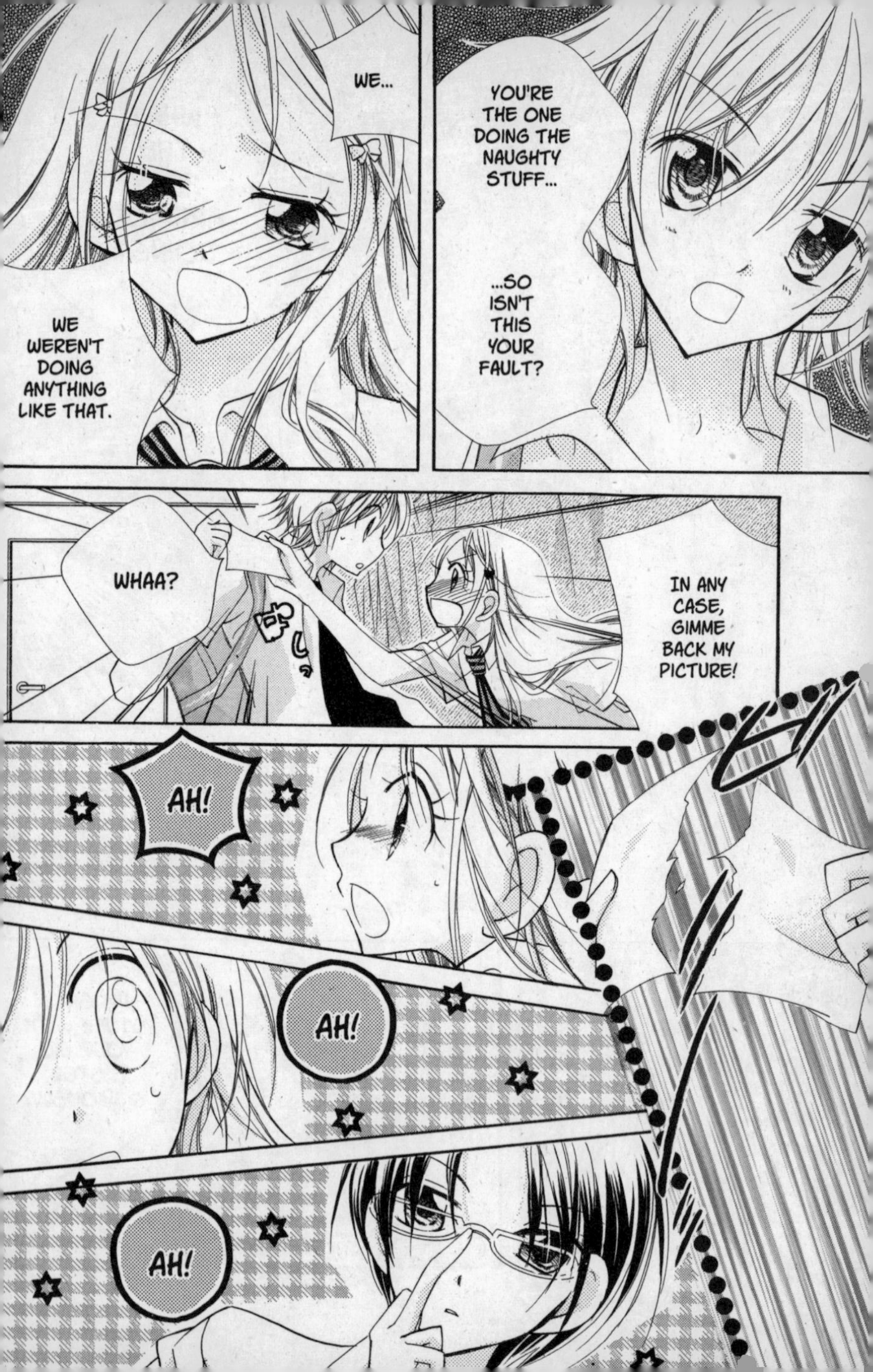
YOU'RE THE ONE DOING THE NAUGHTY STUFF...
...SO ISN'T THIS YOUR FAULT?
WE...
WE WEREN'T DOING ANYTHING LIKE THAT.
IN ANY CASE, GIMME BACK MY PICTURE!
WHAA?
AH!
AH!
AH!

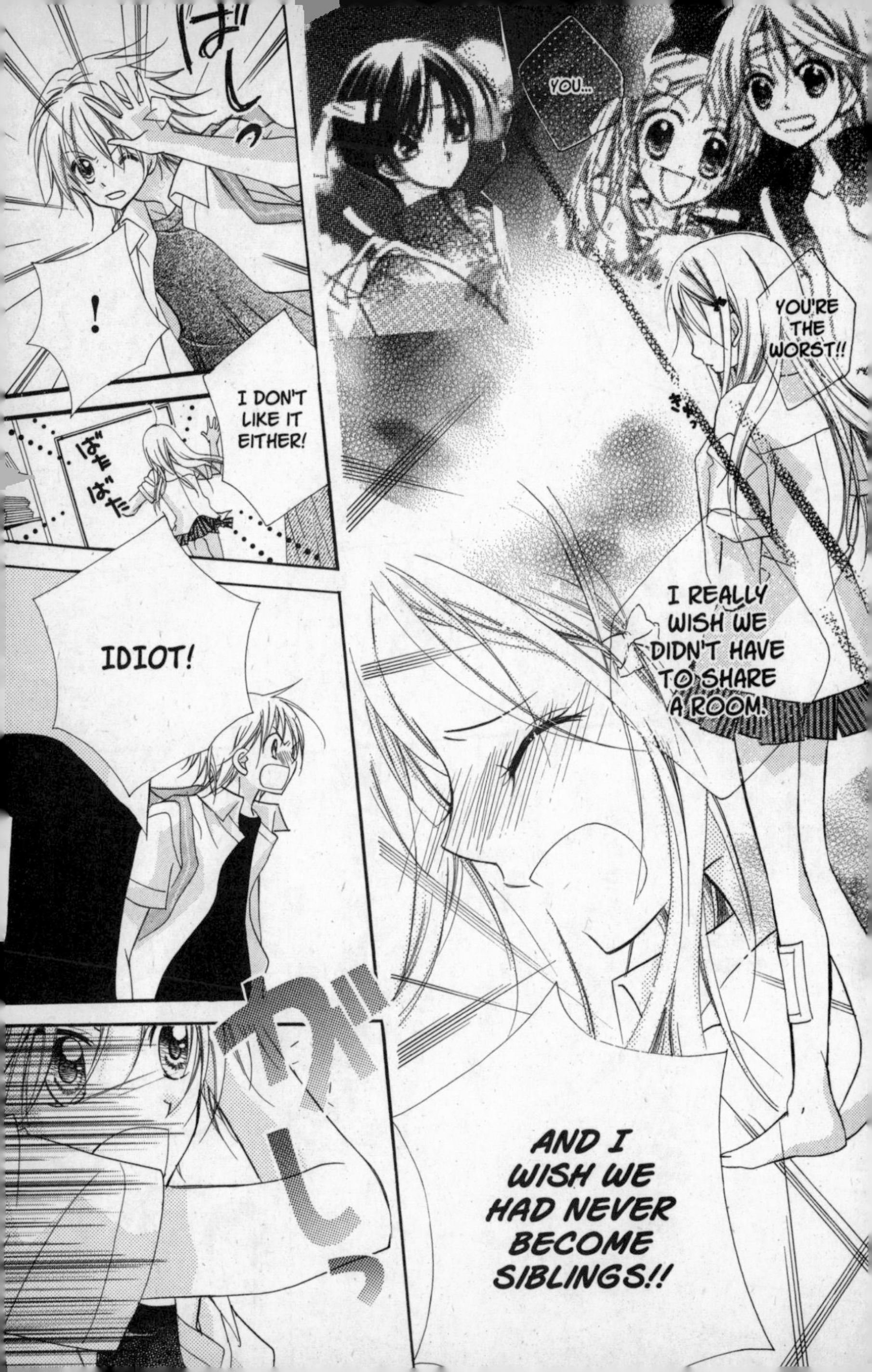
YOU...
YOU'RE THE WORST!!
I REALLY WISH WE DIDN'T HAVE TO SHARE A ROOM.
AND I WISH WE HAD NEVER BECOME SIBLINGS!!
ばしっ
!
I DON'T LIKE IT EITHER!
ぱたぱた
IDIOT!

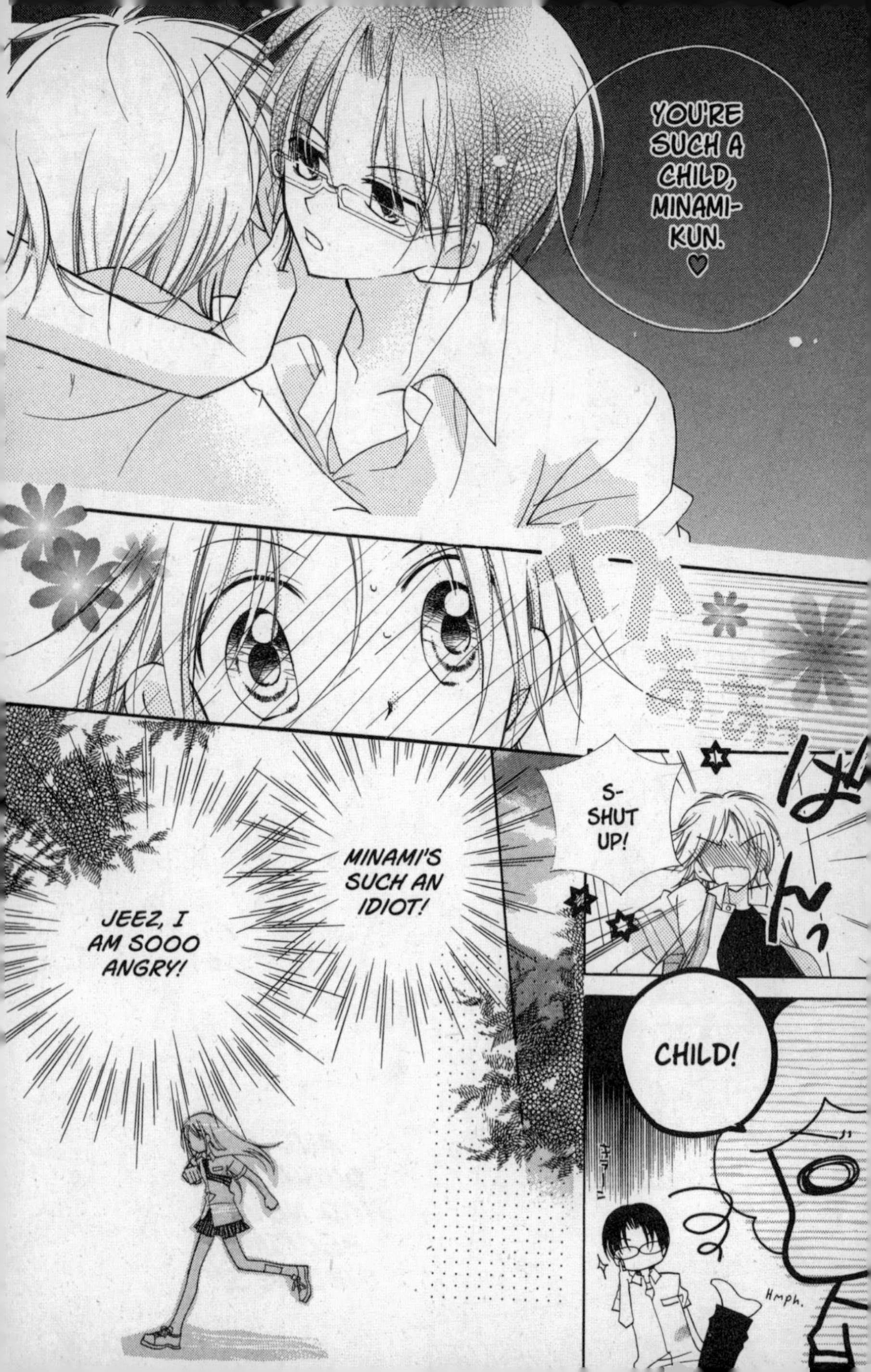
YOU'RE SUCH A CHILD, MINAMI-KUN. ♥
S-SHUT UP!
CHILD!
Hmph.
MINAMI'S SUCH AN IDIOT!
JEEZ, I AM SOOO ANGRY!

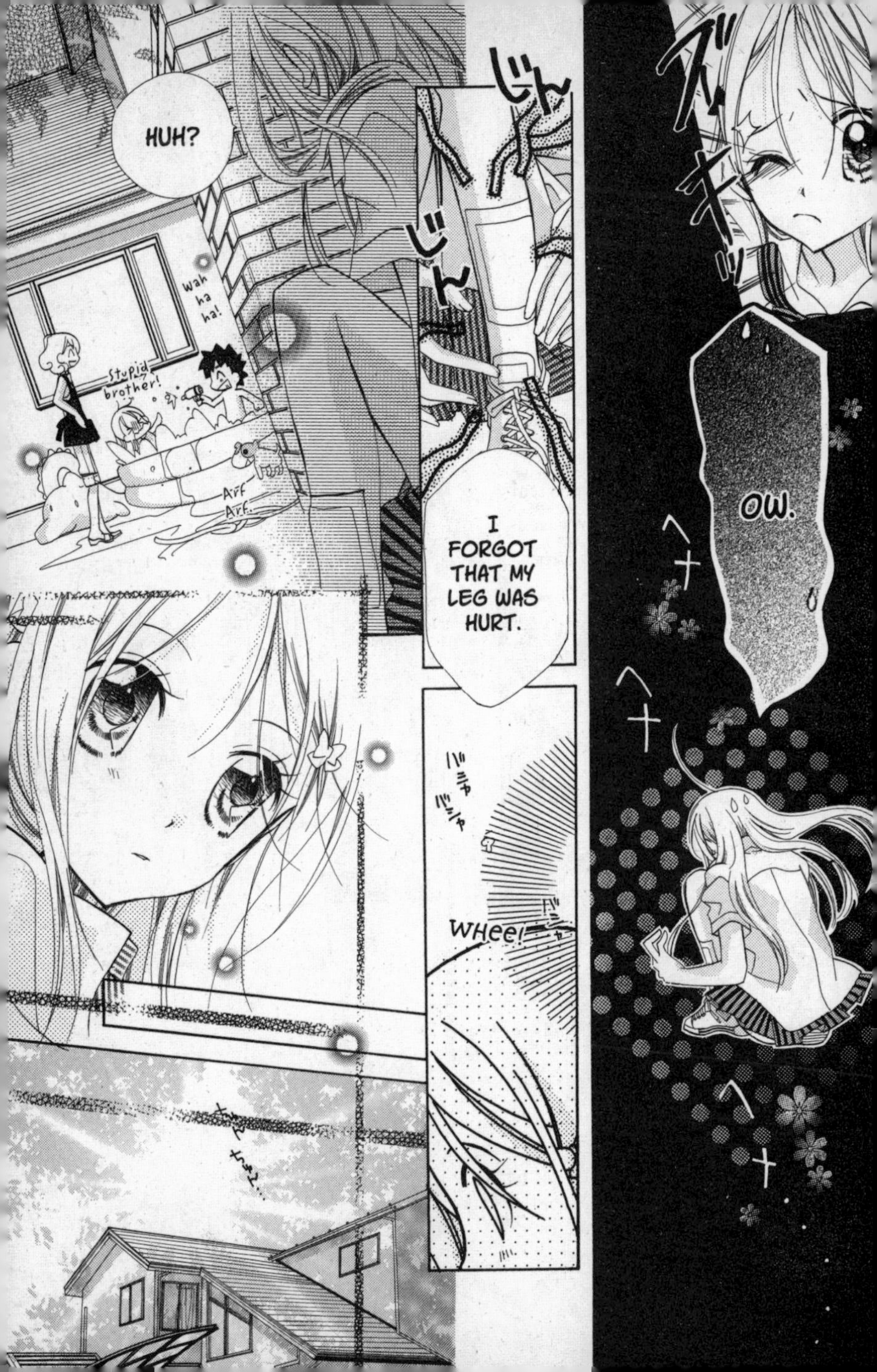
ズキッ
OW.
じん
じん
I FORGOT THAT MY LEG WAS HURT.
HUH?
Wah ha ha!
Stupid brother!
Arf Arf.
WHEE!

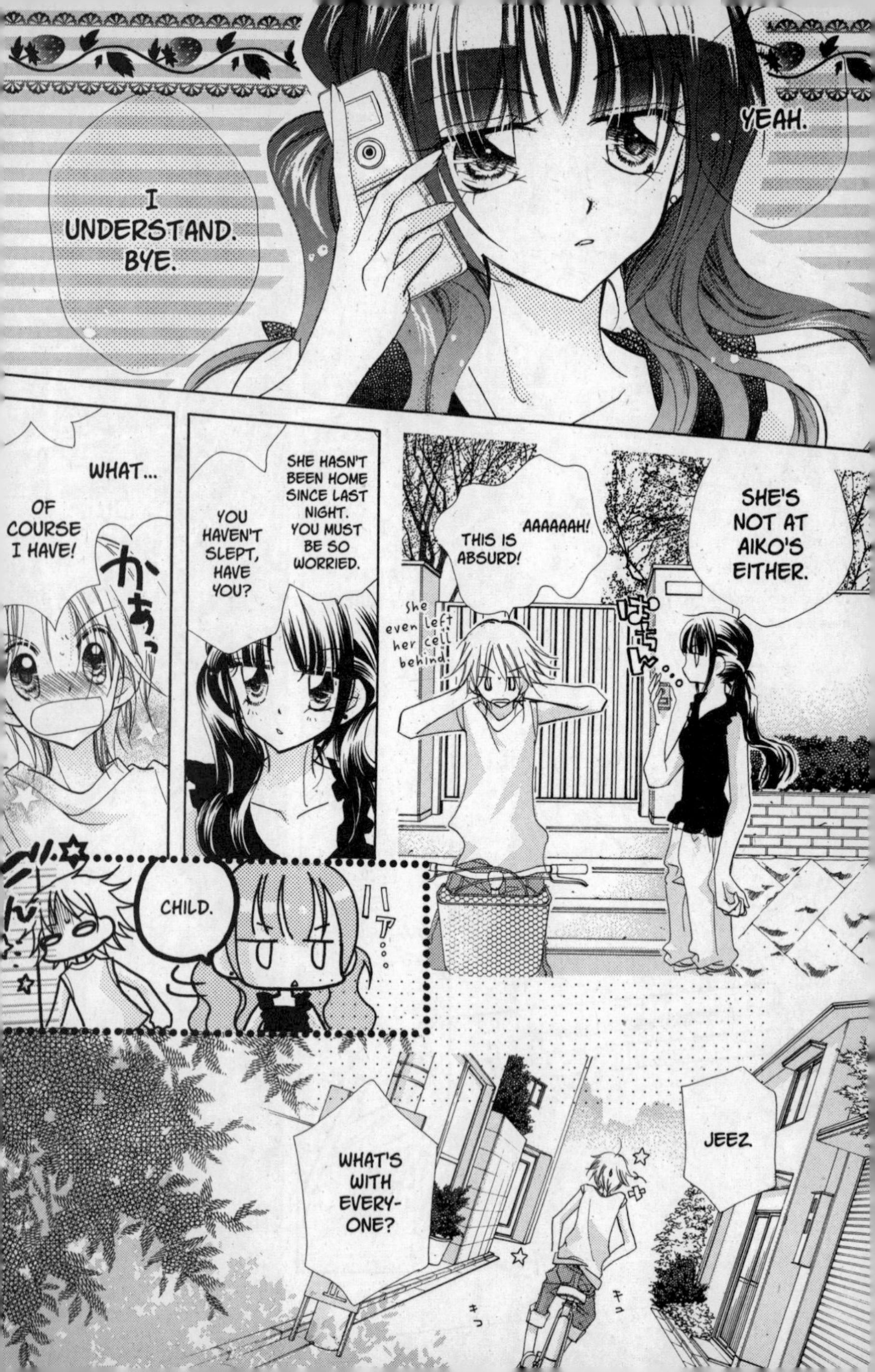
YEAH.
I UNDERSTAND. BYE.
SHE'S NOT AT AIKO'S EITHER.
ぱちん…
AAAAAAH!
THIS IS ABSURD!
She even left her cell behind!
SHE HASN'T BEEN HOME SINCE LAST NIGHT. YOU MUST BE SO WORRIED.
YOU HAVEN'T SLEPT, HAVE YOU?
WHAT...
OF COURSE I HAVE!
かあっ
CHILD.
ハア…
JEEZ.
WHAT'S WITH EVERY-ONE?
キコ
キっ

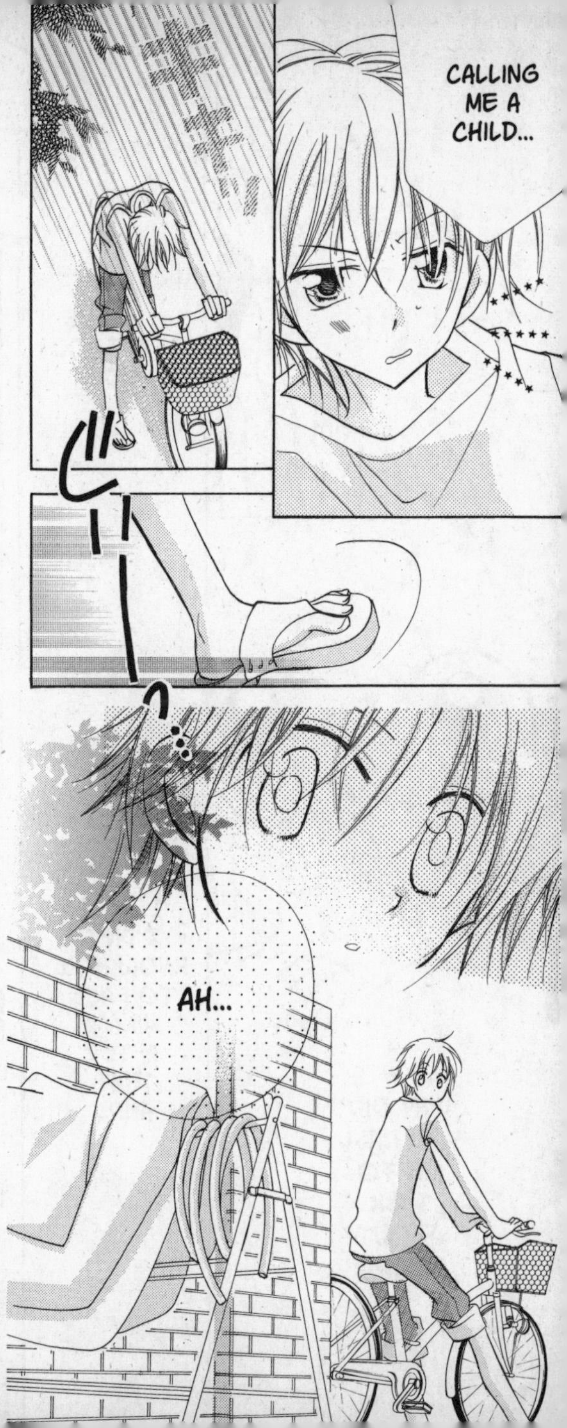
CALLING ME A CHILD...
AH...

E!

I like looking at uniforms, but I also like thinking them up. Besides the one I decided on, I made rough drafts of various others.

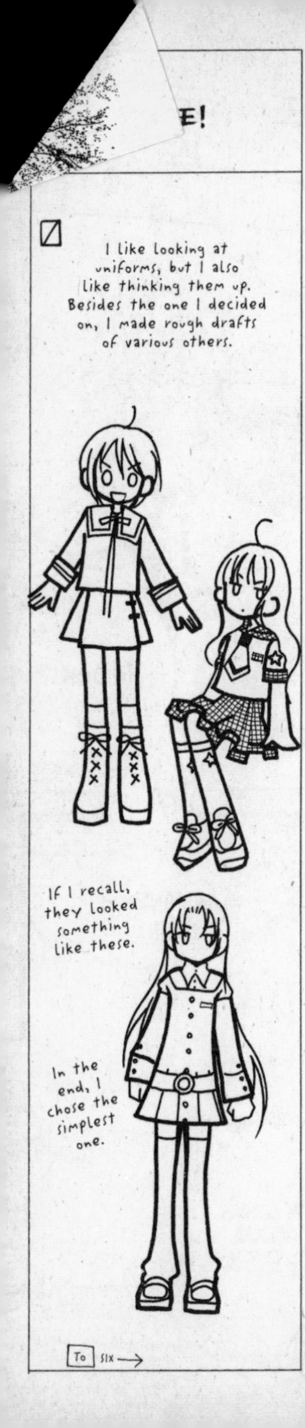

If I recall, they looked something like these.

In the end, I chose the simplest one.

To SIX →

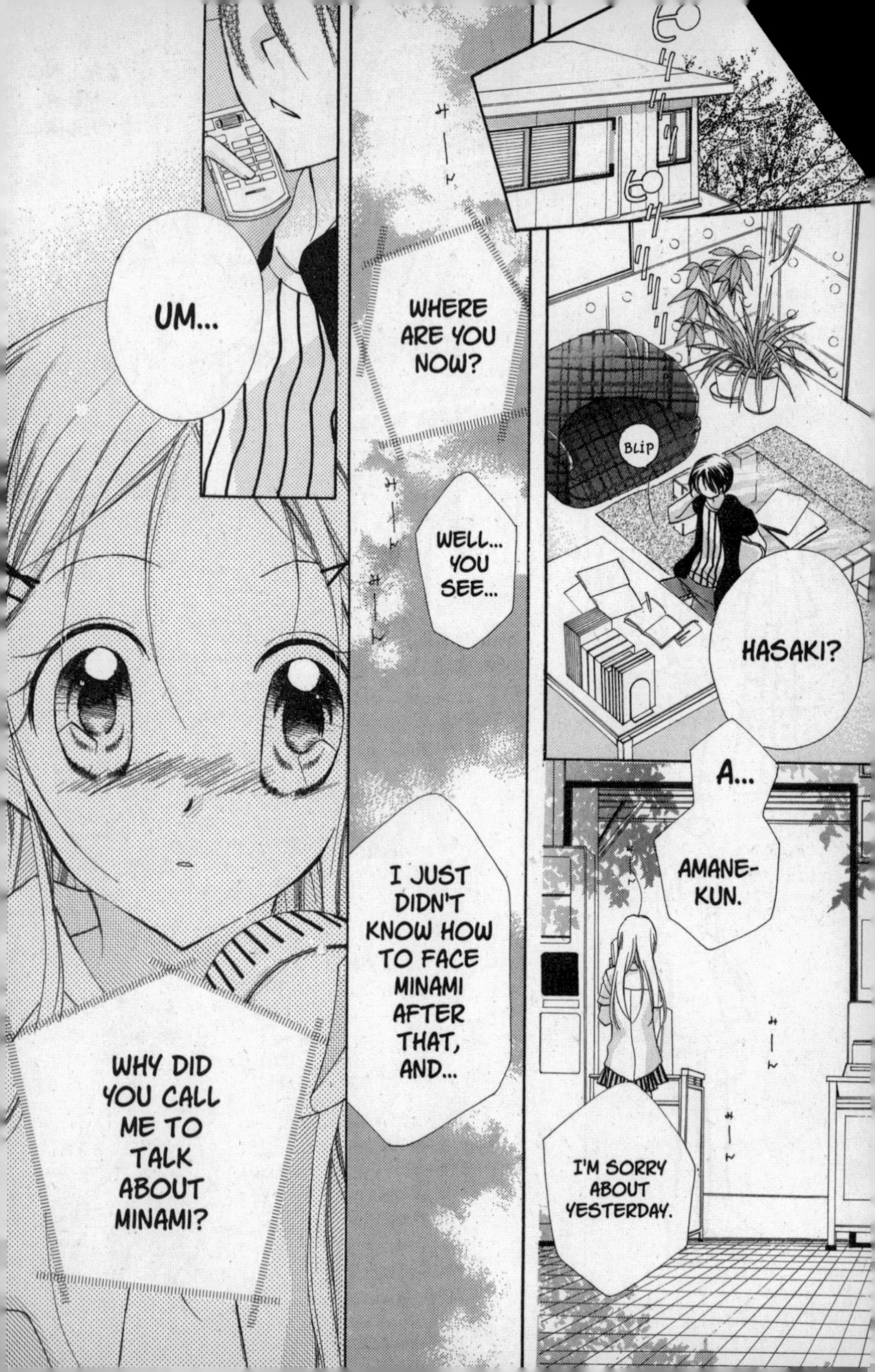
BLIP
HASAKI?
A...
AMANE-KUN.
I'M SORRY ABOUT YESTERDAY.
WHERE ARE YOU NOW?
WELL... YOU SEE...
I JUST DIDN'T KNOW HOW TO FACE MINAMI AFTER THAT, AND...
UM...
WHY DID YOU CALL ME TO TALK ABOUT MINAMI?

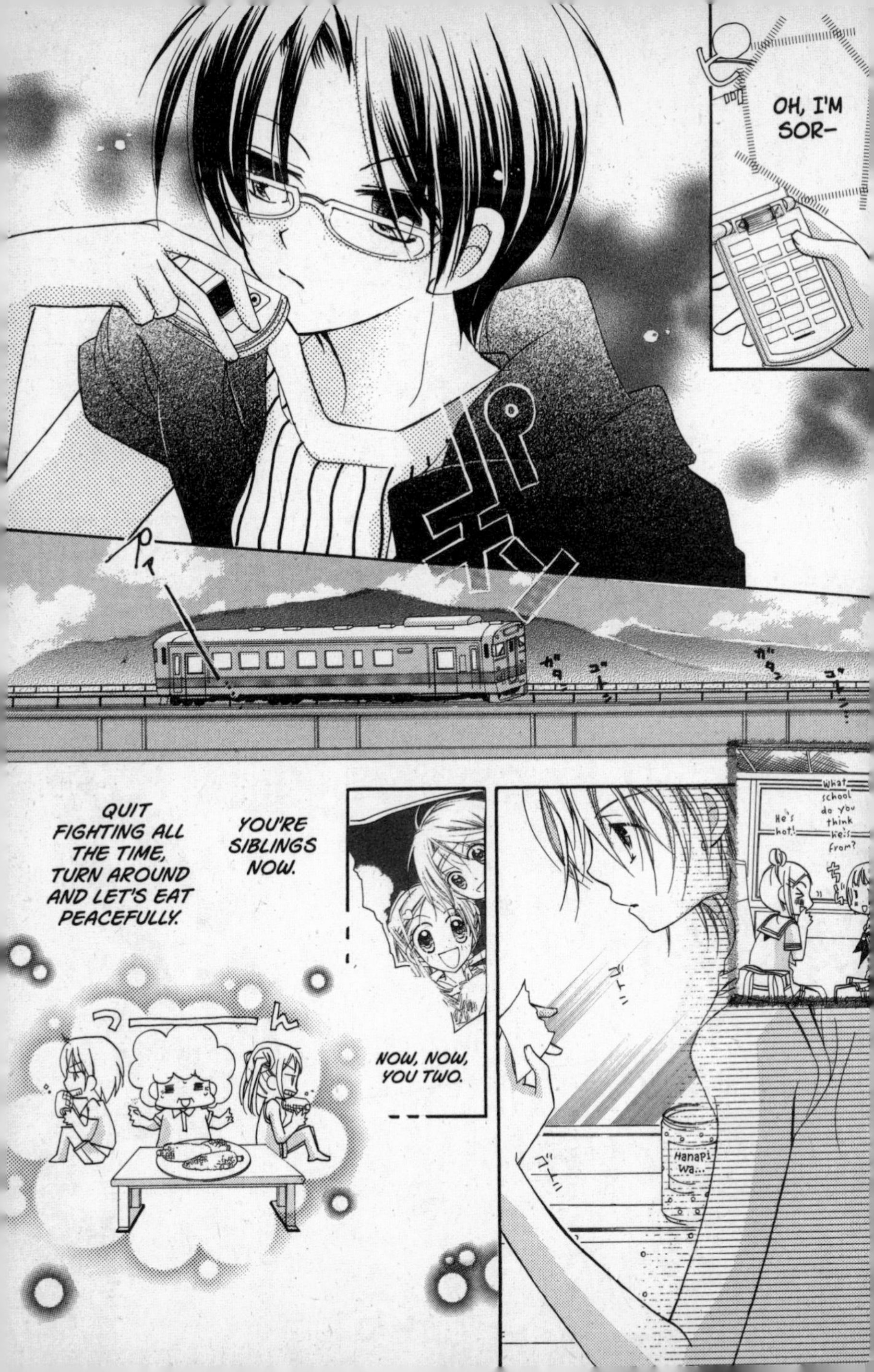
OH, I'M SOR-
What school do you think he's from?
He's hot!
Hanapi wa...
YOU'RE SIBLINGS NOW.
NOW, NOW, YOU TWO.
QUIT FIGHTING ALL THE TIME, TURN AROUND AND LET'S EAT PEACEFULLY.

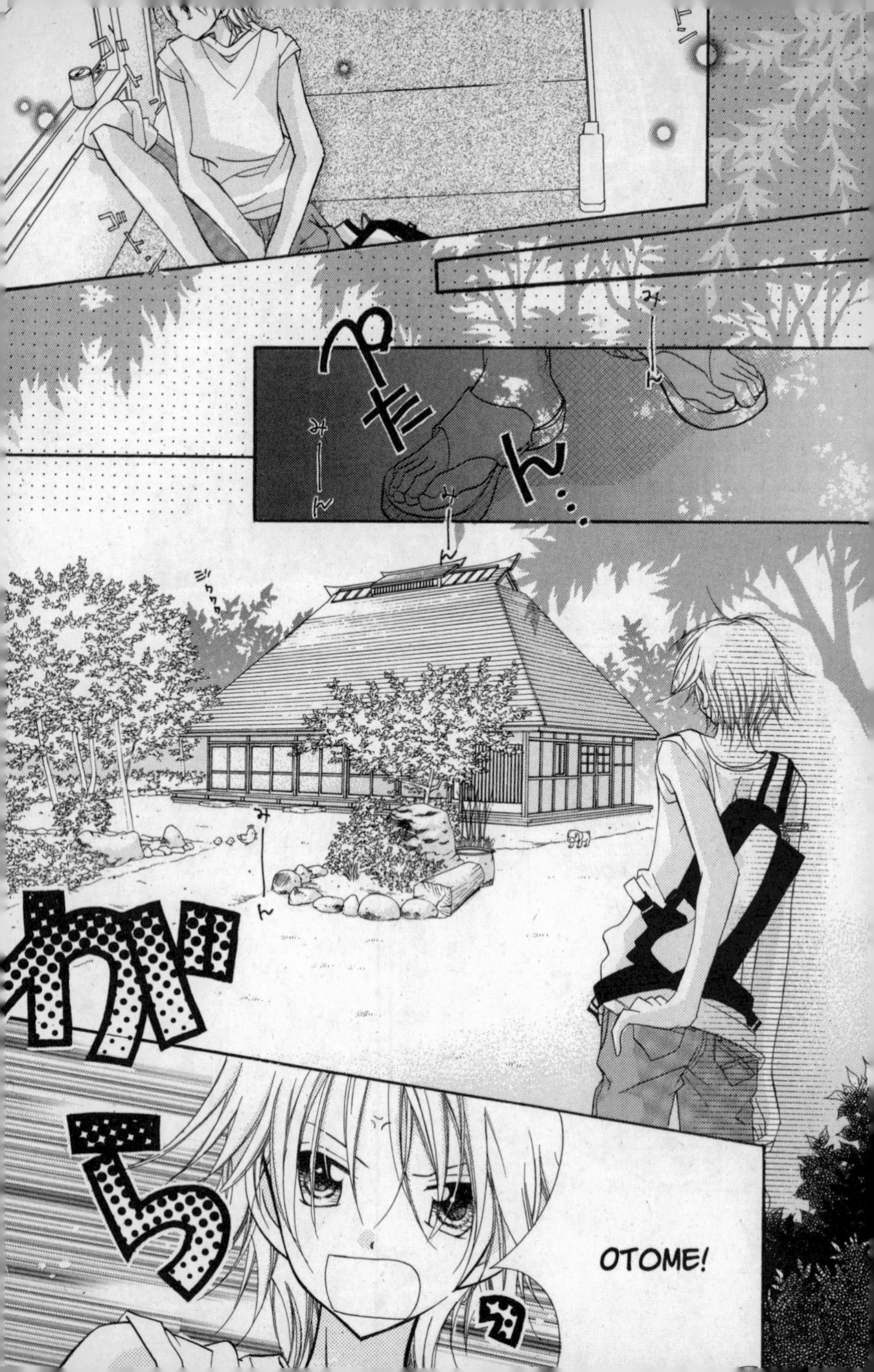
みーん
がらっ
OTOME!

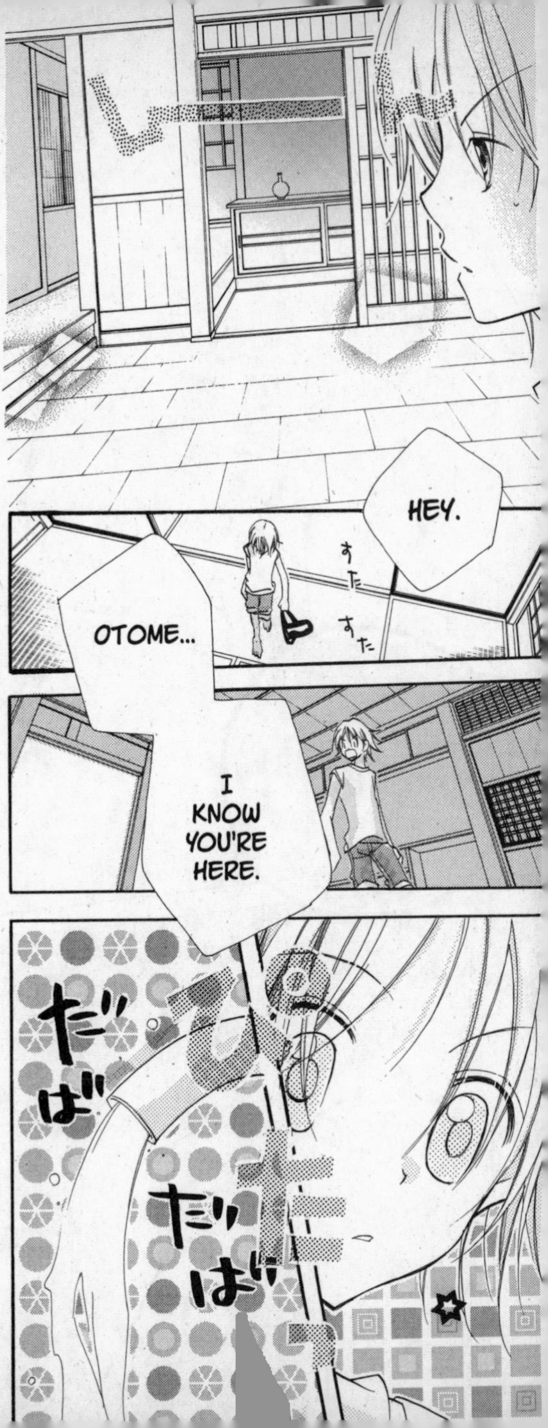
HEY.
すた すた
OTOME...
I KNOW YOU'RE HERE.

SIX!

You might think that I didn't put much love into designing the boy's uniforms, but I did experiment with a couple different versions.

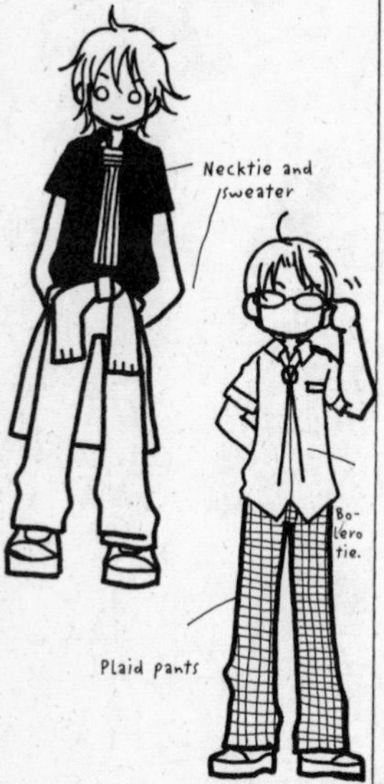
Necktie and sweater
Bolero tie.
Plaid pants

Well, if you say it's plain, then it's plain (heh).

In any case, it was easy to draw the boys wearing something like a parka or t-shirt under their white dress shirts, so I decided to keep it simple.

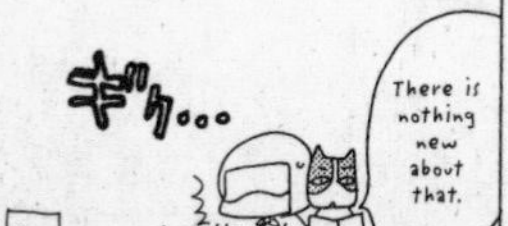
ギク...
There is nothing new about that.

To SEVEN →

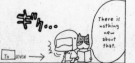

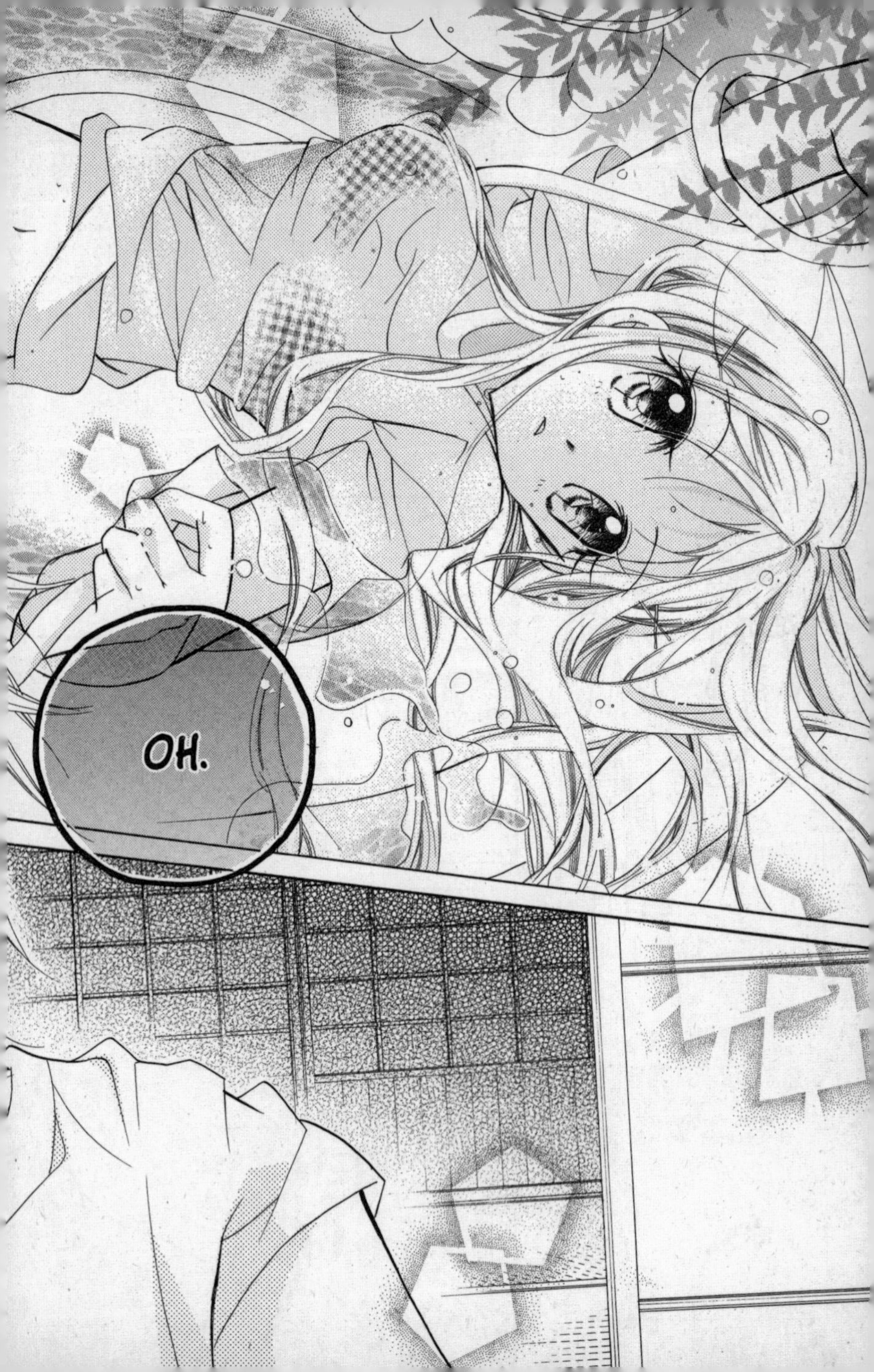
OH.

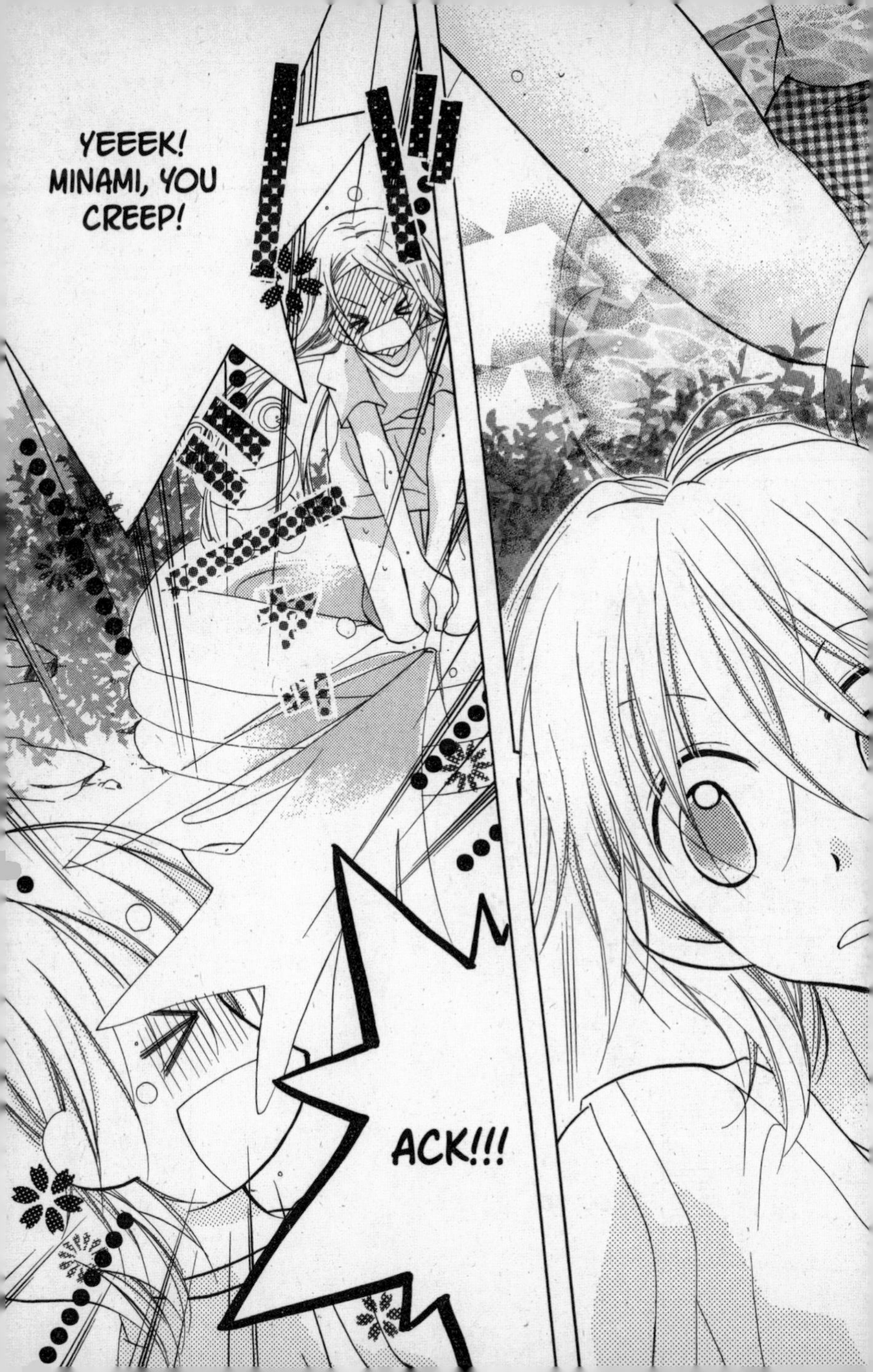
YEEEK! MINAMI, YOU CREEP!
ACK!!!

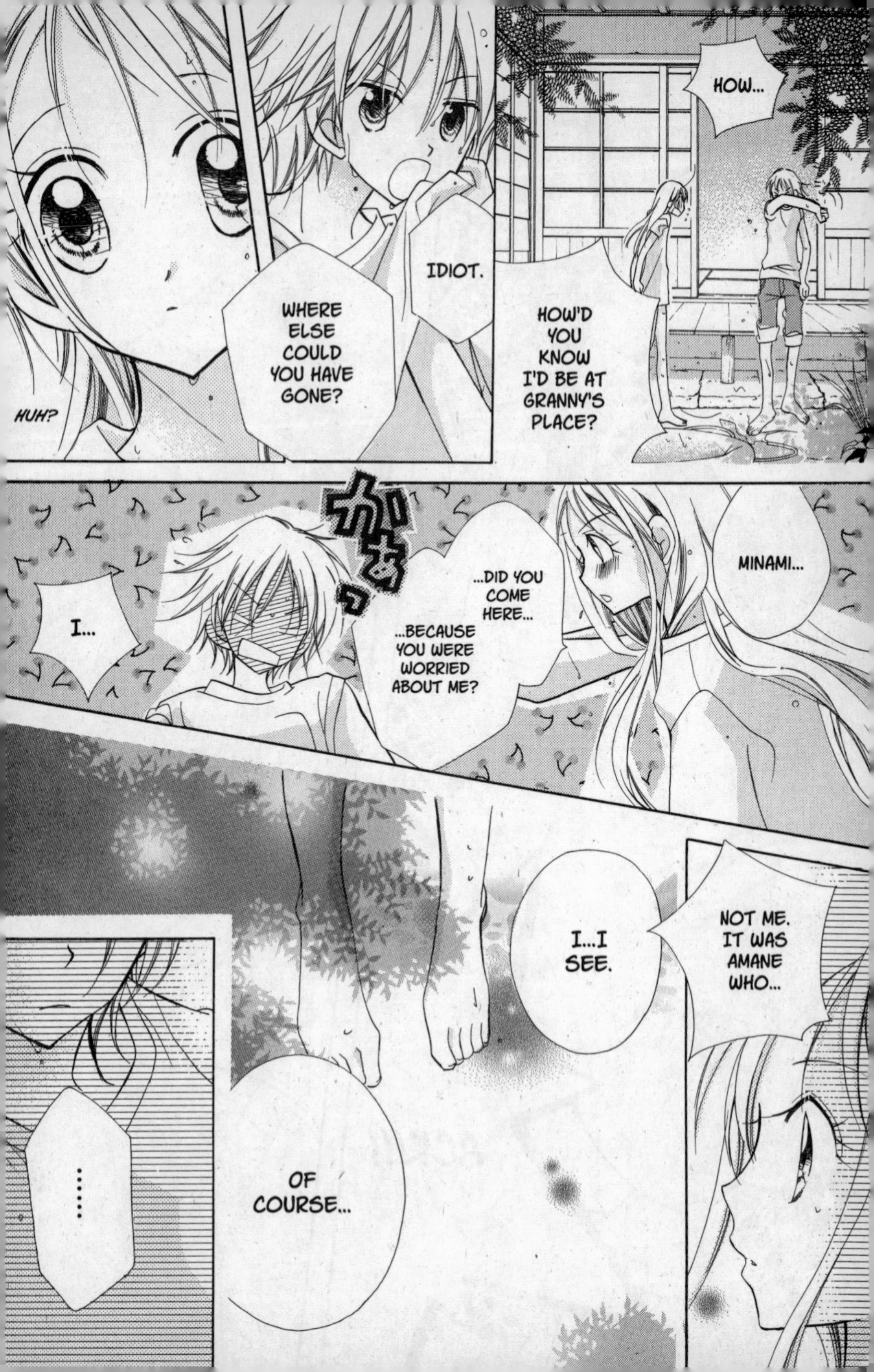
HOW...
HOW'D YOU KNOW I'D BE AT GRANNY'S PLACE?
IDIOT.
WHERE ELSE COULD YOU HAVE GONE?
HUH?
MINAMI...
...DID YOU COME HERE...
...BECAUSE YOU WERE WORRIED ABOUT ME?
かあっ
I...
NOT ME. IT WAS AMANE WHO...
I...I SEE.
OF COURSE...
......

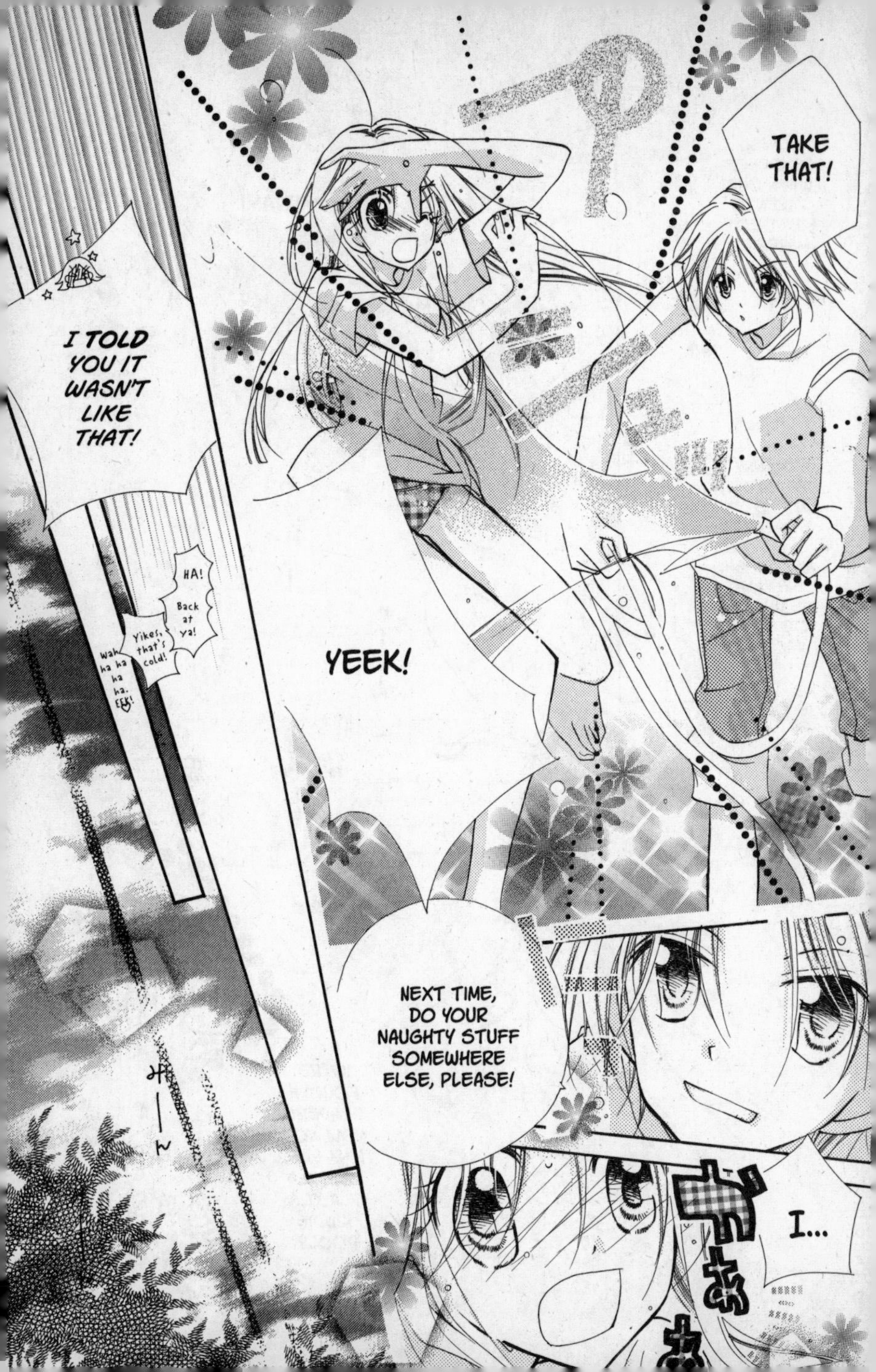
TAKE THAT!
YEEK!
NEXT TIME, DO YOUR NAUGHTY STUFF SOMEWHERE ELSE, PLEASE!
I...
I TOLD YOU IT WASN'T LIKE THAT!
HA! Back at ya!
Yikes, that's cold!
Wah ha ha ha. EEK!

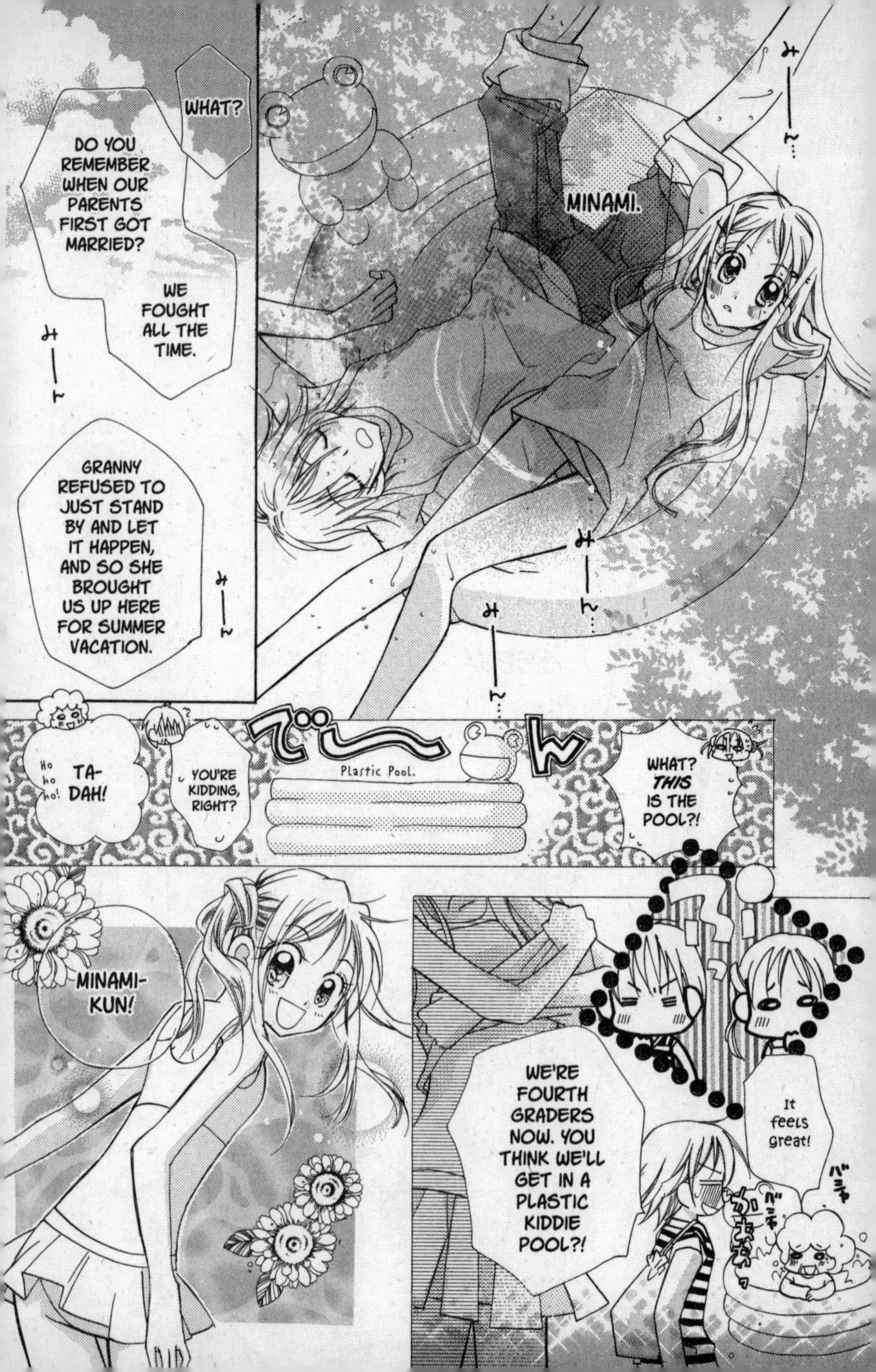
みーん…
MINAMI.
みーん…
みーん…
WHAT?
DO YOU REMEMBER WHEN OUR PARENTS FIRST GOT MARRIED?
WE FOUGHT ALL THE TIME.
みーん
GRANNY REFUSED TO JUST STAND BY AND LET IT HAPPEN, AND SO SHE BROUGHT US UP HERE FOR SUMMER VACATION.
みーん
WHAT? *THIS* IS THE POOL?!
でーん
Plastic Pool.
YOU'RE KIDDING, RIGHT?
TA-DAH!
Ho ho ho!
WE'RE FOURTH GRADERS NOW. YOU THINK WE'LL GET IN A PLASTIC KIDDIE POOL?!
It feels great!
MINAMI-KUN!

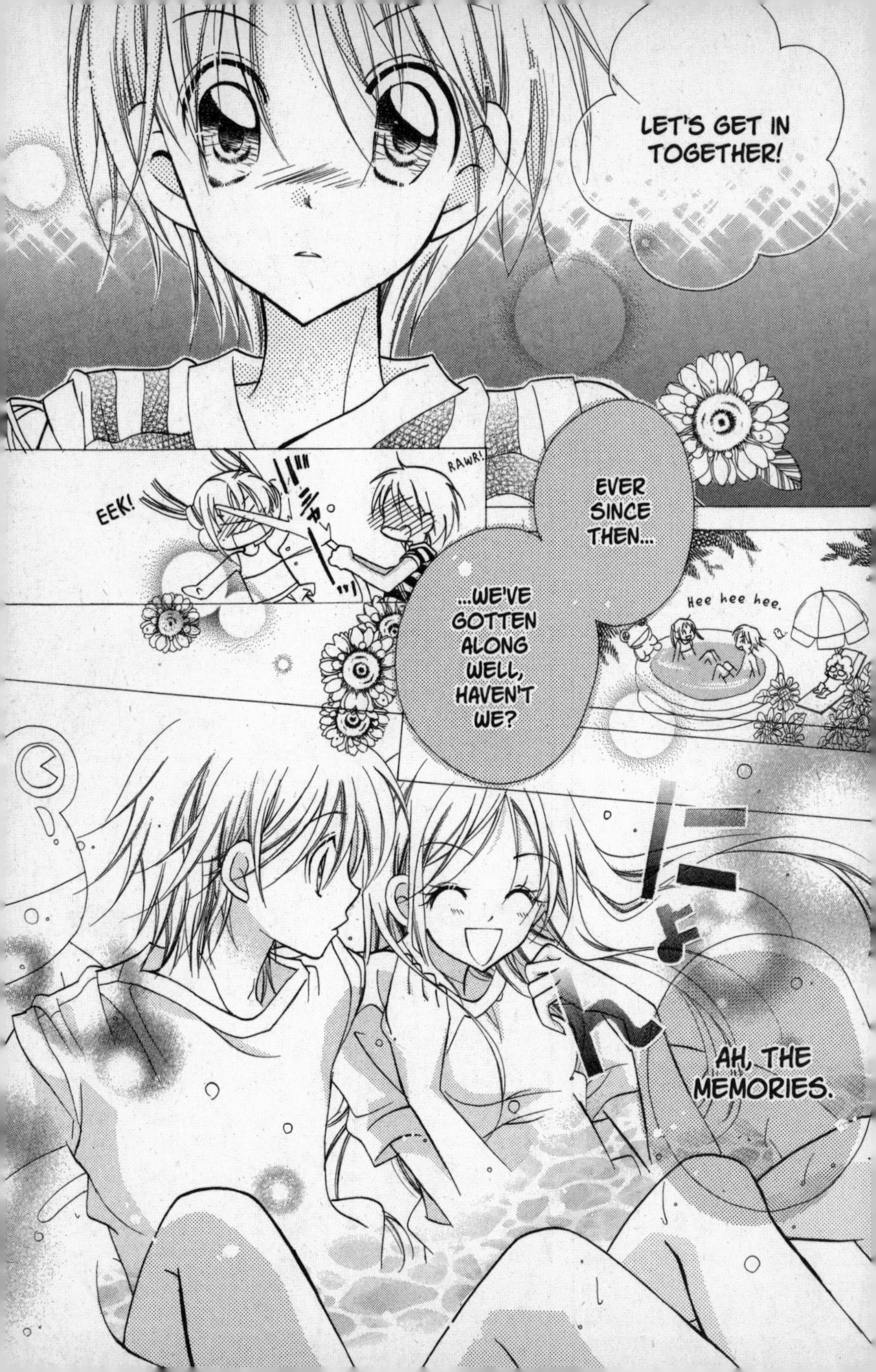
LET'S GET IN TOGETHER!
EVER SINCE THEN...
...WE'VE GOTTEN ALONG WELL, HAVEN'T WE?
RAWR!
EEK!
Hee hee hee.
AH, THE MEMORIES.

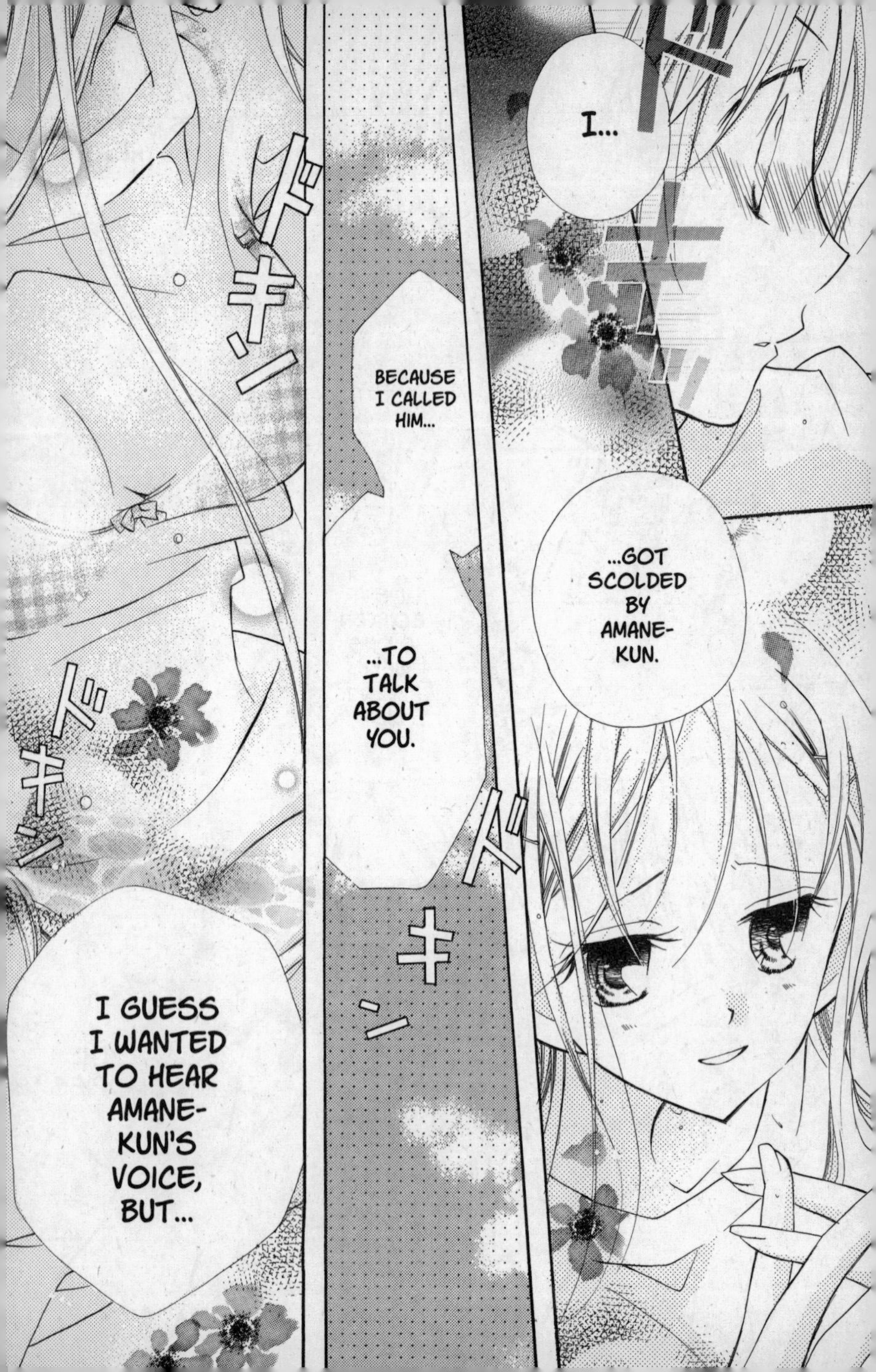
I...
...GOT SCOLDED BY AMANE-KUN.
BECAUSE I CALLED HIM...
...TO TALK ABOUT YOU.
I GUESS I WANTED TO HEAR AMANE-KUN'S VOICE, BUT...

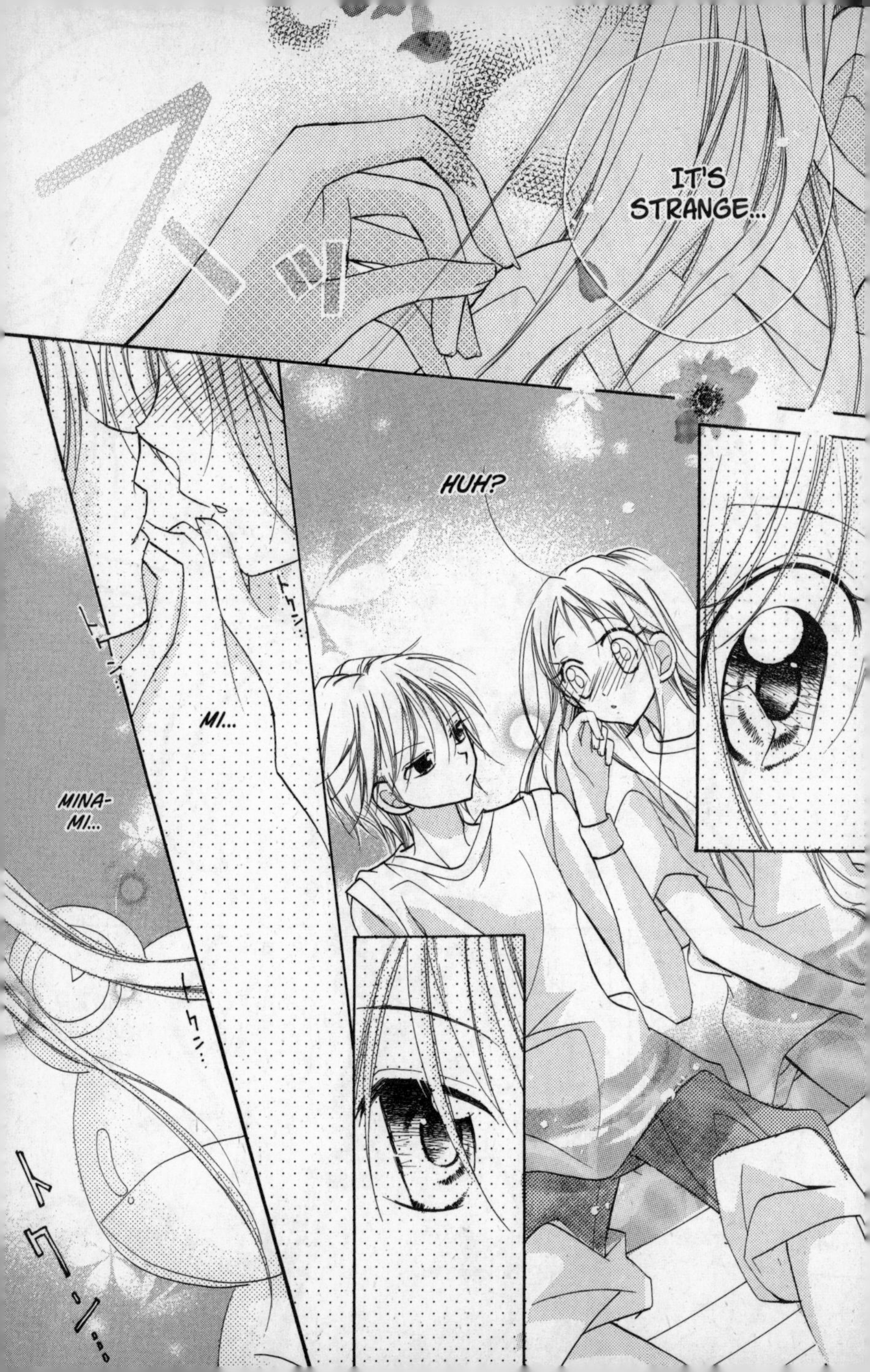
IT'S STRANGE...
HUH?
MI...
MINA-MI...

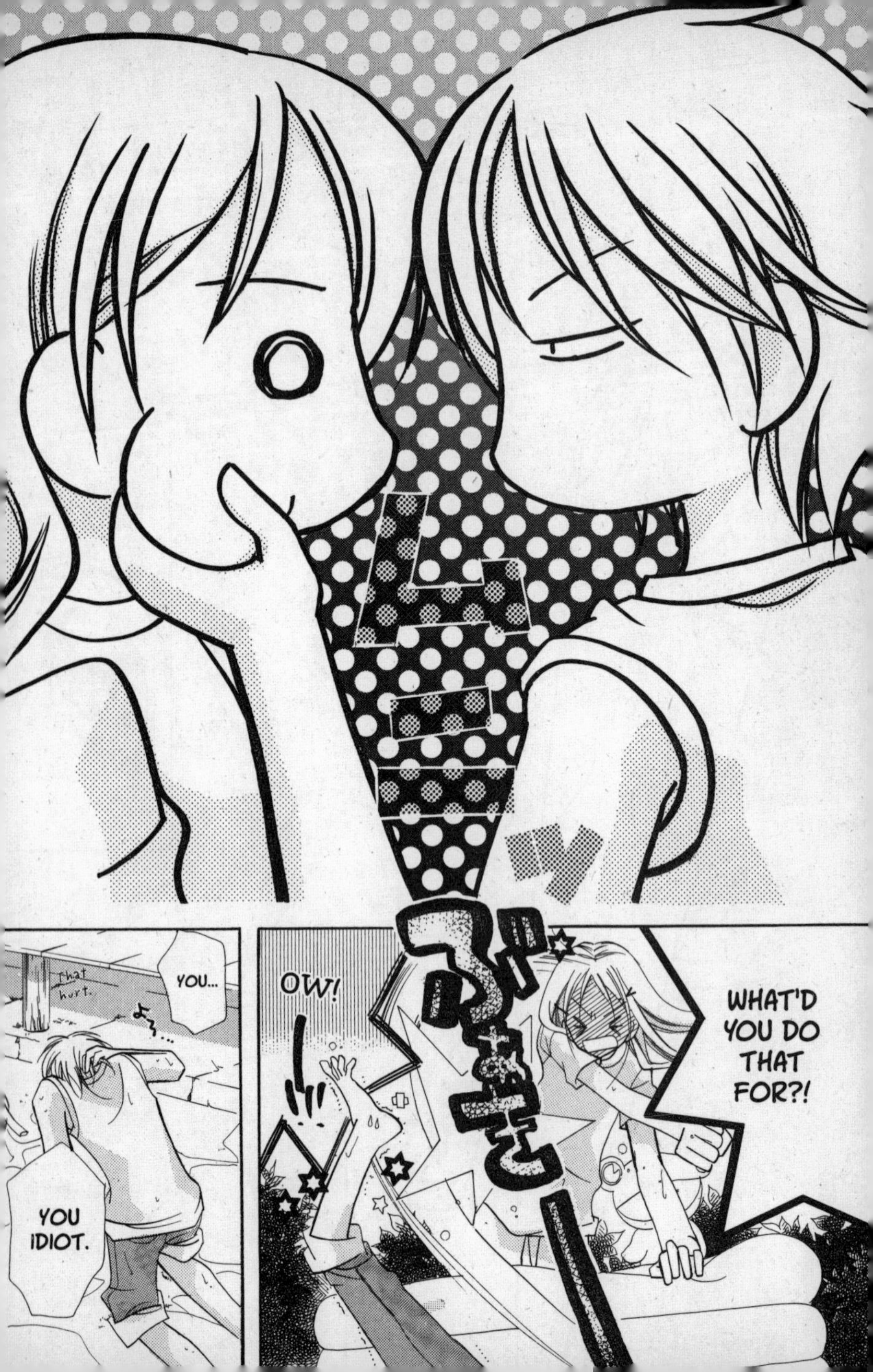
WHAT'D YOU DO THAT FOR?!
OW!
YOU...
that hurt.
YOU IDIOT.

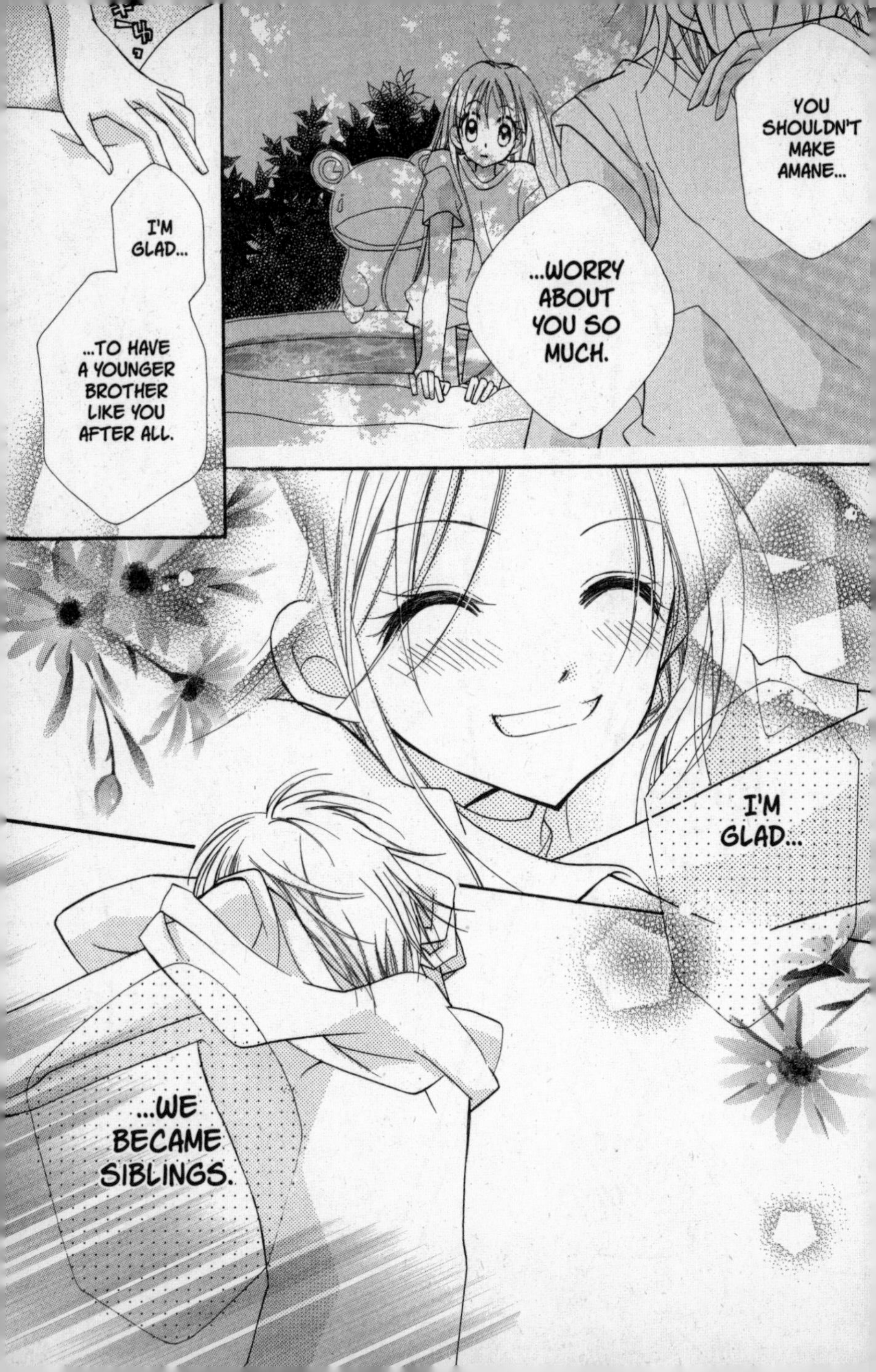
YOU SHOULDN'T MAKE AMANE...
...WORRY ABOUT YOU SO MUCH.
I'M GLAD...
...TO HAVE A YOUNGER BROTHER LIKE YOU AFTER ALL.
I'M GLAD...
...WE BECAME SIBLINGS.

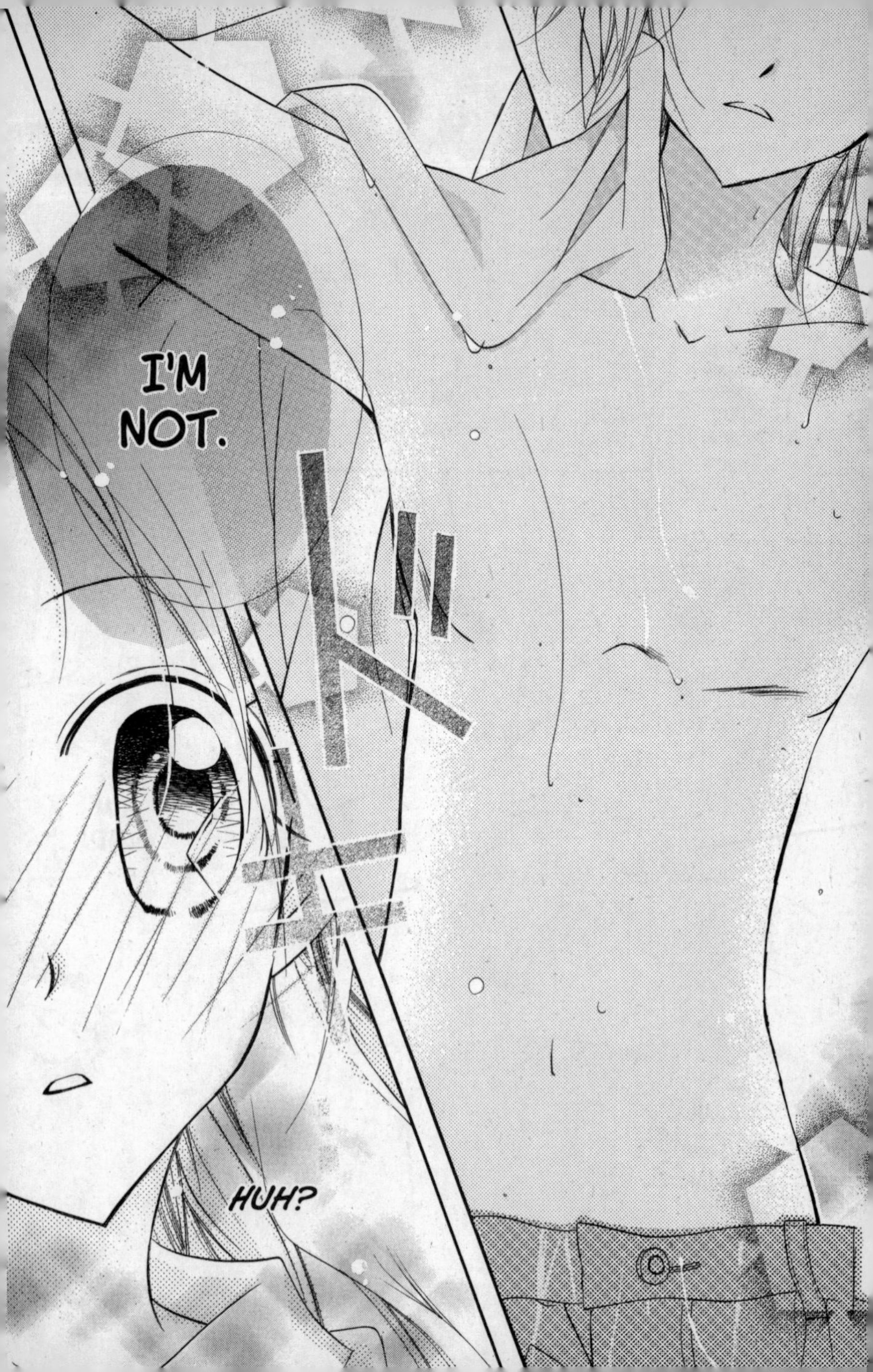
I'M NOT.
HUH?

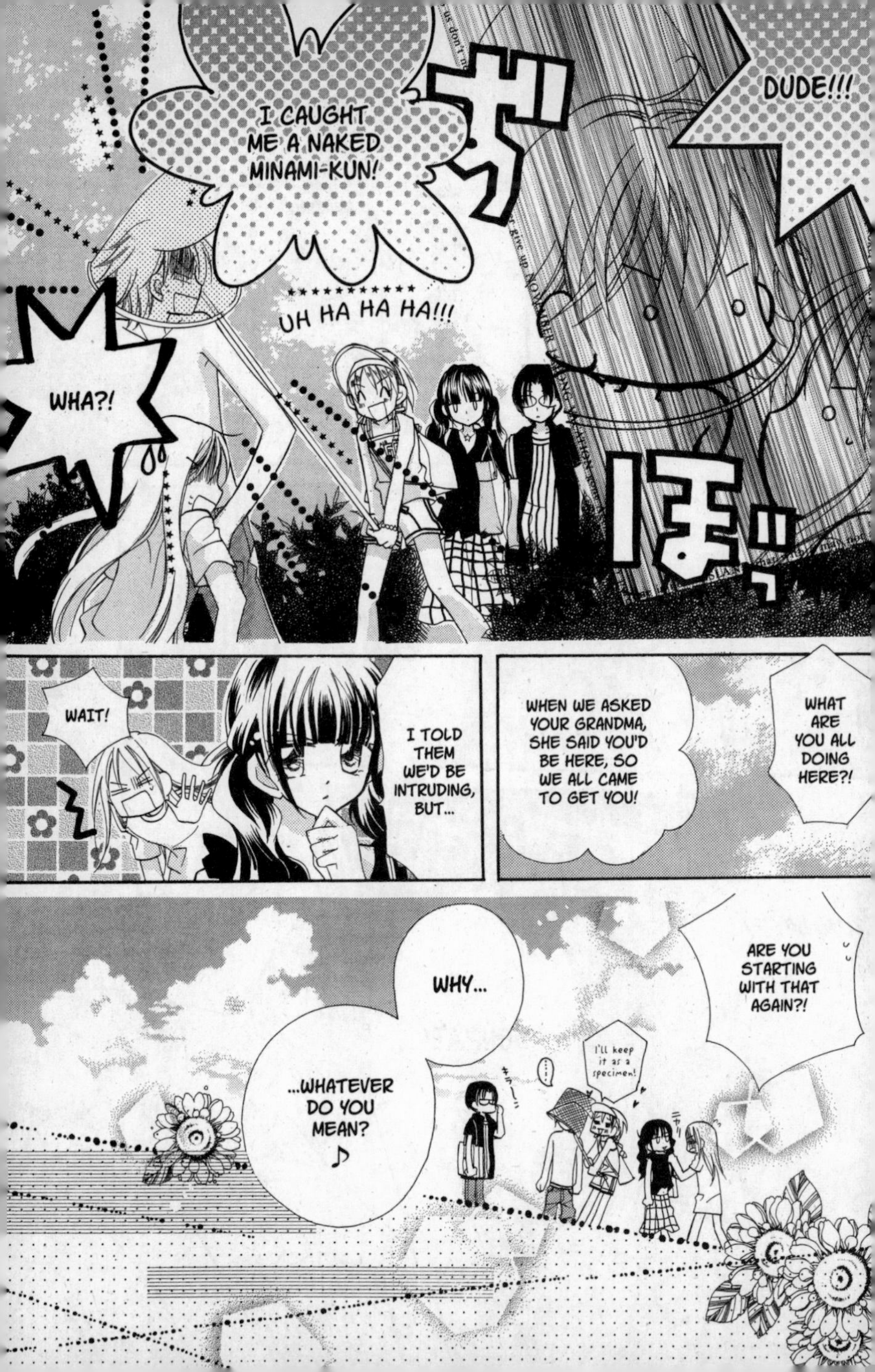

DUDE!!!
I CAUGHT ME A NAKED MINAMI-KUN!
UH HA HA HA!!!
WHA?!
WHAT ARE YOU ALL DOING HERE?!
WHEN WE ASKED YOUR GRANDMA, SHE SAID YOU'D BE HERE, SO WE ALL CAME TO GET YOU!
I TOLD THEM WE'D BE INTRUDING, BUT...
WAIT!
ARE YOU STARTING WITH THAT AGAIN?!
I'll keep it as a specimen!
...
WHY...
...WHATEVER DO YOU MEAN? ♪

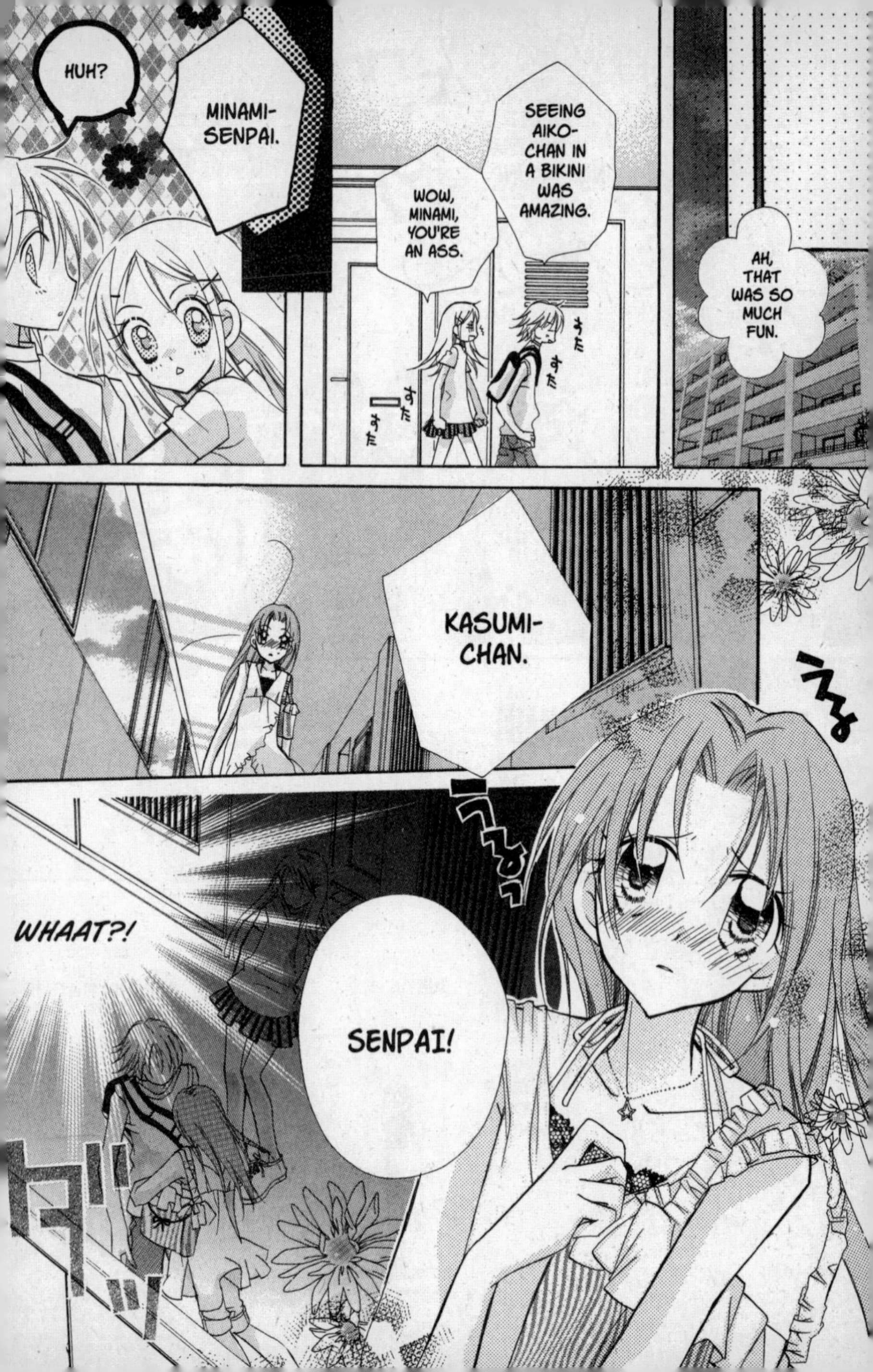
AH, THAT WAS SO MUCH FUN.
SEEING AIKO-CHAN IN A BIKINI WAS AMAZING.
WOW, MINAMI, YOU'RE AN ASS.
すた すた
すた すた
MINAMI-SENPAI.
HUH?
KASUMI-CHAN.
SENPAI!
WHAAT?!

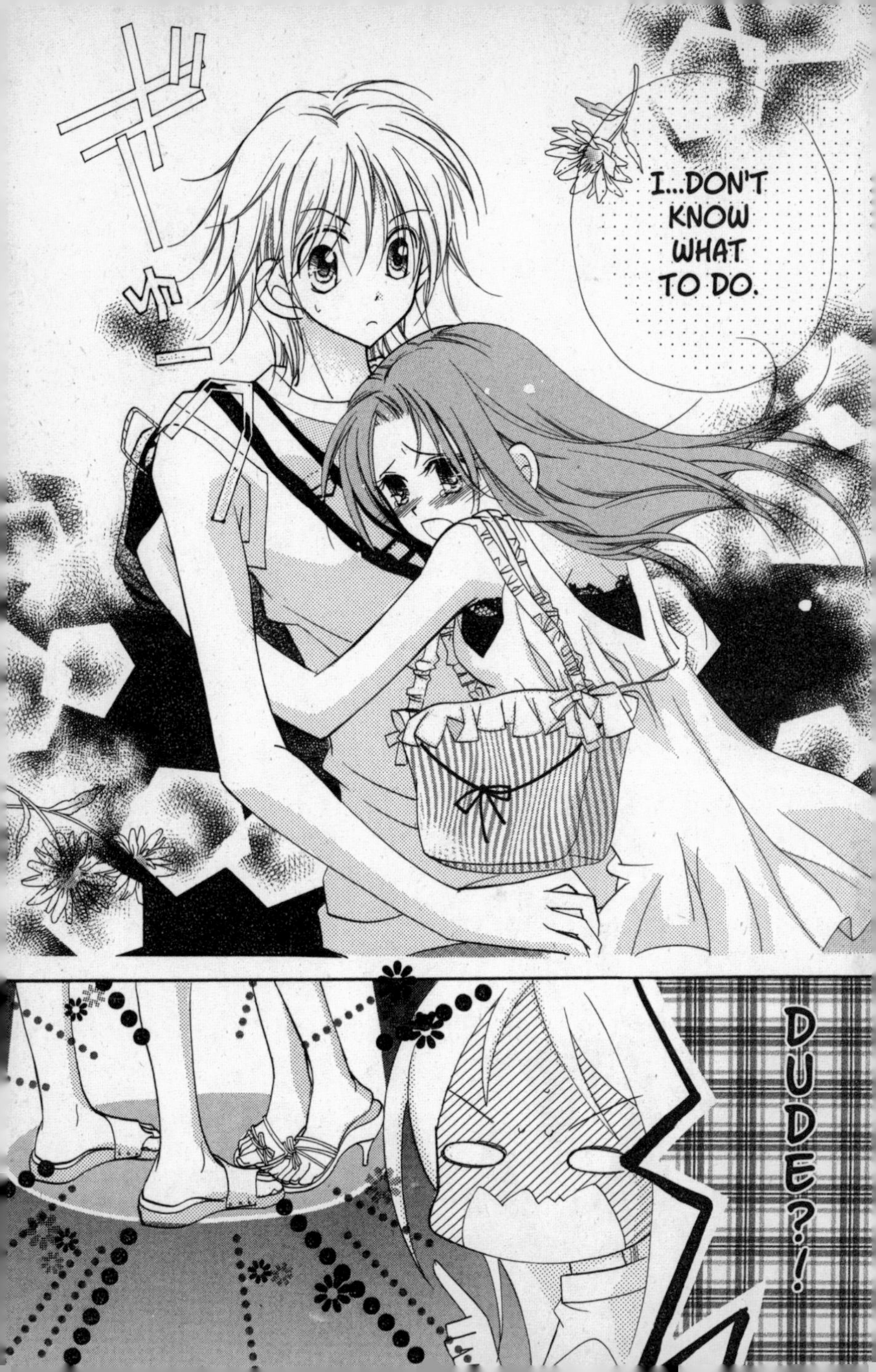
I...DON'T KNOW WHAT TO DO.
ギュー
DUDE?!

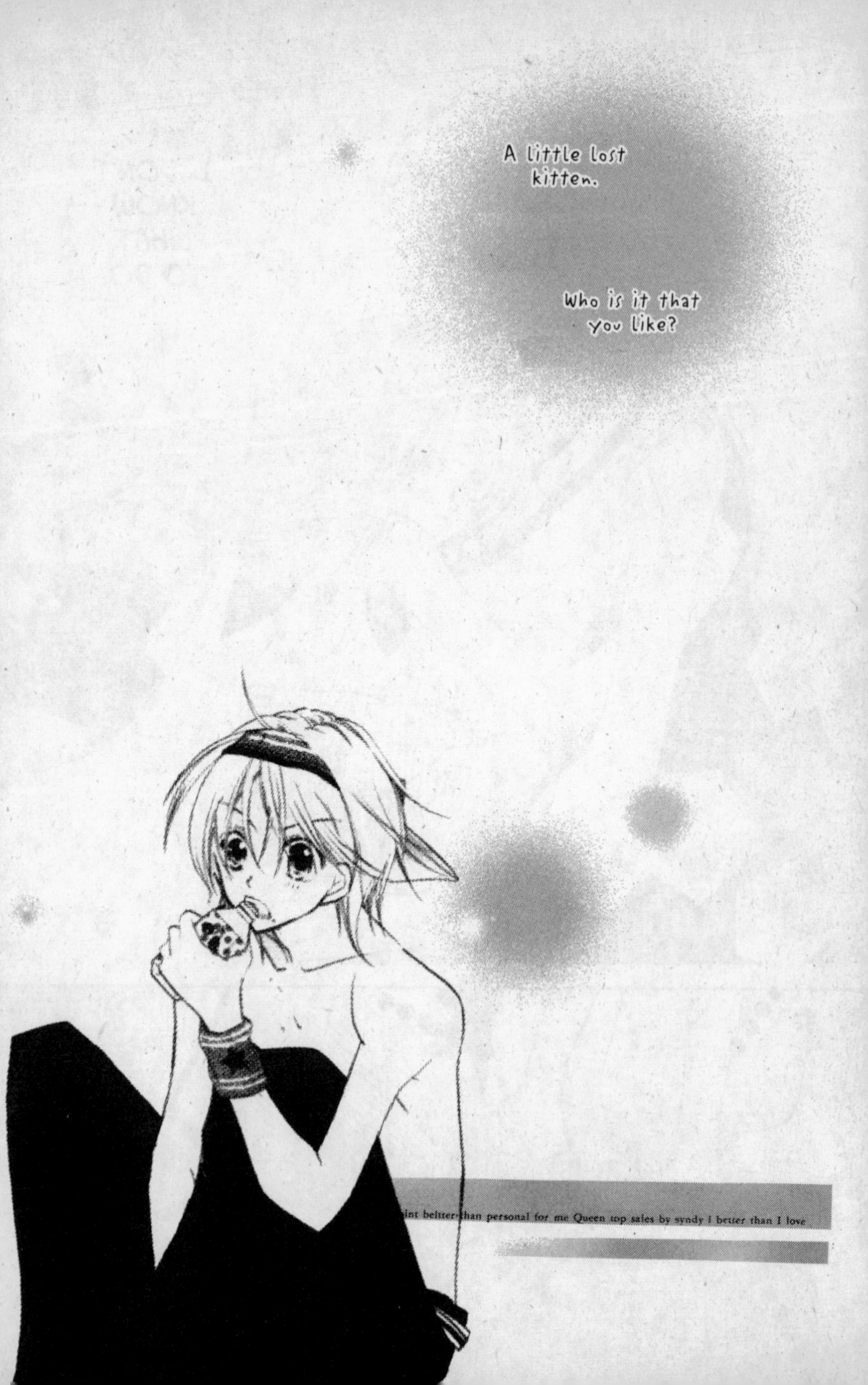
A little lost kitten.
Who is it that you like?
int belter than personal for me Queen top sales by syndy i better than I love

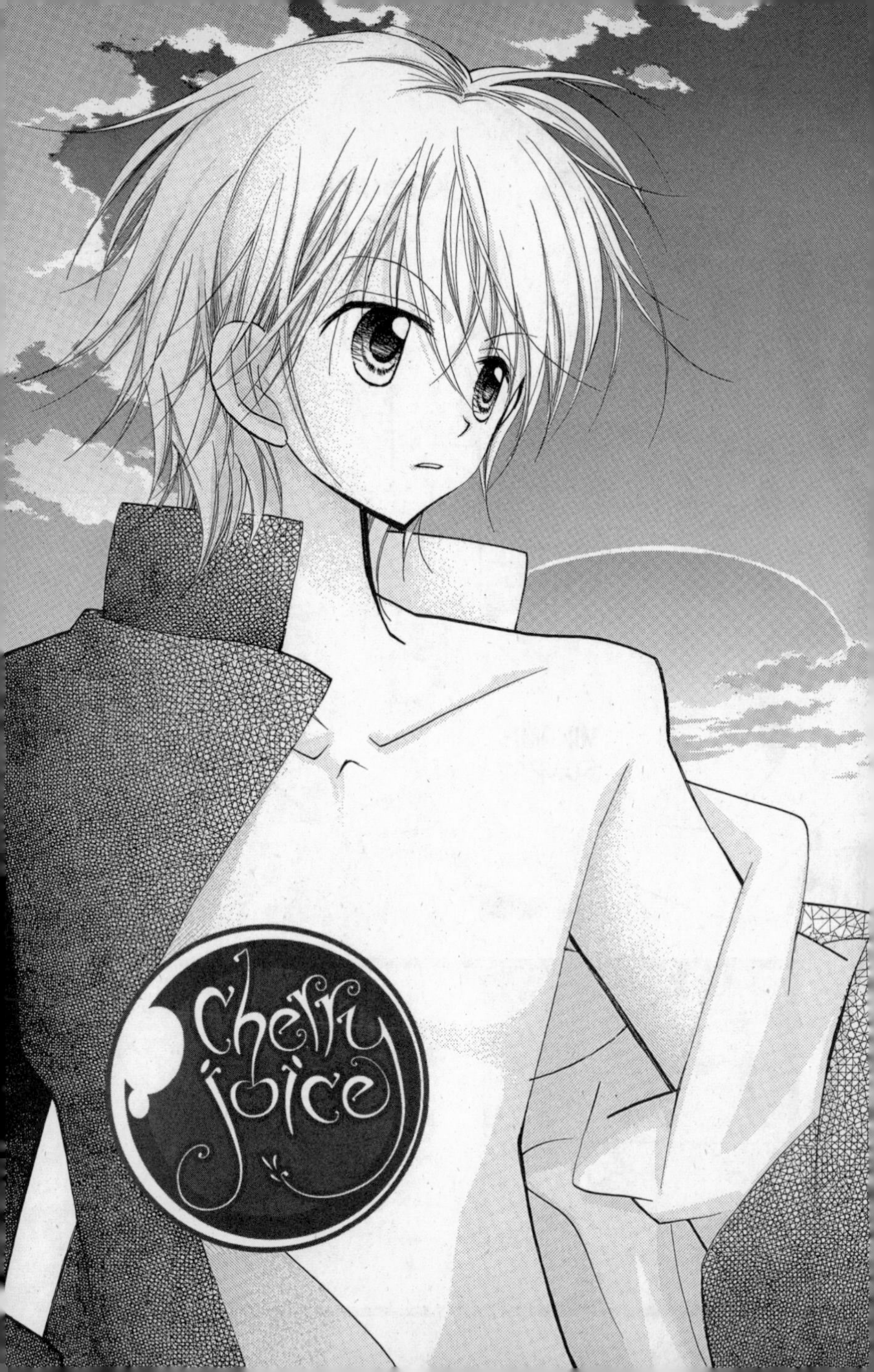
Cherry Juice

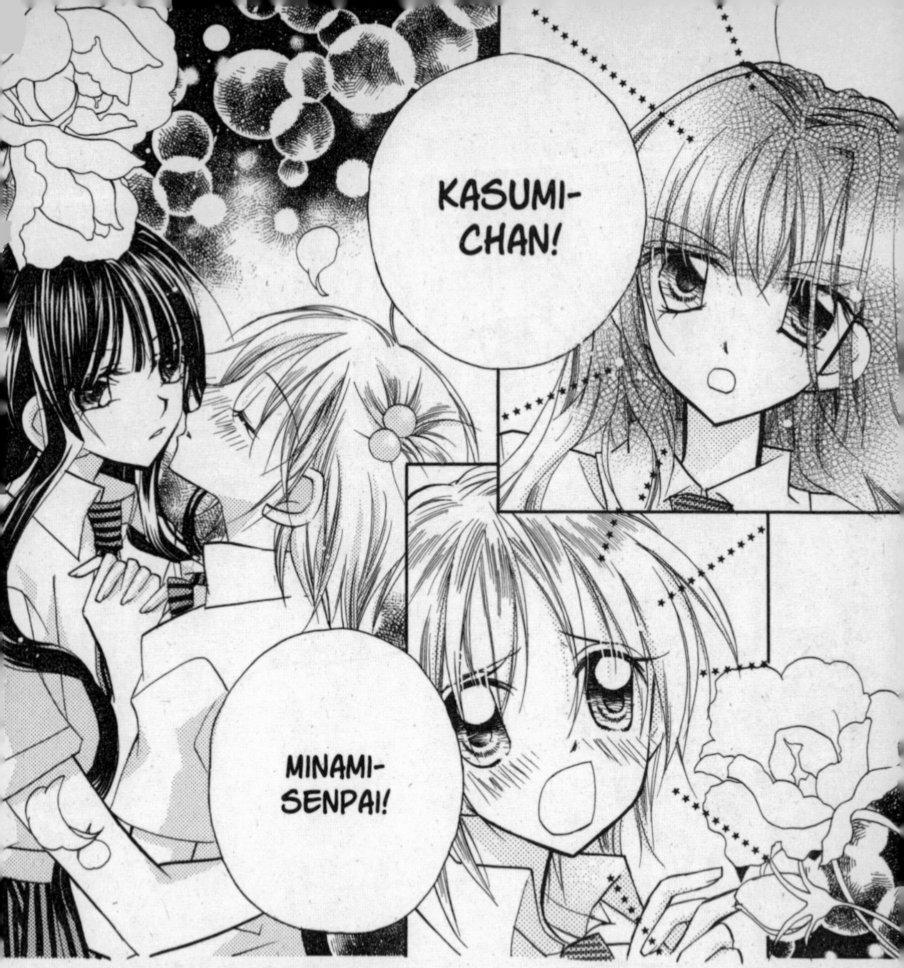
KASUMI-CHAN!
MINAMI-SENPAI!

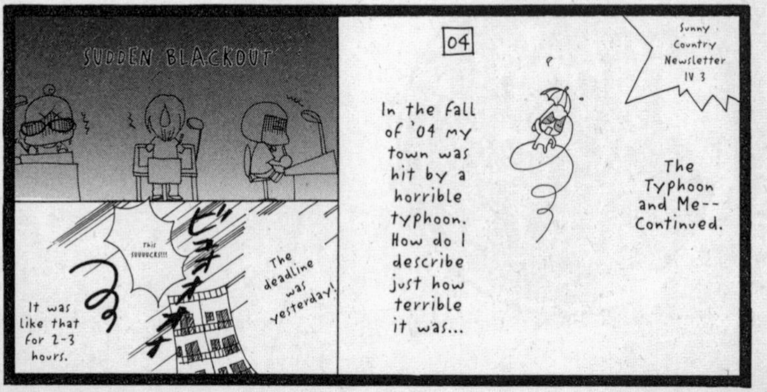
Sunny Country Newsletter IV 3
04
The Typhoon and Me-- Continued.
In the fall of '04 my town was hit by a horrible typhoon. How do I describe just how terrible it was...
SUDDEN BLACKOUT
The deadline was yesterday!
This SUUUUCKS!!!
It was like that for 2-3 hours.

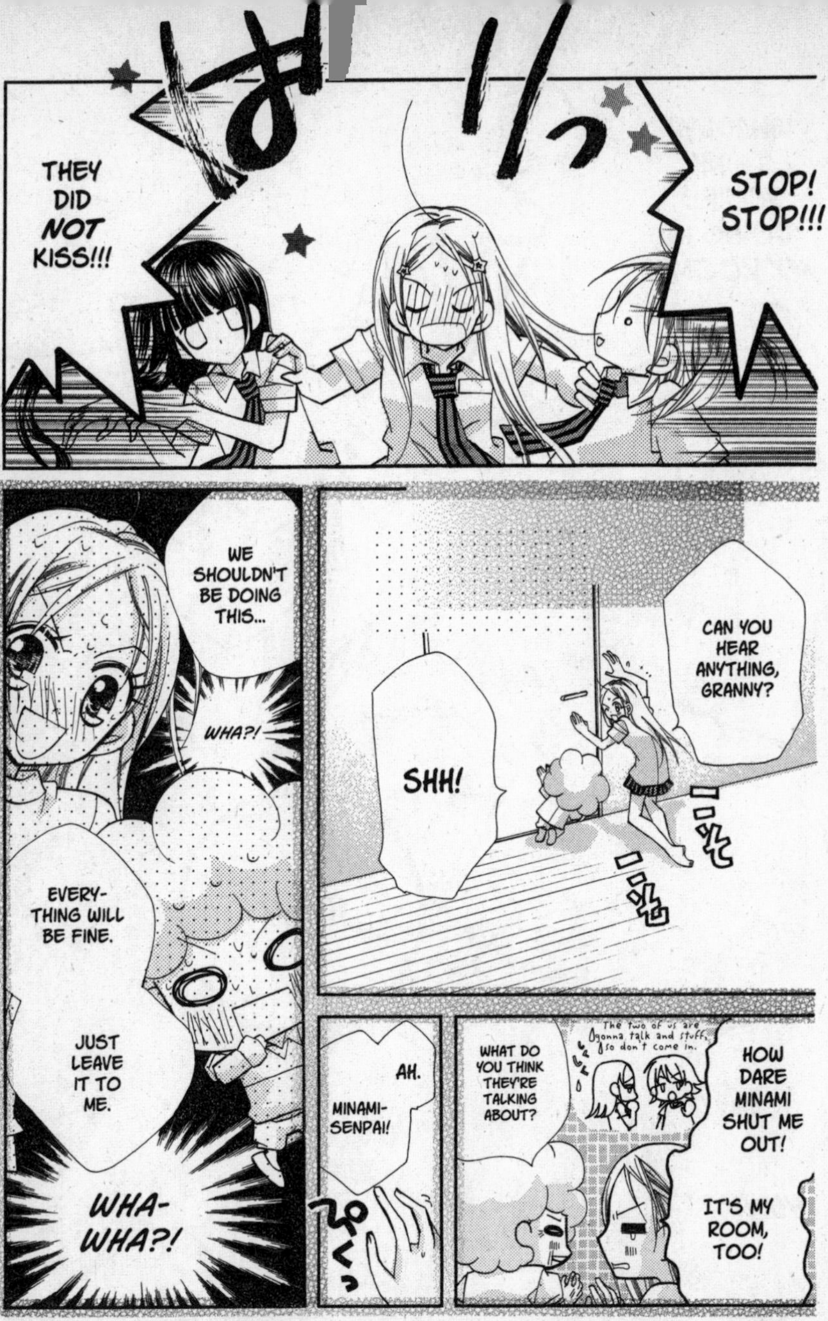
ばりっ
STOP! STOP!!!
THEY DID NOT KISS!!!
CAN YOU HEAR ANYTHING, GRANNY?
SHH!
HOW DARE MINAMI SHUT ME OUT!
IT'S MY ROOM, TOO!
The two of us are gonna talk and stuff, so don't come in.
WHAT DO YOU THINK THEY'RE TALKING ABOUT?
AH.
MINAMI-SENPAI!
WE SHOULDN'T BE DOING THIS...
WHA?!
EVERY-THING WILL BE FINE.
JUST LEAVE IT TO ME.
WHA-WHA?!

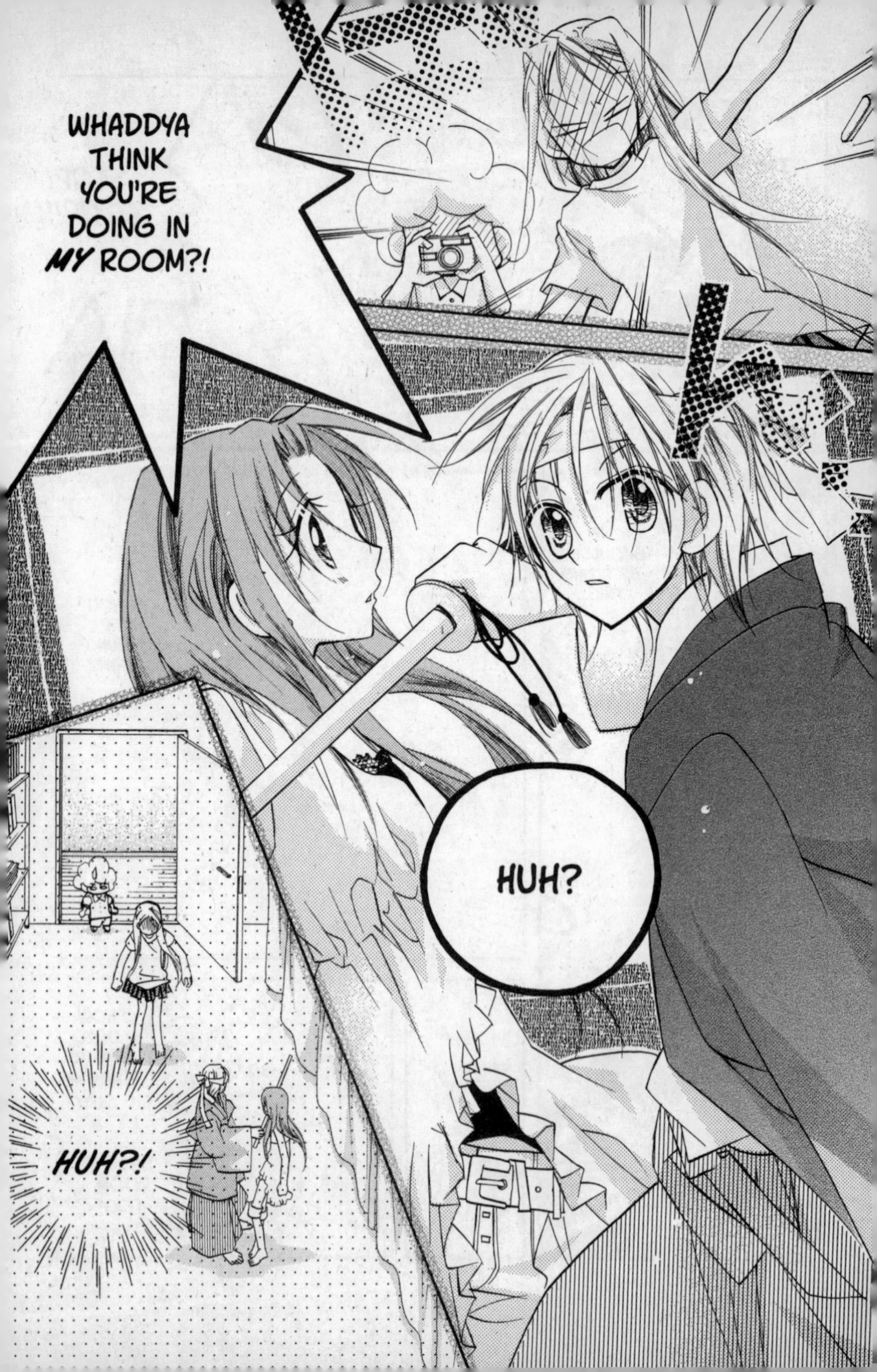
WHADDYA THINK YOU'RE DOING IN *MY* ROOM?!
HUH?
HUH?!

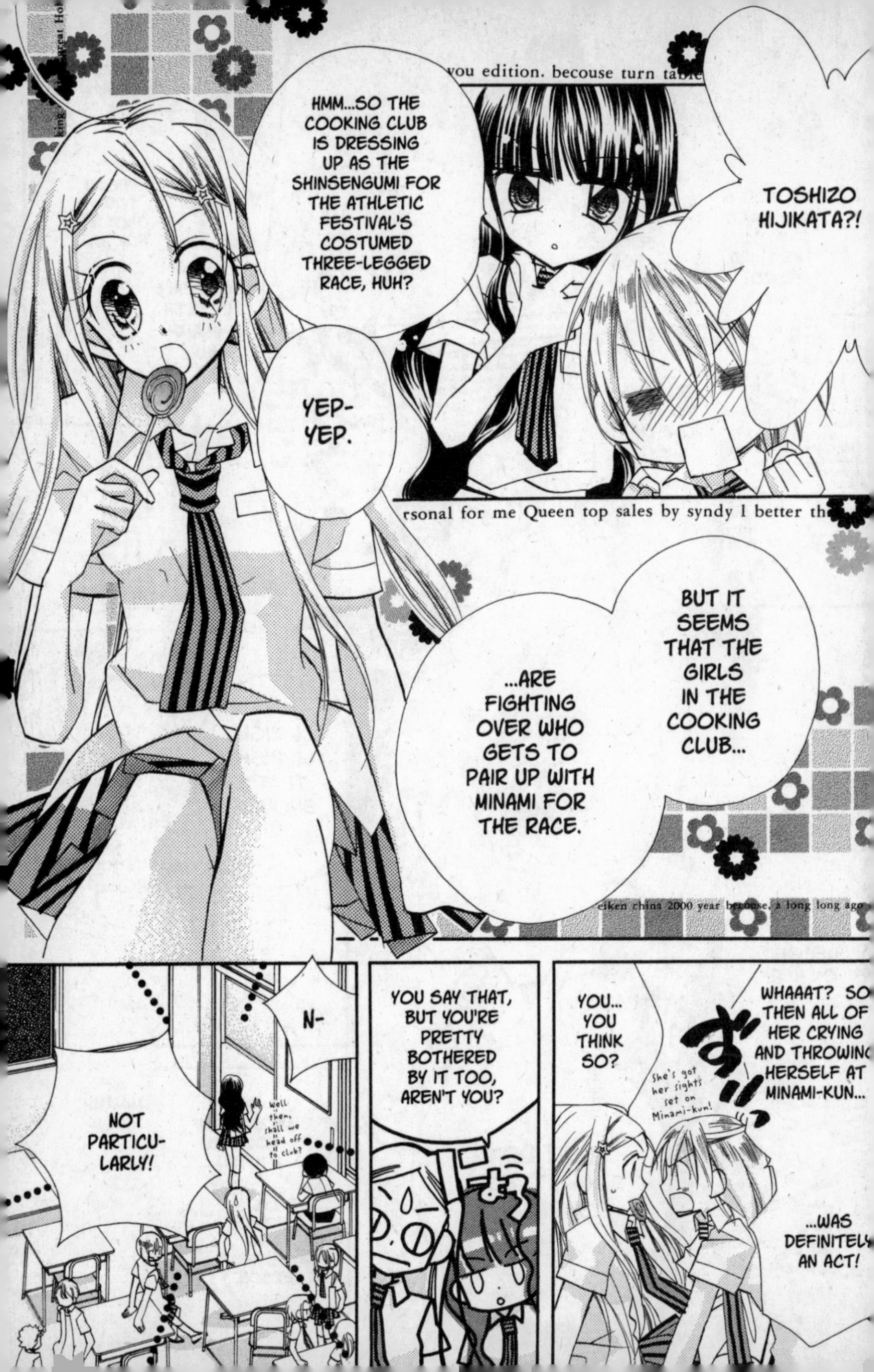
you edition. becouse turn table
HMM...SO THE COOKING CLUB IS DRESSING UP AS THE SHINSENGUMI FOR THE ATHLETIC FESTIVAL'S COSTUMED THREE-LEGGED RACE, HUH?
TOSHIZO HIJIKATA?!
YEP-YEP.
rsonal for me Queen top sales by syndy l better th
BUT IT SEEMS THAT THE GIRLS IN THE COOKING CLUB...
...ARE FIGHTING OVER WHO GETS TO PAIR UP WITH MINAMI FOR THE RACE.
eiken china 2000 year becouse, a long long ago
WHAAAT? SO THEN ALL OF HER CRYING AND THROWIN HERSELF AT MINAMI-KUN...
YOU... YOU THINK SO?
She's got her sights set on Minami-kun!
...WAS DEFINITEL AN ACT!
YOU SAY THAT, BUT YOU'RE PRETTY BOTHERED BY IT TOO, AREN'T YOU?
N-
NOT PARTICU-LARLY!
Well then, shall we head off to club?

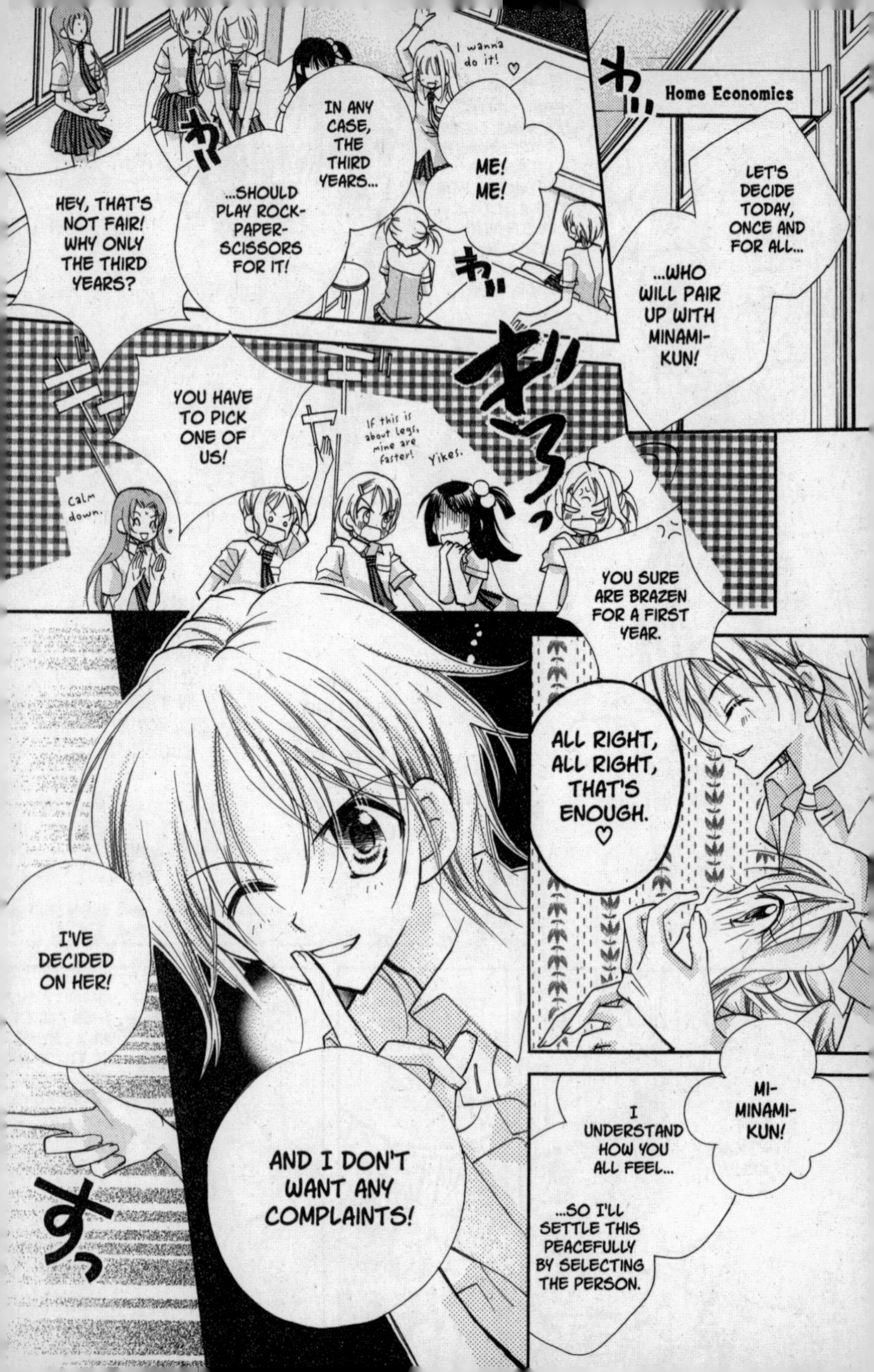
Home Economics
LET'S DECIDE TODAY, ONCE AND FOR ALL...
...WHO WILL PAIR UP WITH MINAMI-KUN!
ME! ME!
I wanna do it! ♡
IN ANY CASE, THE THIRD YEARS...
...SHOULD PLAY ROCK-PAPER-SCISSORS FOR IT!
HEY, THAT'S NOT FAIR! WHY ONLY THE THIRD YEARS?
YOU SURE ARE BRAZEN FOR A FIRST YEAR.
Yikes.
If this is about legs, mine are faster!
YOU HAVE TO PICK ONE OF US!
Calm down.
ALL RIGHT, ALL RIGHT, THAT'S ENOUGH. ♡
MI-MINAMI-KUN!
I UNDERSTAND HOW YOU ALL FEEL...
...SO I'LL SETTLE THIS PEACEFULLY BY SELECTING THE PERSON.
I'VE DECIDED ON HER!
AND I DON'T WANT ANY COMPLAINTS!

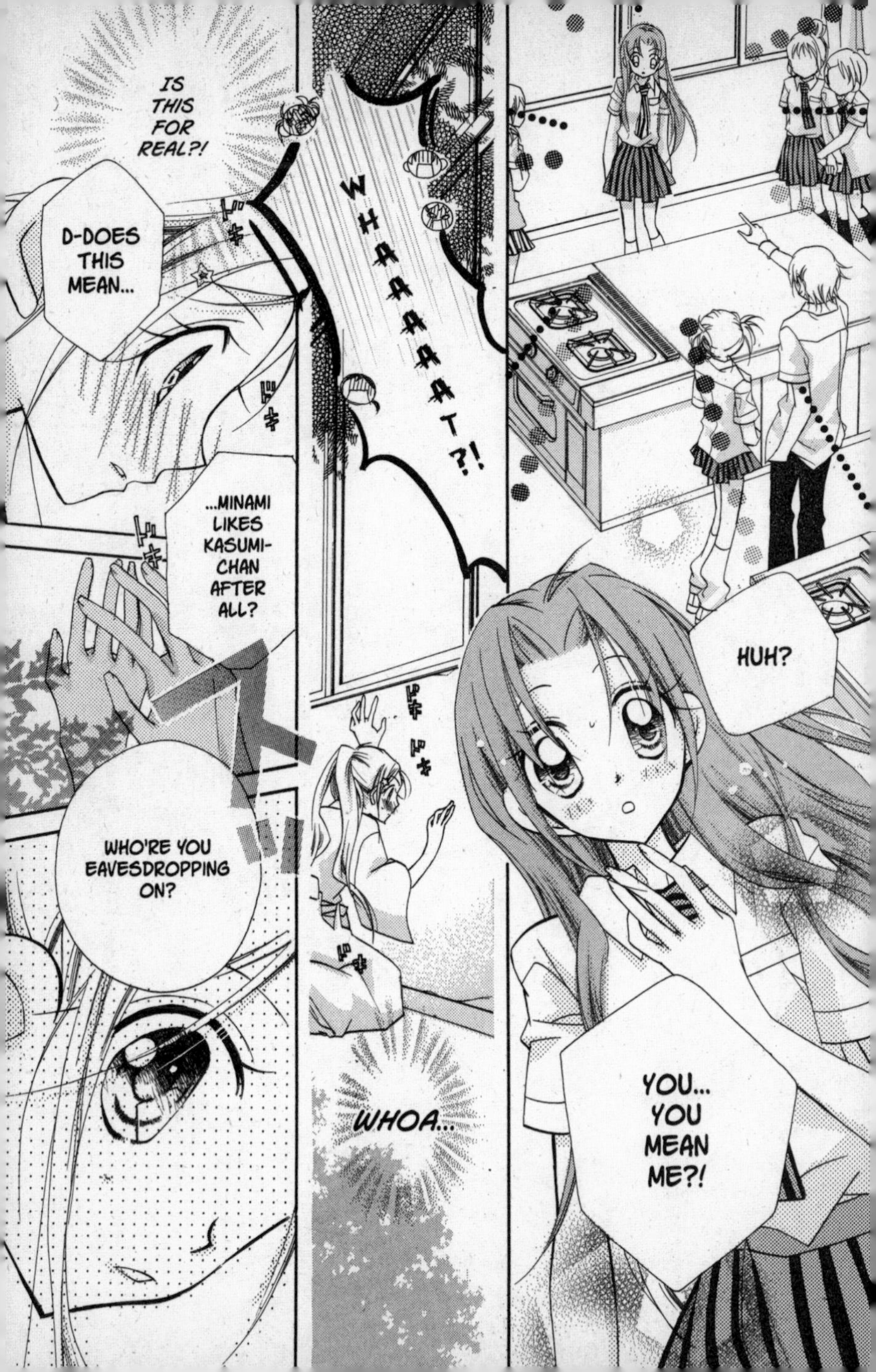
HUH?
YOU... YOU MEAN ME?!
WHAAAAAT?!
WHOA...
IS THIS FOR REAL?!
D-DOES THIS MEAN...
...MINAMI LIKES KASUMI-CHAN AFTER ALL?
WHO'RE YOU EAVESDROPPING ON?

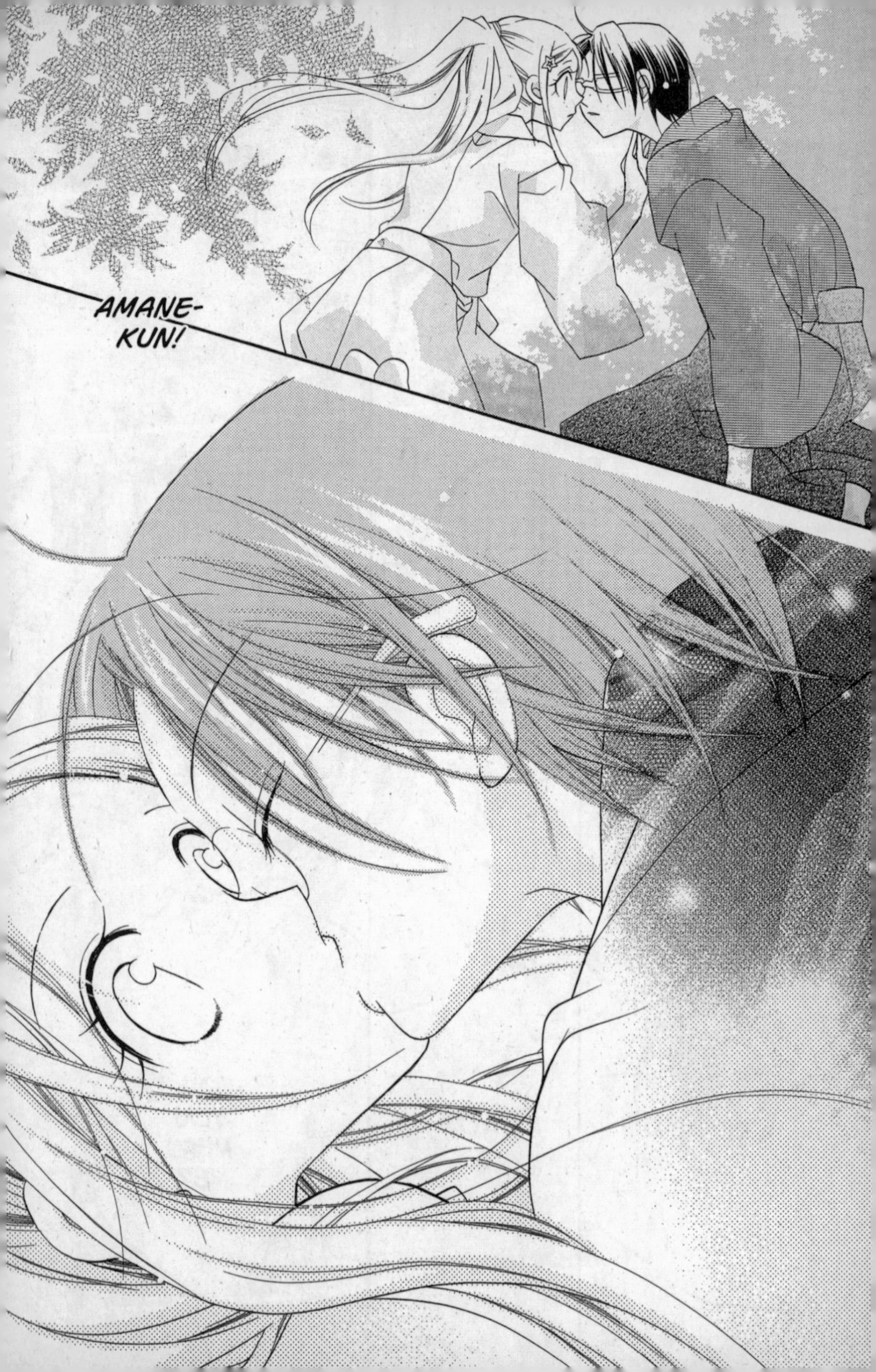
AMANE-KUN!

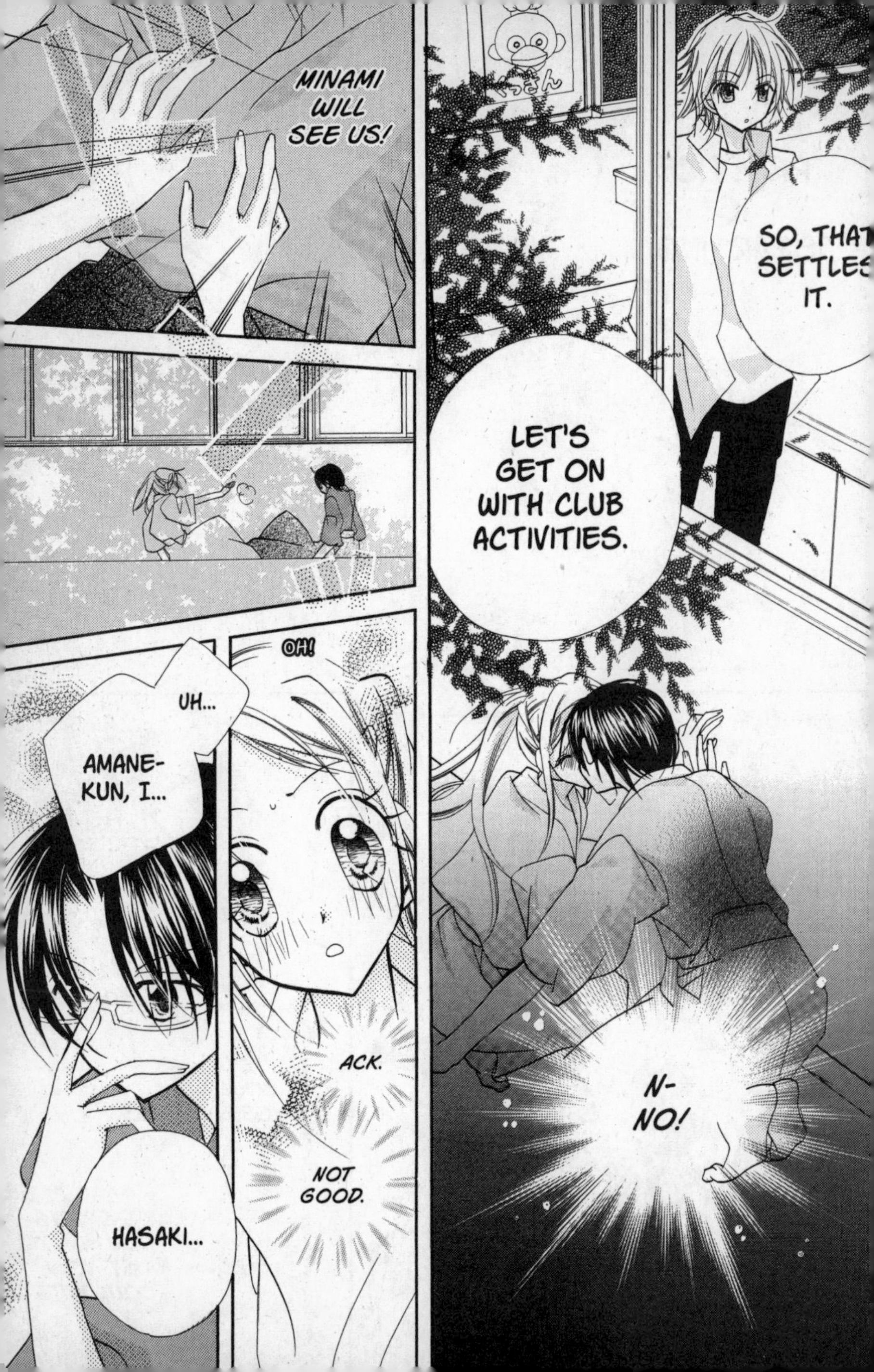
SO, THAT SETTLES IT.
LET'S GET ON WITH CLUB ACTIVITIES.
N-NO!
MINAMI WILL SEE US!
OH!
ACK.
NOT GOOD.
UH...
AMANE-KUN, I...
HASAKI...

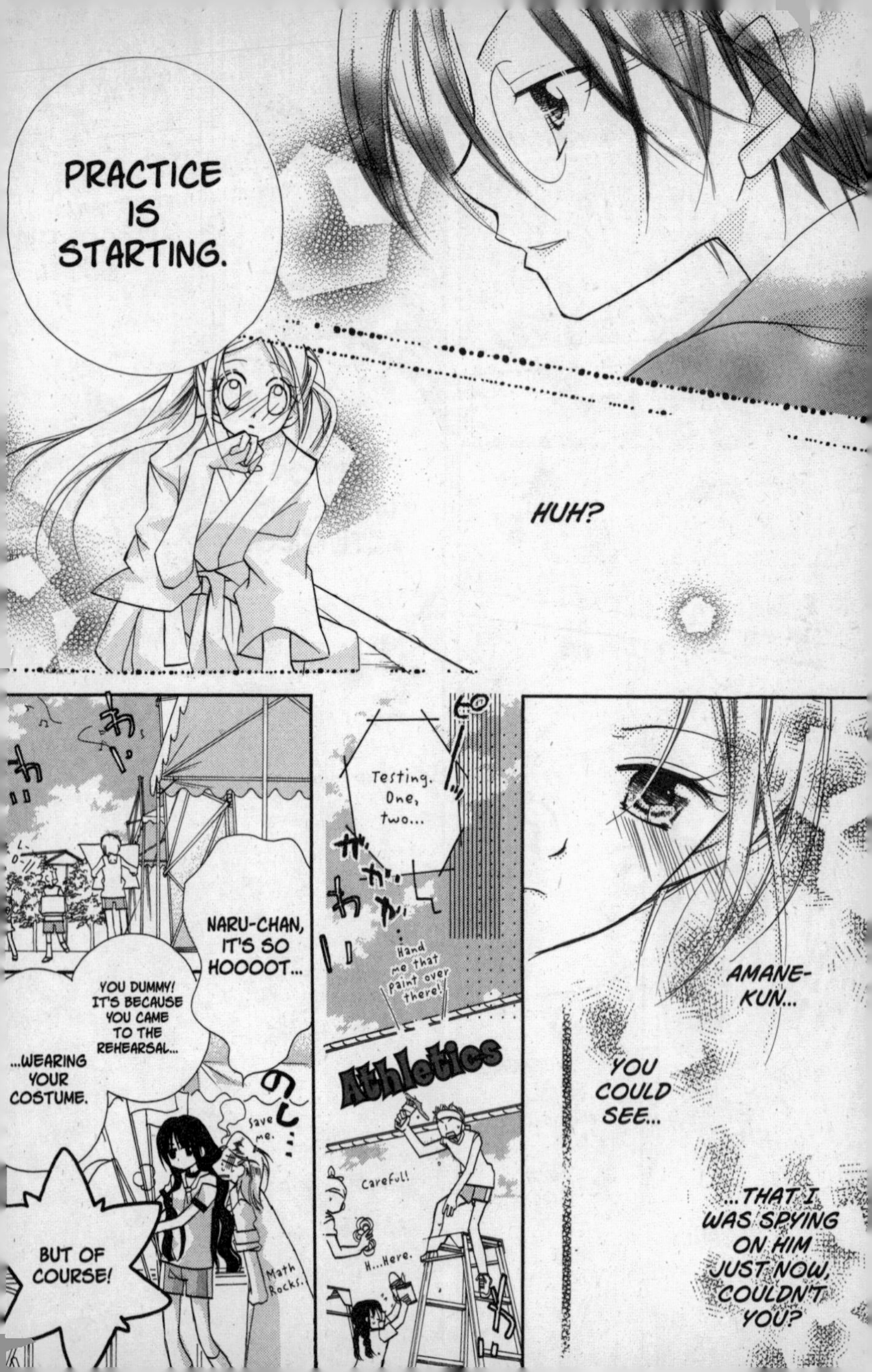
PRACTICE IS STARTING.
HUH?
AMANE-KUN...
YOU COULD SEE...
...THAT I WAS SPYING ON HIM JUST NOW, COULDN'T YOU?
Testing. One, two...
Hand me that paint over there!
Athletics
Careful!
H...Here.
NARU-CHAN, IT'S SO HOOOOT...
YOU DUMMY! IT'S BECAUSE YOU CAME TO THE REHEARSAL...
...WEARING YOUR COSTUME.
Save me.
BUT OF COURSE!
Math Rocks.

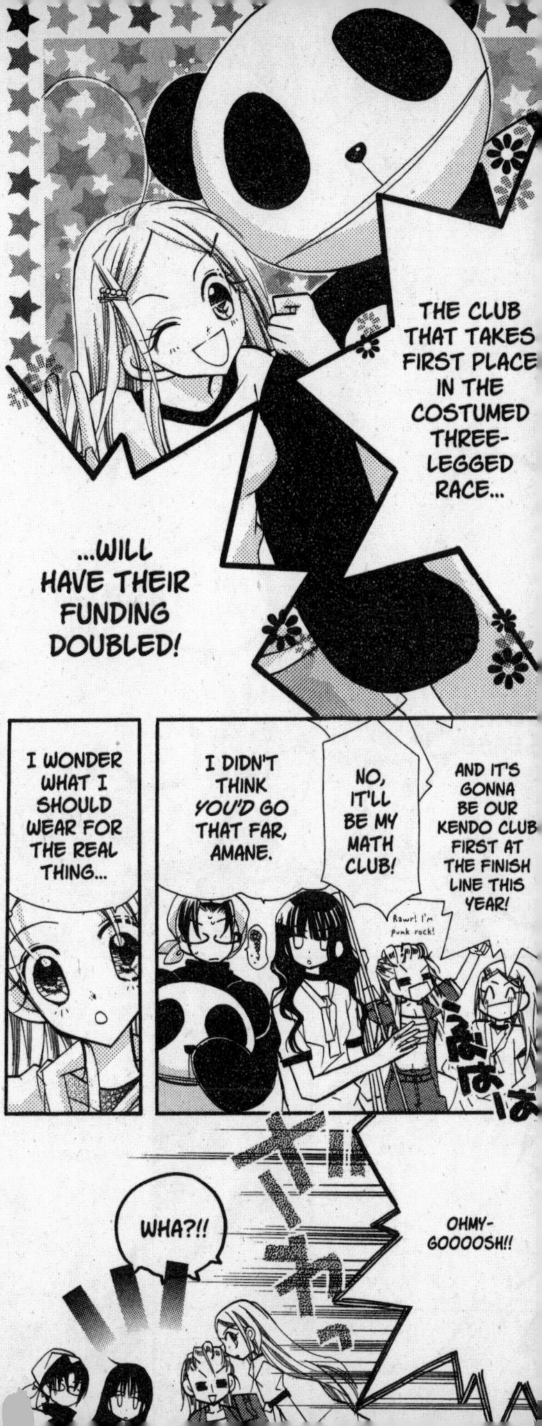
THE CLUB THAT TAKES FIRST PLACE IN THE COSTUMED THREE-LEGGED RACE...
...WILL HAVE THEIR FUNDING DOUBLED!
AND IT'S GONNA BE OUR KENDO CLUB FIRST AT THE FINISH LINE THIS YEAR!
Rawr! I'm Punk rock!
NO, IT'LL BE MY MATH CLUB!
I DIDN'T THINK YOU'D GO THAT FAR, AMANE.
I WONDER WHAT I SHOULD WEAR FOR THE REAL THING...
OHMY-GOOOOSH!!
WHA?!!

SEVEN!

☑ The girl's uniform I decided on was based on a high school (or was it junior high?) uniform I'd seen often at the train station and had fallen in love with at first sight. There was also a sailor-style one from an all-girl's school that had stars and stuff on it. Its cuteness was unrivaled!

☑ Whenever I hit the streets I transform into a suspicious creature whose eyes are unconsciously drawn to uniforms.

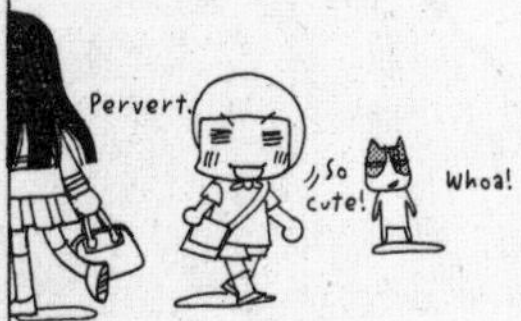
Pervert.
So cute!
Whoa!

☑ As for boy's uniforms, I'm a gakuran fan by far. Each boy wears his gakuran uniquely, and I never get tired of looking at them.

Be that as it may, if I am able to write about Otome and Minami as high-school students, I'll probably have them wear blazers.

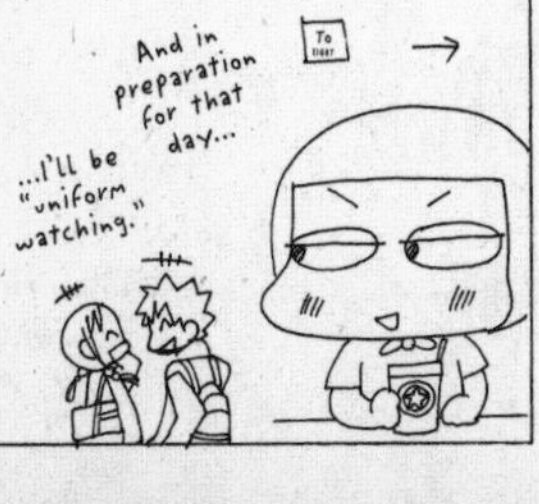
And in preparation for that day...
...I'll be "uniform watching."

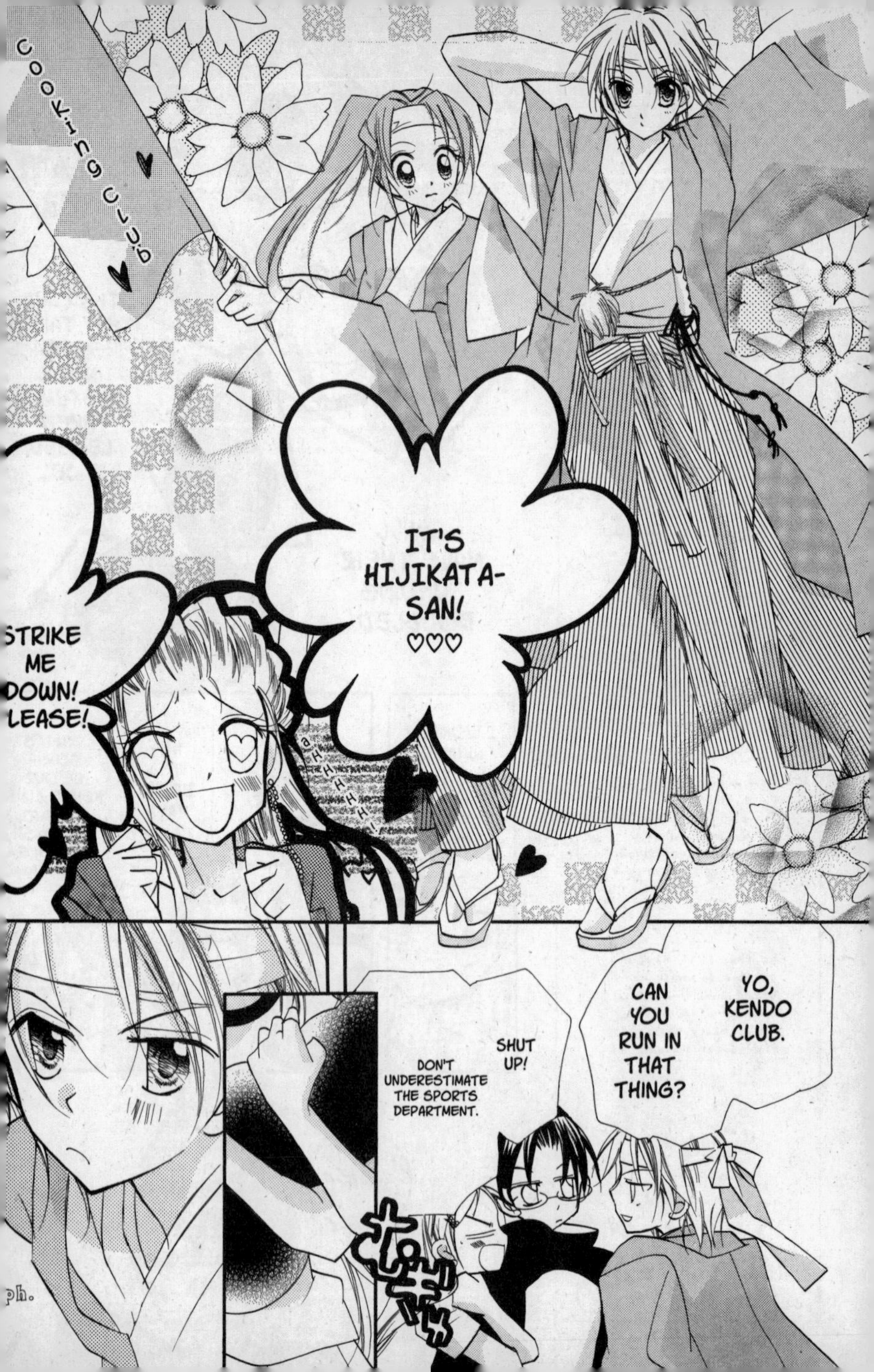

Cooking Club
IT'S HIJIKATA-SAN! ♡♡♡
aHHHHHH!
STRIKE ME DOWN! LEASE!
YO, KENDO CLUB.
CAN YOU RUN IN THAT THING?
SHUT UP!
DON'T UNDERESTIMATE THE SPORTS DEPARTMENT.

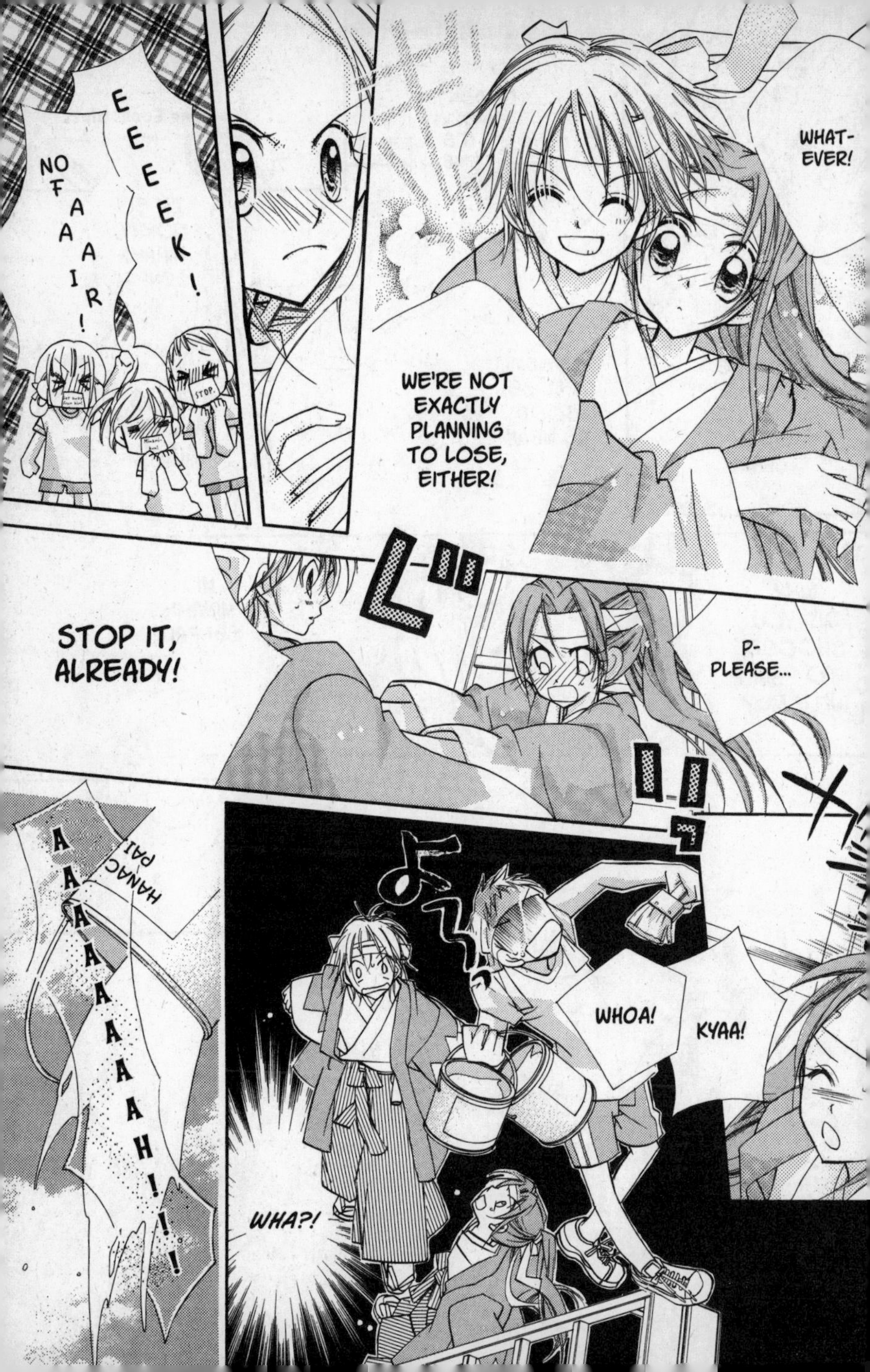
WHAT-EVER!
WE'RE NOT EXACTLY PLANNING TO LOSE, EITHER!
EEEEEK!
NO FAAAIR!
STOP.
P-PLEASE...
STOP IT, ALREADY!
KYAA!
WHOA!
WHA?!
AAAAAAAAAAH!!!!

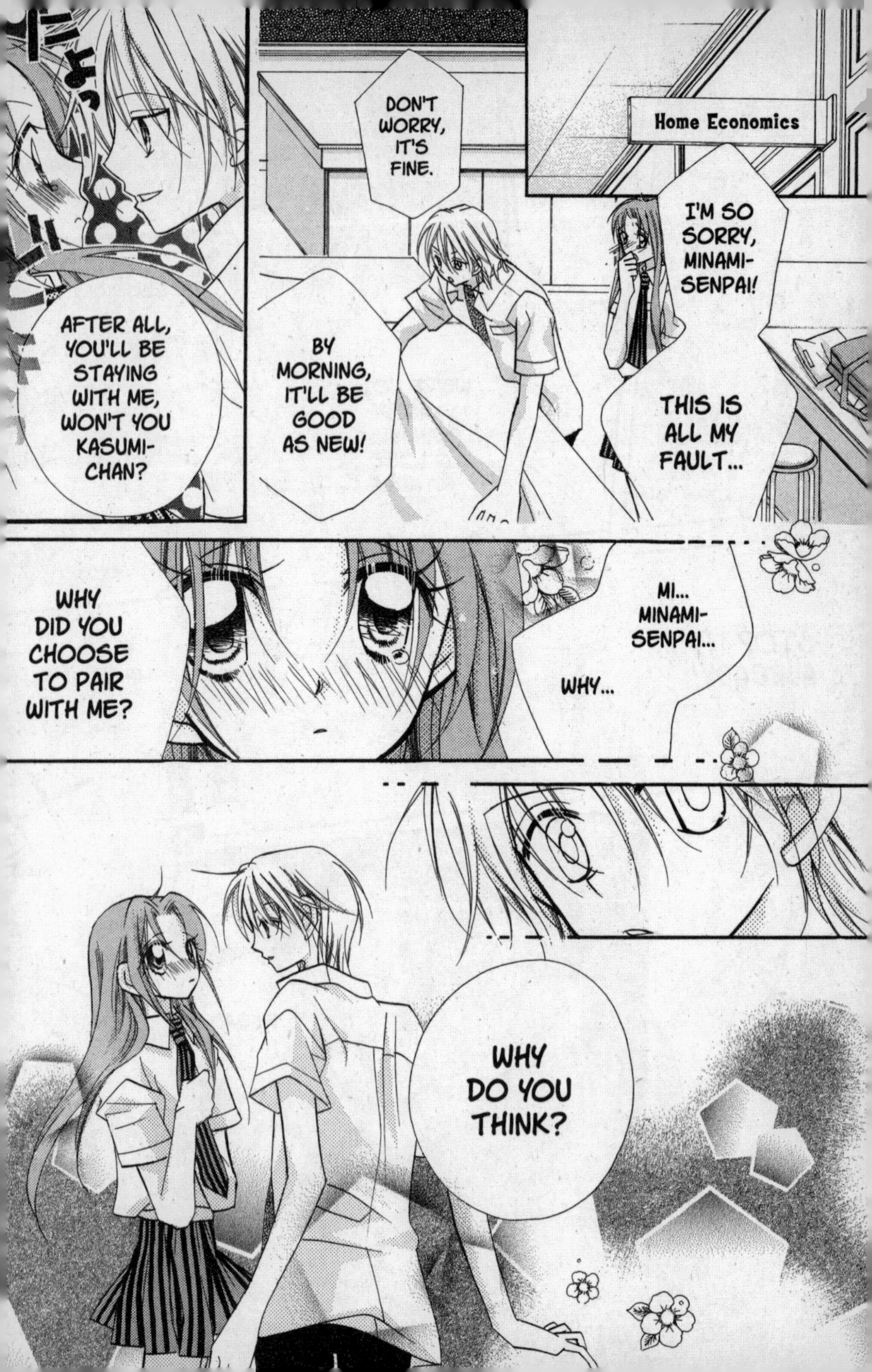
Home Economics
I'M SO SORRY, MINAMI-SENPAI!
DON'T WORRY, IT'S FINE.
THIS IS ALL MY FAULT...
BY MORNING, IT'LL BE GOOD AS NEW!
AFTER ALL, YOU'LL BE STAYING WITH ME, WON'T YOU KASUMI-CHAN?
MI... MINAMI-SENPAI...
WHY...
WHY DID YOU CHOOSE TO PAIR WITH ME?
WHY DO YOU THINK?

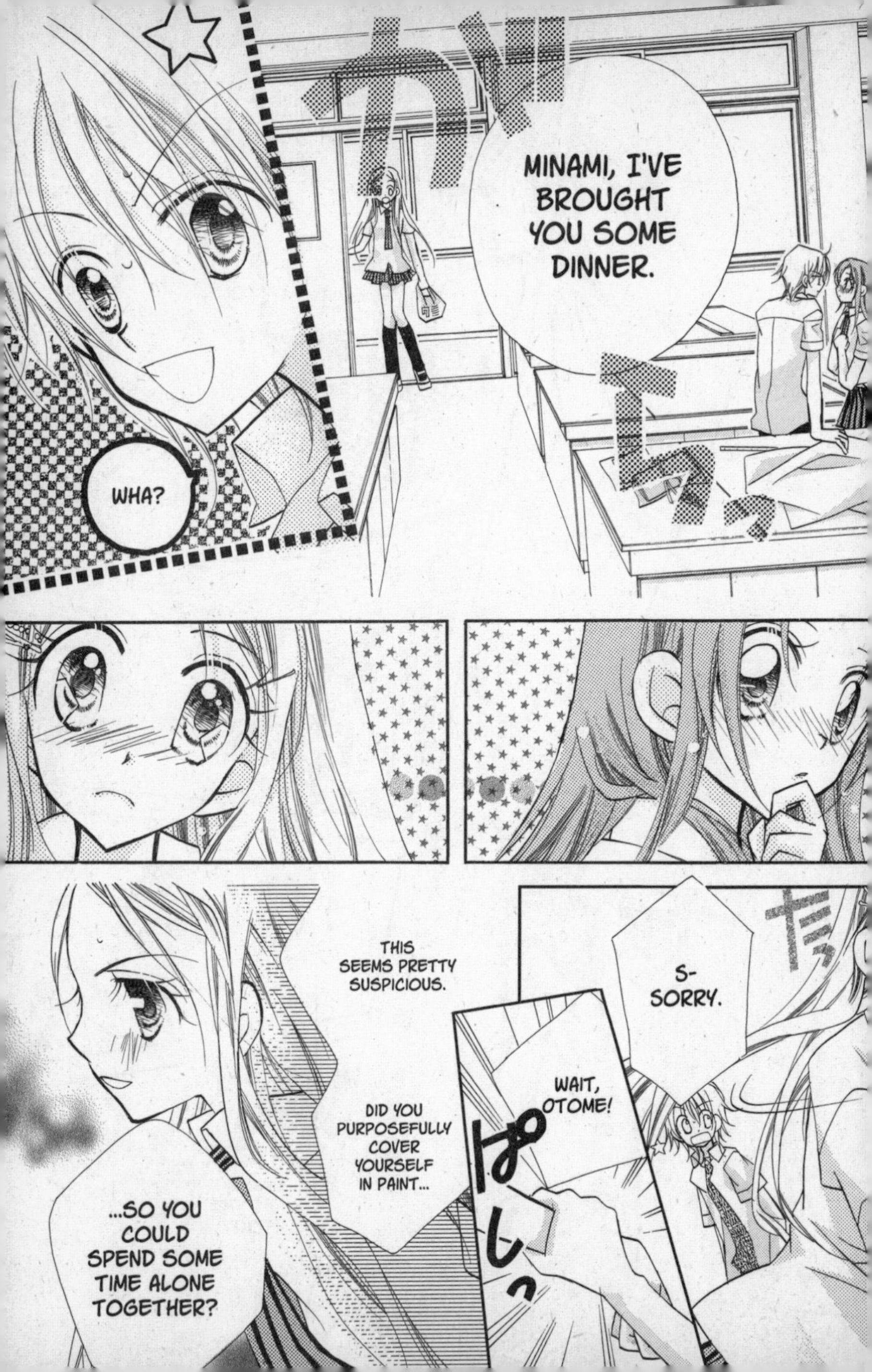
MINAMI, I'VE BROUGHT YOU SOME DINNER.
WHA?
S-SORRY.
WAIT, OTOME!
THIS SEEMS PRETTY SUSPICIOUS.
DID YOU PURPOSEFULLY COVER YOURSELF IN PAINT...
...SO YOU COULD SPEND SOME TIME ALONE TOGETHER?

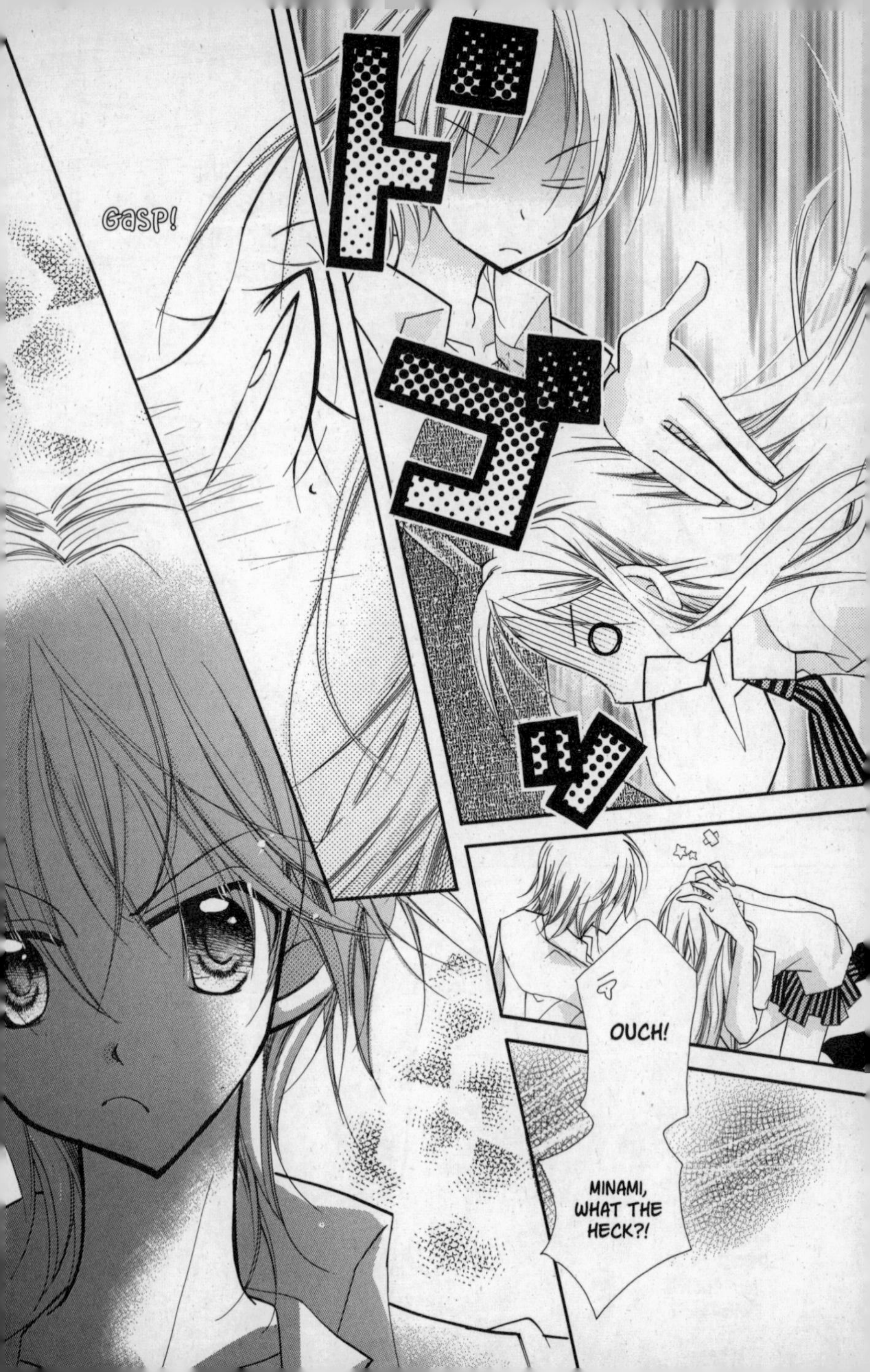
ドゴッ
OUCH!
MINAMI, WHAT THE HECK?!
GASP!

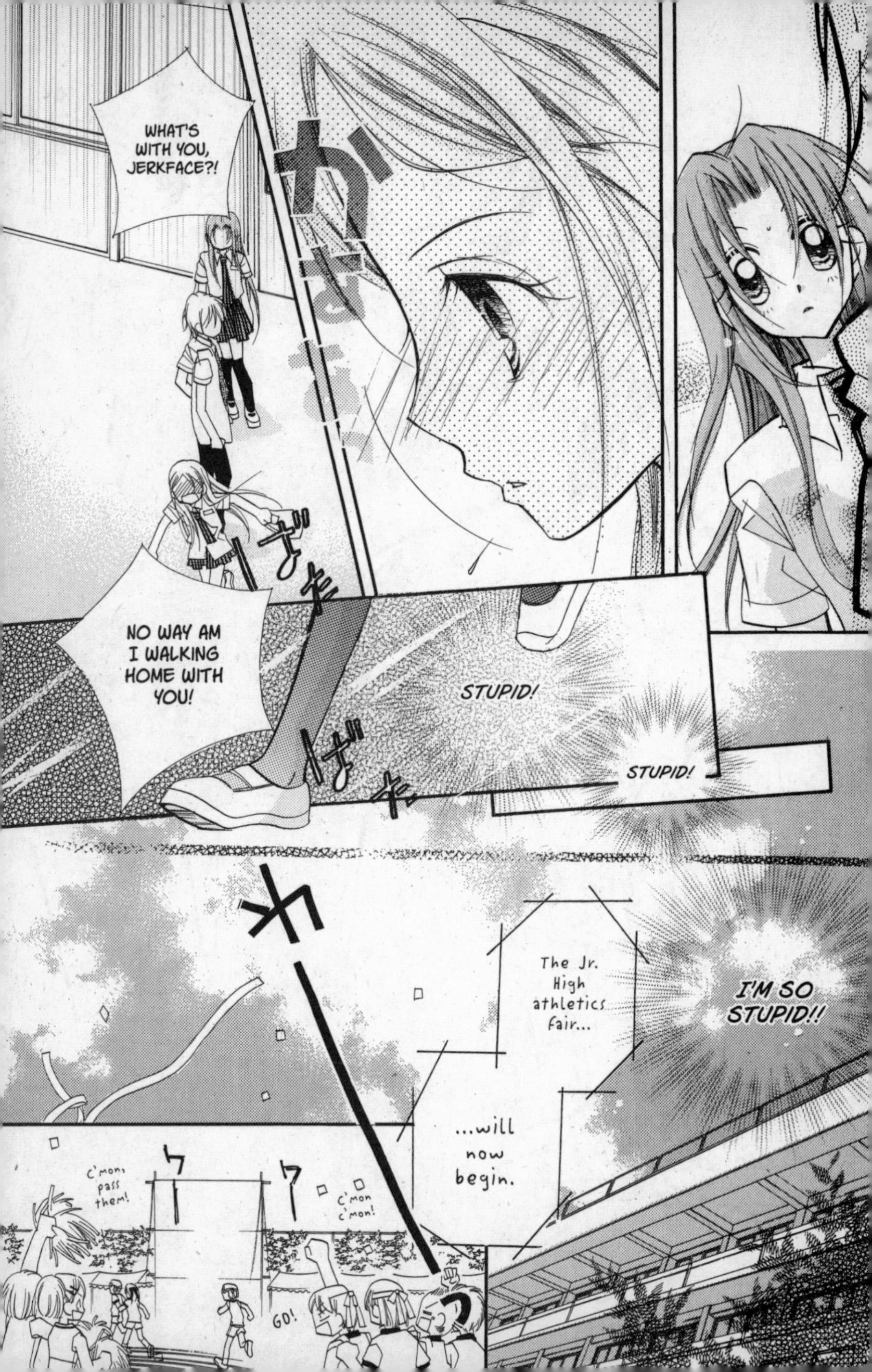
WHAT'S WITH YOU, JERKFACE?!
NO WAY AM I WALKING HOME WITH YOU!
STUPID!
STUPID!
I'M SO STUPID!!
The Jr. High athletics fair...
...will now begin.
C'mon c'mon!
C'mon, pass them!
GO!

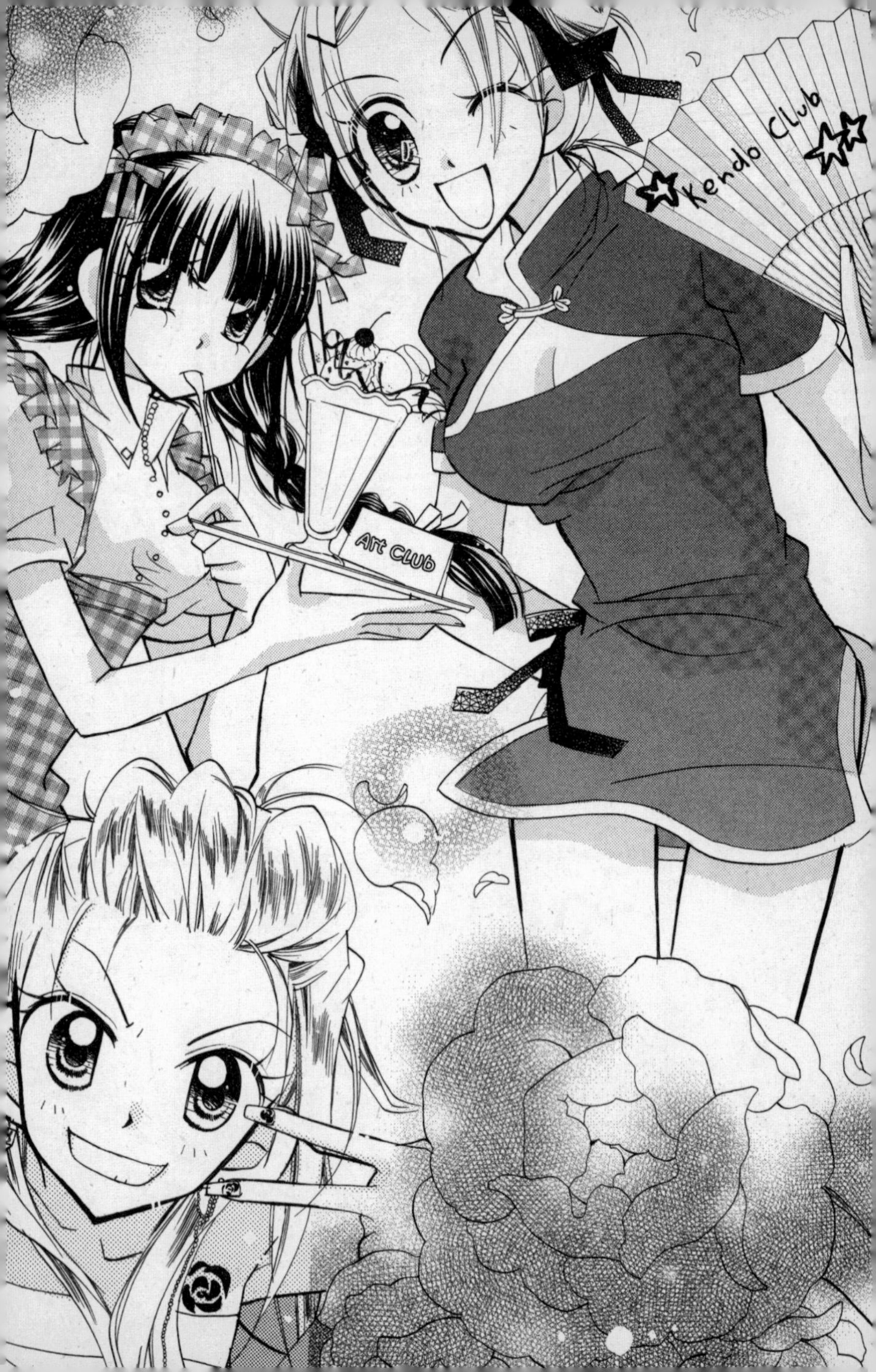
Kendo Club
Art Club

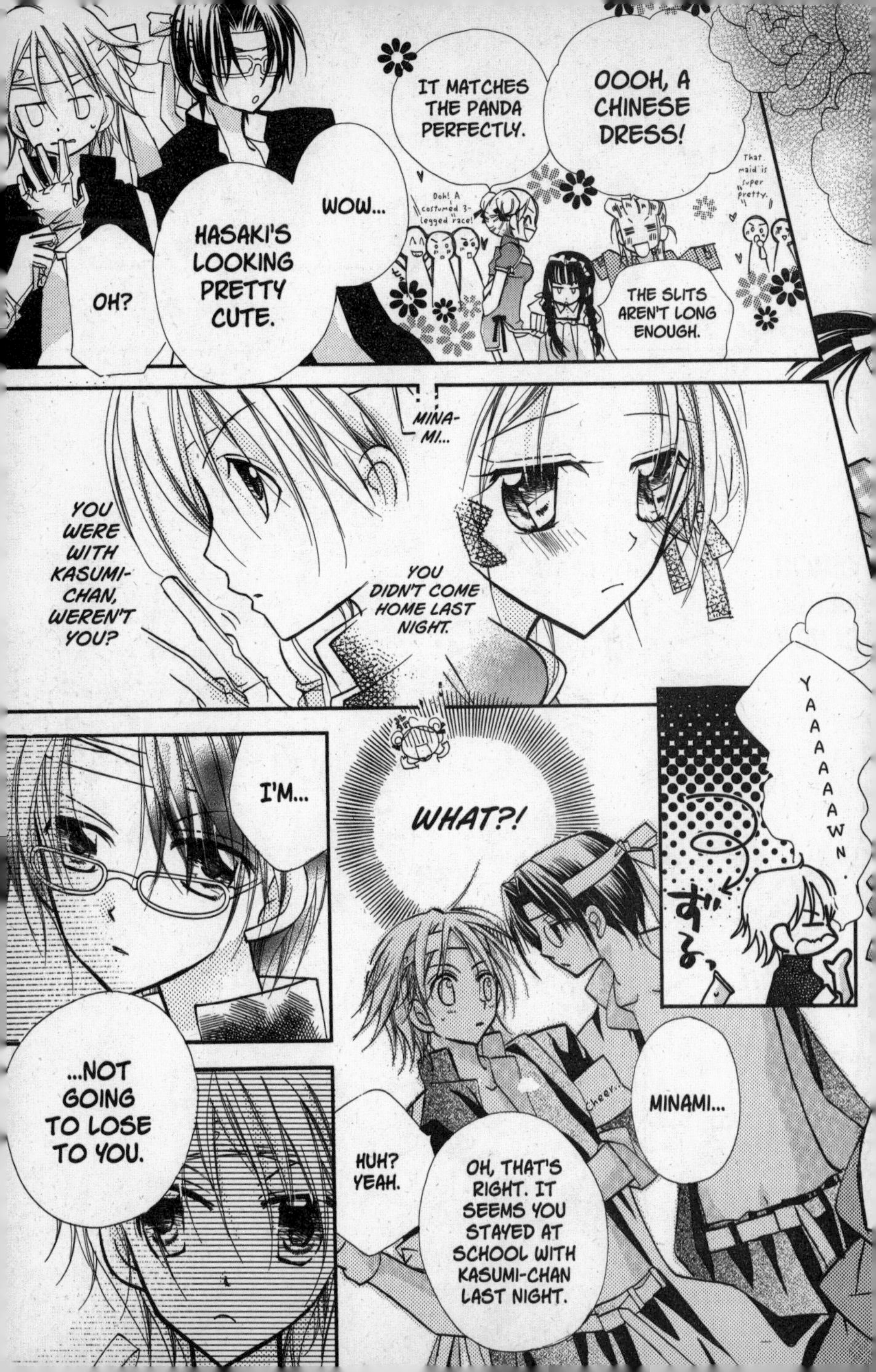
OOOH, A CHINESE DRESS!
IT MATCHES THE PANDA PERFECTLY.
That maid is super pretty.
Doh! A costumed 3-legged race!
THE SLITS AREN'T LONG ENOUGH.
WOW...
HASAKI'S LOOKING PRETTY CUTE.
OH?
MINA-MI...
YOU DIDN'T COME HOME LAST NIGHT.
YOU WERE WITH KASUMI-CHAN, WEREN'T YOU?
YAAAAAAAWN
ずる
WHAT?!
MINAMI...
OH, THAT'S RIGHT. IT SEEMS YOU STAYED AT SCHOOL WITH KASUMI-CHAN LAST NIGHT.
Cheer...
HUH? YEAH.
I'M...
...NOT GOING TO LOSE TO YOU.

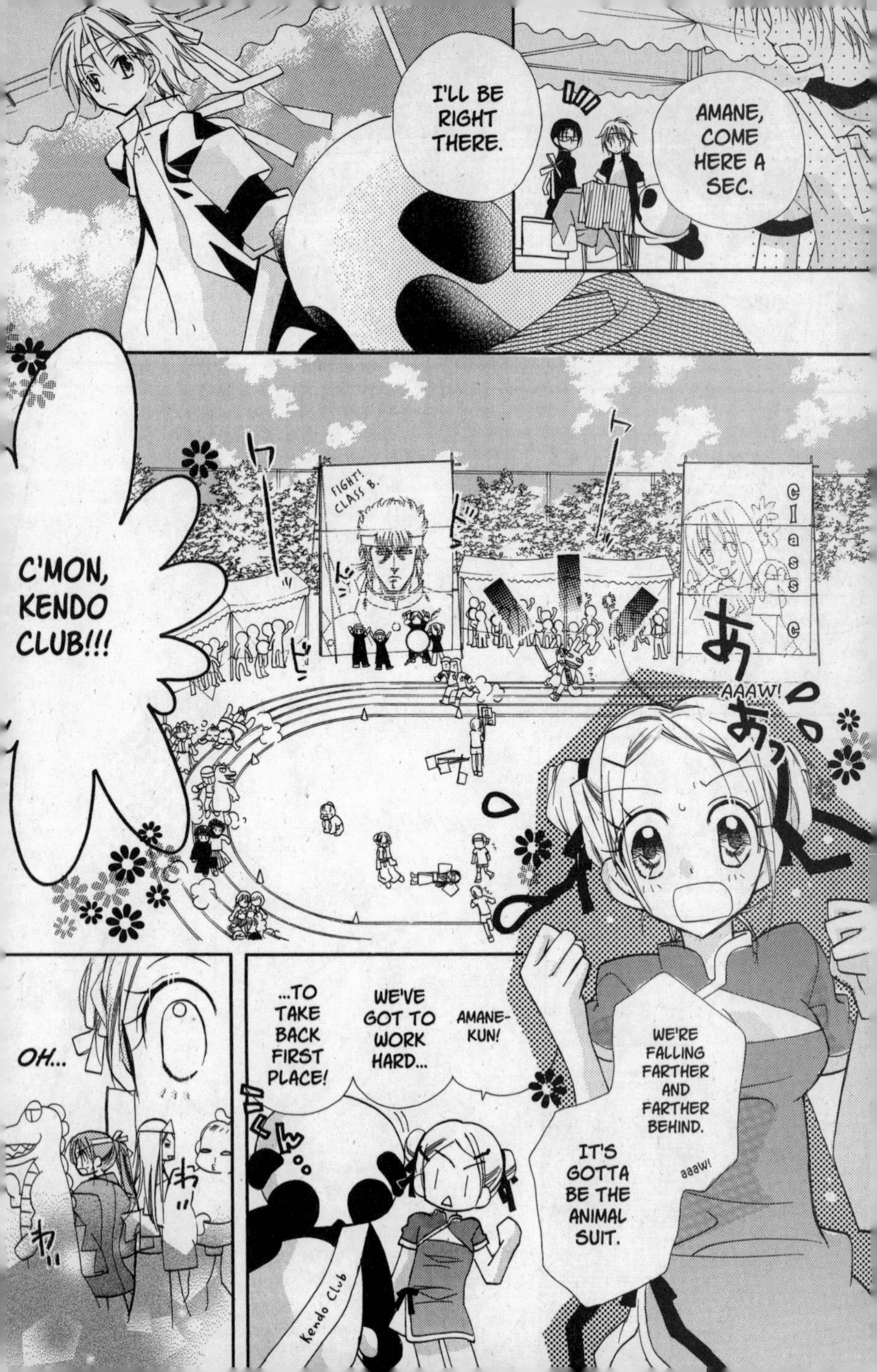
AMANE, COME HERE A SEC.
I'LL BE RIGHT THERE.
FIGHT! CLASS B.
class c
C'MON, KENDO CLUB!!!
AAAW!
WE'RE FALLING FARTHER AND FARTHER BEHIND.
IT'S GOTTA BE THE ANIMAL SUIT.
aaaw!
AMANE-KUN!
WE'VE GOT TO WORK HARD...
...TO TAKE BACK FIRST PLACE!
Kendo Club
OH...

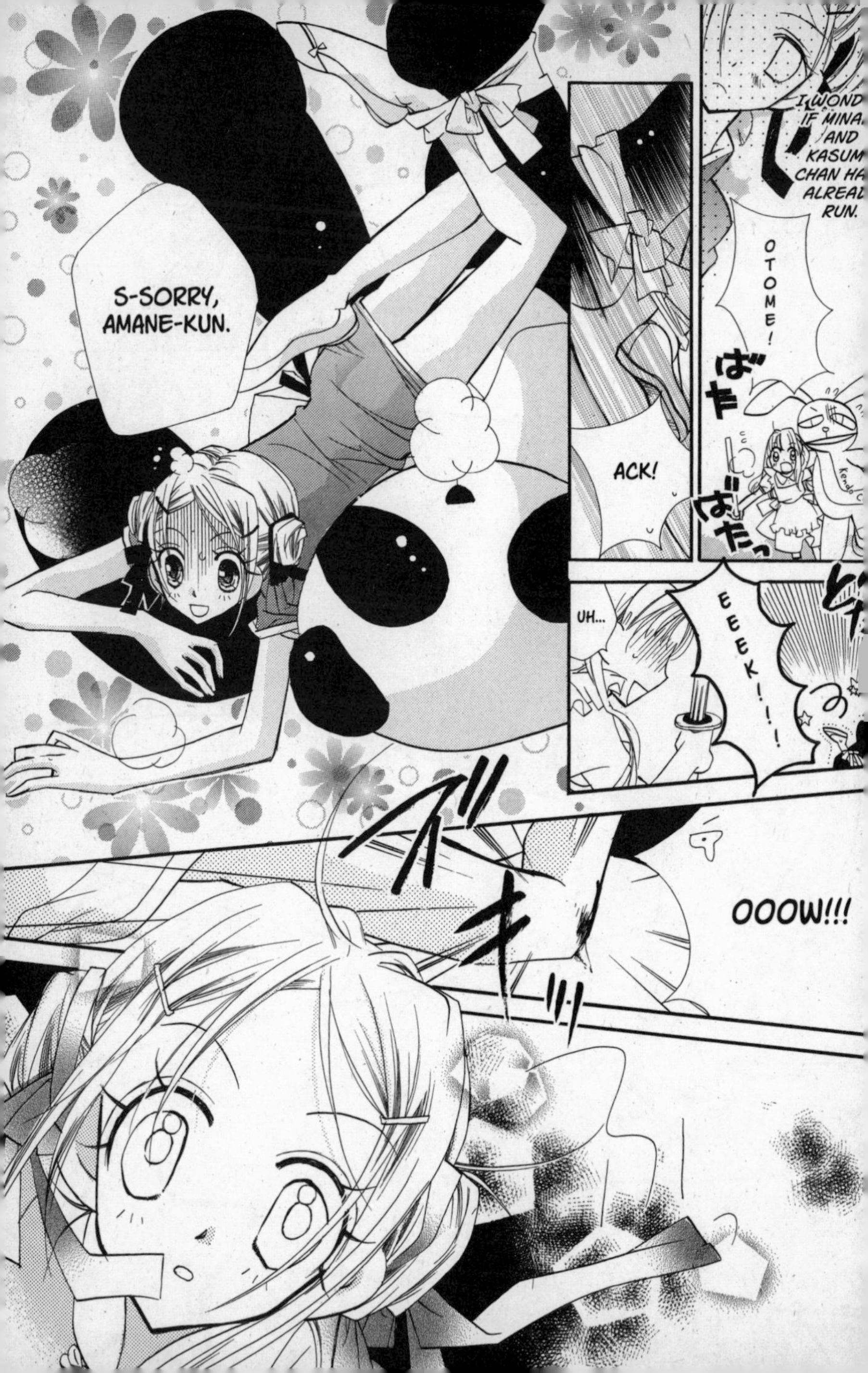
I WOND
IF MINA
AND
KASUM
CHAN HA
ALREAD
RUN.
OTOME!
ばた
ばたっ
ACK!
S-SORRY, AMANE-KUN.
EEEEK!!!
UH...
OOOW!!!

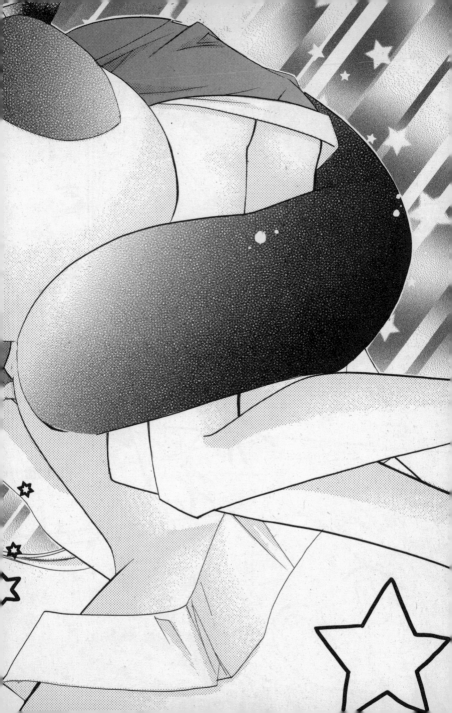

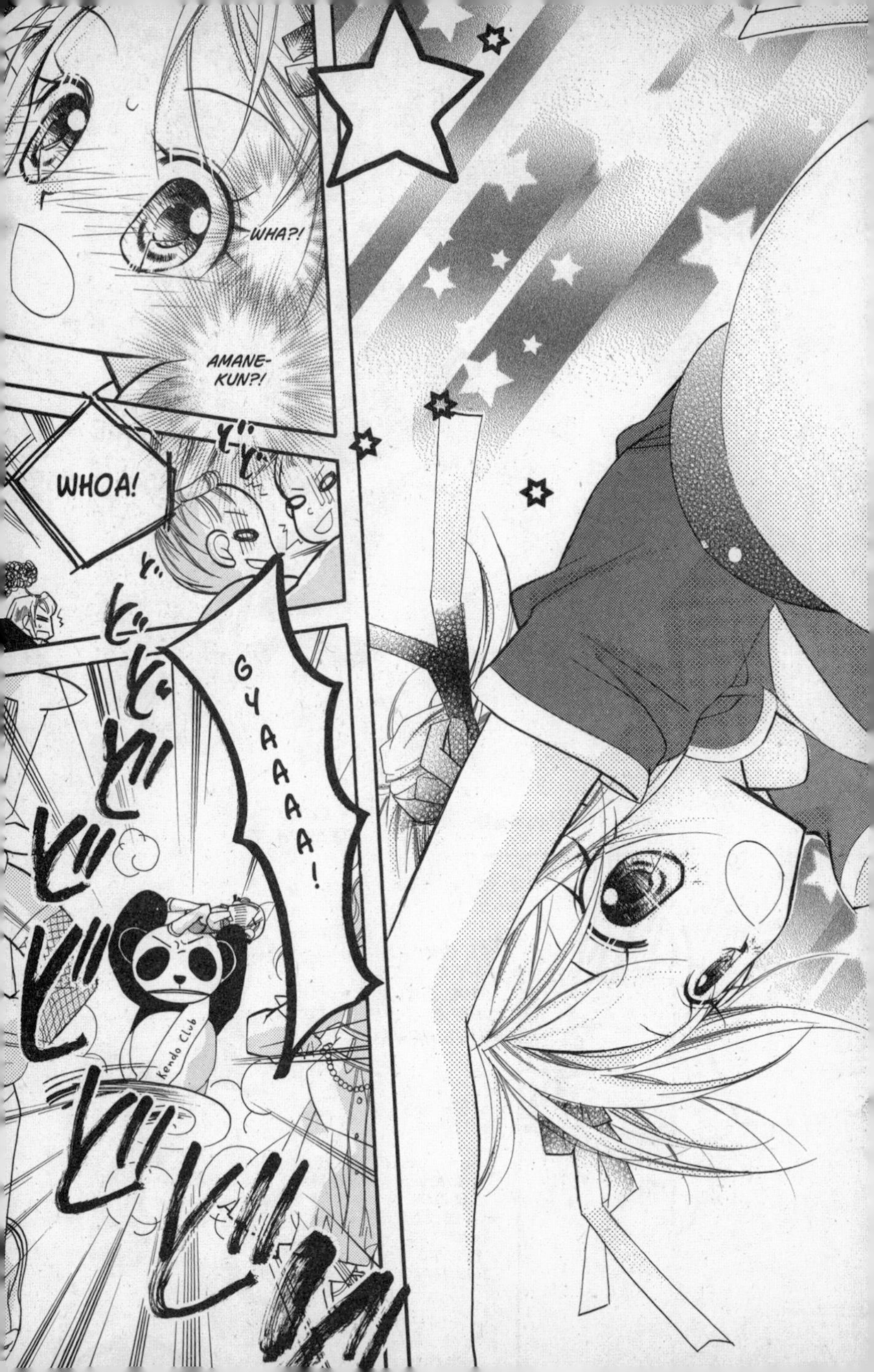
WHA?!
AMANE-KUN?!
WHOA!
GYAAAAA!
Kendo Club

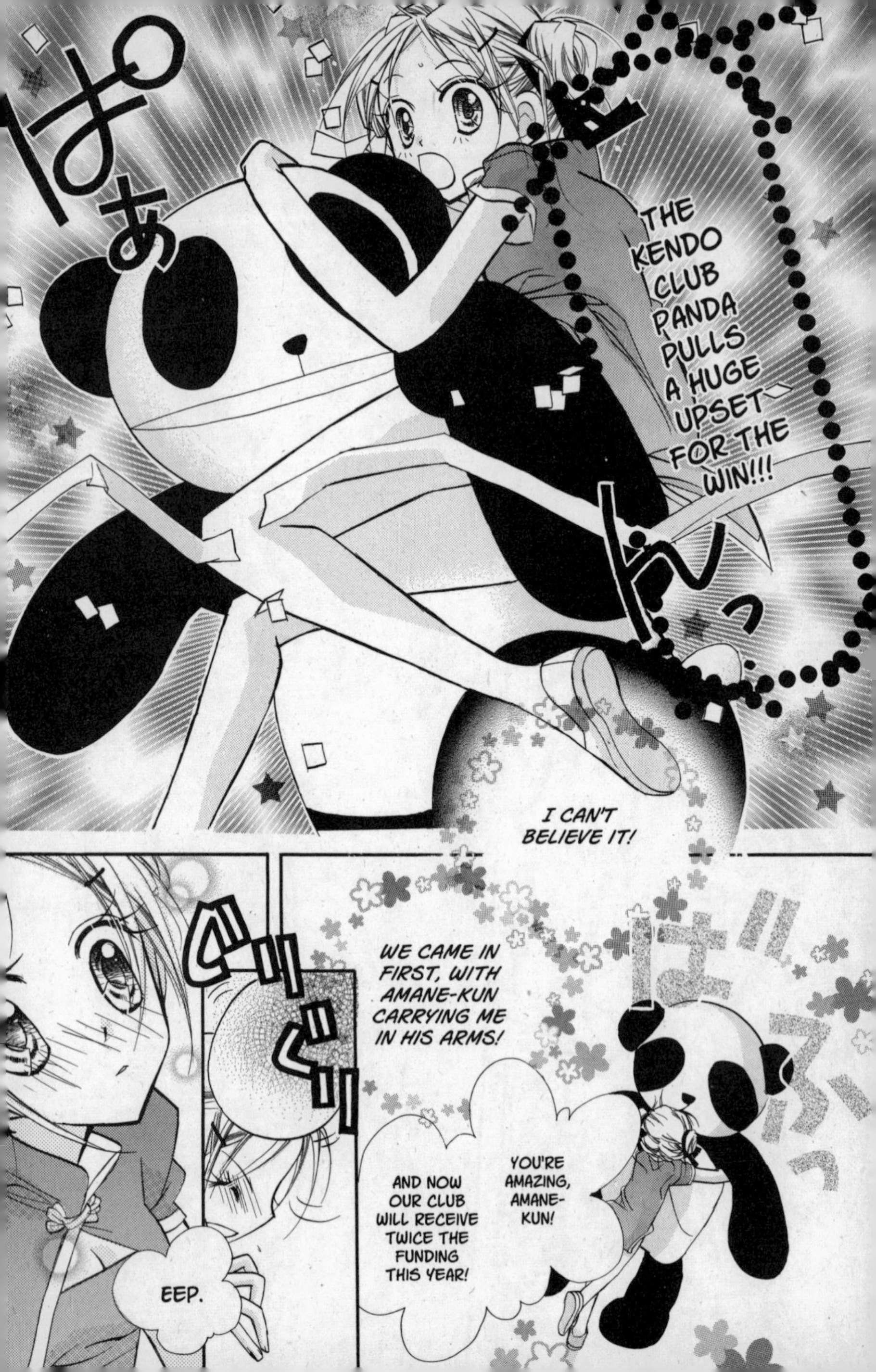
THE KENDO CLUB PANDA PULLS A HUGE UPSET FOR THE WIN!!!
I CAN'T BELIEVE IT!
WE CAME IN FIRST, WITH AMANE-KUN CARRYING ME IN HIS ARMS!
YOU'RE AMAZING, AMANE-KUN!
AND NOW OUR CLUB WILL RECEIVE TWICE THE FUNDING THIS YEAR!
EEP.

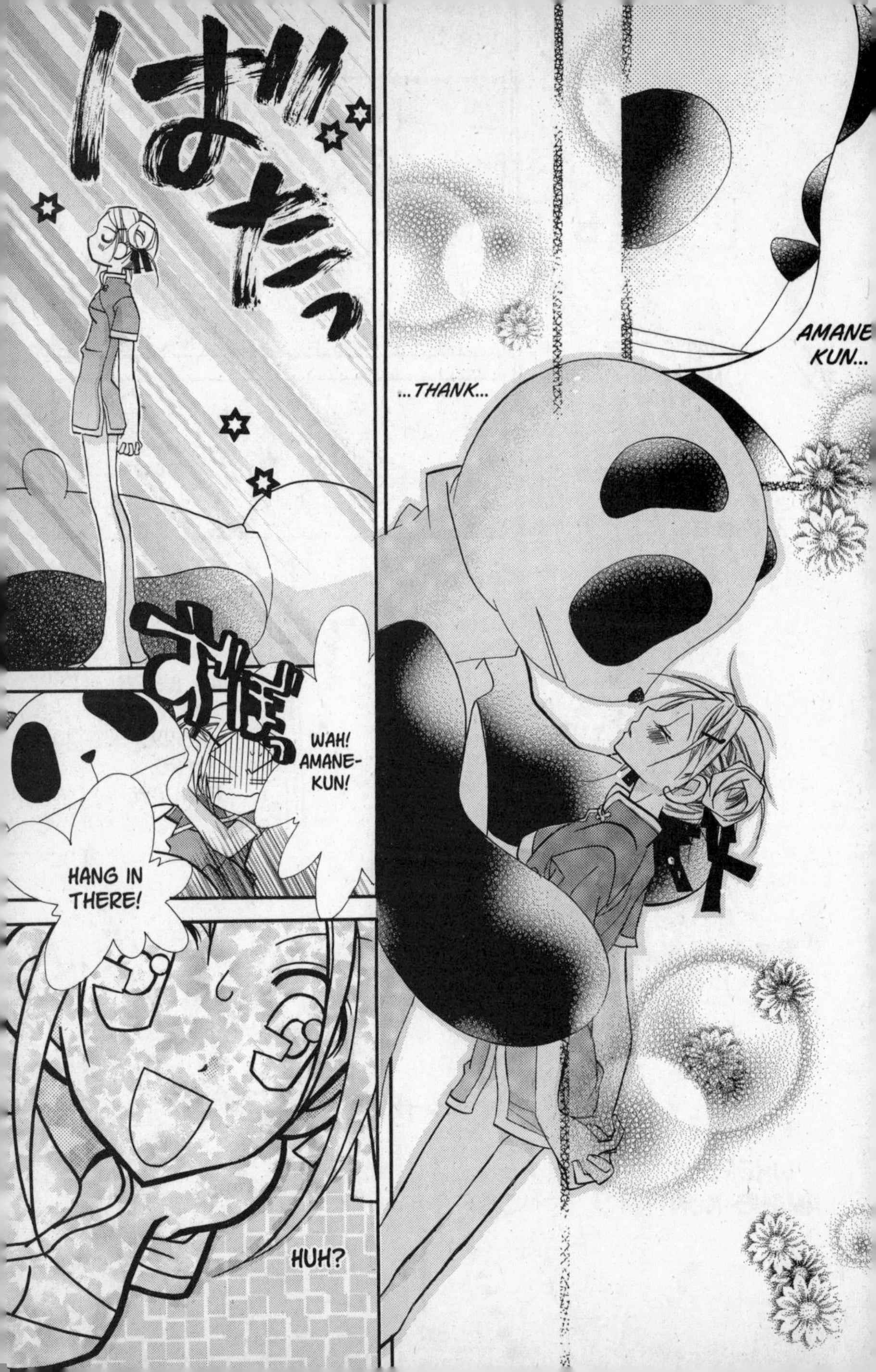
AMANE KUN...
...THANK...
WAH! AMANE-KUN!
HANG IN THERE!
HUH?

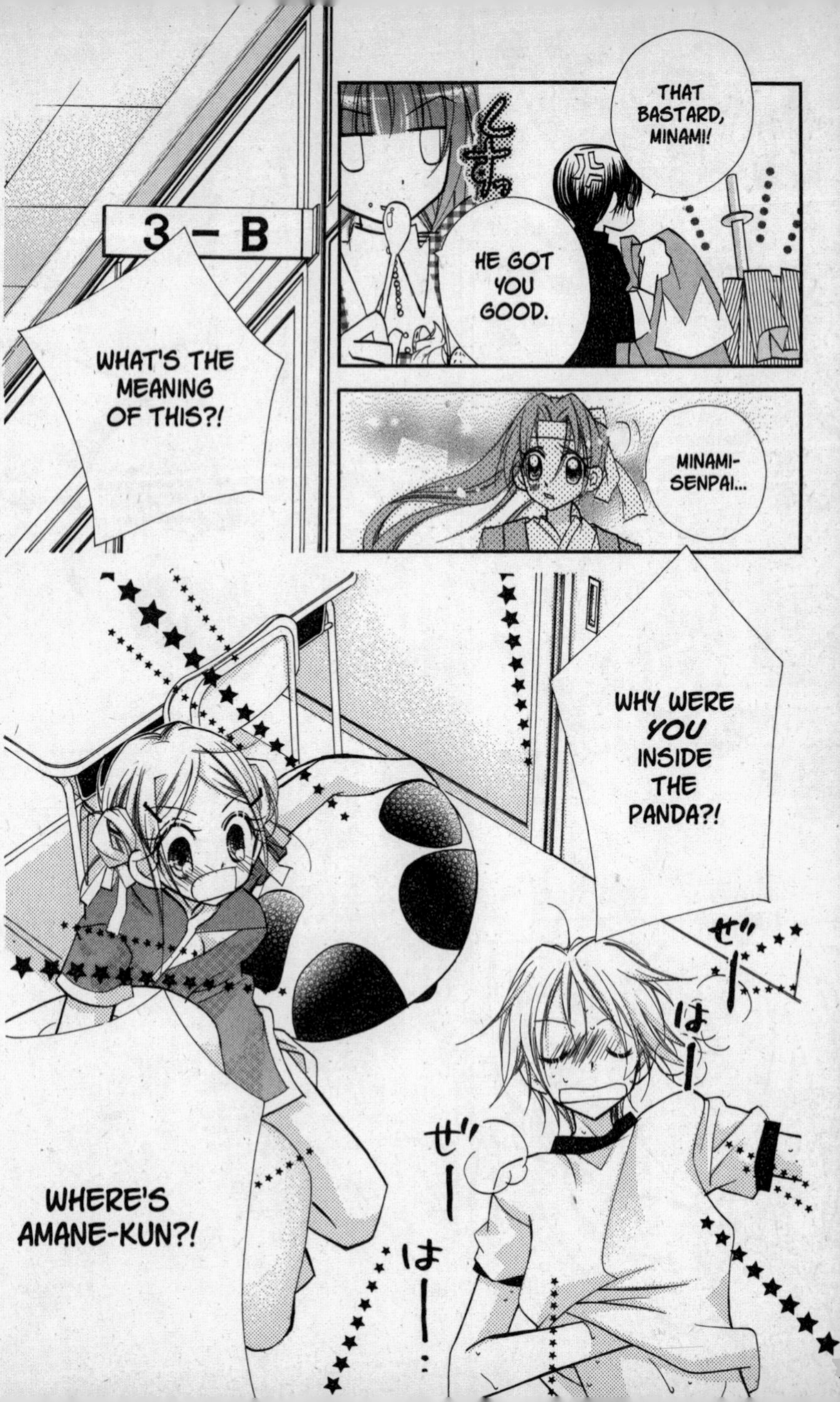

THAT BASTARD, MINAMI!
くす
HE GOT YOU GOOD.
MINAMI-SENPAI...
WHAT'S THE MEANING OF THIS?!
ぜーはー
WHY WERE *YOU* INSIDE THE PANDA?!
ぜーはー
WHERE'S AMANE-KUN?!

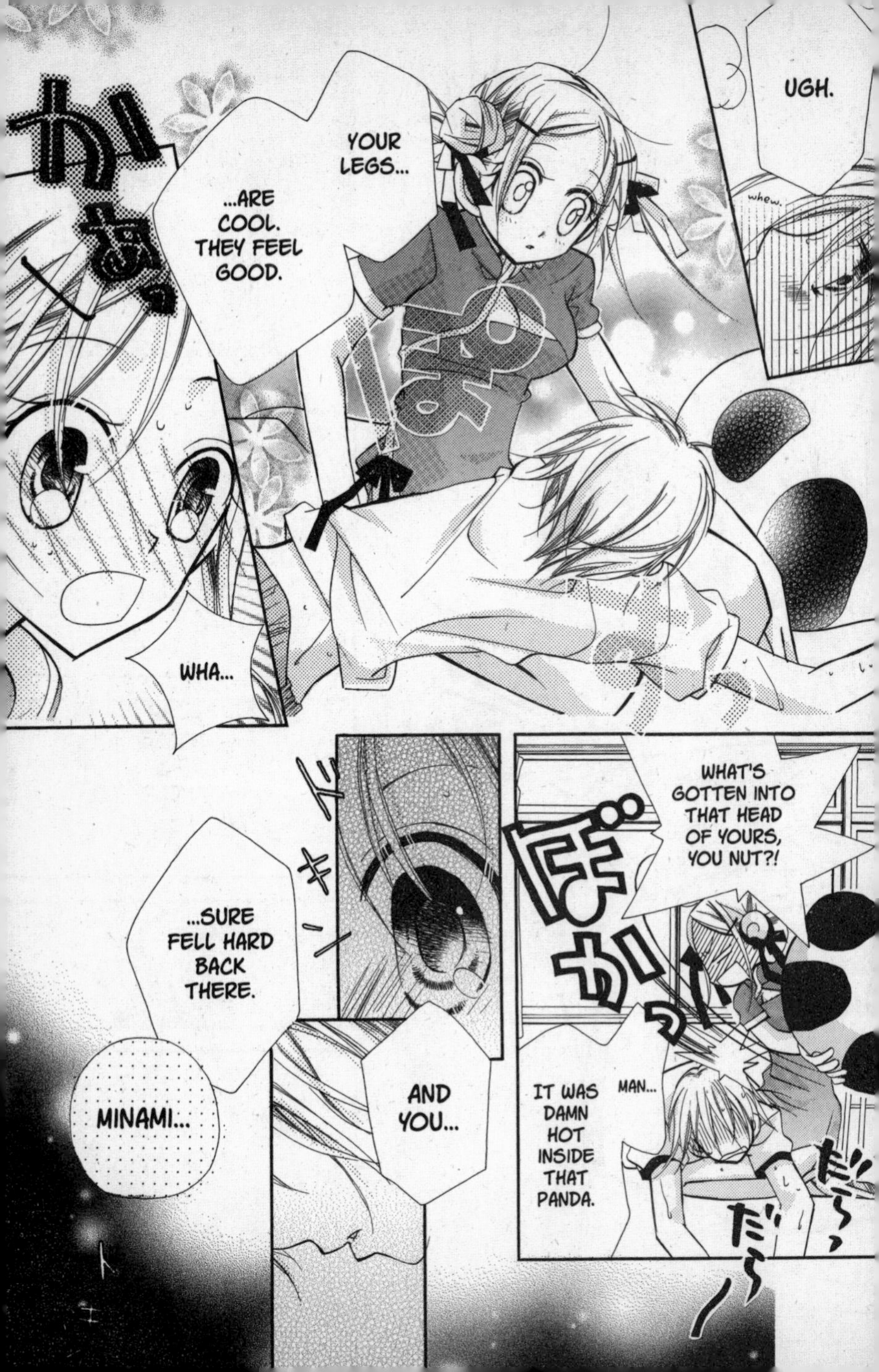
UGH.
whew.
YOUR LEGS...
...ARE COOL. THEY FEEL GOOD.
WHA...
WHAT'S GOTTEN INTO THAT HEAD OF YOURS, YOU NUT?!
MAN...
IT WAS DAMN HOT INSIDE THAT PANDA.
AND YOU...
...SURE FELL HARD BACK THERE.
MINAMI...

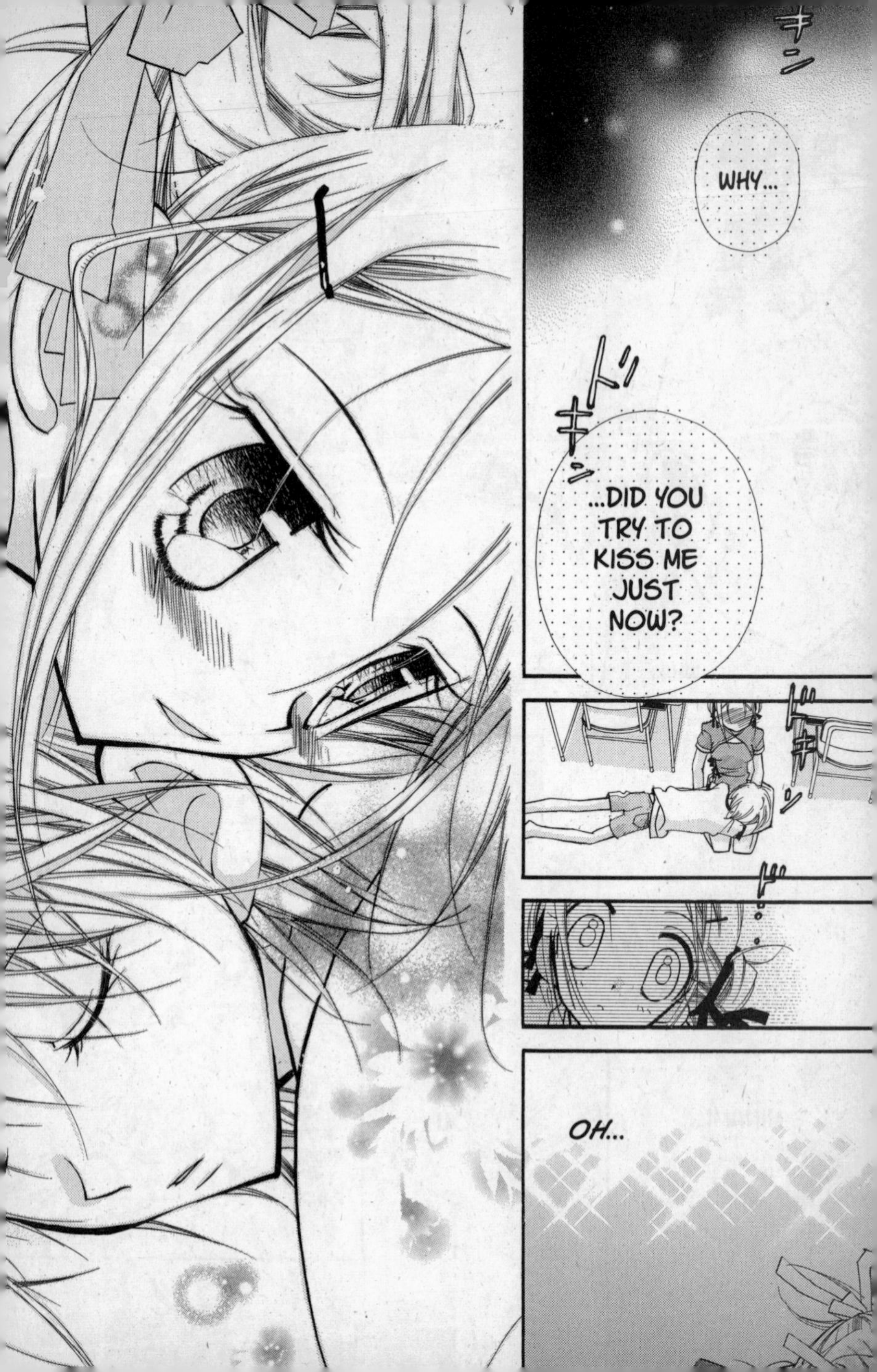
WHY...
...DID YOU TRY TO KISS ME JUST NOW?
OH...

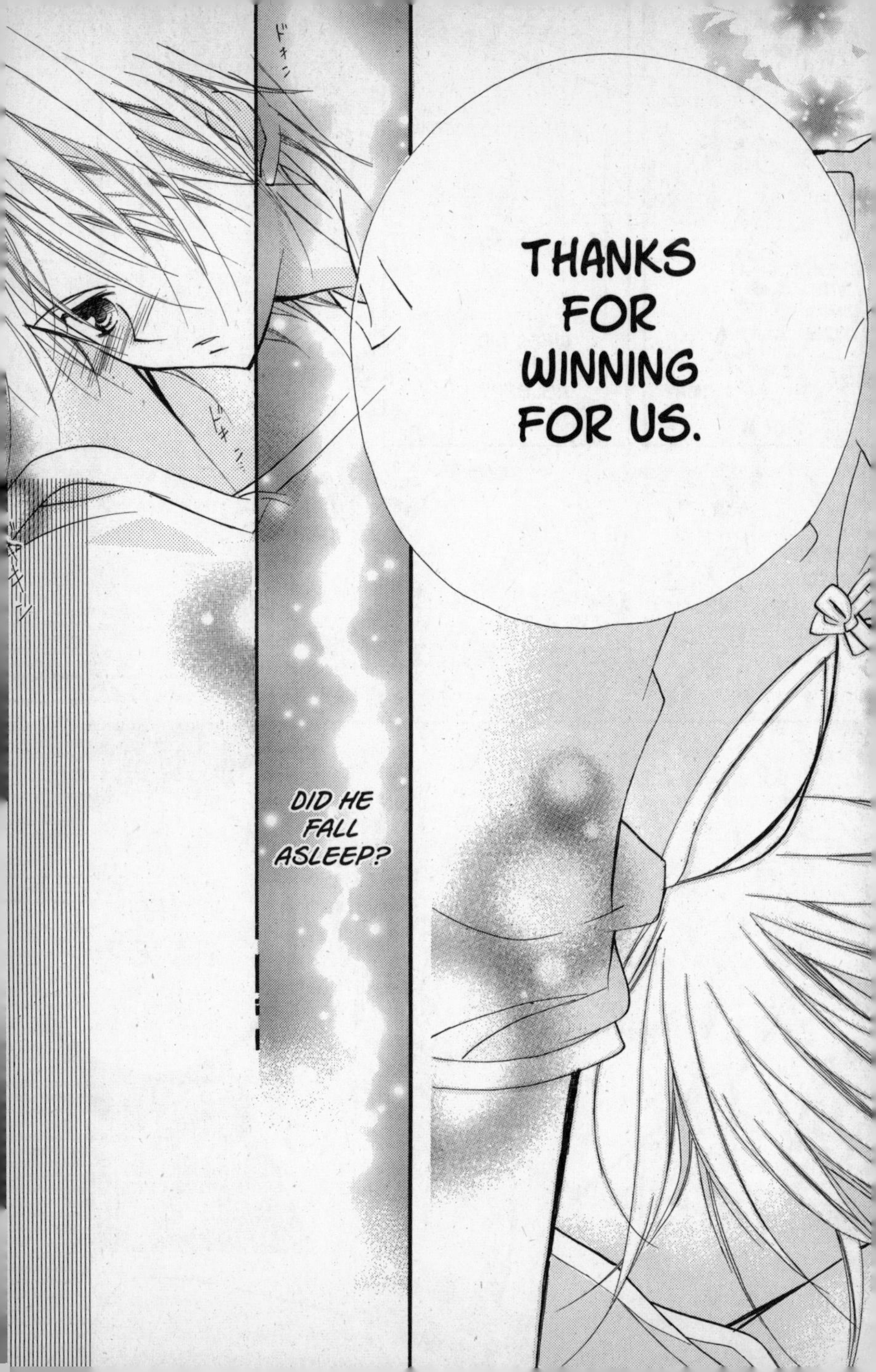
THANKS FOR WINNING FOR US.
DID HE FALL ASLEEP?

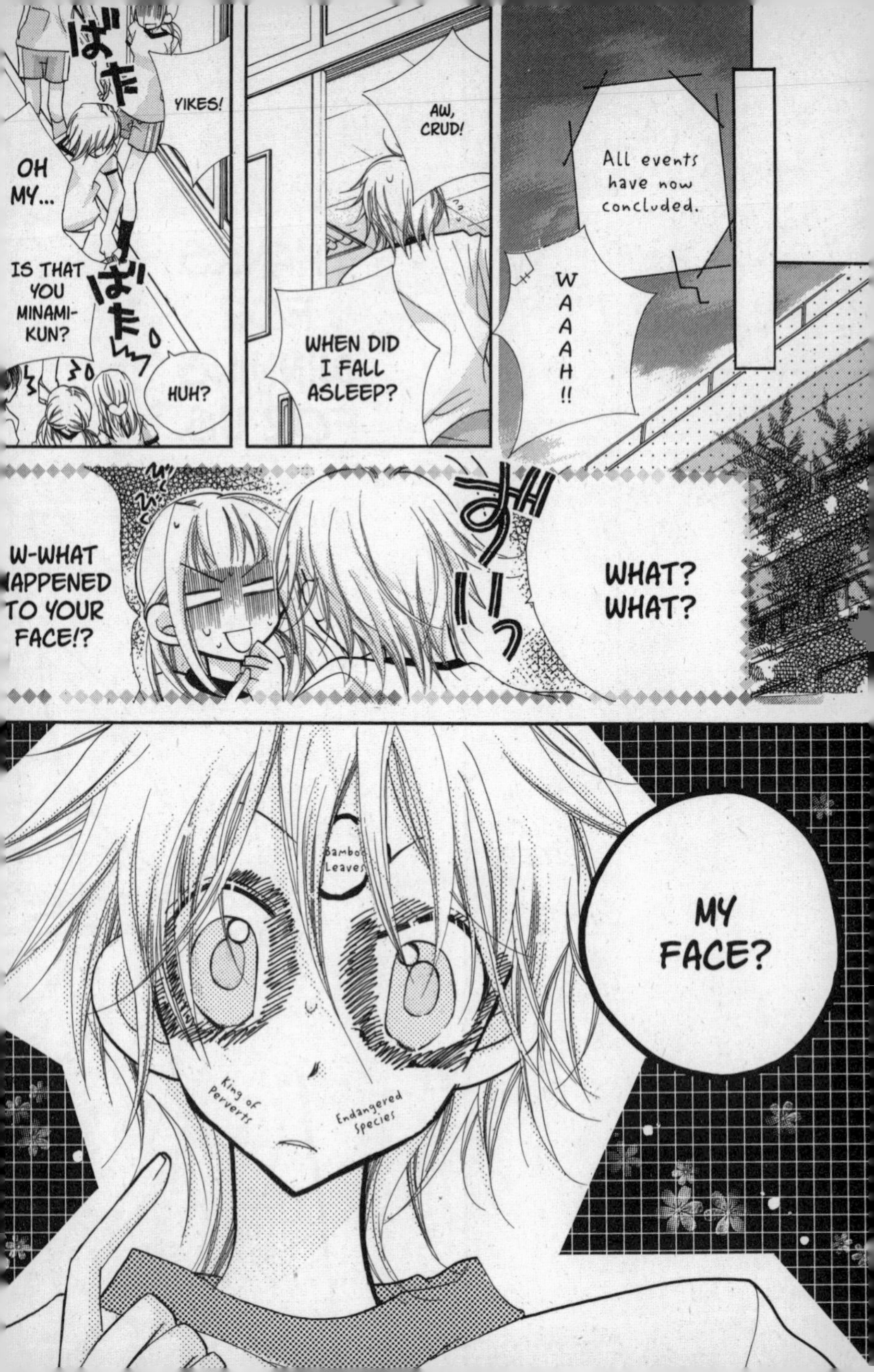
All events have now concluded.
WAAAAH!!
AW, CRUD!
WHEN DID I FALL ASLEEP?
YIKES!
OH MY...
IS THAT YOU MINAMI-KUN?
HUH?
WHAT? WHAT?
W-WHAT HAPPENED TO YOUR FACE!?
MY FACE?
Bamboo Leaves
Endangered Species
King of Perverts

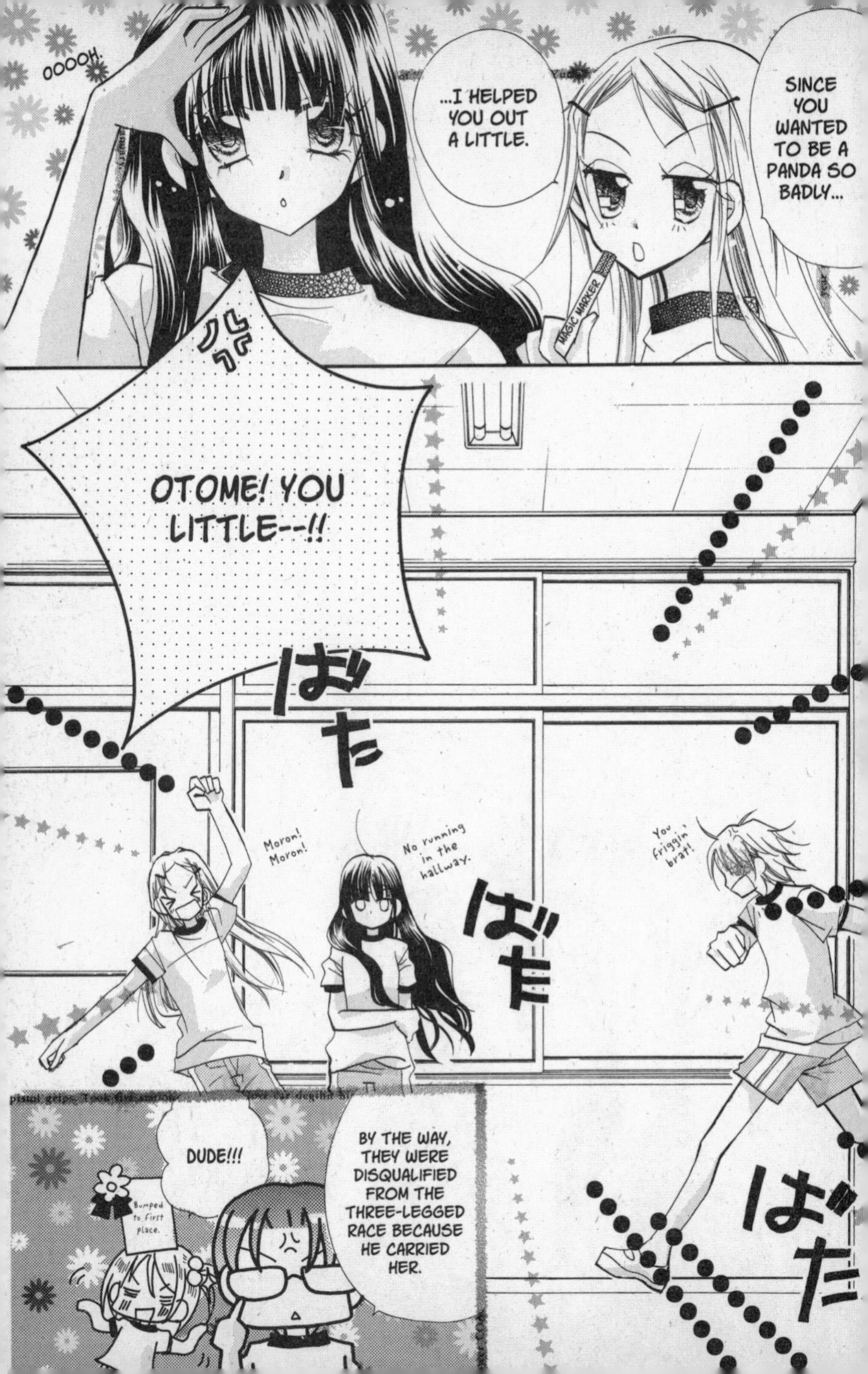
SINCE YOU WANTED TO BE A PANDA SO BADLY...
...I HELPED YOU OUT A LITTLE.
OOOOH.
MAGIC MARKER
OTOME! YOU LITTLE--!!
You friggin brat!
ばた
No running in the hallway.
Moron! Moron!
ばた
ばた
BY THE WAY, THEY WERE DISQUALIFIED FROM THE THREE-LEGGED RACE BECAUSE HE CARRIED HER.
DUDE!!!
Bumped to first place.

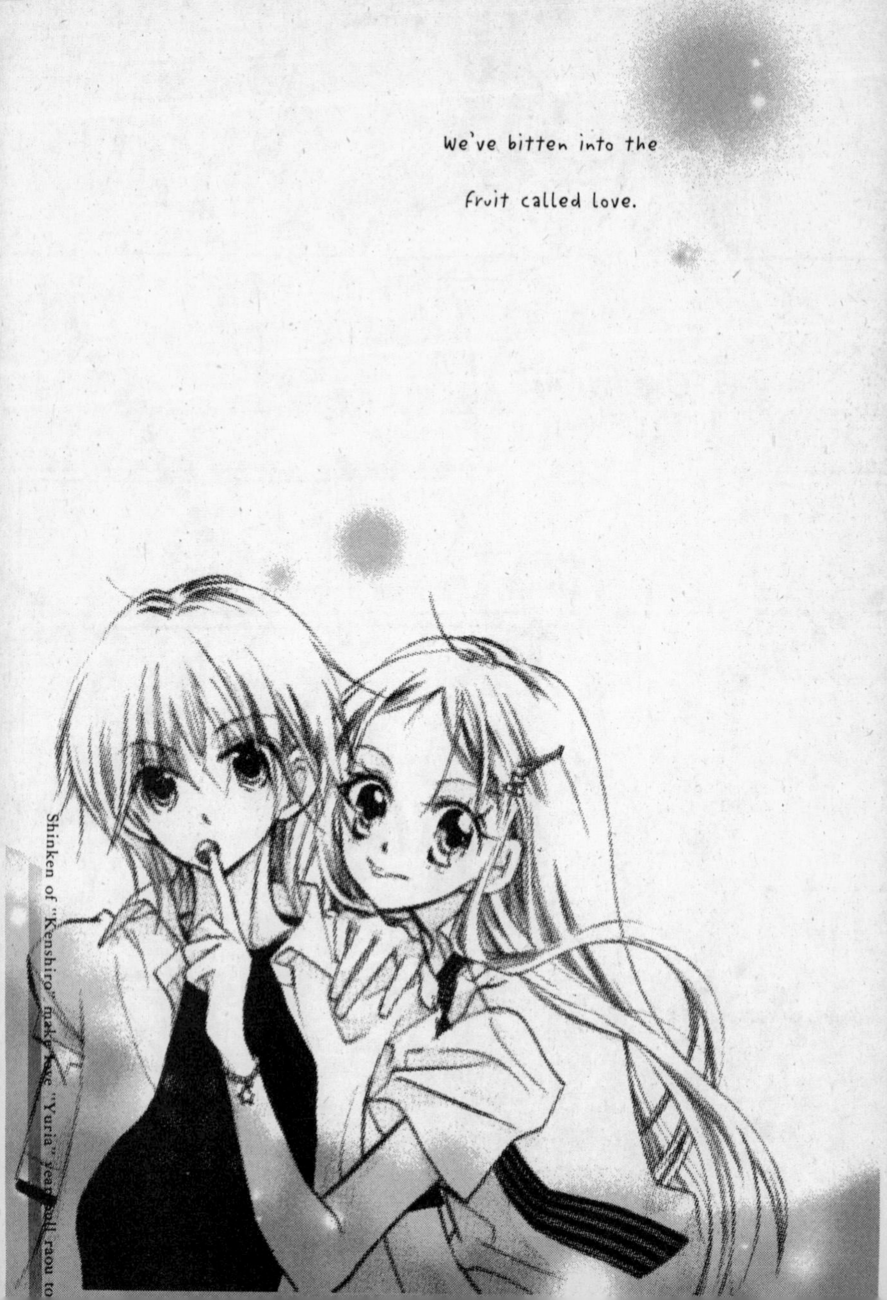
We've bitten into the
fruit called love.

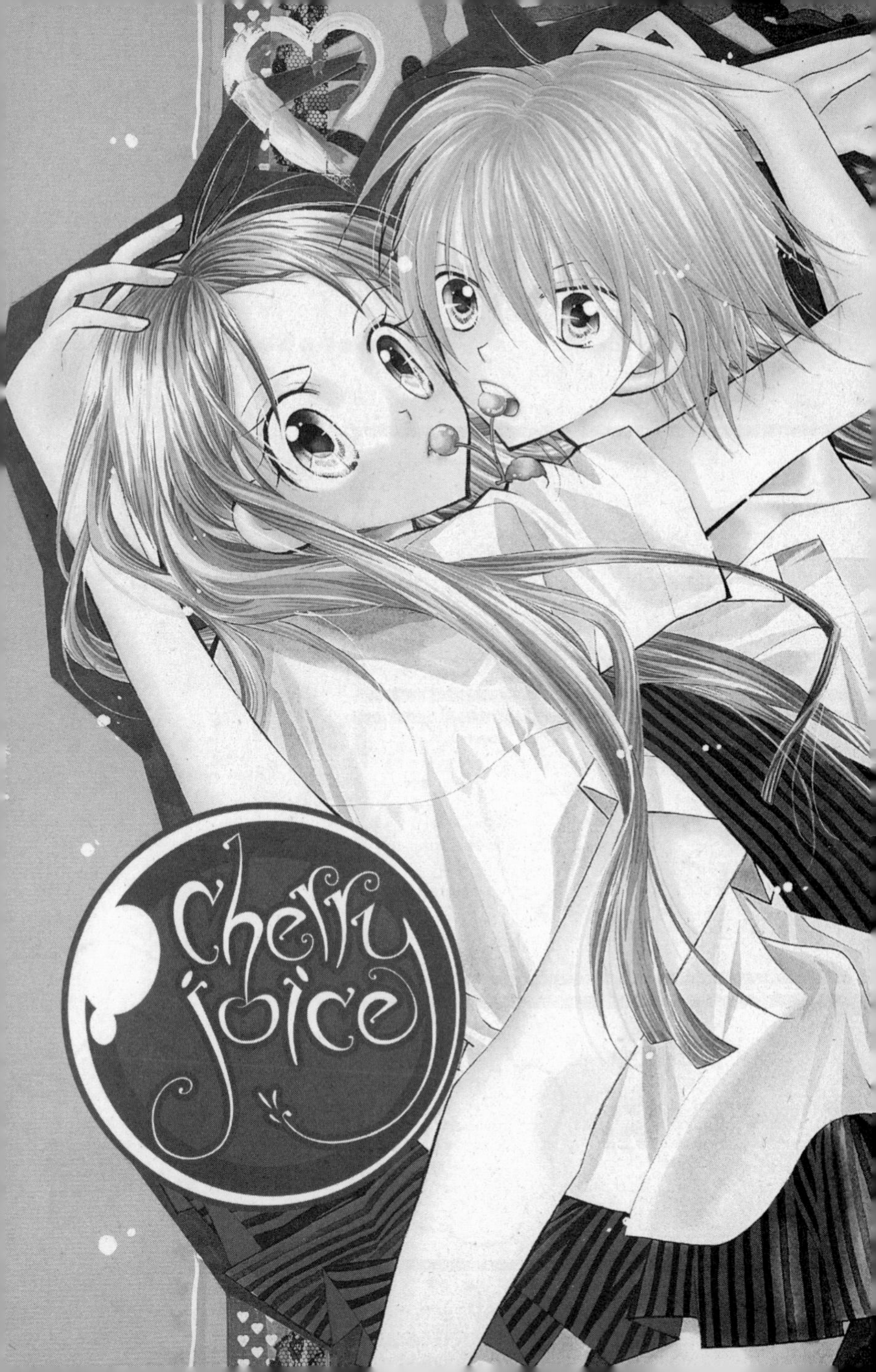
Cherry juice

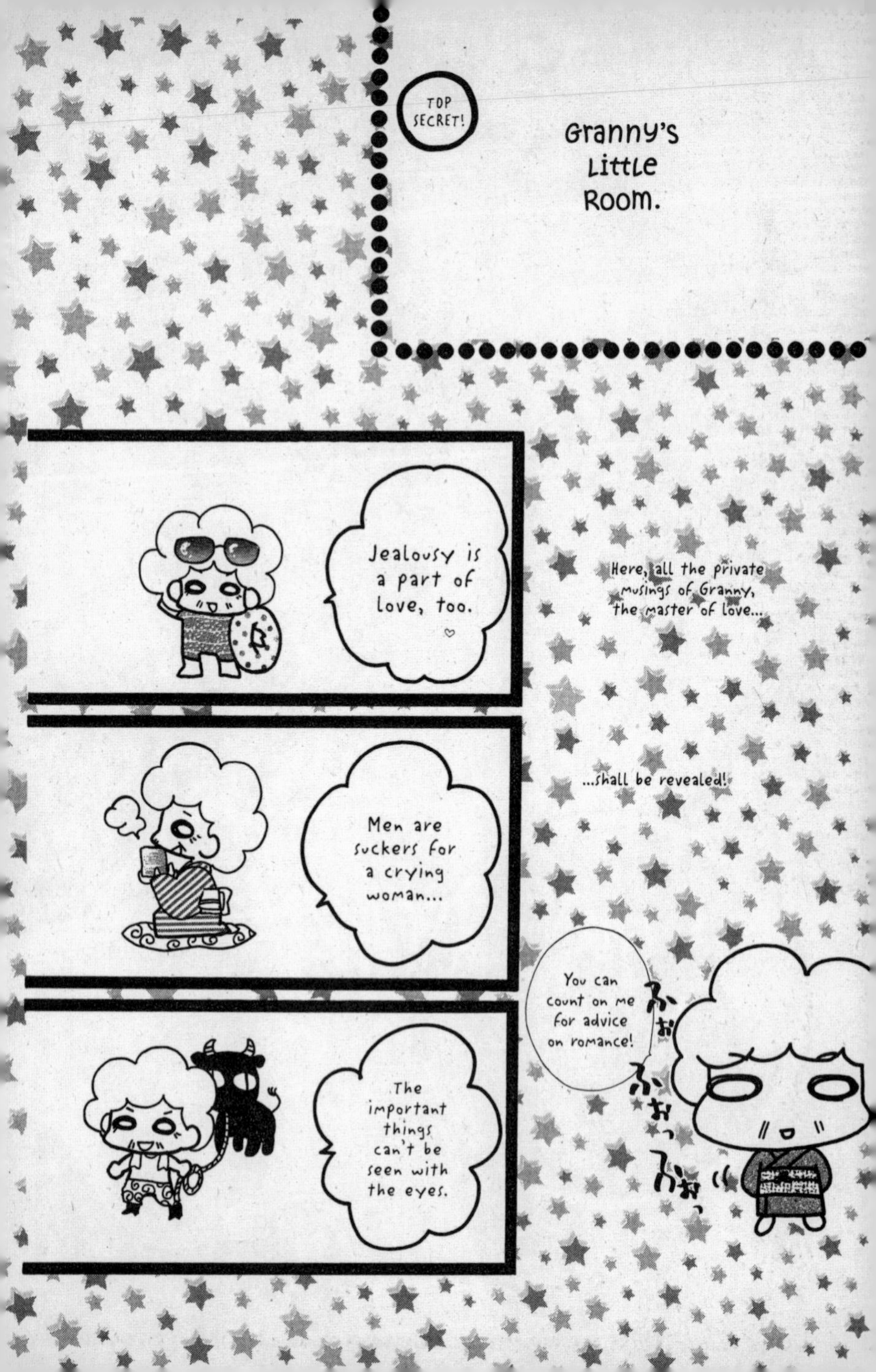
TOP SECRET!
Granny's Little Room.
Here, all the private musings of Granny, the master of love...
...shall be revealed!
You can count on me for advice on romance!
ふぉ ふぉっ ふぉっ
Jealousy is a part of love, too. ♡
Men are suckers for a crying woman...
The important things can't be seen with the eyes.

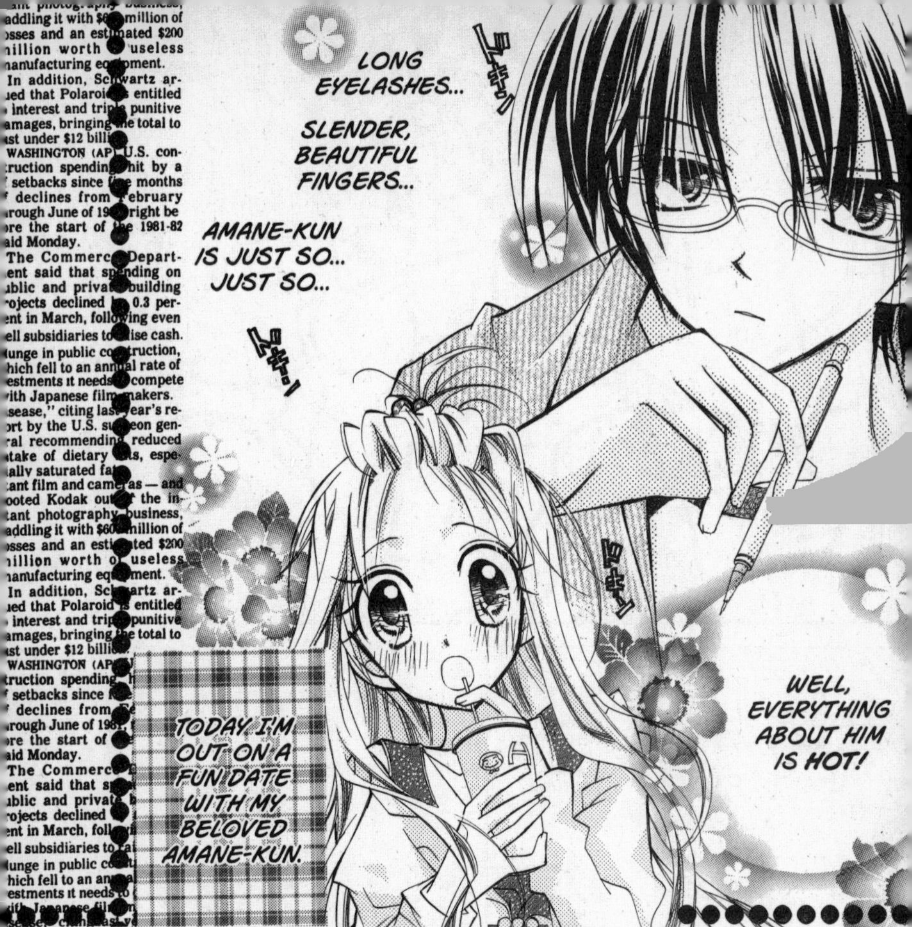
LONG EYELASHES...
SLENDER, BEAUTIFUL FINGERS...
AMANE-KUN IS JUST SO... JUST SO...
WELL, EVERYTHING ABOUT HIM IS HOT!
TODAY I'M OUT ON A FUN DATE WITH MY BELOVED AMANE-KUN.

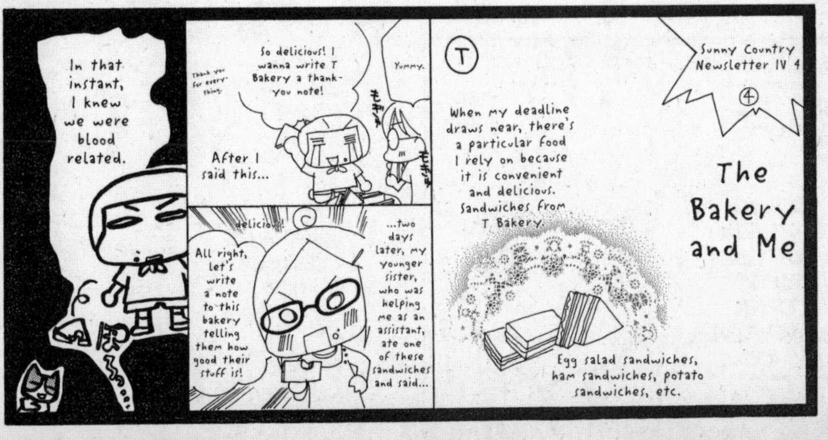
Sunny Country Newsletter IV 4
④
The Bakery and Me
T
When my deadline draws near, there's a particular food I rely on because it is convenient and delicious. Sandwiches from T Bakery.
Egg salad sandwiches, ham sandwiches, potato sandwiches, etc.
Yummy.
So delicious! I wanna write T Bakery a thank-you note!
Thank you for everything.
After I said this...
...two days later, my younger sister, who was helping me as an assistant, ate one of these sandwiches and said...
delicious!
All right, let's write a note to this bakery telling them how good their stuff is!
In that instant, I knew we were blood related.

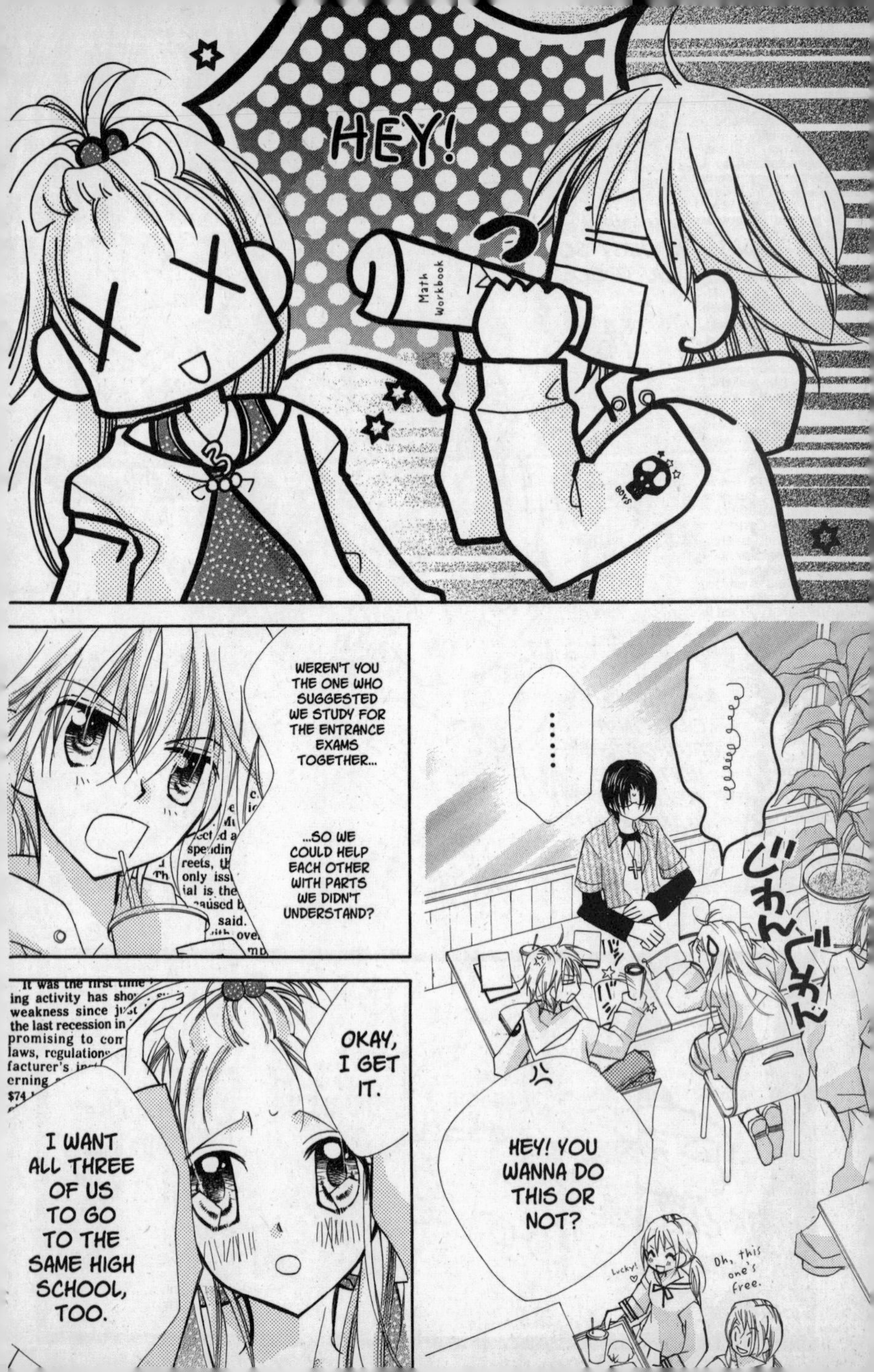
HEY!
Math Workbook
BOYS
......
じわんじわん
HEY! YOU WANNA DO THIS OR NOT?
Lucky!
Oh, this one's free.
WEREN'T YOU THE ONE WHO SUGGESTED WE STUDY FOR THE ENTRANCE EXAMS TOGETHER...
...SO WE COULD HELP EACH OTHER WITH PARTS WE DIDN'T UNDERSTAND?
OKAY, I GET IT.
I WANT ALL THREE OF US TO GO TO THE SAME HIGH SCHOOL, TOO.

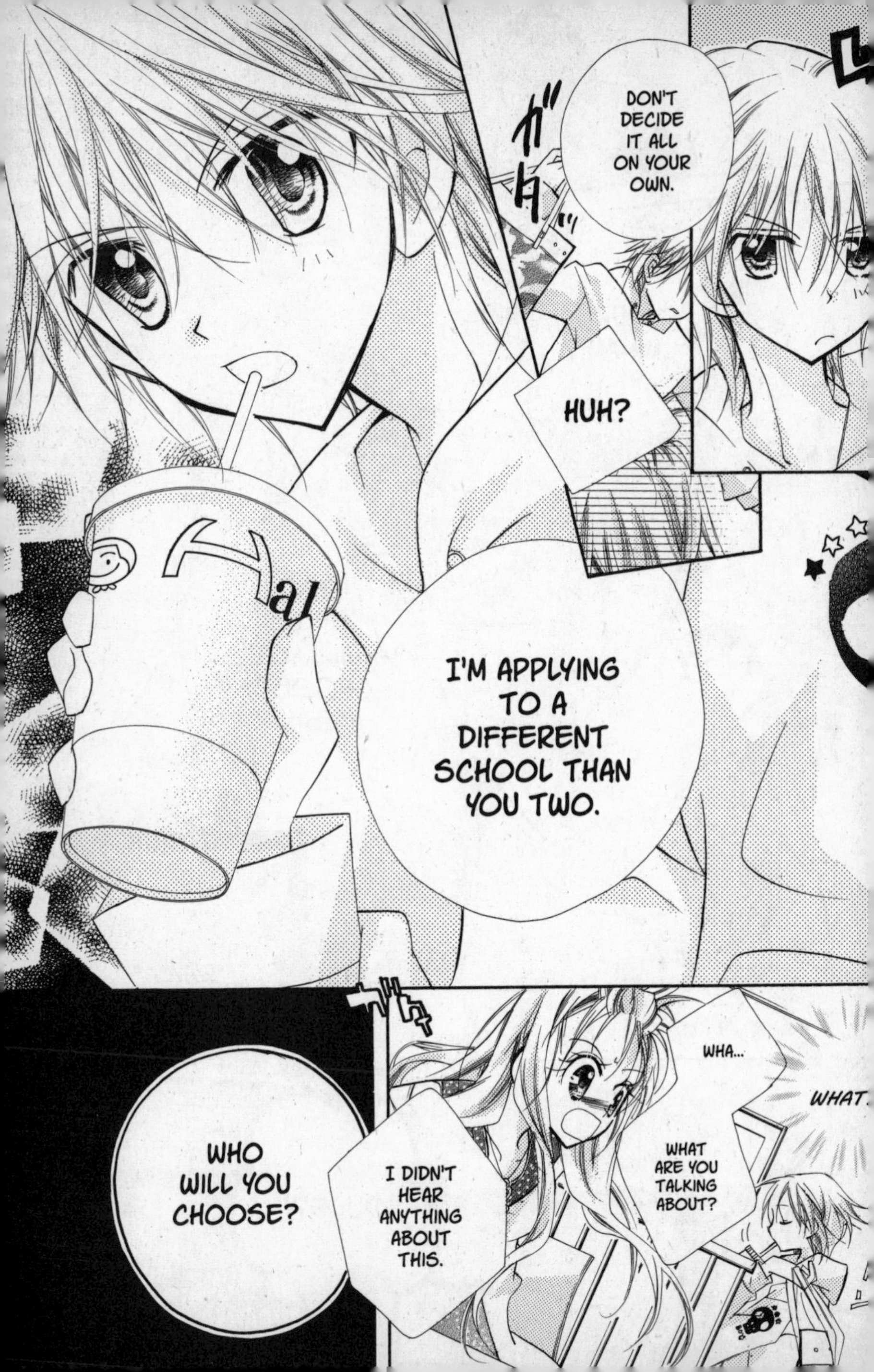
DON'T DECIDE IT ALL ON YOUR OWN.
HUH?
I'M APPLYING TO A DIFFERENT SCHOOL THAN YOU TWO.
WHA...
WHAT.
WHAT ARE YOU TALKING ABOUT?
I DIDN'T HEAR ANYTHING ABOUT THIS.
WHO WILL YOU CHOOSE?

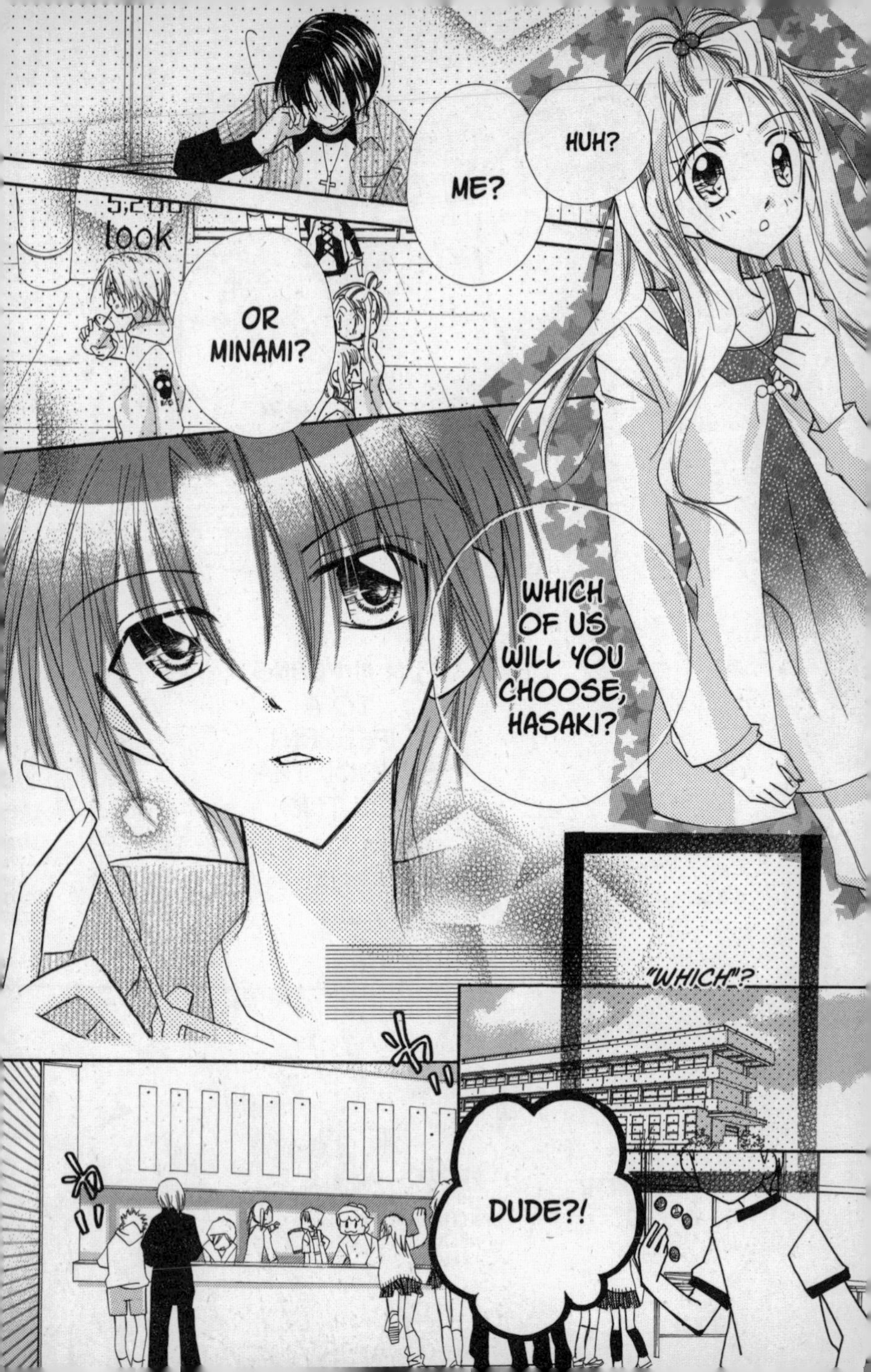
HUH?
ME?
look
OR MINAMI?
WHICH OF US WILL YOU CHOOSE, HASAKI?
"WHICH"?
DUDE?!

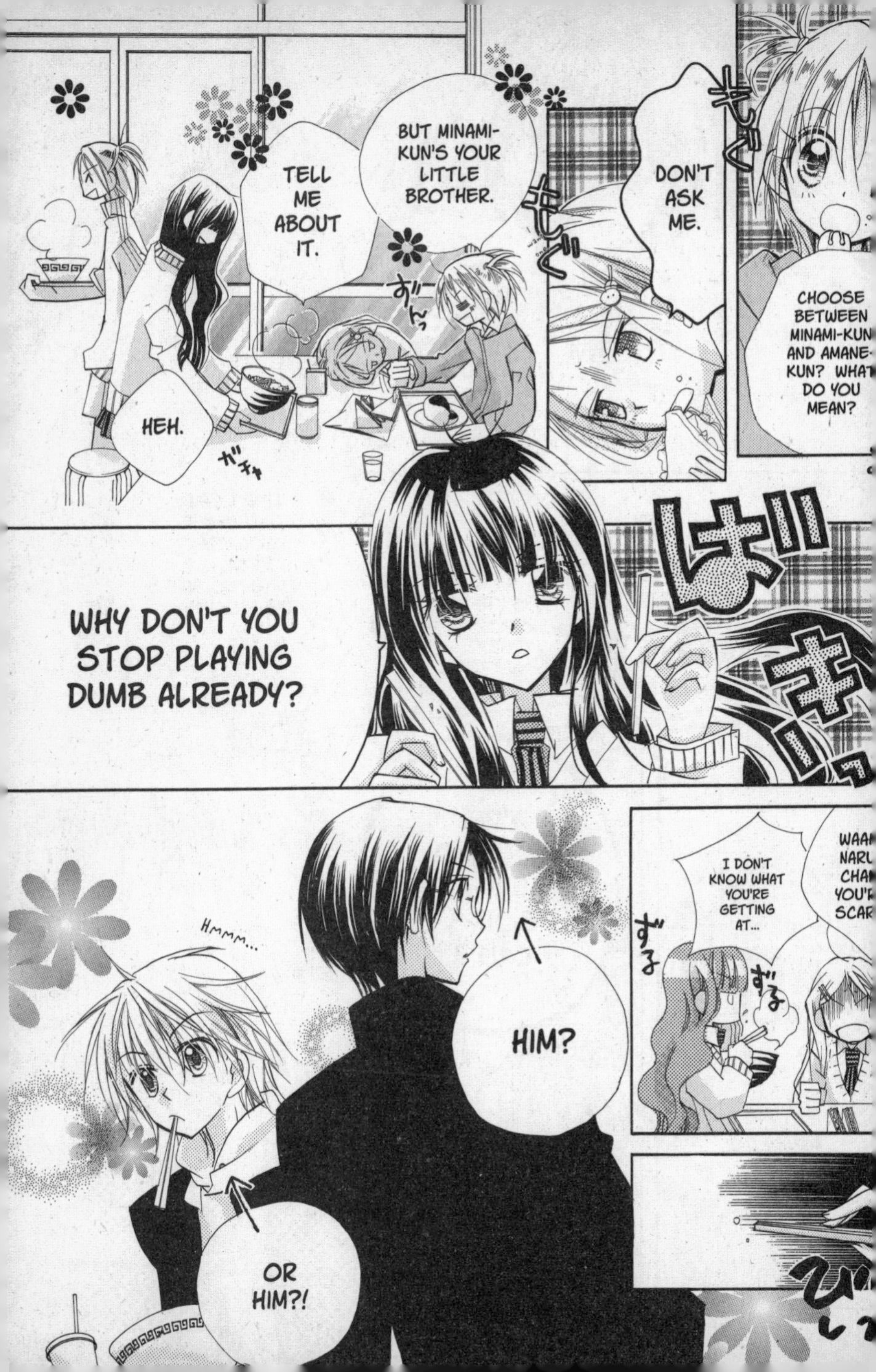
CHOOSE BETWEEN MINAMI-KUN AND AMANE-KUN? WHAT DO YOU MEAN?
DON'T ASK ME.
BUT MINAMI-KUN'S YOUR LITTLE BROTHER.
TELL ME ABOUT IT.
HEH.
WHY DON'T YOU STOP PLAYING DUMB ALREADY?
I DON'T KNOW WHAT YOU'RE GETTING AT...
HIM?
HMMM...
OR HIM?!

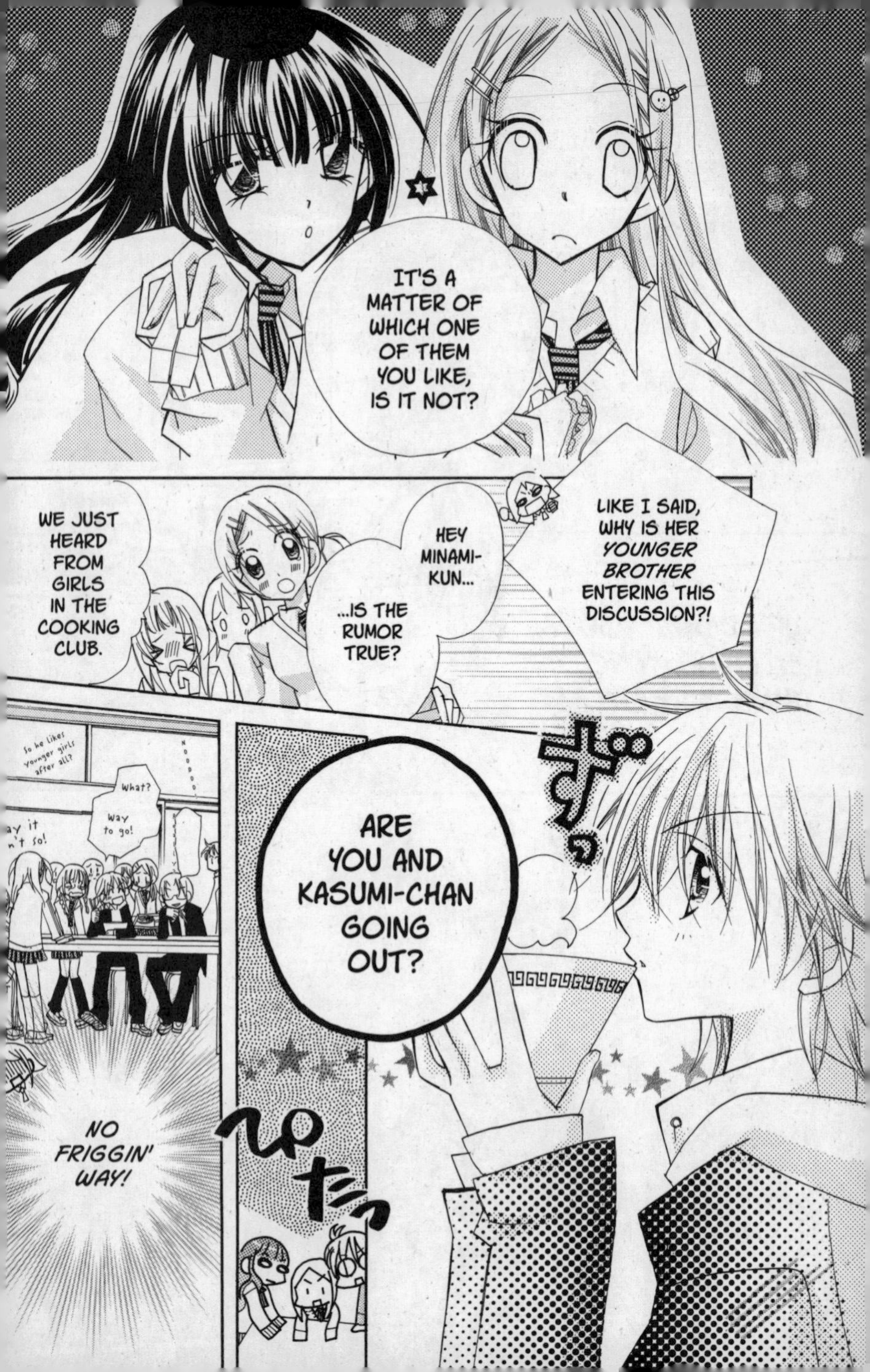
IT'S A MATTER OF WHICH ONE OF THEM YOU LIKE, IS IT NOT?
LIKE I SAID, WHY IS HER *YOUNGER BROTHER* ENTERING THIS DISCUSSION?!
HEY MINAMI-KUN...
...IS THE RUMOR TRUE?
WE JUST HEARD FROM GIRLS IN THE COOKING CLUB.
ARE YOU AND KASUMI-CHAN GOING OUT?
NOOOOOO
What?
Way to go!
So he likes younger girls after all?
NO FRIGGIN' WAY!

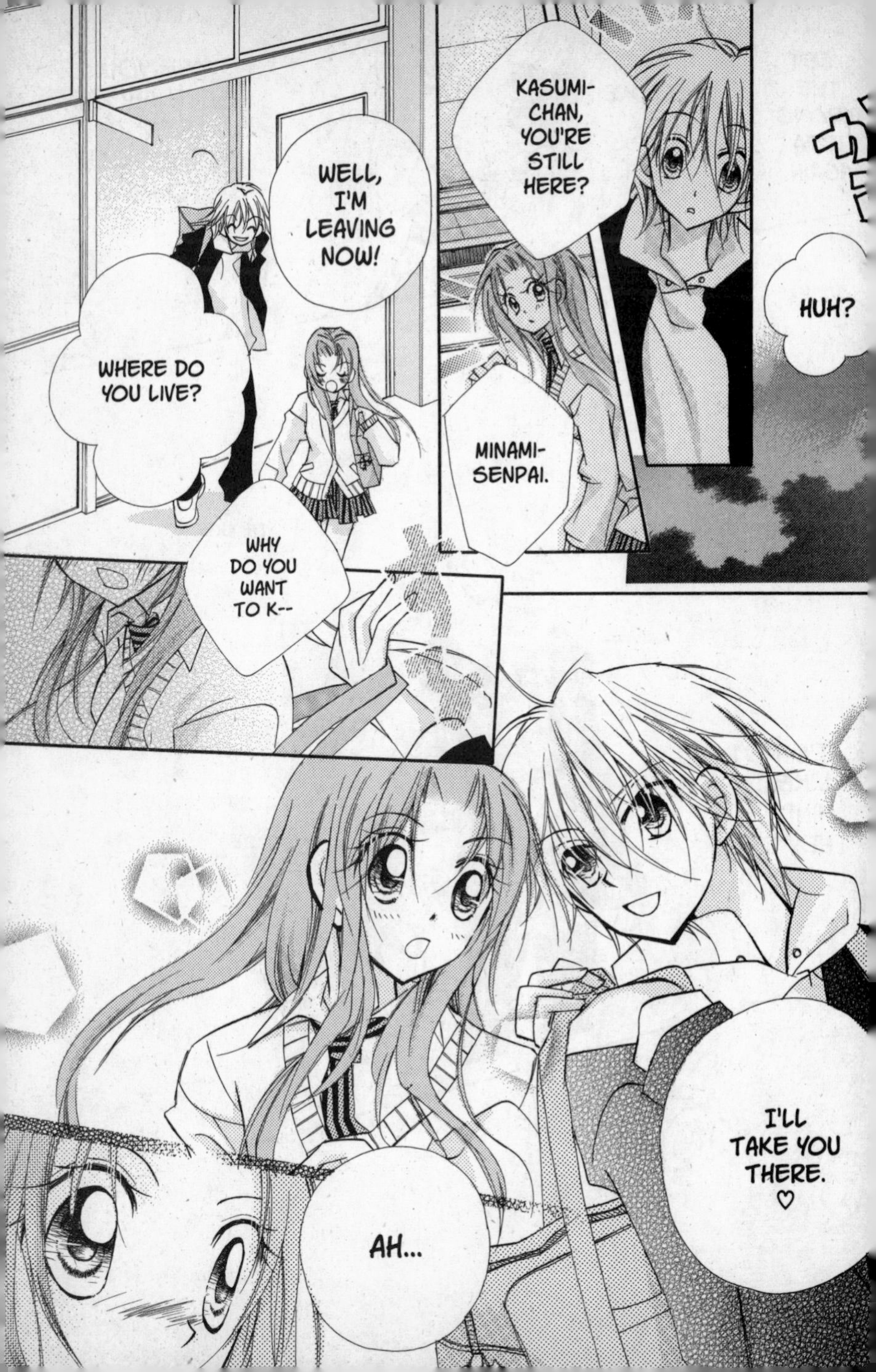
KASUMI-CHAN, YOU'RE STILL HERE?
HUH?
MINAMI-SENPAI.
WELL, I'M LEAVING NOW!
WHERE DO YOU LIVE?
WHY DO YOU WANT TO K--
I'LL TAKE YOU THERE. ♡
AH...

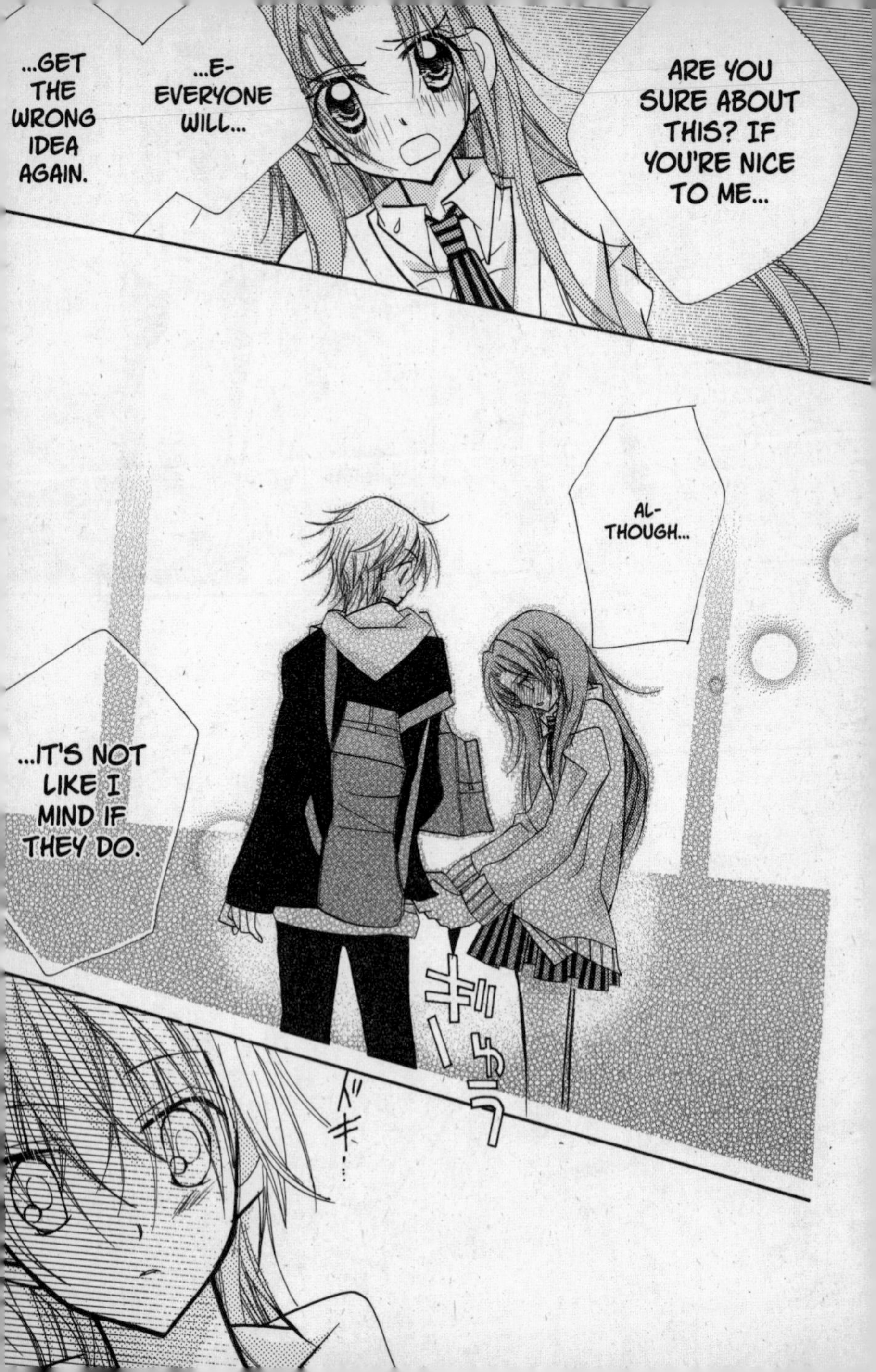
ARE YOU SURE ABOUT THIS? IF YOU'RE NICE TO ME...
...E- EVERYONE WILL...
...GET THE WRONG IDEA AGAIN.
AL- THOUGH...
...IT'S NOT LIKE I MIND IF THEY DO.
ぎゅう
ドキ…

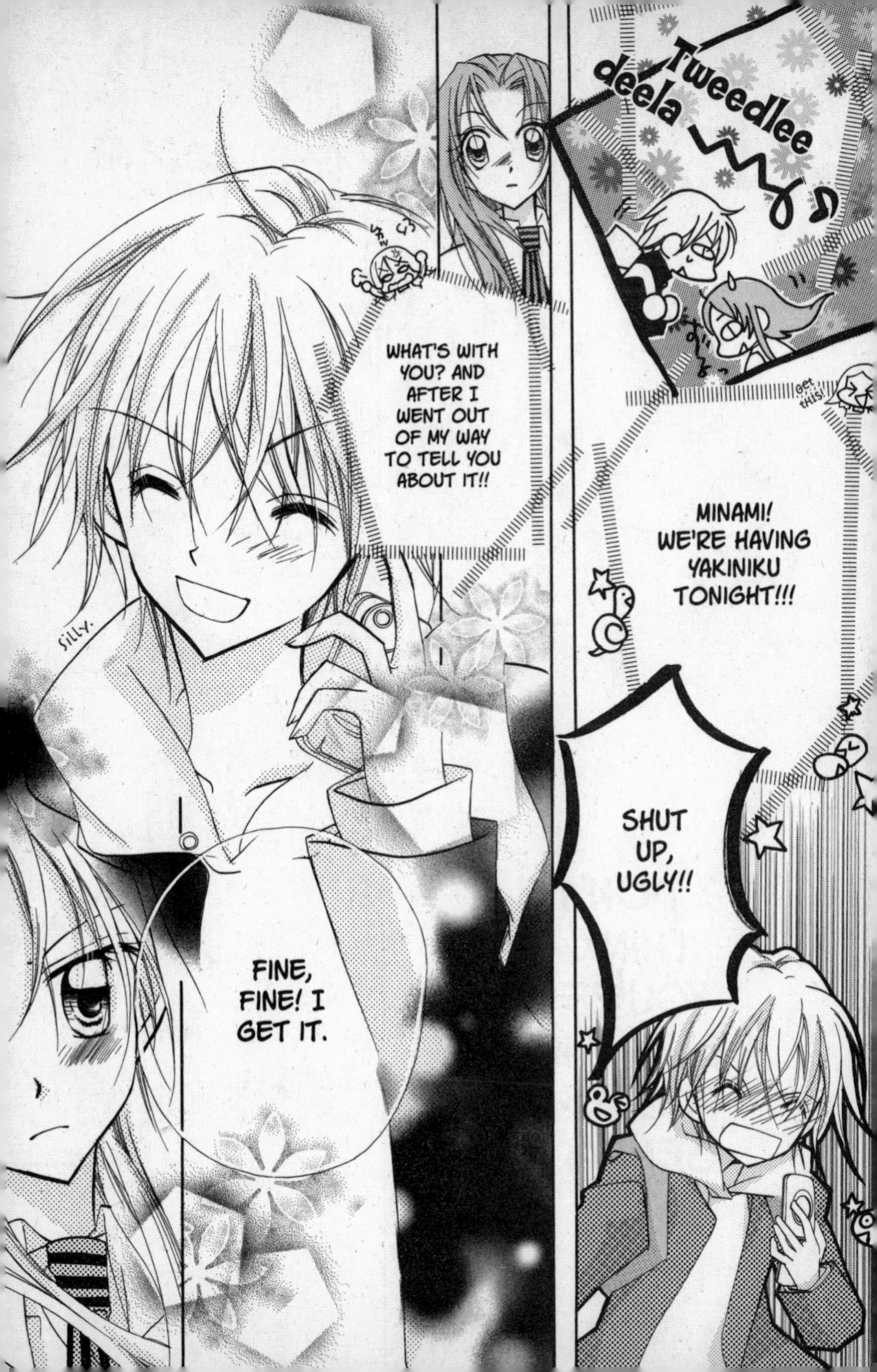
Tweedlee deela
Get this!
MINAMI! WE'RE HAVING YAKINIKU TONIGHT!!!
SHUT UP, UGLY!!
WHAT'S WITH YOU? AND AFTER I WENT OUT OF MY WAY TO TELL YOU ABOUT IT!!
silly.
FINE, FINE! I GET IT.

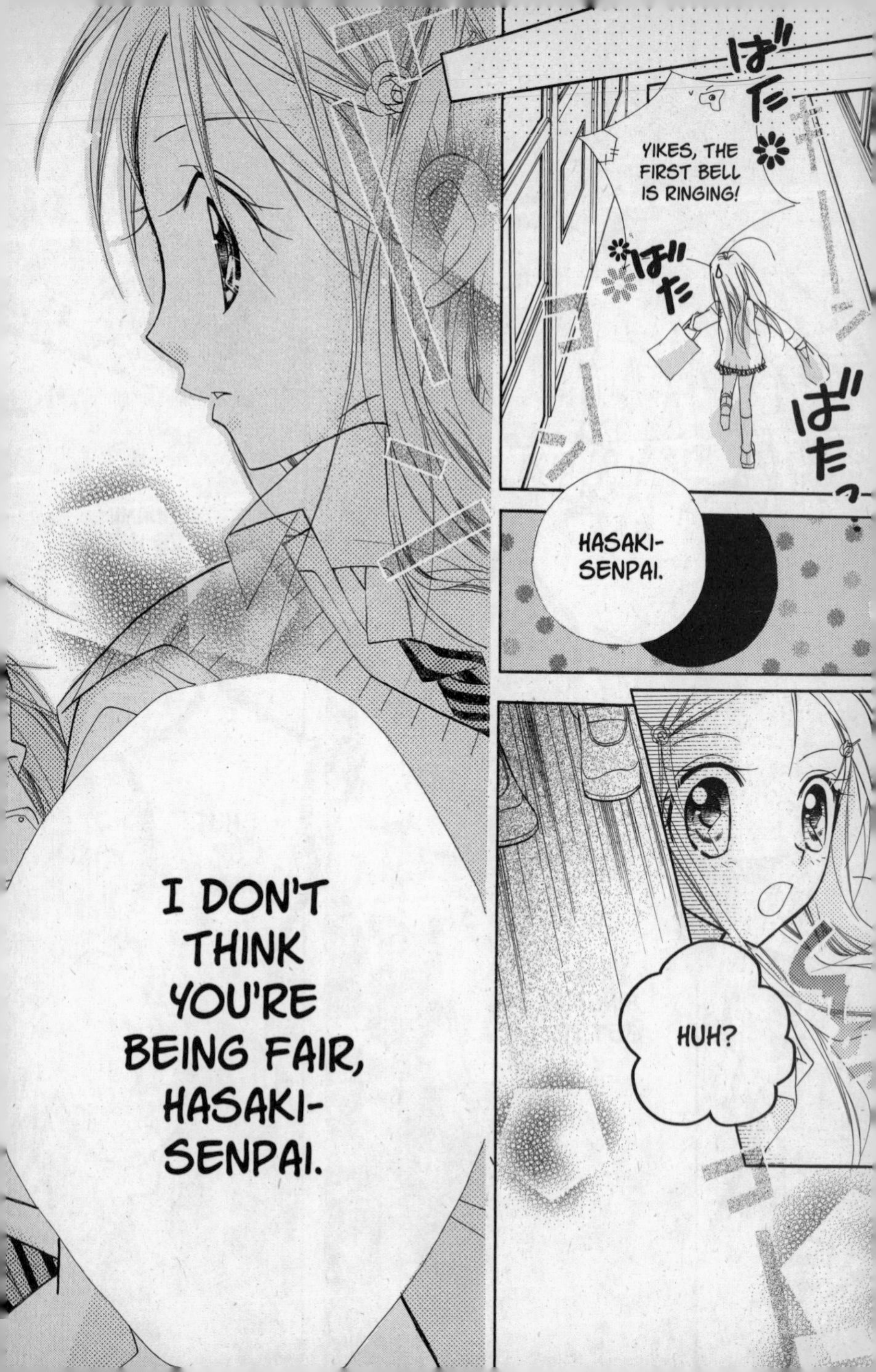
ばた
YIKES, THE FIRST BELL IS RINGING!
ばた
ばたっ
HASAKI-SENPAI.
HUH?
I DON'T THINK YOU'RE BEING FAIR, HASAKI-SENPAI.

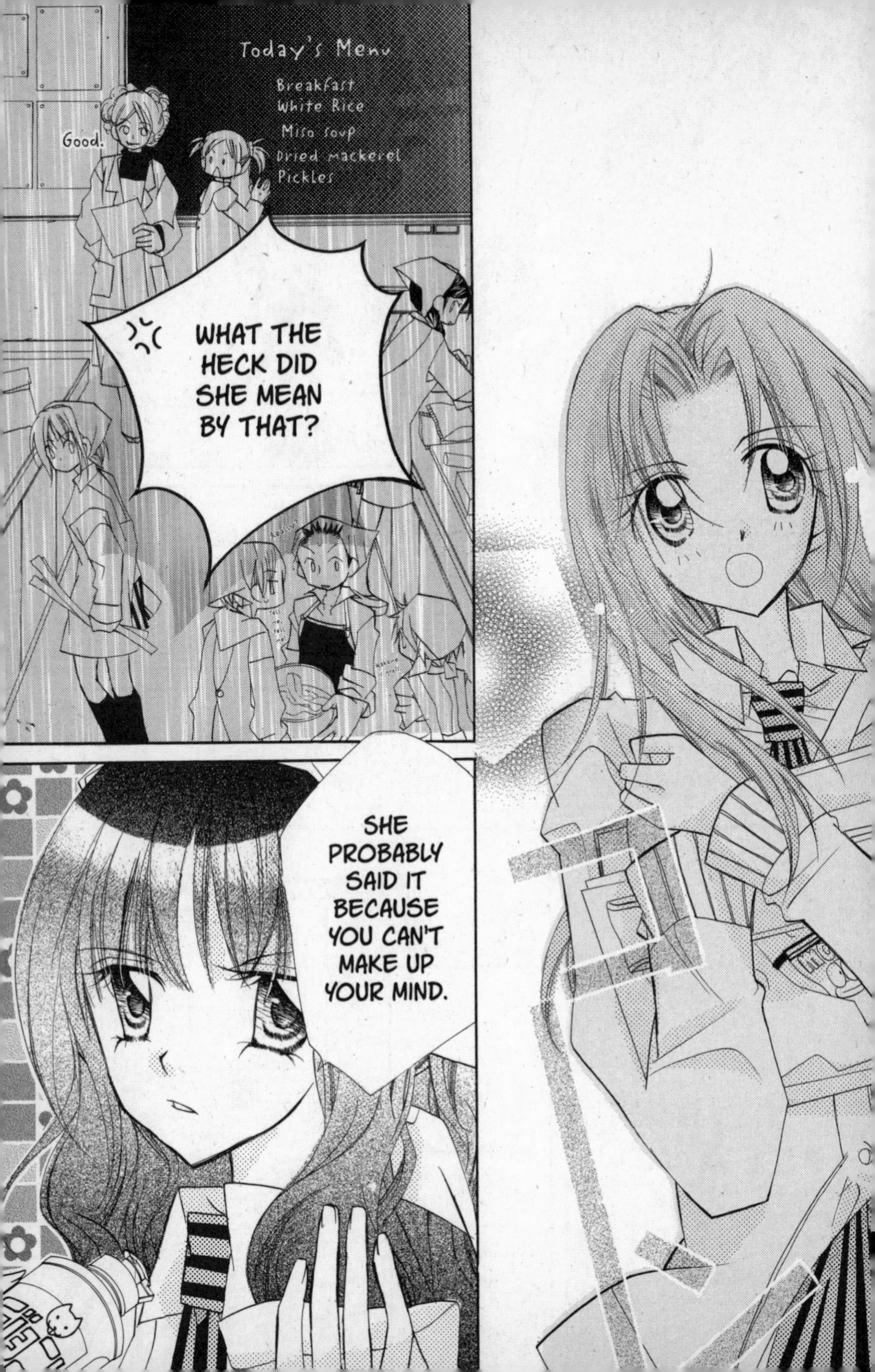
Today's Menu
Breakfast
White Rice
Miso soup
Dried mackerel
Pickles
Good.
WHAT THE HECK DID SHE MEAN BY THAT?
SHE PROBABLY SAID IT BECAUSE YOU CAN'T MAKE UP YOUR MIND.

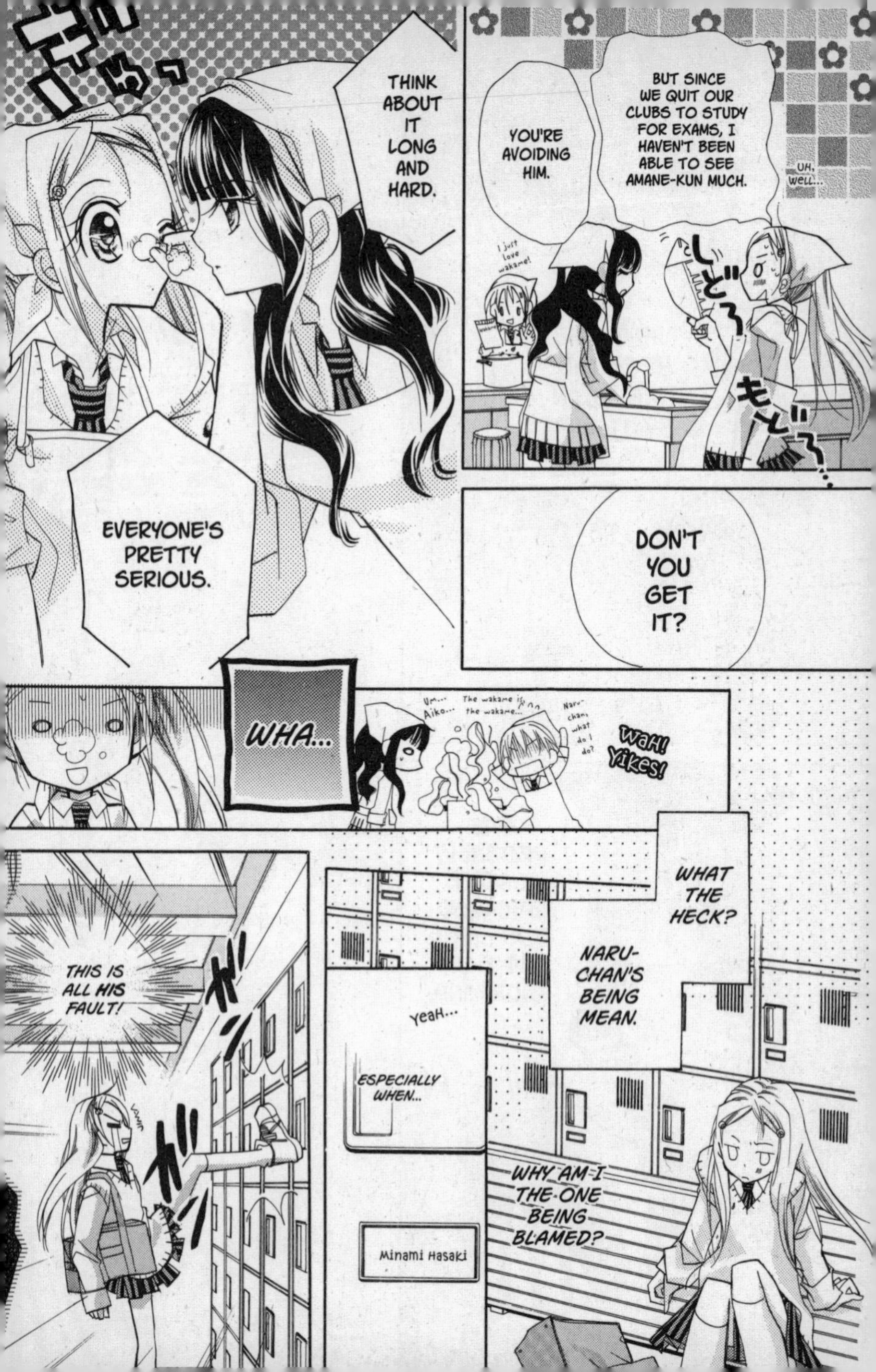
Uh, well...
But since we quit our clubs to study for exams, I haven't been able to see Amane-kun much.
You're avoiding him.
I just love wakame!
Don't you get it?
Think about it long and hard.
Everyone's pretty serious.
Wah! Yikes!
Naru-chan, what do I do?
The wakame is, the wakame...
Um... Aiko...
WHA...
What the heck?
Naru-chan's being mean.
Why am I the one being blamed?
Yeah...
Especially when...
Minami Hasaki
This is all his fault!

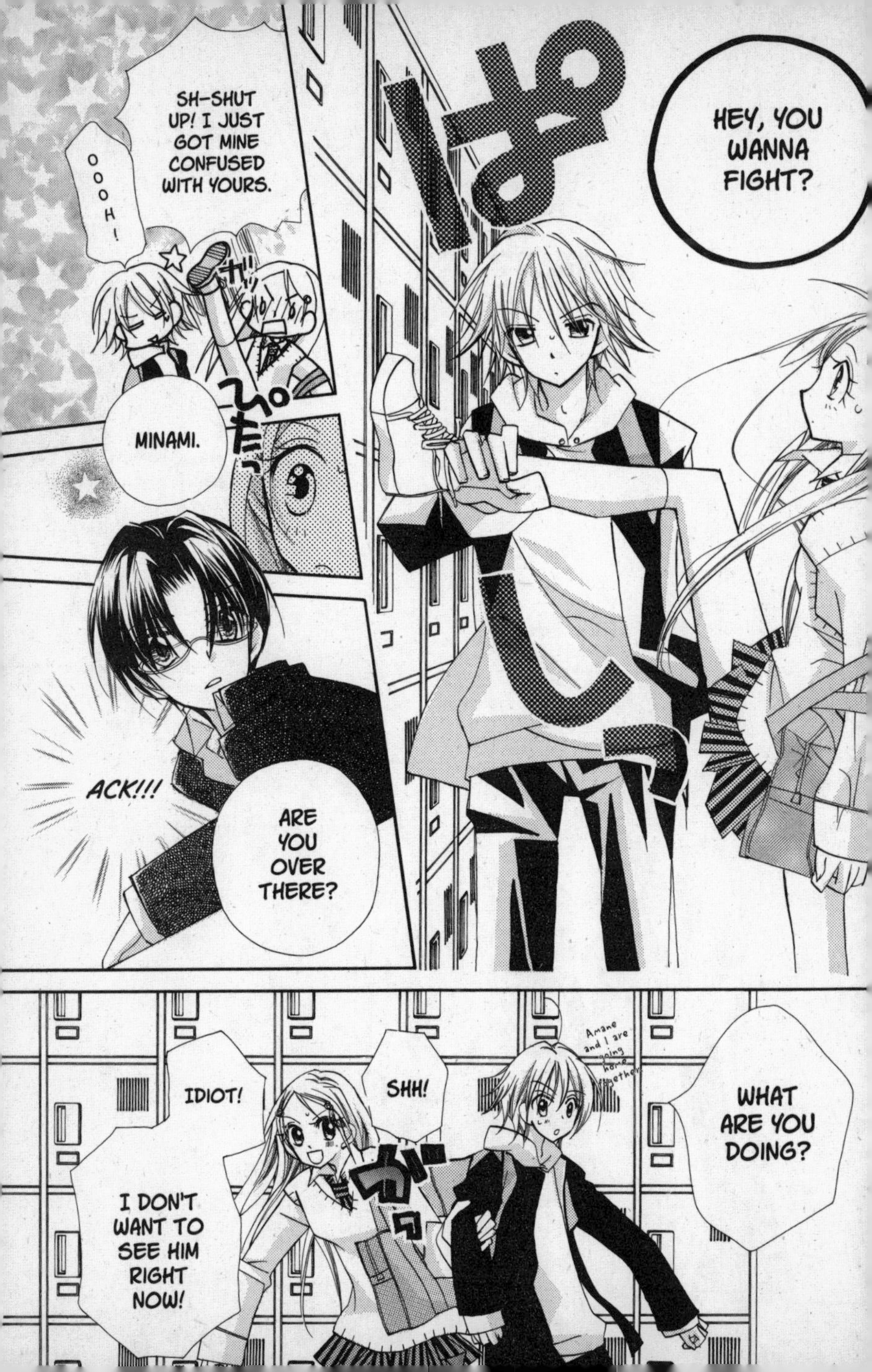
HEY, YOU WANNA FIGHT?
SH-SHUT UP! I JUST GOT MINE CONFUSED WITH YOURS.
OOOH!
MINAMI.
ARE YOU OVER THERE?
ACK!!!
WHAT ARE YOU DOING?
Amane and I are going home together.
SHH!
IDIOT!
I DON'T WANT TO SEE HIM RIGHT NOW!

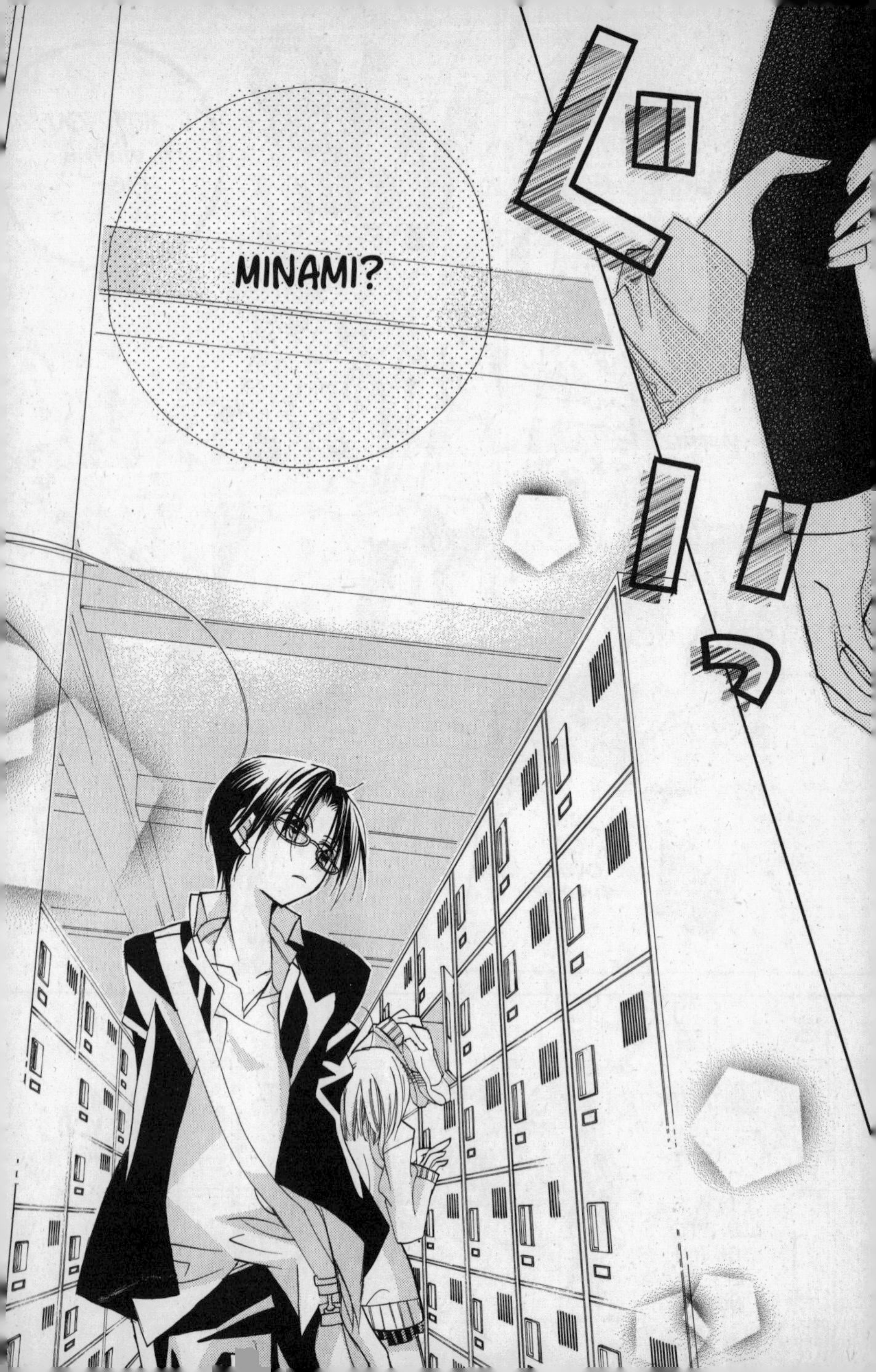
MINAMI?

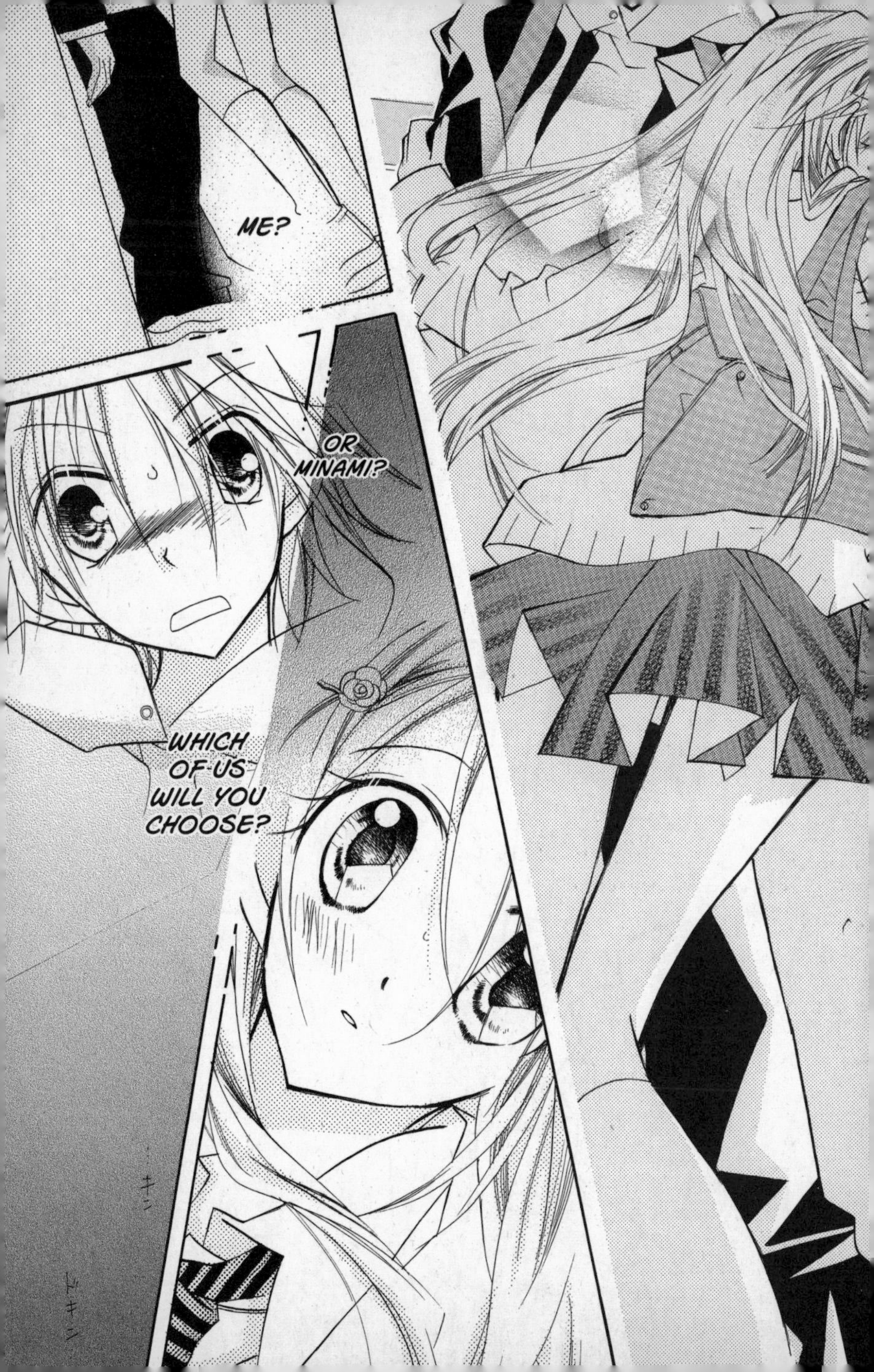
ME?
OR MINAMI?
WHICH OF US WILL YOU CHOOSE?
ドキン

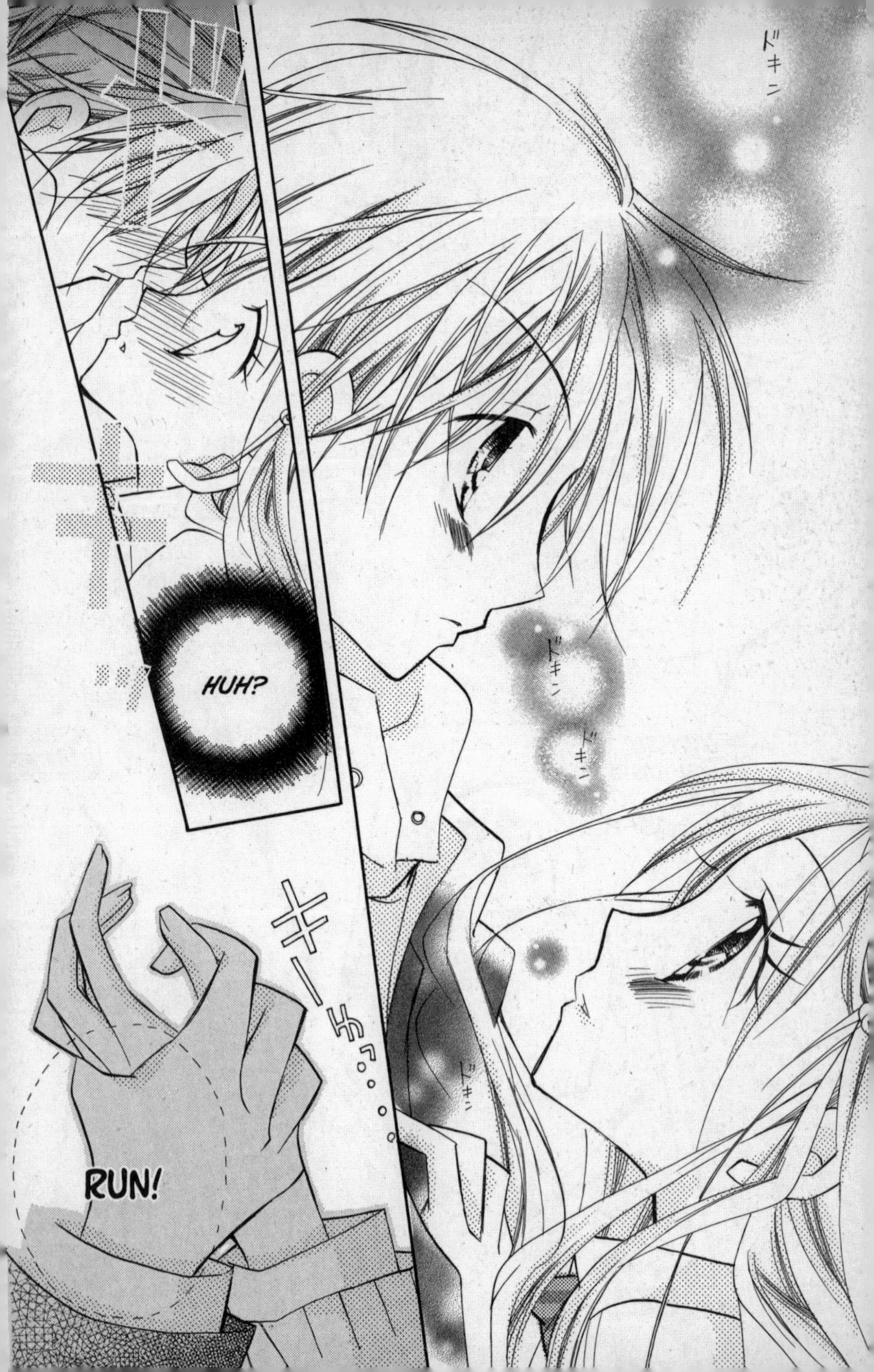
ドキン
ドキン
ドキン
ドキン
HUH?
RUN!

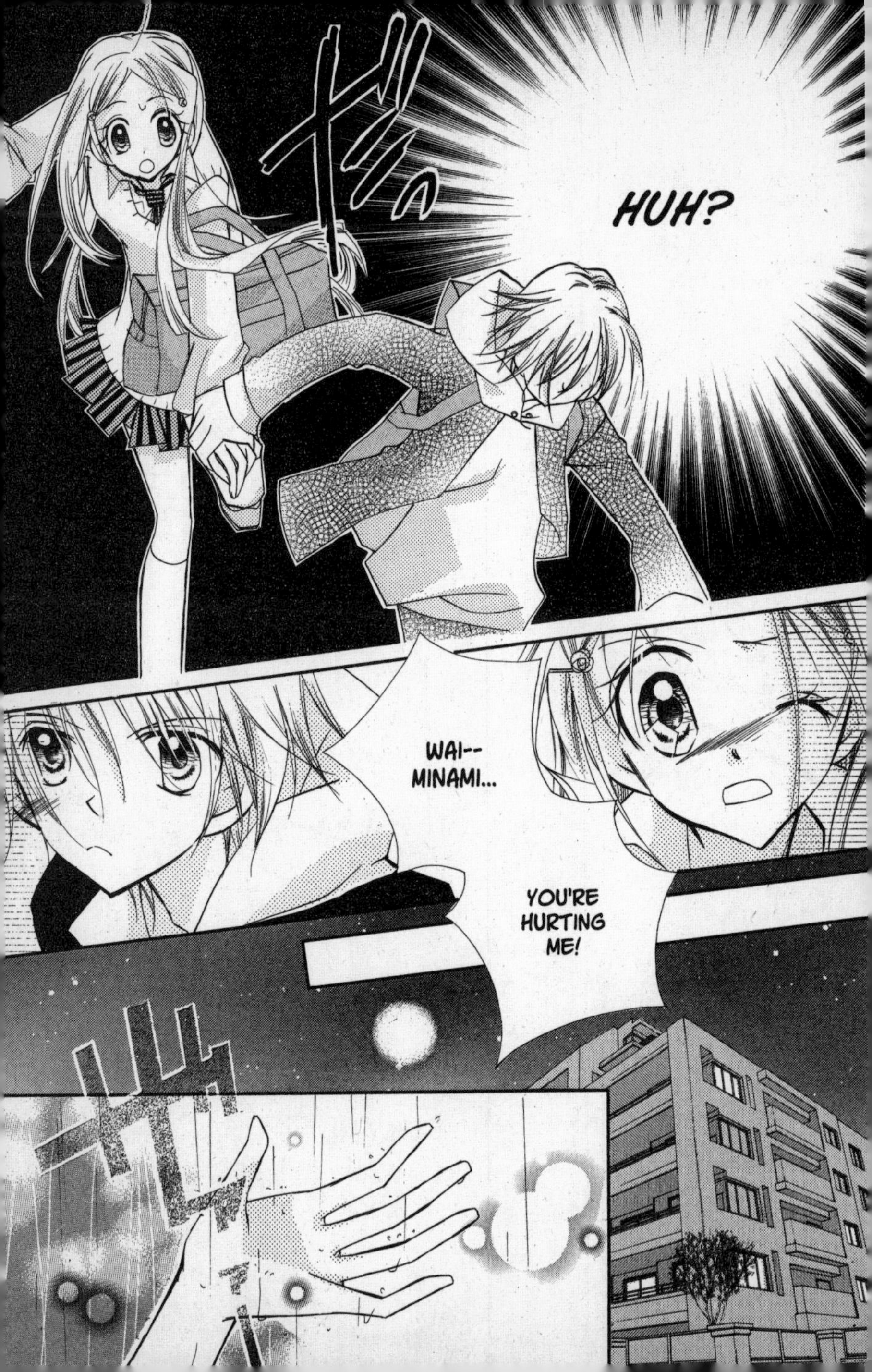
HUH?
WAI--
MINAMI...
YOU'RE
HURTING
ME!

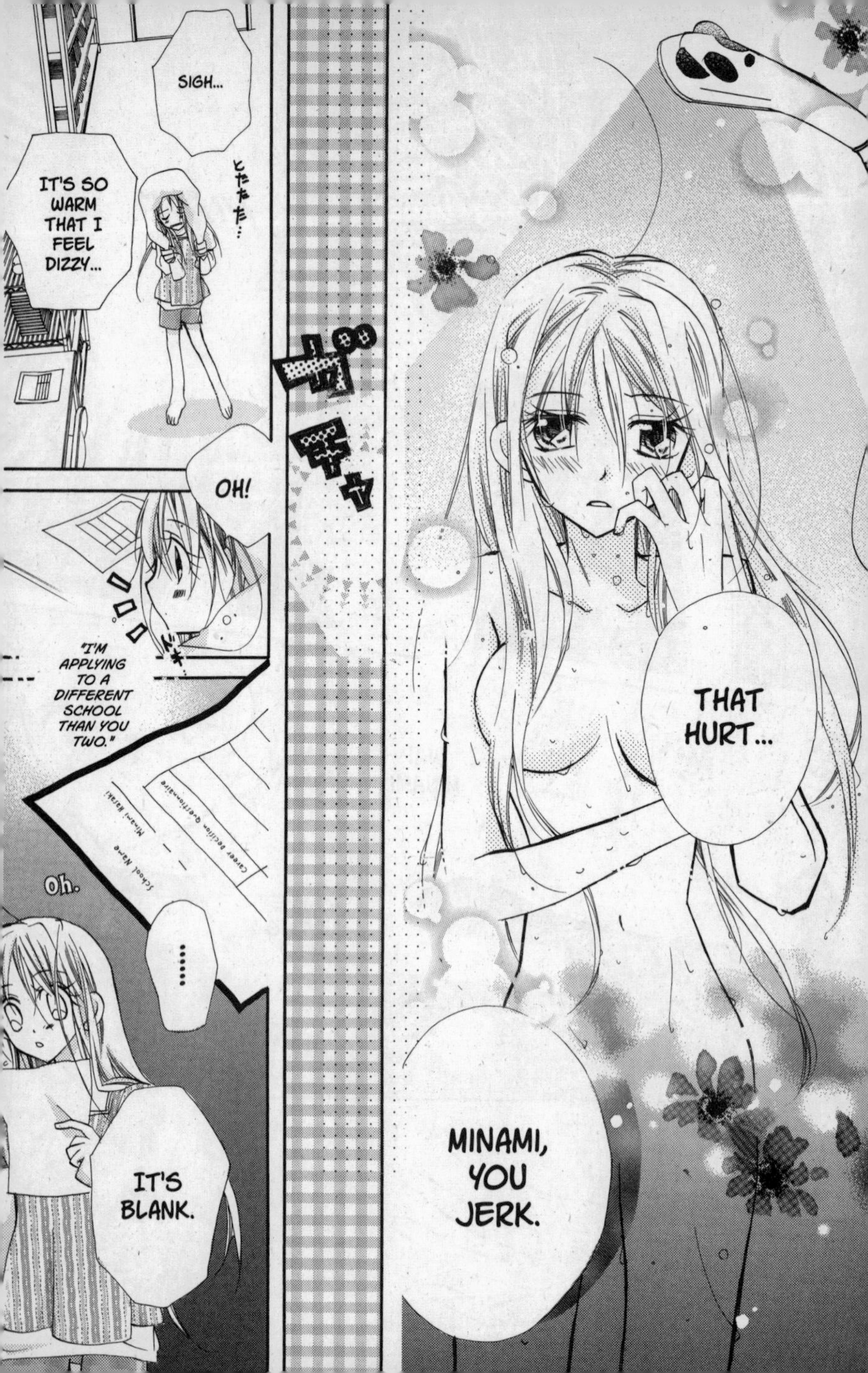
THAT HURT...
MINAMI, YOU JERK.
SIGH...
IT'S SO WARM THAT I FEEL DIZZY...
とたたた…
OH!
"I'M APPLYING TO A DIFFERENT SCHOOL THAN YOU TWO."
Career Decision Questionnaire
Minami Kazaki
School Name
Oh.
......
IT'S BLANK.

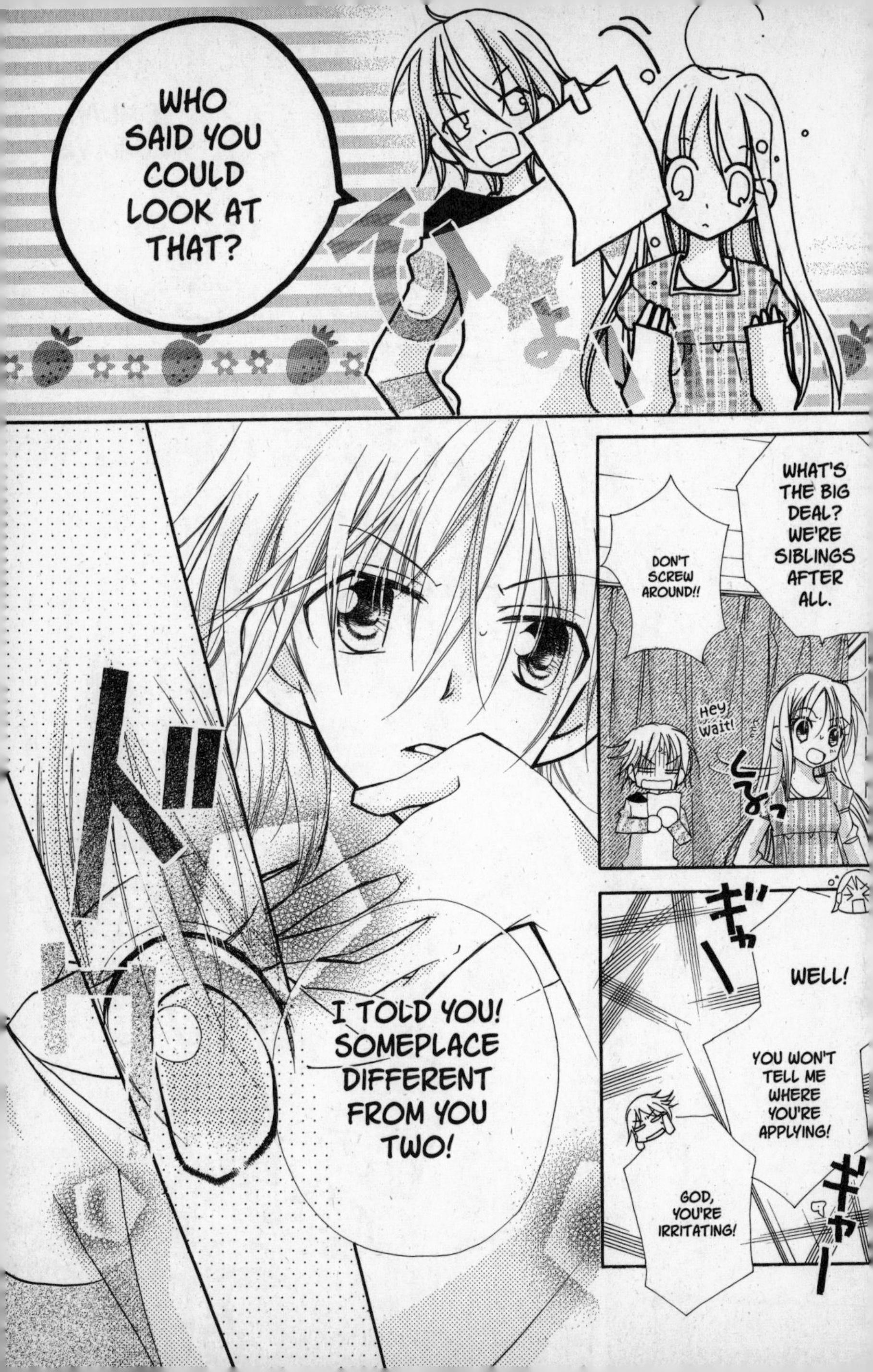
WHO SAID YOU COULD LOOK AT THAT?
WHAT'S THE BIG DEAL? WE'RE SIBLINGS AFTER ALL.
DON'T SCREW AROUND!!
Hey Wait!
ギャー
WELL!
YOU WON'T TELL ME WHERE YOU'RE APPLYING!
GOD, YOU'RE IRRITATING!
ギャー
I TOLD YOU! SOMEPLACE DIFFERENT FROM YOU TWO!

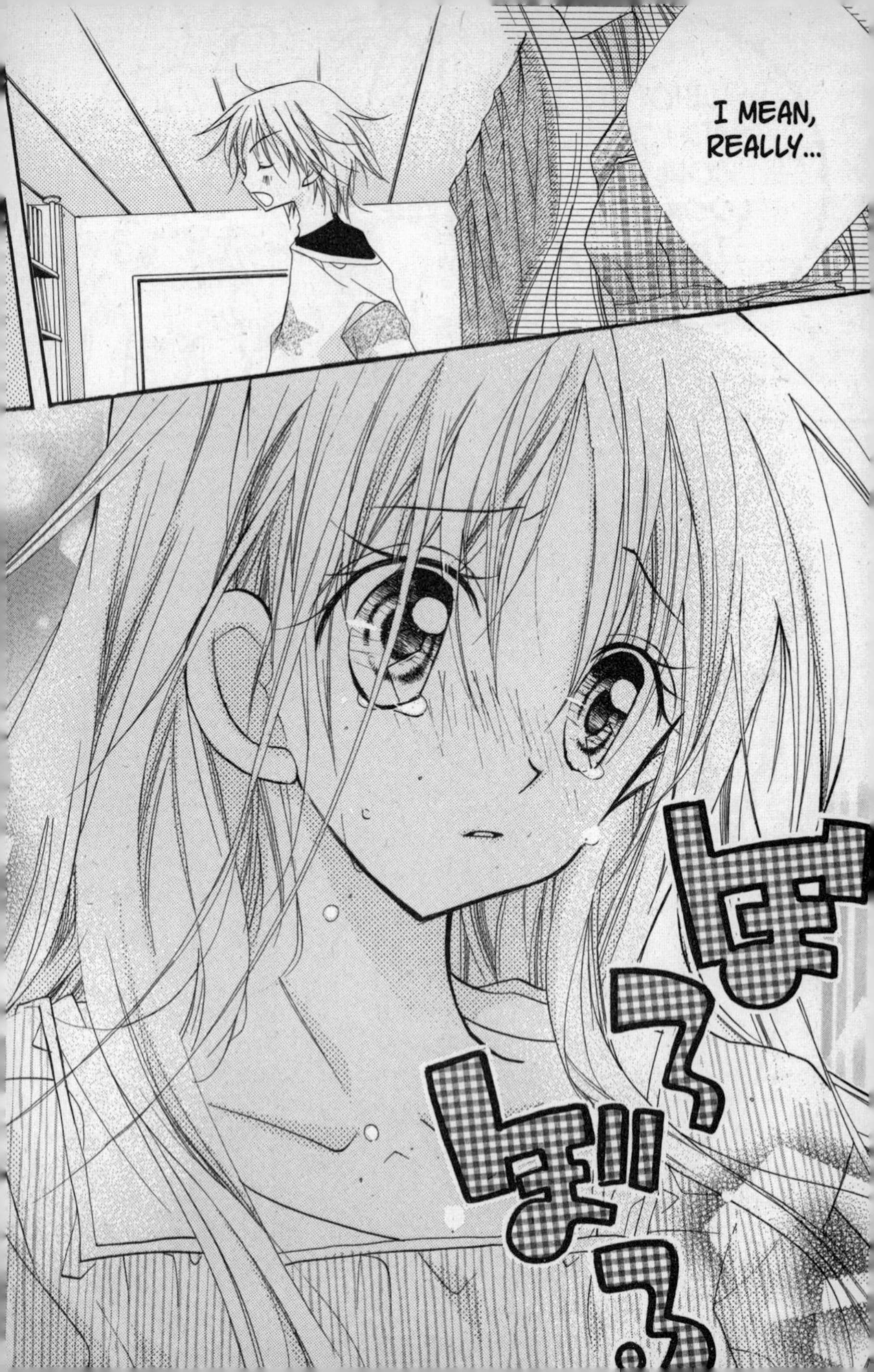
I MEAN, REALLY...

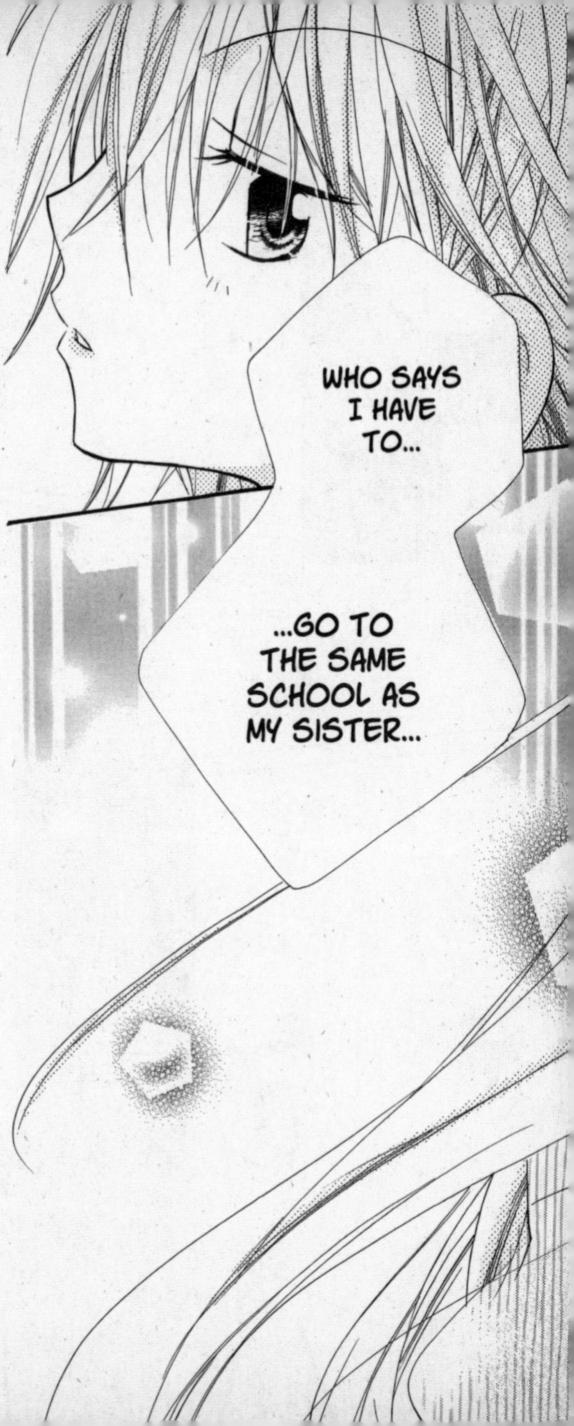
WHO SAYS I HAVE TO...
...GO TO THE SAME SCHOOL AS MY SISTER...

EIGHT!

☐ It's interesting how many different styles of uniforms there are these days. Students wear them, of course, but the uniforms of working adults are sometimes so cute I could puke. The other day, I met my friend on her way home from the office, and I was blown away by how adorable her uniform was.

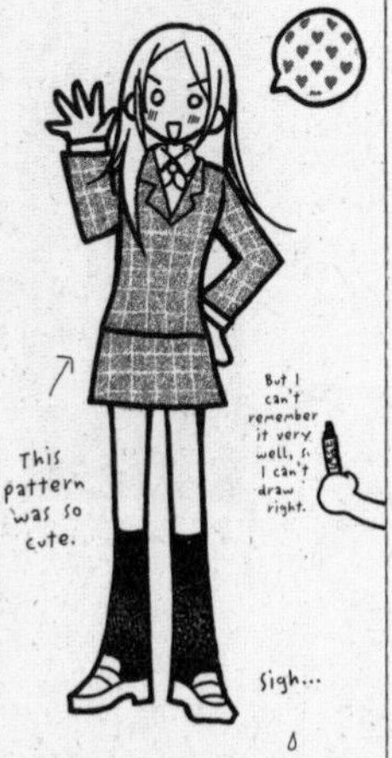
This pattern was so cute.
But I can't remember it very well, so I can't draw right.
Sigh...

☐ My friend has the build of a model, though, so that could have been part of how great she looked.

So magnificent...

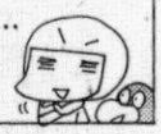

To Nine →

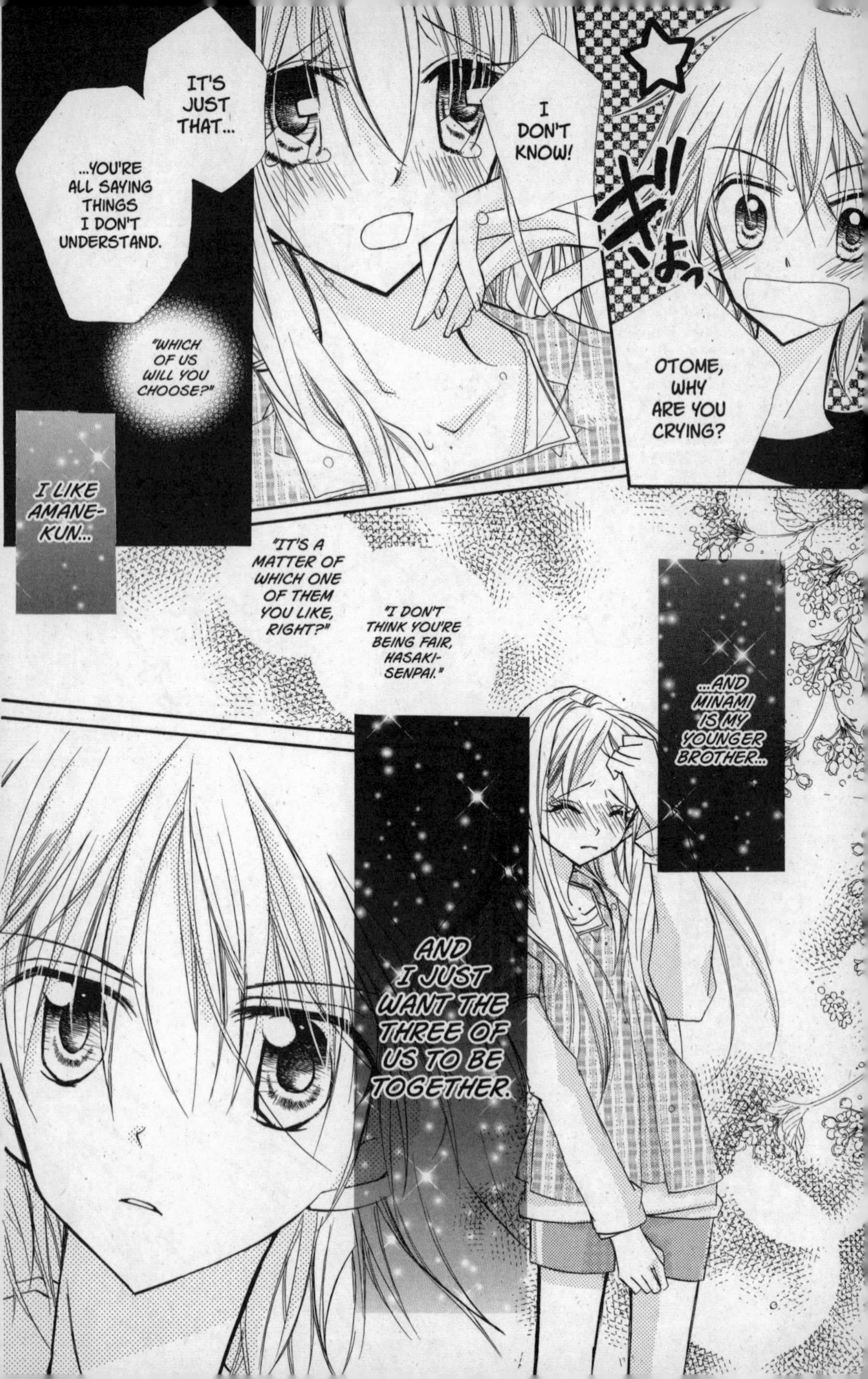
ギョッ
OTOME, WHY ARE YOU CRYING?
I DON'T KNOW!
IT'S JUST THAT...
...YOU'RE ALL SAYING THINGS I DON'T UNDERSTAND.
"WHICH OF US WILL YOU CHOOSE?"
I LIKE AMANE-KUN...
"I DON'T THINK YOU'RE BEING FAIR, HASAKI-SENPAI."
"IT'S A MATTER OF WHICH ONE OF THEM YOU LIKE, RIGHT?"
...AND MINAMI IS MY YOUNGER BROTHER...
AND I JUST WANT THE THREE OF US TO BE TOGETHER.

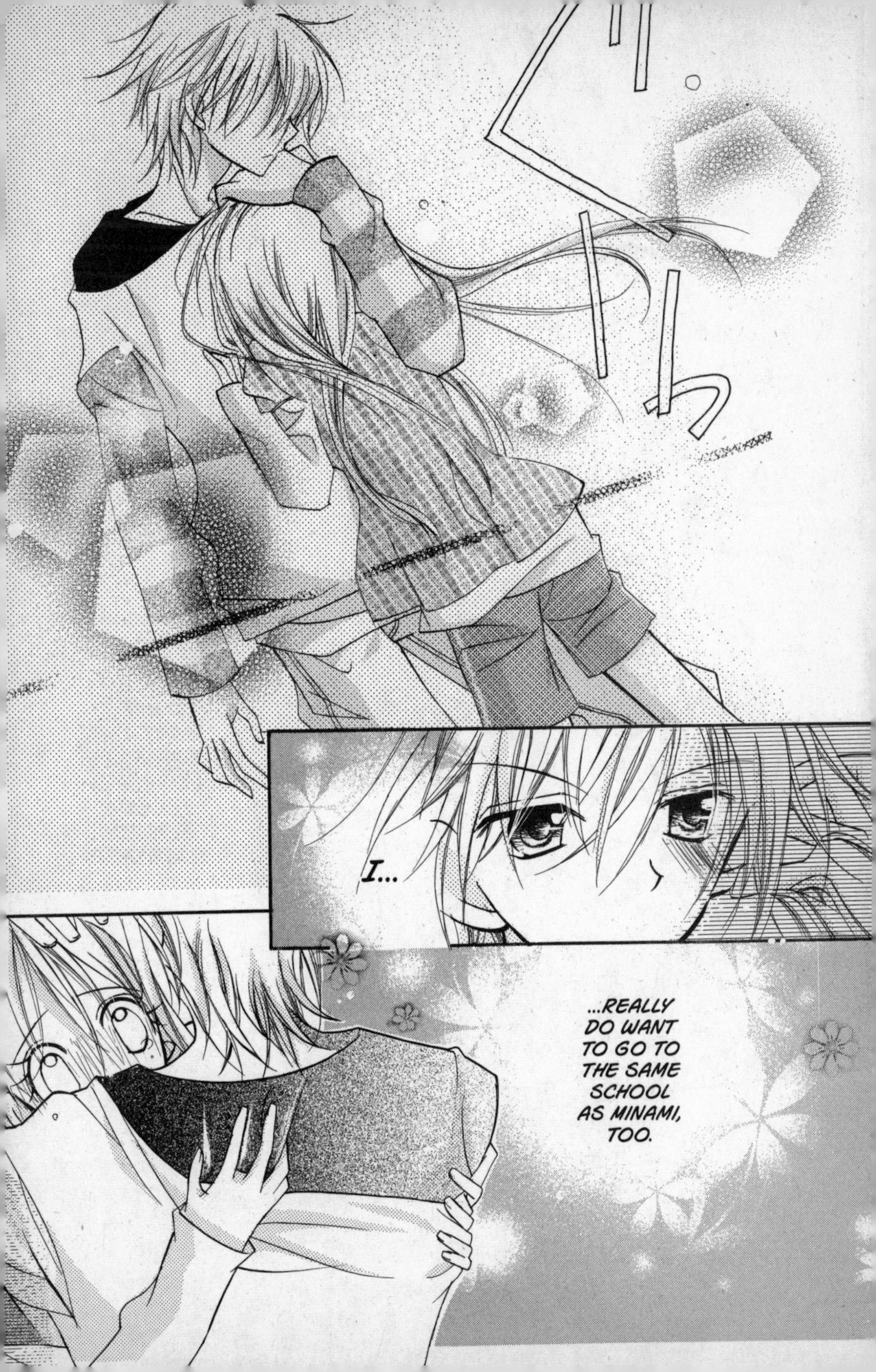
I...
...REALLY DO WANT TO GO TO THE SAME SCHOOL AS MINAMI, TOO.

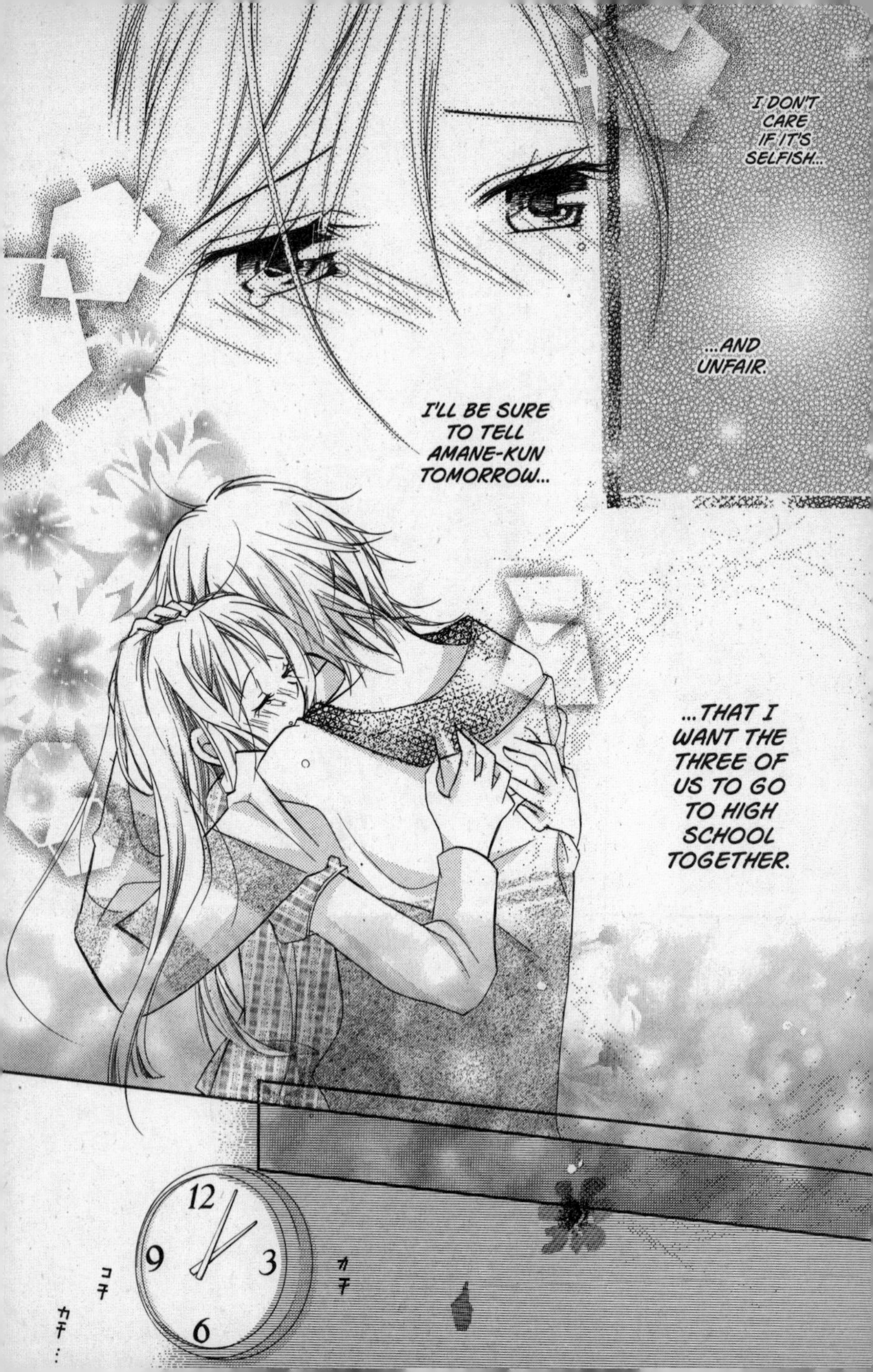
I DON'T CARE IF IT'S SELFISH...
...AND UNFAIR.
I'LL BE SURE TO TELL AMANE-KUN TOMORROW...
...THAT I WANT THE THREE OF US TO GO TO HIGH SCHOOL TOGETHER.
カチ
コチ
カチ‥

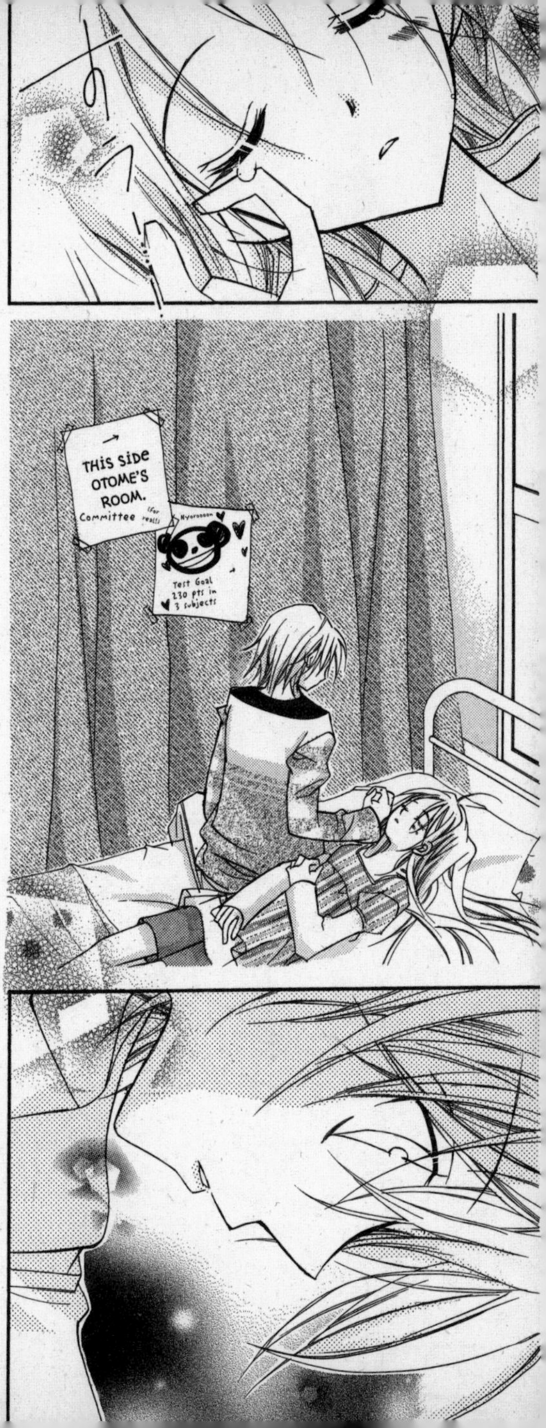
→
THIS SIDE
OTOME'S
ROOM.
Committee (for real!)
Nyoroooon
Test Goal
230 pts in
3 subjects

NINE

☑

Oh...so we've come to the end already? I still haven't finished my story. I hope I'll be able to keep talking about uniforms in the next volume, too. And I'd love it if you all told me about your school's uniforms or other uniforms you admire.

And with that, it's about time to say...

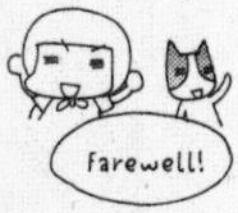
Farewell!

Special Thanks!

- ☐ T. Katada
- ☐ S. Hironaka
- ☐ N. Tsubota
- ☐ M. Fukushima
- ☐ My family
- ☐ My friends

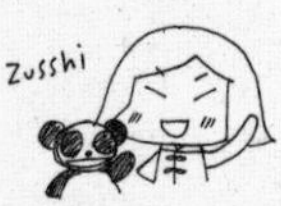
Zusshi

2004. 10.28

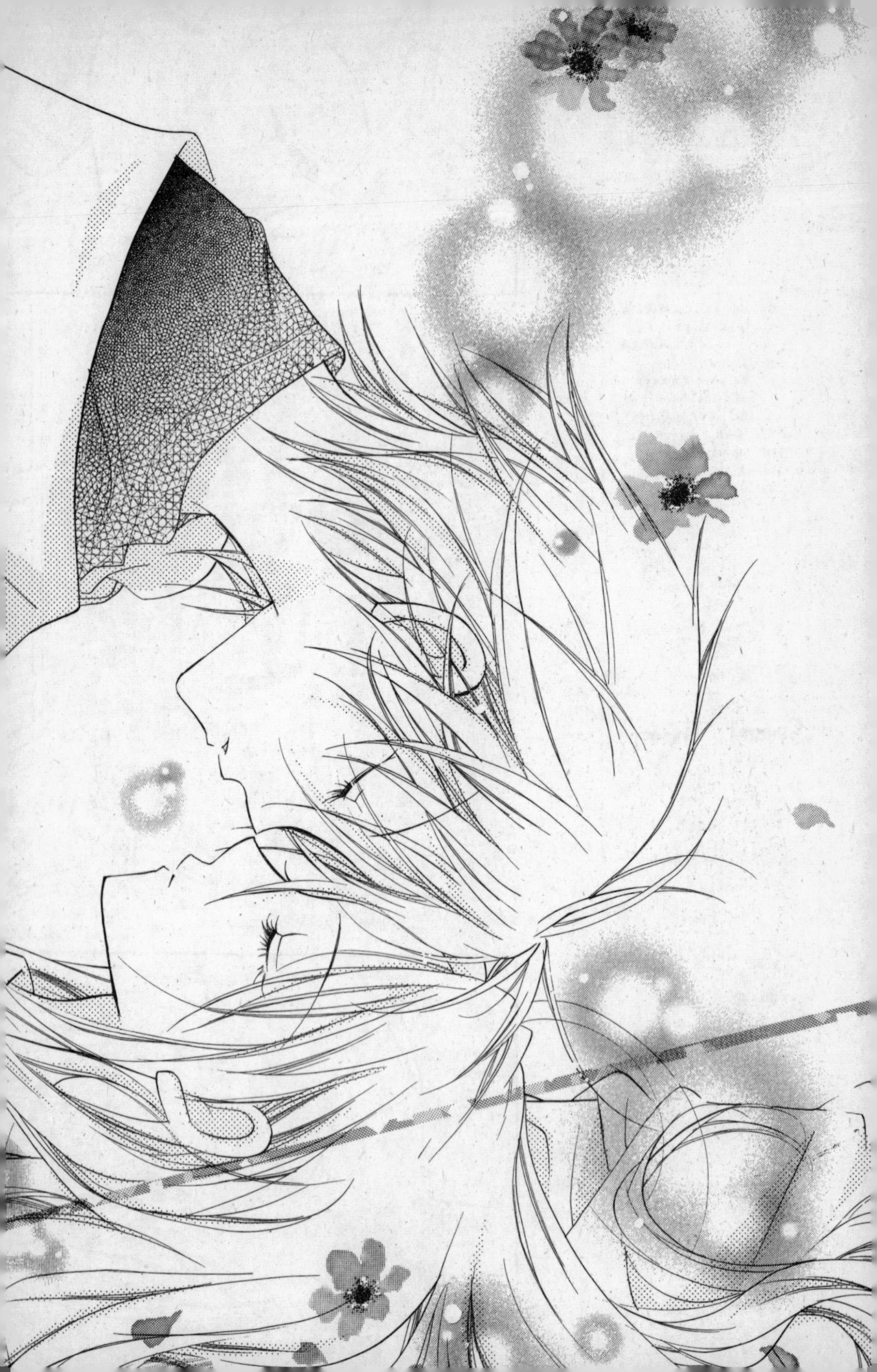

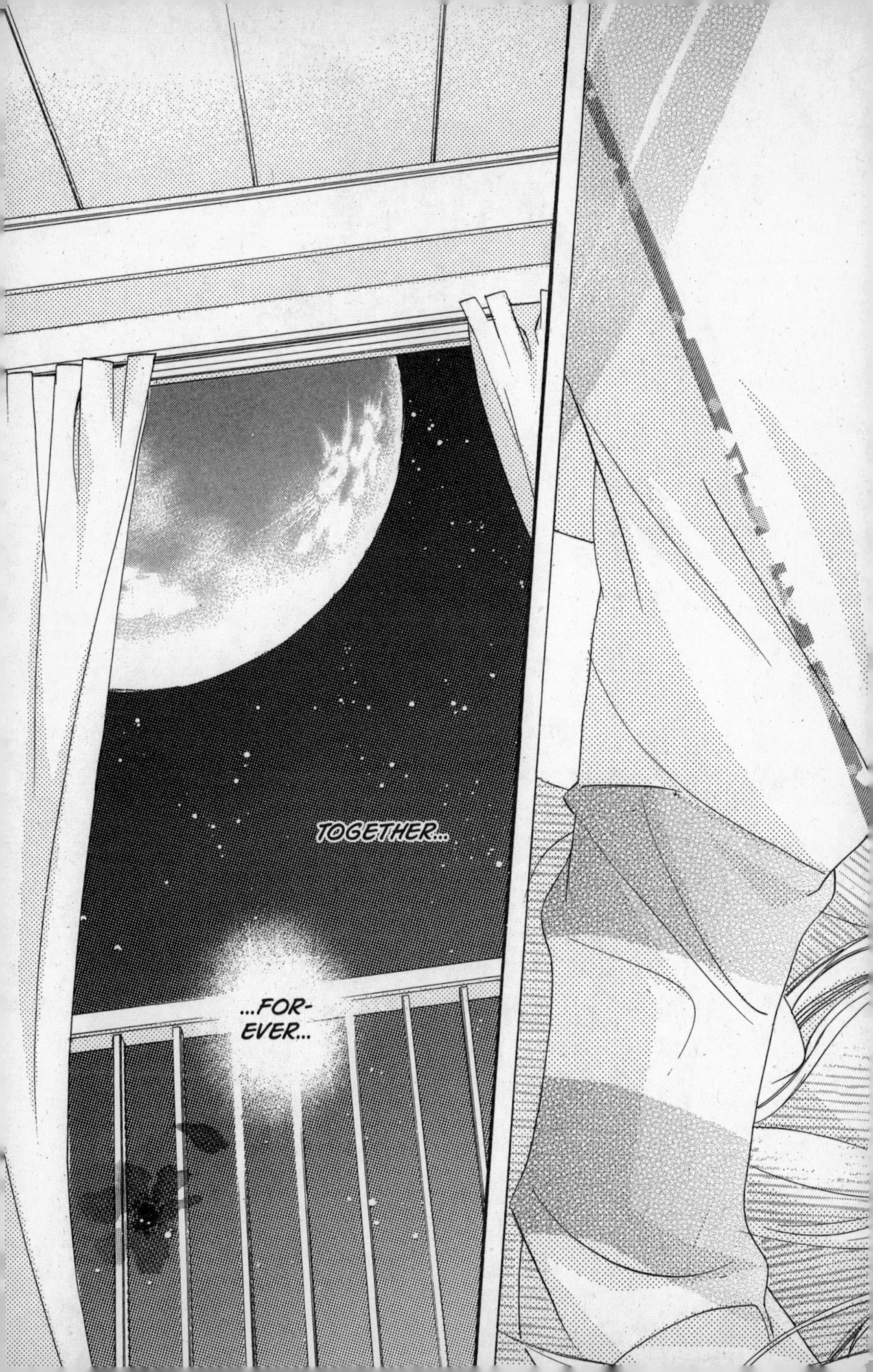
TOGETHER...
...FOR-
EVER...

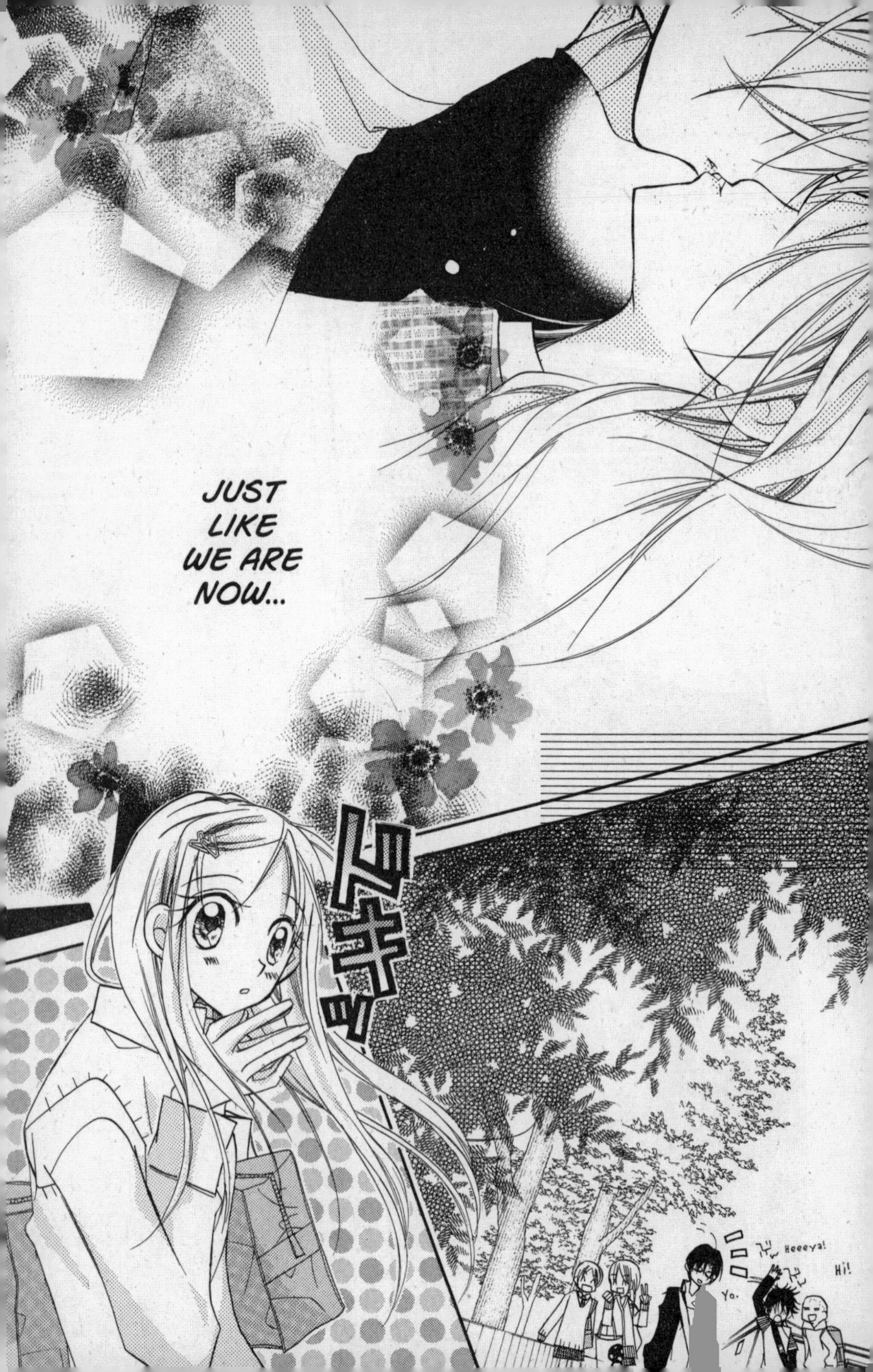
JUST LIKE WE ARE NOW...
ドキッ
Heeeya!
Hi!
Yo.

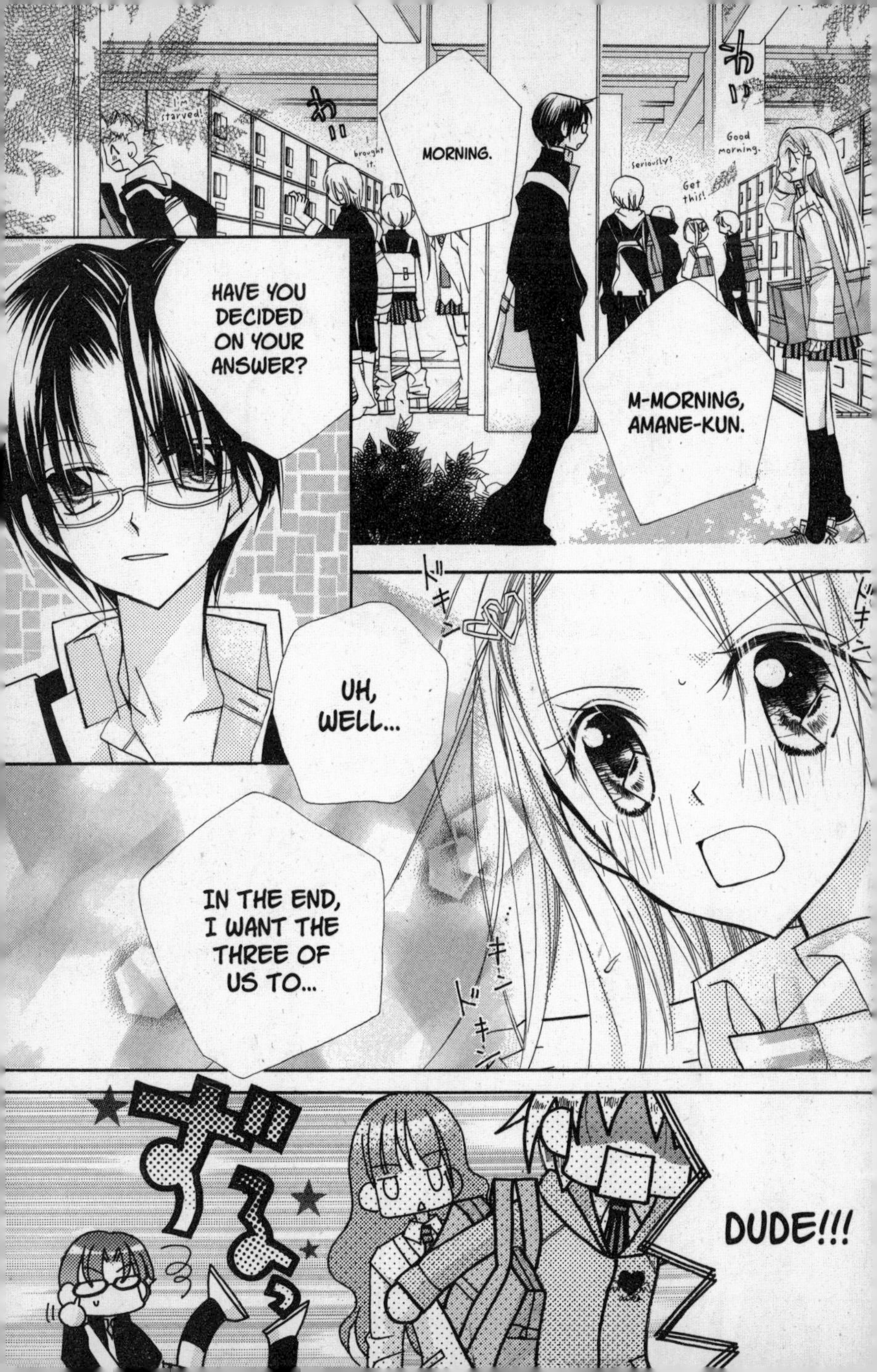

Good morning.
Get this!
seriously?
MORNING.
I brought it.
I'm starved!
M-MORNING, AMANE-KUN.
HAVE YOU DECIDED ON YOUR ANSWER?
UH, WELL...
IN THE END, I WANT THE THREE OF US TO...
DUDE!!!

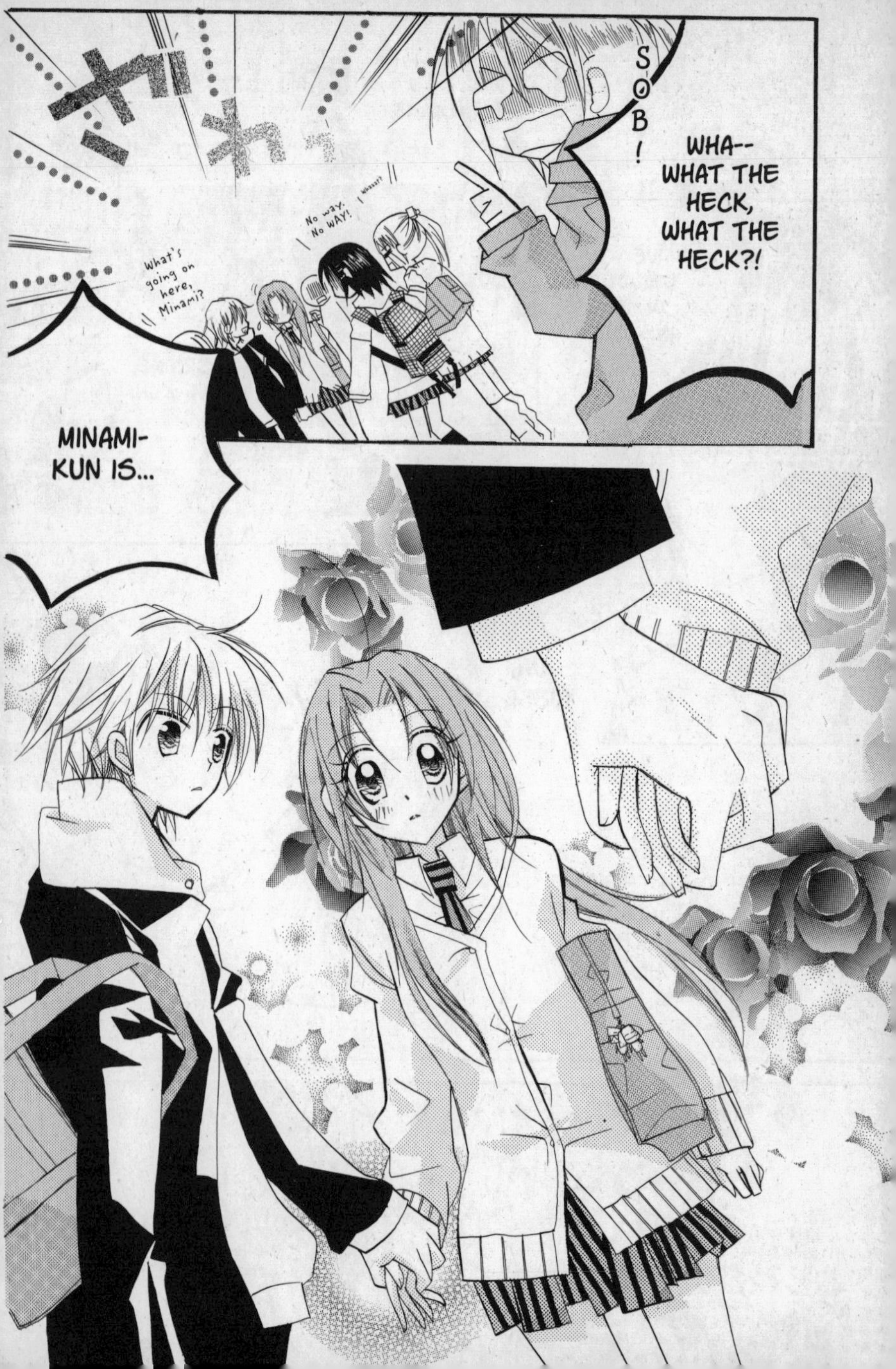
SOB!
WHA-- WHAT THE HECK, WHAT THE HECK?!
Whaaa?
No way. No WAY!
What's going on here, Minami?
MINAMI-KUN IS...

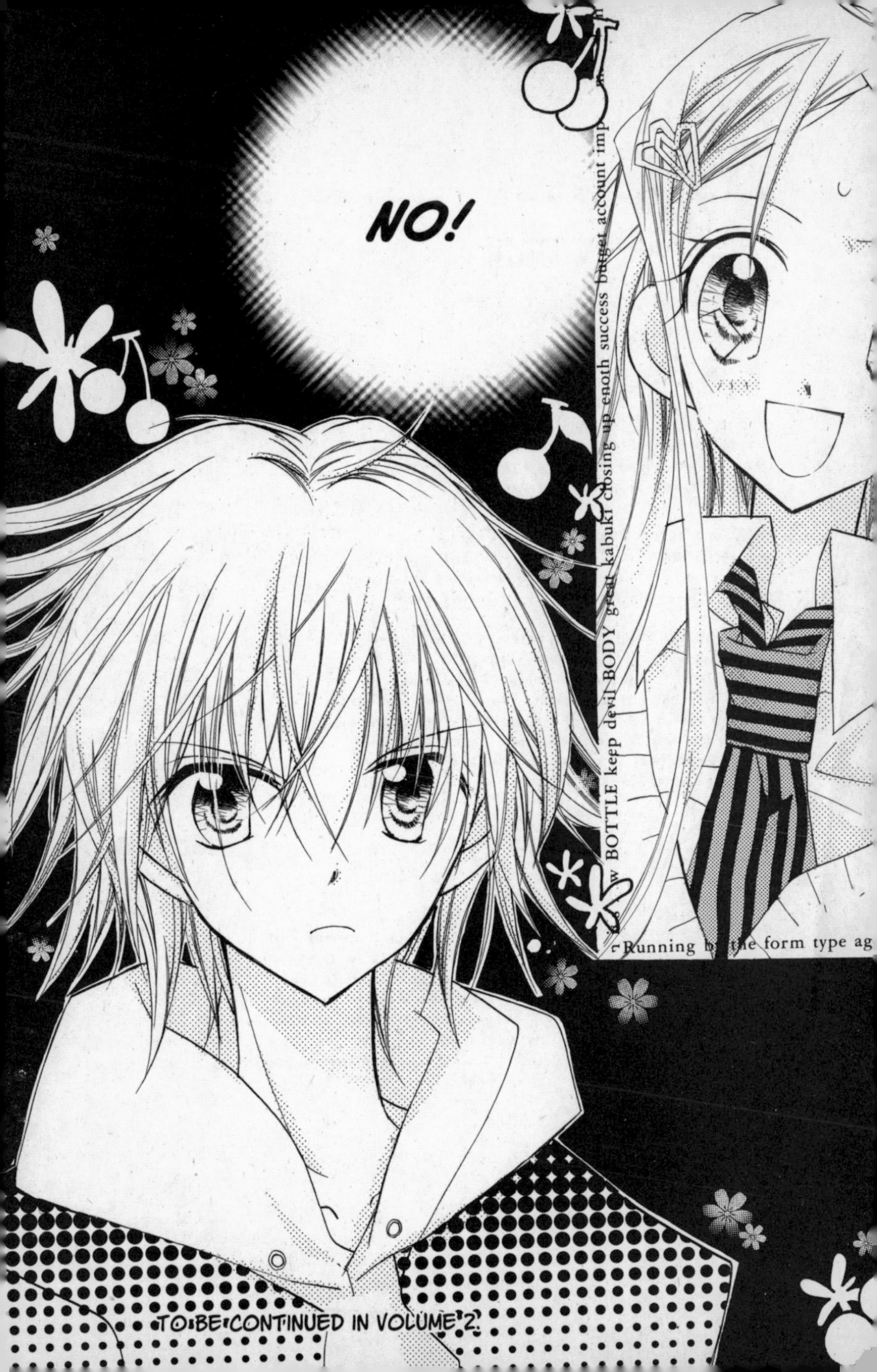
NO!
BOTTLE keep devil BODY great kabuki closing up enoth success budget account imp
Running b the form type ag
TO BE CONTINUED IN VOLUME 2.

☐ And with that...

Thank you very much for reading all the way up to this point.

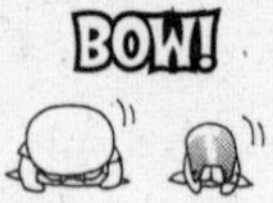
BOW!

☐ It's finally been half a year since the start of *Cherry Juice*. I've continued to release a chapter month after month, ever since my debut years ago, but, in my haste, I've probably made mistakes, so please forgive me.

☐ Many characters that appear in *Cherry Juice* are unlike any from my other manga. I like each and every character and have delusions about someday drawing side stories featuring them.

As for my favorite characters, I like Minami, of course, but I also like Naru-chan. She's fun to draw. When I'm drawing in color, I like Aiko-chan. (I like her colors.) Wondering who you, my readers liked, I took a look at the illustrations received on postcards for Illustration Corner. There were more than I expected of Granny and Amane, so I secretly wondered if those two are unexpectedly popular.

☐ By the way, this summer ('04) I got to participate in autograph sessions at K-Fes (Tokyo) and at a bookstore in Kyoto. Since becoming a mangaka, I've had several of such experiences, but I'm always nervous to the point of death about them (heh).

To p.182 →

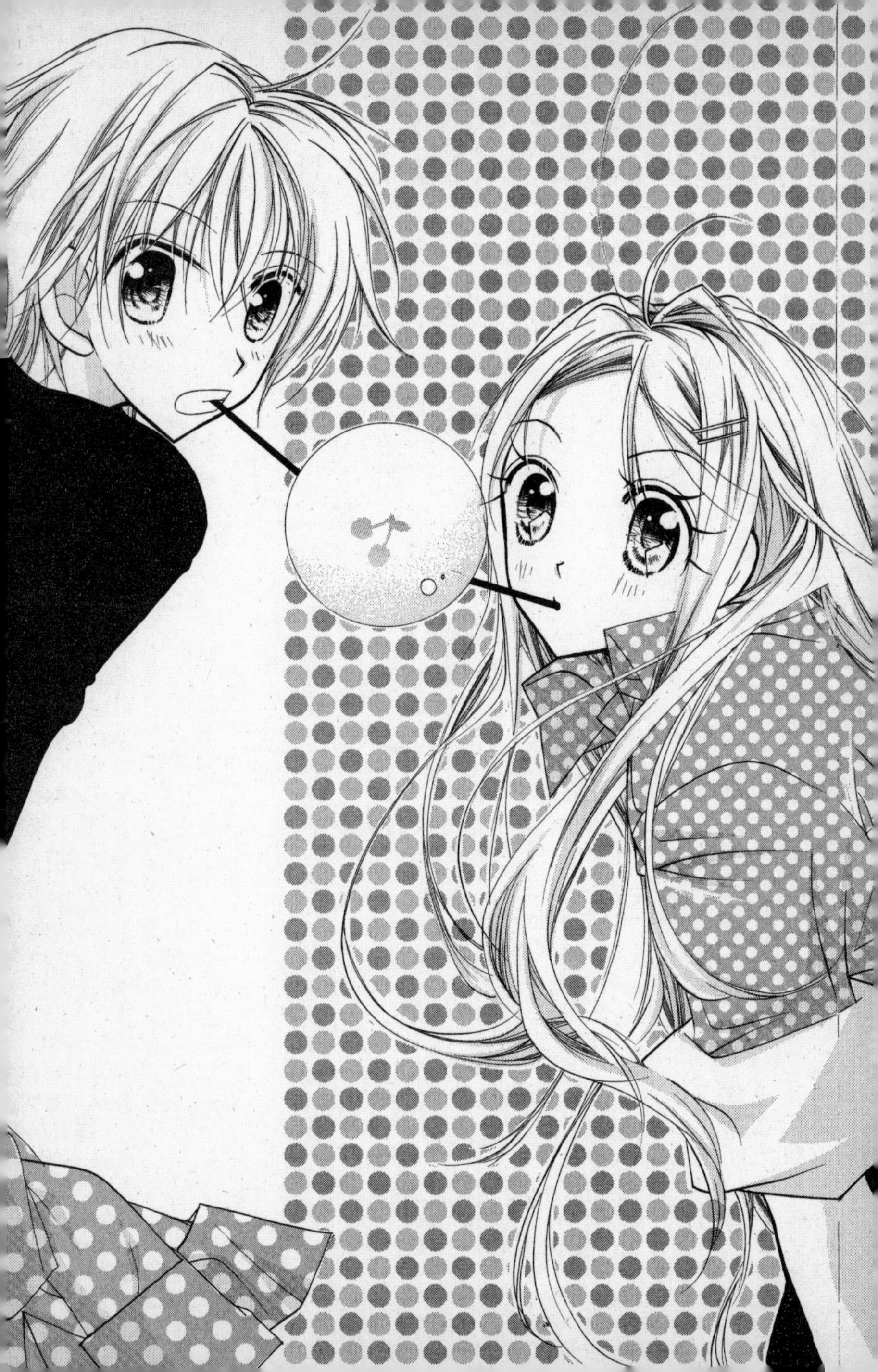

→ Continued from p.180 → →

☑ In addition, when I'm confused by someone's dialect, I keep silent.

I'm terribly sorry if I appeared rude.

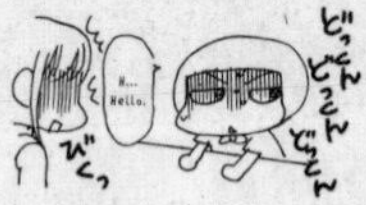
H... Hello.

You came all the way out to see me, so I'm sorry for being so rude. Come to think of it, there was someone in Kyoto who bought just about all of my books and got in line for each one (sob)!

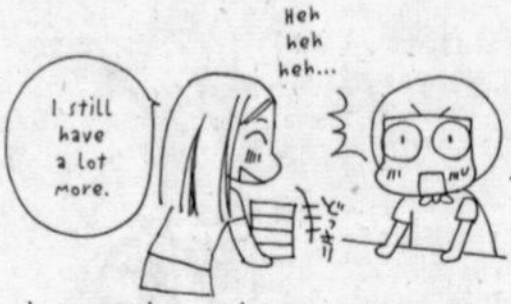
You were just here!
Heh heh heh...
I still have a lot more.

Also, the interesting thing was that there was some kind of theatrical event or something being held in the same building.

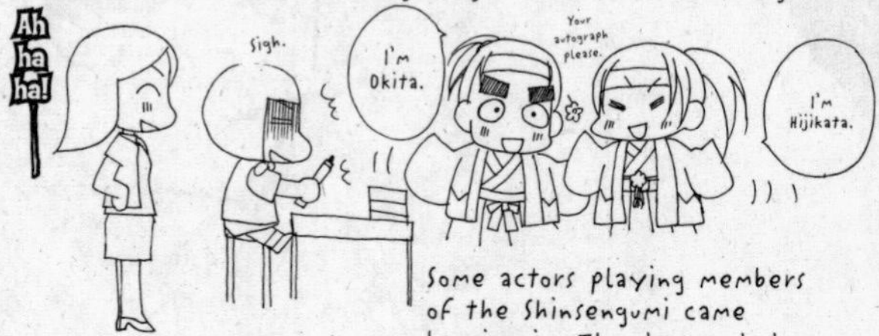
I'm Hijikata.
Your autograph please.
I'm Okita.
Sigh.
Ah ha ha!

Some actors playing members of the Shinsengumi came barging in. The day ended on a pretty wild note.

Thanks to all of you who came, to the bookstore employees who collaborated with us and to everyone else who helped out.

And I hope for your continued support in the future.

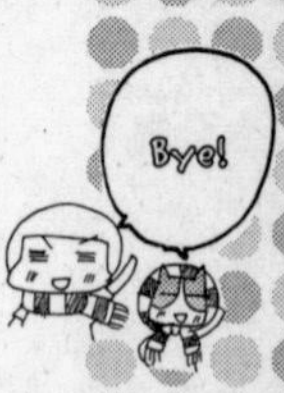
Bye!

Best wishes! See you soon!

P.S. I'm afraid a reply will be slow in coming, but if you have any feedback, please send it here.

Tokyopop, Inc.
5900 Wilshire Blvd.
Ste 2000
Los Angeles CA. 90036

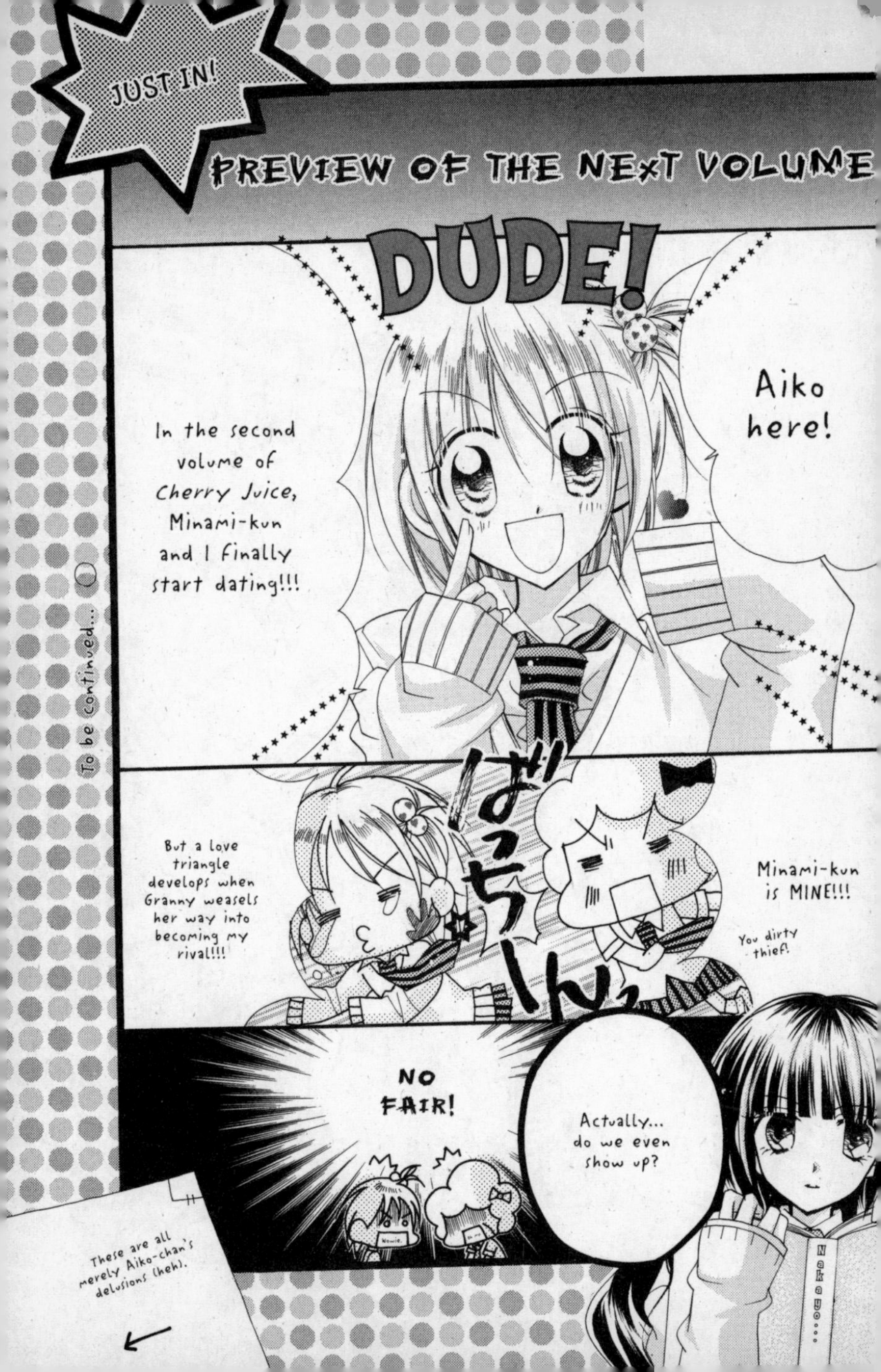
JUST IN!
PREVIEW OF THE NEXT VOLUME
DUDE!
Aiko here!
In the second volume of Cherry Juice, Minami-kun and I finally start dating!!!
ばっちーん
Minami-kun is MINE!!!
You dirty thief!
But a love triangle develops when Granny weasels her way into becoming my rival!!!
Actually... do we even show up?
Nakayo...
NO FAIR!
These are all merely Aiko-chan's delusions (heh).
To be continued...

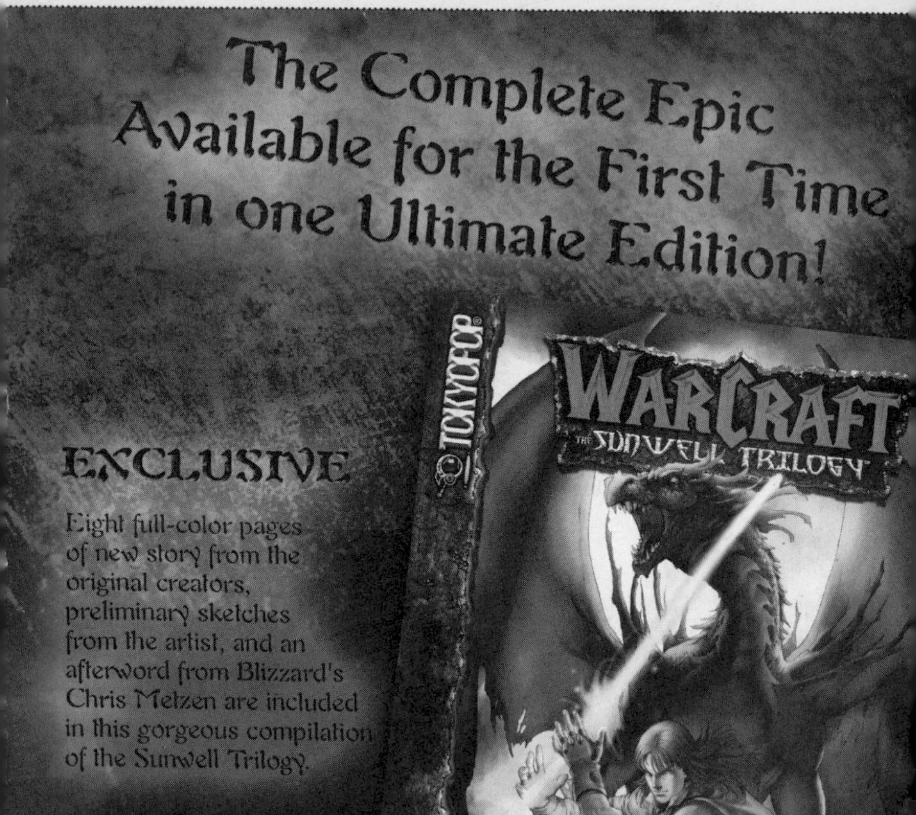
The Complete Epic Available for the First Time in one Ultimate Edition!
EXCLUSIVE
Eight full-color pages of new story from the original creators, preliminary sketches from the artist, and an afterword from Blizzard's Chris Metzen are included in this gorgeous compilation of the Sunwell Trilogy.
TOKYOPOP
WARCRAFT
THE SUNWELL TRILOGY
ULTIMATE EDITION
RICHARD A. KNAAK · JAE-HWAN KIM
ACTION
T
TEEN AGE 13+
© 2007 Blizzard Entertainment, Inc. All Rights Reserved.

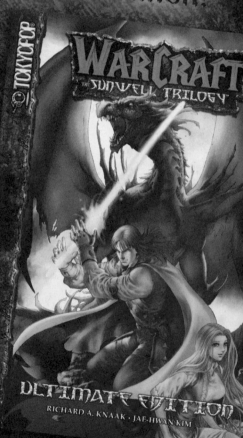

STOP!

This is the back of the book.
You wouldn't want to spoil a great ending!

This book is printed "manga-style," in the authentic Japanese right-to-left format. Since none of the artwork has been flipped or altered, readers get to experience the story just as the creator intended. You've been asking for it, so TOKYOPOP® delivered: authentic, hot-off-the-press, and far more fun!

DIRECTIONS

1
2
3
4
5
6
7
8
9
10

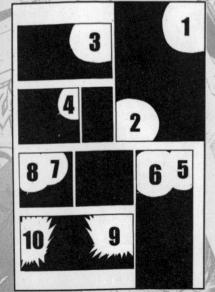

If this is your first time reading manga-style, here's a quick guide to help you understand how it works.

It's easy... just start in the top right panel and follow the numbers. Have fun, and look for more 100% authentic manga from TOKYOPOP®!

THE MANGA REVOLUTION · LEADING · 漫画革命

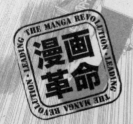